PERICLES AND THE CONQUEST OF HISTORY
A *Political Biography*

As the most famous and important political leader in Athenian history, Pericles has featured prominently in descriptions and analyses of Athenian democracy from antiquity to the present day. Although contemporary historians have tended to treat him as representative of values like liberty and equality, Loren J. Samons II demonstrates that the quest to make Athens the preeminent power in Greece served as the central theme of Pericles' career. More nationalist than humanist and less rationalist than populist, Pericles' vision for Athens rested on the establishment of an Athenian reputation for military success and on the citizens' willingness to sacrifice in the service of this goal. Despite his own aristocratic (if checkered) ancestry, Pericles offered the common and collective Athenian people the kind of fame previously available only to heroes and noblemen, a goal made all the more attractive because of the Athenians' defensiveness about Athens' lackluster early history.

LOREN J. SAMONS II is Professor of Classical Studies at Boston University. He was born in Little Rock, Arkansas, and studied classics and history at Baylor University before earning his PhD in ancient history at Brown University. Samons has published widely on Greek politics and history and on the relationship between ancient and modern democracy. His books include *What's Wrong with Democracy? From Athenian Practice to American Worship* (2004), *Empire of the Owl: Athenian Imperial Finance* (2000), and (with C. W. Fornara) *Athens from Cleisthenes to Pericles* (1991). He is the editor of *The Cambridge Companion to the Age of Pericles* (Cambridge University Press, 2007) and has published articles in such journals as *Historia, Hesperia, Classical Quarterly, Zeitschrift für Papyrologie und Epigraphik,* and the *Classical Journal.*

Pericles of Athens. Photo: Getty Images.

PERICLES
AND THE
CONQUEST OF HISTORY

A Political Biography

LOREN J. SAMONS II

Boston University

CAMBRIDGE
UNIVERSITY PRESS

CAMBRIDGE
UNIVERSITY PRESS

32 Avenue of the Americas, New York, NY 10013-2473, USA

Cambridge University Press is part of the University of Cambridge.

It furthers the University's mission by disseminating knowledge in the pursuit of
education, learning, and research at the highest international levels of excellence.

www.cambridge.org
Information on this title: www.cambridge.org/9781107526020

First published 2016

Printed in the United Kingdom by Clays, St Ives plc.

A catalog record for this publication is available from the British Library.

Library of Congress Cataloging in Publication Data
Samons, Loren J., author.
Pericles and the conquest of history : a political biography / Loren J. Samons.
pages   cm
Includes bibliographical references and index.
ISBN 978-1-107-11014-4 (hardback : alkaline paper)
1. Pericles, approximately 495 B.C.-429 B.C.   2. Greece – History – Athenian supremacy,
479-431 B.C.   3. Athens (Greece) – Politics and government.   4. Democracy – Greece –
Athens – History – To 1500.   5. Statesmen – Greece – Athens – Biography.   I. Title.
DF228.P4S26   2015
938′.04092–dc23
[B]
2015024720

ISBN 978-1-107-11014-4 Hardback
ISBN 978-1-107-52602-0 Paperback

To the river

and

to my teachers
Tommye Lou Davis
Robert Reid†
Randy Todd
Wallace Daniel
David Herlihy†
Michael Putnam
Kurt Raaflaub
and
Charles Fornara

Exiled Thucydides knew
All that a speech can say
About Democracy
And what dictators do,
The elderly rubbish they talk
To an apathetic grave;
Analysed all in his book,
The enlightenment driven away,
The habit-forming pain,
Mismanagement and grief:
We must suffer them all again.
                  – W. H. Auden, from "September 1, 1939"

Many things escape us.
                  – Aristophanes, *Peace* 618

The true history of these events is unknown.
                  – Plutarch, *Pericles* 32.6

Contents

Figures and Maps

Preface

A vortex. For me, Pericles has been a vortex. Perhaps any student of fifth-century Athenian history, literature, philosophy, art, or architecture must eventually think – at least for a few minutes – about Pericles. A scholar interested in classical Athenian politics, foreign relations, historiography, and warfare simply cannot escape him.

I never wanted to write a biography, and I certainly did not want to write a biography of Pericles. Nevertheless, questions about why Athens went to war with Sparta in 431, what the Athenians thought about themselves (and other Greeks), how Thucydides constructed his history, and what the Athenian people sought in a leader forced me to accept my fate. The figure of Pericles ultimately sucks all these questions into his powerful, churning maw. The historian Thucydides deserves a great deal of blame for this, as do the comic poets and philosophers who loved to skewer the Athenian states-man and whose works played a major role in the construction of Plutarch's biography. Then there are the fantastic buildings constructed with (at least) Pericles' encouragement, the modern fascination with democratic Athens under its greatest leader, and, especially, the empire over other Greeks that Pericles and his fellow Athenians built and exploited while expanding their own political freedoms and privileges. Perhaps, in the end, Pericles should be forgiven for demanding our attention.

The principal question this work seeks to answer is what circumstances and ideas led Pericles to take the actions he (and Athens) took in the fifth century BC. The guiding hypothesis is that Thucydides has attempted to present us with a picture of Pericles that is not misleading. Like Thucydides,

I am interested in Pericles' ideas and in his role as a leader. However, unlike Thucydides, I attempt to elucidate or reconstruct the factors that made Pericles into the man Thucydides and Plutarch found so fascinating.

It has become fashionable to avoid using admittedly anachronistic terms like "state," "conservative," and "progressive" in descriptions of classical Athenian politics and foreign policy. I hope I may be forgiven for employing them for the purpose of convenience. I use the term "state" to refer to sovereign political entities. By "conservative" I mean simply those Athenians who preferred good relations with Sparta to enmity with that city-state and who wished to maintain the political status quo rather than extending more power to the poorer elements in society, an action favored by those I call "progressive" or "more democratic." Of course, nothing like political parties existed in ancient Athens, but some individuals did tend to support or pursue policies that fell into one of these two schools of thought. On the other hand, sometimes other considerations (like family relationships or status) seem to have trumped political concerns.

I employ no fixed system, but I usually spell Greek names in the ways that seem most readily recognizable to the nonspecialist reader without doing violence to the original Greek (hence "Pericles" instead of "Perikles," but "Kimon," which does not run the risk of mispronunciation faced by "Cimon"). In cases where the mispronunciation or Latinization has become endemic (e.g., Thucydides, Alcibiades), I usually bow to tradition and apologize to my Greek friends: Συγγνώμη.

I want to thank several people for their help or inspiration. Robert Reid brought the ancient world to life for me and many other Baylor students in his Waco, Texas, classroom. Wallace Daniel showed me (or, rather, became) the Platonic form of a college professor, providing an ideal standard to which I could only aspire. Tommye Lou Davis taught me Latin and the beauty of grammar. Randy Todd introduced me to the Greek of Homer and Herodotus with great patience and generosity. Michael Putnam showed me why Vergil is wonderful, and David Herlihy explained new ways to study and understand late antiquity and the Middle Ages. Charles Fornara introduced me to the professional study of Pericles and fifth-century Athens about thirty years ago. He forced me to become a classicist when I wanted only to be a historian. My great debts to him will be obvious to anyone who knows his work.

The anonymous readers for Cambridge University Press offered invaluable corrections and suggestions for this work. However, above all I am grateful to my former teacher and longtime friend, Kurt Raaflaub, who read an earlier version of the entire manuscript and offered me numerous ideas, suggestions, and pointed criticisms. His reading caused me to correct many errors and to rethink several important issues. Because he is perhaps the most generous scholar I have ever known, Kurt will forgive me for the places where I have chosen to be stubborn. For me, Pericles remains a disquieting figure, whose intelligence, idealism, sagacity, ambition, and political honesty present aspects both attractive and foreboding.

The classical studies faculty at Dickinson College generously invited me to give the Christopher Roberts Lectures in the fall of 2013. Some of the ideas appearing here were developed or put into their final form during that delightful visit with my good friends in Carlisle, Pennsylvania. I want especially to thank Marc Mastrangelo and Chris Francese for their hospitality. I must also thank Brendan McConville for joining me in a presentation there and Ted Lendon for serving as the (appallingly frank) commentator. Dickinson College seems to me an ideal place to study the ancient world.

Other scholars who have helped along the way with this project (at times unwittingly) include Jim Sickinger, Tom Figueira, Peter Rhodes, Mortimer Chambers, Lucia Athanassaki, Jim Kennelly, and Don Kagan.

Friends at Boston University have made the writing of this book much easier than it would otherwise have been. I must single out Steve Esposito, Wolfgang Haase, Brian Jorgensen, Peter Michelli, Stephanie Nelson, Kelly Polychroniou, Wayne Snyder, James Uden, and Ann Vasaly.

My wife Jamie, my family, my students, and my friends have endured my harangues about fifth-century Athens, Pericles, and many other things for far too long. I offer this book to all of them as an act of expiation and exorcism.

Jay Samons
Athens, Agia Paraskevi
July 2015

Important Dates

546/5	Peisistratus establishes tyranny firmly in Athens
528/7	Death of Peisistratus; Hippias becomes tyrant
525/4	Cleisthenes is archon eponymous
524/3	Miltiades is archon eponymous
514	Murder of Hipparchus, brother of tyrant Hippias
511/10	Tyranny of Hippias in Athens overthrown by Spartans
ca. 510?	Kimon's birth
ca. 507	Cleisthenes' reforms (*demokratia*)
ca. 500–495?	Pericles' birth
493	Miltiades returns to Athens; tried for tyranny
490	Battle of Marathon
489	Miltiades' second trial; Xanthippus prosecutes
485/4	Ostracism of Pericles' father, Xanthippus
483/2	Themistocles' proposal to use silver revenues for fleet
481	Recall of Xanthippus and other ostracized Athenians
480	Battles of Thermopylae and Salamis
479	Persians defeated at Plataea and Mycale
478/7	Foundation of Delian League
473/2	Pericles serves as *choregos*
ca. 471	Themistocles ostracized
ca. 466	Kimon's victory at the Eurymedon
465–463	Thasos' revolt and suppression
463	Pericles' prosecution of Kimon

INTRODUCTION

Biography and History

There must be a special place in hell reserved for biographers. And in the lowest part of the inferno suffer the biographers of ancient figures.

Plutarch wisely informed his readers that he was not a historian but a biographer, and was therefore more interested in the chance remark or anecdote revealing the subject's character than in the narrative of battles and great events.[1] But Plutarch should have gone further, admitting that even the best descriptions of jokes, personal demeanor, and physical appearance cannot capture a human being's actual nature. A biographer – a word derived from Greek roots meaning "life writer" – remains a kind of charlatan, presenting depictions that may gain credence more by verisimilitude than by accuracy. By contrast, a historian who seeks to describe (say) a battle may have accounts of dozens of eyewitnesses and the testimony of commanding officers as well as the battlefield topography to help him reconstruct his nonetheless imperfect account of the event. But his object of study – the battle itself – remains insensate, without its own will or purpose, unconflicted by emotions and morals, without lost loves, false hopes, or crushed dreams. While a battle can be misrepresented, it cannot be defamed, its character or reputation cruelly twisted by the caprice, malice, or incompetence of the historian.

Perhaps this very fact about biography – its willingness to attempt the impossible while running the risk of either maligning or deifying its subject – has made it such a popular genre from antiquity to the present. Every reader of a biography knows (or should know) that the figure in the volume he is reading cannot be the real person, that something essential has been lost in the process of reducing a human life to a few thousand words. And yet we eagerly read on, gauging the written "life" against our own experience and estimates of plausibility.

Pericles of Athens lived before the creation of biography. Certainly during his lifetime and shortly thereafter Greeks composed works that included biographical information, especially anecdotes (often unflattering) about famous Athenians or other Greeks. Such stories often reflected the very obvious biases of their ultimate sources, a fact that will be helpful to keep in mind when we attempt to analyze them. But no one in the fifth century BC attempted to document Pericles' life or career. No person or institution saved his letters or copies of his speeches. No journalists composed accounts of his day-to-day dealings with other statesmen or foreign dignitaries. None of his wives, sons, friends, or lovers wrote an account of "life with Pericles." Even the statesman's younger contemporary Thucydides, who had heard Pericles speak and undoubtedly knew him personally, made almost no effort to inform us about the statesman's *life* (as opposed to his public policies and beliefs).

Given these circumstances, can one write a proper biography of Pericles more than 2,400 years after his death? The obvious answer to this question is no. Plutarch's own *Life of Pericles*, written some 500 years after the statesman's death, if anything confirms the impossibility of the undertaking. The "real" Pericles arguably does not emerge from that text, despite the fact that Plutarch had access to many precious contemporary documents and accounts now lost to us. Plutarch, for example, had the scandalous pamphlet on Pericles, Themistocles, and Thucydides son of Melesias (a different Thucydides than the historian) by Stesimbrotus of Thasos, a work that apparently included considerable information about private matters like the sexual liaisons of his subjects. He also had many contemporary Athenian comedies that made Pericles the butt of numerous jokes about matters ranging from his physical appearance to his relationship with his notorious consort Aspasia. Plutarch possessed the histories written in the fourth century BC and later, especially the lost account of Ephorus of Cyme.[2] Plutarch, moreover, could walk through an Athens that still boasted an unspoiled acropolis, where the Periclean constructions of the Parthenon and Propylaia testified eloquently to the greatness of the Athenian statesman's vision.

And yet Plutarch's brief biography, if intriguing, remains deeply unsatisfying, as much for what it does not tell us as for what it does.[3] Perhaps it was not so to the ancients themselves. They were, after all, not inured to the obscene amounts of personal detail and popular media analysis of public figures that moderns take for granted. We inhabit a world in which public figures strive to project a personal biography – indeed, the construction of that very public biography features as a crucial part of their strategy to sell themselves or their works. The personal and biographical attract so much of modern society's interest that we arguably often lose sight of the actual public policies our leaders pursue. It seems we want to feel good about or empathize with the men and women who serve in office or make the music or movies we like. Thus, we want to know as much as possible about their lives, even as some of us realize that the picture presented is hardly real.

A reader of Plutarch's biography might object that the work does provide us with a remarkable number of stories about Pericles' personal life. Some of the tales could easily feature prominently in Yahoo! News or on the front page of today's *People* magazine. Since I make no effort in this book to deal with the scandalous aspects of Pericles' personal life except insofar as they could affect his political life, some readers may find Plutarch's attention to this aspect of Pericles' biography more satisfactory than the present volume. However that may be, where Plutarch fails by the standards of modern biography, one could argue, is that he provides the reader with no sustained analysis of Pericles' family, education, or environment in order to help us understand how the Athenian became the man he did. Plutarch also fails to provide any clear thesis about Pericles' thought and political ideals, beyond his view that the Athenian acted as a demagogue early in his career and a statesman after he had achieved predominance. What, in short, did Pericles want for Athens? What drove him to take the actions and support the policies he did? Finally, did Pericles succeed?[4]

The last question had an obvious answer for Plutarch and others of his day and thus had no need to be asked. Any leader who had left such an indelible mark on his world had surely been a success. Plutarch's admiration of the Athenian – if not unbounded – could hardly be more clear. It remains striking, therefore, that some Athenians in the years just before and after Pericles' death had a different view. Here again, Plutarch fails us. For while he admits that Pericles had serious detractors and opponents while he was alive, the biographer does little to show us what happened to Pericles' reputation after his death.

Here we must call on Thucydides, whose defense of Pericles (2.65) clearly aims to counter attacks on the leader's reputation in the years just after Athens had lost the great Peloponnesian War against Sparta (404 BC). In those days – two and a half decades after Pericles' death in 429 – and in subsequent years, some Athenian elites had grave questions about Pericles and his policies. He had, after all, driven Athens into the war that led to the loss of its empire and the bankrupting of its public treasuries, not to mention the deaths of thousands of Athenians and other Greeks. Plutarch, writing around AD 100 and thus looking back on Pericles' life after more than five centuries, gives us little sense of the way in which Pericles' reputation had fallen and then recovered. By the time of Plutarch, Pericles and fifth-century Athens – the greatest Athenian and the period of Athens' greatest achievements – had both already achieved an exalted if not mythic status. By Plutarch's day, no one expected the Athenians ever to produce another Sophocles, Pheidias, or Socrates. If, by that time, the "Age of Pericles" had not yet crystallized into a moment when literature, architecture, philosophy, and empire had reached unprecedented and unequaled heights in classical Greece, it was still true that no Greek in AD 100 living under Roman domination could write about once independent, formidable, and remarkable Periclean Athens – and its foremost leader – with anything other than a degree of respect.[5]

In the almost two millennia since Plutarch, views of Pericles and Periclean Athens have not remained perfectly constant. The Italian humanists of the Renaissance, for example, generally found Athenian democracy unstable and problematic but occasionally found a way to praise Pericles.[6] The American Founders saw in Periclean Athens a dangerous tendency to mob rule that made the idea of direct democracy anathema.[7] And yet by the late twentieth century Pericles and his Athens had attained (or regained) something like heroic status. Today's English-speaking scholars have tended to see Pericles and his Athens as potential models for the contemporary world.[8] And while a few have begun to question the popular view that Thucydides presents Pericles as a kind of hero, even they have usually claimed to be speaking only of "Thucydides' Pericles," a character in a literary work rather than the historical figure. Pericles himself – the real man – it seems, remains virtually untouchable, an ostensible and perpetual champion of modern democratic and cultural values like freedom and diversity.[9]

This book attempts to recapture the critical spirit of those against whom Thucydides so vehemently argued (even as he often provided ammunition for future attacks). Pericles, as we shall see, did inspire the Athenians to make war on the Spartans and numerous other Greek states. Pericles intensified the long-standing Athenian tradition of aggression and acted as an amplifier for the Athenian people's desire to dominate other Greeks. In domestic affairs, Pericles introduced the idea that the Athenians should pay themselves from public moneys (including moneys collected from their allies under compulsion) for public services like sitting on juries, a policy that had a debilitating effect on Athenian (and later) democratic practice and ideology. Pericles pursued an ideal of moral and public excellence (*arete*) that placed the greatest emphasis on an individual's service to the state, while he held up the acquisition of future glory for that state as the citizenry's highest possible goal. To secure these ends, Pericles played on the Athenians' native discomfort with their heritage and emphasized their supposedly unique identity when compared with other Greeks. Though sprung from the ancient Athenian aristocracy, Pericles sacrificed certain privileges of his class in order to raise Athens (and himself) to new heights. Athens' greatness, he saw, depended on a relatively underutilized resource: the common Athenian populace. By empowering and ennobling Athens itself, Pericles believed all Athenians could partake in the old heroic ideal of *kleos* – a fame that included the renown the future grants to the past.[10] To achieve this goal, no sacrifice was too great, and the deaths of thousands of Athenians and other Greeks constituted a price Pericles was all too ready to pay in order to achieve his vision of securing Athens' place in history.

And yet this is not the whole picture. Thucydides rightly argued that Pericles far surpassed those who followed him in terms of his integrity and wisdom. Pericles, at least by the 430s BC, was no mere demagogue, manipulating the populace and playing on the electorate's hopes and fears in order to empower himself. Pericles' political honesty – his willingness to oppose the Athenian people and tell them what they did not wish to hear – marked him as a true leader in a sense modern democratic governments rarely experience. These qualities gave Pericles a kind of moral authority that none of his successors and few democratic politicians in any period have possessed. They made Pericles, in short, the greatest and the most dangerous leader in Athenian history.

Analysis of Pericles' career requires that we pay special attention to the contemporary evidence provided by Thucydides and by Athenian inscriptions. The public records, laws, and decrees the Athenians inscribed on stone in the fifth century provide a marvelous if often problematic and controversial source of information about Periclean Athens. A recent (and long overdue) reassessment of the orthodox dating of these documents has removed many of them from the Periclean age and moved them to later periods.[11] Nonetheless, our inscriptional record of this period remains relatively strong, often informing us about the environment in which Pericles operated even if telling us little about Pericles himself. Indeed, to evaluate Pericles' political career we must rely heavily on the literary record.[12]

Thucydides remains our most important witness for any attempt to reconstruct the historical Pericles, and the three speeches he puts into the mouth of the statesman in his great history of the war between Athens and Sparta arguably provide invaluable evidence for the thought and policies of Pericles. His report of the Funeral Oration that Pericles delivered after the first year of the Peloponnesian War contains the most influential description of Athenian culture and government to survive antiquity. Scholars have long debated whether this speech (and Pericles' other orations in Thucydides) should be treated as mainly the words and ideas of Pericles or the words and ideas of the historian, with the latter view now clearly holding sway. Thucydides tells us (1.22.1) that he has made the speakers in his history say "what it seemed to me was required" (*ta deonta*), "while holding as closely as possible to the general sense of what they actually said." The historian thus asserts that he knew the "general sense of what was actually said" for each speech he recounts, while admitting that he has elaborated on those themes by making the speakers say what seemed necessary given their general drift and purpose.[13]

My own view is that the speeches in the history do not reflect Thucydides' own views on any particular subject, but rather reflect what Thucydides believed the speaker could or *should* have said given the demands of the occasion and the general sense of his actual speech. What this means for Pericles' speeches – which were heard by many thousands of

Athenians – is that we should usually, I believe, treat the major themes of the speeches as Periclean and the actual words as Thucydidean. Thucydides has elaborated on the theses of these speeches, adhering to them "as closely as possible" given the situation without having the speaker say types of things he never would have said.[14]

I want to make it clear that I treat these speeches not as verbatim accounts of Pericles' orations but rather as the works of a contemporary of Pericles who had heard the leader speak, knew him personally, and had every reason not to have the Pericles of his history speak in a way that his contemporary readers would recognize as grossly inauthentic.[15] Thucydides, who is at such pains to explain his desire for accuracy (1.22), would not have provided us with a Pericles who was more or less sheer invention. I take it that the things Pericles says in Thucydides are usually the kinds of things Pericles did say, even if Thucydides has put them into his own extremely idiosyncratic language. I do not, therefore, rest my arguments on the *ipsissima verba* ("the very words") of Pericles' speeches in Thucydides, but I do maintain that ideas and themes from those speeches that comport with our knowledge of Athenian history and Pericles' biography, and especially those ideas that appear repeatedly in the speeches Thucydides puts in Pericles' mouth, should be treated as "Periclean." The issue is not, therefore, "Did Pericles actually say that?" The issue is whether Pericles could have said something like that and whether his contemporaries would have recognized Periclean ideas and themes in the speeches they read in Thucydides.[16]

I must emphasize that my interpretation of Pericles' career and policies does not depend on the historical content of his speeches in Thucydides. The actual history of Athens over the 20 to 30 years that Pericles acted as the city's leading statesman amply demonstrates that the belligerent and nationalistic picture painted in Pericles' speeches in Thucydides reflects an accurate picture of mid-fifth-century Athenians. Indeed, if the Pericles in Thucydides had spoken in a less bellicose fashion we would be more than justified in questioning whether Thucydides had given us a relatively authentic picture of the statesman. As it stands, the events of Athenian history support the conclusion that Thucydides' Pericles is closer to his actual historical model than to a fictional character.[17]

I make no apology for using Pericles' speeches in Thucydides in an attempt to flesh out our understanding of Periclean thought, goals, and policies. Thucydides surely included these speeches precisely to allow us better to grasp the figure of Pericles as well as the historical situation he faced. And while I do not claim Thucydides has given us the very words of Pericles, I remain quite comfortable with the conclusion that he has not attempted to mislead us or to make *his* Pericles into someone different from the man Athenians encountered in the fifth century. Historians have been unapologetically using Pericles' words about democracy in Thucydides to characterize Athenian government and society for many decades. It is time to use the speeches – treated carefully and informed by our other evidence – to help us characterize Pericles himself.

The reader will not always like the Pericles he encounters in these pages. One is, indeed, hard-pressed to find evidence of likability in our evidence about the Athenian statesman. Pericles resembled nothing so little as the "man of the people" image we moderns so often claim to seek in democratic leaders (and yet we will see that his relationship with the Athenian people was remarkably strong). Pericles also had troubled relations with his own family and friends. Scandalous rumors circulated about his private life. He was not a particularly handsome man, or at least had some unusual physical features that could be considered unattractive. And yet all these factors make his political success all the more remarkable. Pericles did not try to whip up the crowd after the fashion of the later demagogue Cleon or offer an attractive physical appearance and seductive manner as did his young relation and ward Alcibiades. What Pericles offered, I will suggest, was a vision of Athenian power and greatness that resonated very deeply with the Athenian people even as he showed how that power could benefit them in very tangible terms. Pericles offered the Athenians political, economic, and emotional satisfaction. This required only that the Athenians accept the need for almost constant warfare. Pericles' ability to convince the Athenians to make this kind of exchange tells us a great deal about fifth-century Athens and the belligerent environment in which democracy first arose.

Pericles embodied and fostered the links between Athens' democratic government and the Athenians' drive to control other Greeks. The greatest lesson of Pericles' biography may be that a people who prize their own freedom may happily vote – and then march or sail out – to take it away from others.

ONE

To Be an Athenian

The unique profile and history of Athens spawned Pericles and provided him with the raw material and tools with which he constructed his career. While sharing many characteristics with their Greek contemporaries, the fifth-century Athenians possessed unusual traits and traditions that would ultimately play considerable roles in Athens' rise to political and cultural hegemony.

The Athenians' heroic-age heritage was weak and suspect compared with the traditions of Thebes, Sparta, Argos, and even (by the classical age, relatively backward) Thessaly. The fame of the Athenians' national hero Theseus rested largely on remedial feats that all too often mimicked those of the great Herakles, merely placed Athens on a more equal footing with other important Hellenic states, or transplanted classical Athenian accomplishments (especially democracy) to the heroic past. The Athenians' claim to "autochthony" – the idea that they were Attica's original inhabitants, sprung from the very soil – perhaps bespeaks a recognition of their tenuous connection with the great Hellenic achievements and migrations of the late or just post-heroic age, including the return of the descendants of Herakles and the wanderings of the Ionian Greeks.

Ultimately the Athenians would make much of their claim to have offered organization, protection, and respite to the Ionian Greeks (who were on their way to Asia Minor and the islands). Their putative role as metropolis ("mother city") to these Hellenes came to figure prominently in tyrannic and democratic imperial propaganda. Yet the Ionian connection cut two ways, and the Athenians appear to have been acutely aware of the disadvantages the connection transmitted when it came to their mainland (and often

Dorian) Greek neighbors. The latter saw the Ionian branch of the Greek people as weak, effeminate, and inured to luxury and slavery.

Indeed, while inhabiting the largely Doric (and Aeolic) mainland, the Athenians had much in common with the Ionian islanders to their east. Athens' external ambitions looked to the Aegean long before attempting major conquests on the mainland. The Athenians had already incorporated the nearby island of Salamis by the early sixth century, and not long after this they began a pursuit of interests in the northeastern Aegean and Hellespont that would not end until the age of Alexander. Athens' aggressive foreign policy predated the sixth-century tyranny of the Peisistratids, and the city's attempt to control areas of the Aegean remained largely immune to changes in Athens' government over almost two centuries: aristocratic, tyrannic, democratic, and oligarchic regimes all sought to project Athens' power into the islands and especially into the Hellespont, a trade route crucial for the city's grain supply.

Many Athenians by Pericles' day had come to view the tyranny of the Peisistratids (ca. 546 to 510) as a period of oppression. But a different and much more positive tradition remained alive. Peisistratus and his sons enjoyed a largely successful reign until the murder of Hipparchus, brother of the ruling tyrant Hippias, caused a falling-out with certain aristocratic families. Ultimately the Spartans (and not the Athenian people) overthrew Athens' tyrants, but the tyranny had made Athens a more urban and self-assured polis, weakened entrenched aristocratic power, and provided the demos (common people) with a new view of itself as a political and social force. During the same period, the Athenians had probably begun to exploit their local silver mines, a source of wealth that was without parallel on the Greek mainland and that would provide Athens with a fundamental source of its power in the classical age.

All these factors (and others) combined to provide the Athenians of Pericles' day with a complicated self-image. Moreover, early fifth-century victories allowed the Athenians to make previously unwarranted claims about their military standing. The Athenians ultimately placed much more emphasis on their martial prowess than on their cultural or political advances.

Like all men, Pericles emerged from a particular environment, and the culture, history, and traditions of his city and his family left indelible marks on the statesman's character and career. Yet Pericles also demonstrated a remarkable ability to abstract himself and his contemporaries from their environment – to think beyond the world of fifth-century Athens to consider Athens' potential role in history. Indeed, Pericles urged the Athenians to attempt to shape their own place in history and to do so in a way that was both radically innovative – redefining excellence (*arete*) as service to the city-state – and deeply traditional – promising fame in the future (which Homer called *kleos*) as a reward for present-day *arete*.

Our attempt to recover Pericles and the world he inhabited must focus on both components in this compound – his inheritance and his attempt to forge a new vision of Athens. We should begin by attempting to understand what Athens, and the city's history and culture, gave to Pericles.

ATHENIAN AGGRESSION

Sometime before about 700 BC the residents of the town of Athens began to incorporate the other, smaller towns and villages of Attica into the larger political entity we know historically as Athens. Attica, a region in central Greece about the size of Rhode Island, comprises a very large area for an ancient Greek polis or city-state (an entity closer in size to a modern city than to a state but nonetheless independent and politically sovereign, making its own laws and foreign policy). No other ancient Greek polis beyond Sparta controlled so much territory directly, and no other city-state had citizens living as much as thirty miles away from the city center, where the most important political and economic activities occurred.

Athens' absorption of the outlying villages and towns in Attica – a process that the Greeks called *synoicism* ("living together" as one political entity) – involved both peaceful and violent incorporation. The Athenians remembered a time when, for example, they had fought wars with Eleusis, a town in Attica to their northwest that eventually became part of Athens proper and where the famous mysteries of the goddesses Demeter and Kore were celebrated.[1]

Why did the people dwelling in the city center of Athens feel compelled to incorporate the other towns and villages of Attica into this larger political entity? Why did the people of these other settlements (ultimately) accede to this process? We cannot answer these questions beyond admitting that the early history of Attica and Athens reflects a marked interest in expansion of territory and acquisition of resources. Of course, such a desire hardly differentiated the Athenians from other Greeks in the preclassical (archaic) period (ca. 800–500 BC). In this period, Greek city-states launched colonizing projects all over the Mediterranean and Black Sea, from Spain to the Crimea. The Athenians,[2] somewhat oddly, played almost no role in the early period of colonization, preferring to consolidate their hold on the very large and perhaps relatively underexploited region of Attica itself.[3] Yet by at least 600 BC or so, they were attempting to gain control over a crucial region (Sigeion) commanding the Hellespont, the narrow neck of water that acted as the gateway to the Black Sea and the grain supply on which Athens would rely for the rest of classical antiquity (see Figure I).[4] Once they had achieved direct control over the region of Attica, the Athenians apparently began rather quickly to search for more distant projects that offered the potential for expansion and economic advantage. But it remains surprising that their first (documented) foreign adventure, as it were, took place more than 175 miles from Athens, in a location that could be reached only by means of sea travel. Like most Greeks, the Athenians, it would seem, were committed seafarers.

From about 600 BC, Athens' foreign policy would remain remarkably consistent. The Athenians sought influence over the Hellespont and the regions on both sides of the straits, the regions along the coast of Macedon and Thrace in the north (where there were mines and timber), and islands in the Aegean (especially those linking Athens to the Hellespont). To understand the Athens of Pericles' day, one must understand that to be an Athenian meant to participate in a long-standing effort to project Athens' power far beyond Attica.[5]

The century immediately before Pericles' birth (which probably occurred sometime around 500–495 BC)[6] saw Athens engaged in a series of aggressive campaigns to extend the city's power.[7] Beyond the effort to gain influence over the Hellespont, Athens fought a war much closer to home. Athens and Megara, a city just to the west of Attica on the isthmus connecting northern Greece to the Peloponnese (see Figure II), contended for control of the island of Salamis.[8] The island's position in the Saronic Gulf, lying just west of Athens and just east of Megara, had probably encouraged long-standing disputes over the territory. Athens asserted a claim on the island based on the descendants of Ajax, the Homeric hero who had sailed to Troy from (then independent) Salamis. The Athenians maintained that Ajax's son Philaeus had become an Athenian, and a very prominent Athenian family (connected with Kimon, Pericles' greatest rival) claimed descent from Ajax through Philaeus.[9] There were counterclaims: some said that lines in Homer's *Iliad* ostensibly showing Salamis as an ally (if not dependency) of Athens had been added by the Athenian lawgiver Solon to justify Athens' claim on the island.[10]

Indeed, even the Athenians could not assert that Athens had actually exercised some sort of ancient control over Salamis itself, as the "Philaeus *became* an Athenian" story shows. Athens could not claim the great Ajax of Salamis as a (technical) Athenian. As we shall see, Athens had a notoriously weak heritage from the heroic age and the Athenians' attempt to capture the glory of Ajax through the rather lame story of his son Philaeus becoming an Athenian bespeaks a desperate attempt to give Athens some praiseworthy connection to the heroes of the Trojan War, the most famous event in Greek history. Athens' own hero at Troy – Menestheus – plays an embarrassingly minor role in the tale.[11]

In any case, by 600 or so the Athenians sought to gain control over Salamis and fought a long war, or perhaps engaged in a series of smaller conflicts, with Megara for control of the island. The future lawgiver Solon and the eventual Athenian tyrant Peisistratus both served in these wars and apparently earned their first fame through their military success.[12] By the end of the sixth century, Athens had incorporated Salamis into the political entity of Athens proper, but this was the last time Athens would add new territory and thus new citizens to the formal, independent polis of Athens: future conquests would provide new resources and opportunities, but not new *citizens*, possessing the privilege of ruling themselves in return for performing civic duties.[13]

In the middle of the sixth century, while the tyrant family of Peisistratus and his sons dominated Athens (ca. 546–511/10 BC), Athens continued its efforts to control the southern side of the Hellespont (via Sigeion) and also moved to control the Chersonese, the spit of land commanding the northern (European) side of the straits. The Athenian Miltiades (uncle to the famous victor at Marathon in 490) became tyrant of the region, eventually passing down that position to other relations. Like the tyrants of Athens, Miltiades would have exercised powers that were largely informal but nonetheless real.[14] Although the family of Miltiades (called Kimonids or Philaids by moderns) apparently later claimed that they had been at odds with the Peisistratids of Athens, the actual events of the period (as

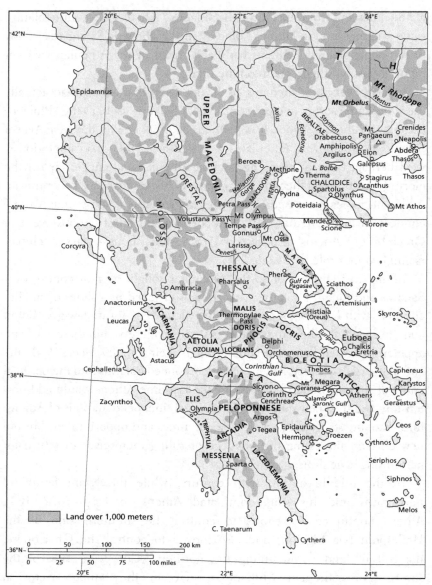

I. Greece and the Aegean Sea. Athenian foreign policy over several centuries demonstrated special interest in the Hellespont and lands on either side of the straits, the Thraceward region (especially the areas around the Strymon River and Amphipolis), and Aegean islands including Euboea, Skyros, Lemnos, and Imbros.

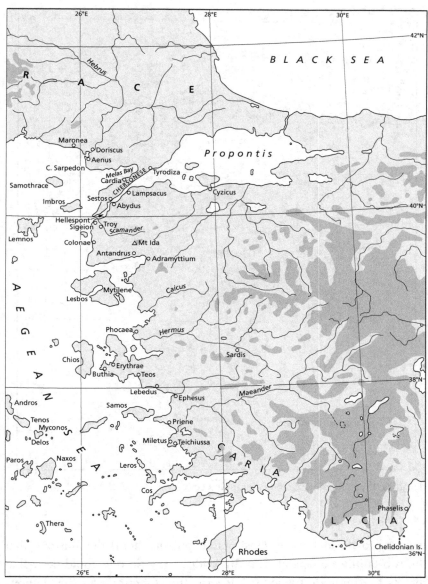

I. (cont.)

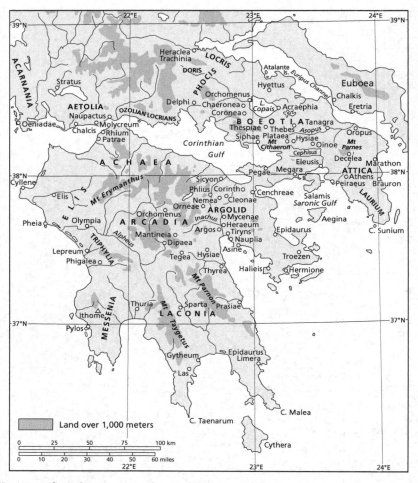

II. Attica, the Peloponnese, and central Greece.

opposed to the defensive construction put on them) demonstrate that the two families cooperated in this endeavor.[15] No one could deny that the last Kimonid/Philaid to govern the Chersonese, the famous Miltiades who would win the battle of Marathon, had gone to the Chersonese with the support of the Peisistratids. Moreover, this Miltiades captured the island of Lemnos (and probably Imbros) around 500 BC and handed it to Athens.[16] In short, with the family of Miltiades in the Chersonese and Athens holding on to Sigeion, the Athenians by the middle of the sixth century BC had achieved enviable positions commanding both sides of the crucial Hellespont.[17]

Other Athenian foreign policy adventures in the sixth century included Peisistratus's conquest of the great island of Naxos in the southern Aegean (where he installed a supporter as tyrant and where he left hostages, undoubtedly members of Athenian families less than cooperative with the Peisistratids) and the purification of Delos, an island sacred to Ionian Greeks.[18] Delos would figure prominently in later Athenian imperial ambitions, and it may well be that by the middle of the sixth century Peisistratus was already attempting to exploit the Athenian tradition as "mother city" of all the Ionians (the Greek ethnic/dialect group that inhabited most of the Aegean islands and much of the coast of Asia Minor).[19] The Peisistratids also derived some kind of revenues from the Thraceward region in the northern Aegean, and it seems likely that Athenians were therefore already involved in the mining interests in the area.[20]

According to Herodotus, the Athenians became an even more formidable military force after the overthrow of the Peisistratids in 511/10.[21] In an act of reprisal for a raid on Attica around 506 BC, the Athenians launched a major expedition to the island of Euboea (to the east of Attica), seized a huge amount of territory there, and ensconced 4,000 Athenians on land formerly belonging to the city of Chalkis.[22]

By the time of Pericles' birth, Athens already had a long-standing tradition of aggression and a kind of nascent empire, in that Athenians sought to exploit and profit from their control of several crucial regions outside of Athens (or Attica) proper. As we shall see, although Athens in the years just after 500 BC faced a major threat posed by an aggressive Persia, the Persian Wars did nothing to slow Athens' attempt to expand its influence over the Aegean basin.[23]

TYRANNY

We have seen that Athens came under the rule of the family of the Peisistratids in the middle of the sixth century (ca. 546 BC, though there were two earlier attempts to seize control).[24] Although the modern word "tyrant" has exclusively negative connotations, the Greek *tyrannos*, from which it derives, originally did not. Tyrants in Greece were simply individuals who achieved an inordinate amount of power and control outside of normal channels. They could be elected officials, former or current military leaders, or even kings (a type of which still existed in some parts of Greece into the historical period) who successfully arrogated enough power to themselves to dominate their respective city-states. While some tyrants came to be viewed as malicious, cruel, arrogant, or hybristic, more typically the view of a particular tyrant depended on the source describing him. Peisistratus and his sons provide an excellent example of this. Although it is true that many Athenians viewed the last years of rule by Peisistratus's son Hippias as a dark period in which the tyrant lorded it over the Athenian people, a strong tradition also existed that praised the Peisistratids for moderate rule. The historian Thucydides tells us that the Peisistratids simply attempted to have "one of their own" in office (he probably means the archonship, Athens' chief magistracy), and Herodotus remarks that the Peisistratids ruled in accordance with laws of the time.[25] For some, the period of Peisistratid rule seemed a golden age in Athens, and indeed there is no record of the Athenian people (as opposed to certain groups of aristocrats) ever mounting a serious effort to oppose the tyrants until the very end of their reign.[26]

But whether we view the Peisistratid tyranny as a golden age or a period of oppression, we must recognize that the period played a major role in shaping the Athens Pericles would inhabit. For one thing, tyrannic government in general and the Peisistratids in particular tended to suppress the power of (at least some of) the aristocratic families and clans that dominated Greek polis government in the archaic period (before 500 BC). Aristocratic families were always vying with one another for influence and control in Greek city-states, but occasionally one family managed to gain enough power that it could supersede the others. This is certainly the process by which at least some tyrants (including those in Athens) achieved power.[27]

Tyrants like the Peisistratids effectively acted as a centralizing force in terms of power in a Greek city-state. And because they wished to exhibit their dominance over other aristocrats, they often carried out major civic projects (such as construction of temples and other buildings or improvements in the water-supply system) that could underscore their power.[28] Our sources also inform us that the Peisistratids levied a tax on Athenian farmers, a story that (if true) very clearly underscores the statist tendency of some

Greek tyrannies.[29] Direct and regular taxation on produce or income (as opposed to occasional levies for special purposes) was very rare and extremely unpopular even in later, classical Greece.

To put it in other terms, tyrants tended to support and fund construction projects and sponsor religious festivals and activities as well as demand the collection and centralization of revenues as part of their program to accumulate *personal* power (at the expense of other aristocratic families). A (probably unintended) result of these actions was the creation of a potential or active central force within the city-state greater than had previously existed. The government of a typical Greek polis (without a tyrant) in the archaic period exhibited decentralization, with nodes of power that included particular aristocratic families, relatively weak government organs like councils of elders or former magistrates, military leaders and other officials elected or chosen by lot, as well as the citizens themselves sitting in assembly, which tended to have sovereign authority over major questions (like war or peace). A tyrant had the potential to bypass some or all of these sources of power and to arrogate to himself and his family a concentration of authority that had not been seen before in a Greek city-state.

But what happened when the tyranny collapsed? In Athens it seems clear that not all of the authority acquired by the family of the Peisistratids devolved on the previous power centers in Athens. Rather, the city-state itself (in the form of its citizen body) retained some of the centralized power created by the tyrants.[30] The aristocrats thus emerged from the tyranny as a weaker (if still very important) group, while the city exhibited an increased willingness and ability to intervene in citizens' economic lives and to undertake massive projects in a way that was hardly conceivable before the tyranny. The tyranny therefore created conditions Pericles and others would exploit in the fifth century by making something like "state power" tangible in Athens, although the ancient Greeks had still not reached the reification of the state and its bureaucracies seen in modern governments. Today we speak of "the government," "the IRS," and the like as if they are independent agents acting on us. The classical Greeks usually expressed the idea of the state – to the extent they employed it all – through the collective citizenry: "the Athenians" took this or that action.

As we shall see, the negative tradition about the Peisistratids (as tyrants in the modern sense of the word) played a major role in shaping Pericles' early career, especially because his family on his mother's side had been deeply involved with the Peisistratids, first as their allies, and later (so they claimed) as their enemies.

SILVER MINES

Athens was the only major Greek power to possess its own native supply of precious metal, and by the middle of the fifth century the Athenians had come to control the other sites in the Aegean with similar capabilities. Although the mines in southern Attica may have been worked for centuries, in the late sixth century the Athenians discovered particularly rich veins of silver there. This metal, extracted perhaps by newly adopted and more efficient methods, soon after made its appearance in Athenian coinage. The best recent scholarship suggests that this occurred late in the Peisistratid period, perhaps circa 520–515, a fact that helps us explain how the Athenians came to consider the mines of Attica public property.[31] It seems likely that the Peisistratid family gained control over these mines and that when the family was deposed in 511/10, the mines remained public property rather than reverting to the private citizens who had presumably owned the land before the Peisistratid takeover.[32]

If this picture is accurate, it shows us a very tangible way in which the tyranny led to greater centralization of control and authority in Athens. Once the tyrants departed, all the powers they had accumulated did not return to private individuals or associations. Rather, some of that authority remained centered on the government – that is to say, in a Greek polis, on the citizenry itself acting as a collective.

In any case, by the early fifth century the Athenians had come to treat the revenues of the mines as public property. This would have a great impact on Athens' history, allowing the Athenians to construct a very large fleet in 483/2 and thus to make themselves almost overnight into a naval superpower.[33] This fleet permitted the Athenians not only to help the Greek allies defeat the Persians in 480–479 but also to extend their sphere of influence and control over the entire Aegean in the following years.

Beyond funding the fleet, the silver of Attica freed up other sources of revenue and allowed the Athenians to spend huge sums on buildings, temples, festivals, and payments to the citizen body. Combined with the money the Athenians collected from other Greek states (using the fleet the silver mines had made possible), Athens' wealth in the time of Pericles surpassed that of any other Greek state.

HEROIC-AGE HERITAGE

I t is perhaps difficult for us to appreciate how great a role the past – or, rather, what was believed about the past – played in many ancient cultures. The Greeks' obsession with their own history confronts the student of Hellenic culture and literature repeatedly, especially their obsession with events that supposedly occurred in the generations before, during, and just after the Trojan War. Many Greeks of Pericles' day undoubtedly realized that some of these accounts were dubious, but it is probably fair to say that most Athenians and other Greeks accepted the basic "facts" of their distant past as more or less established and authentic.[34]

Those facts portrayed certain states[35] – and here we are talking about kingdoms rather than city-states – and individuals as particularly significant and heroic, especially the kingdoms of Thebes, Argos, Mycenae, and Sparta and warriors like Agamemnon and Achilles and the demigod Herakles. Even smallish islands (Salamis, Ithaca) and far-flung, eventual backwaters (Crete) had produced first-rate heroes like Ajax, Odysseus, and Diomedes in the distant past. Yet, as we have already seen, Athens had no great hero and hardly even a discernible presence in Homer's *Iliad* or *Odyssey* or many of the tales surrounding the Trojan War. The greatest story of the Greeks' past in its most repeated form – the seizure (and return) of Helen and the final attack on Troy – offered virtually no scope for Athenian glory.

Yet the Athenians did claim to have a great hero from this age (or, rather, from the period just before the famous war with Troy). Athens' mythical ancient king Theseus figures prominently in the Athenians' stories about themselves. Most famously, Theseus freed Athens from domination by the Cretans and their monstrous Minotaur, a tale that also clearly demonstrates the discomfort Athenians felt about their heroic-age heritage. Why, after all, did great Athens need to be freed from the control of Cretans (!), who by the historical period played a very minor role in Greek history? Such a story would be roughly analogous to an American legend of George Washington freeing the United States from the overlordship of Iceland or Norway. Indeed, if we analyze Theseus's greatest actions, we find that they are usually remedial, attempting to raise Athens to a level with other great, heroic-age states rather than establishing something special about Athens. Theseus, for example, recaptures the Marathonian bull (after Herakles had done so), saves Athens from marauding female warriors (the Amazons), sweeps brigands and robbers off the roads, and brings the residents of Attica together as a single state.[36] These tales did find a way to connect Theseus with the Trojan War cycle, by making him an early abductor of Helen (before Paris's more famous action), but this story, like so many others about Theseus, has the ring of desperation about it.[37]

So intent were the Athenians on improving their hero Theseus's status (and on justifying contemporary actions) that they eventually made him into the founder of Athenian imperialism and of Athenian democracy.[38] Such accomplishments were unlikely to resonate with other Greek states, and they underscore the Athenians' deep need to provide an imposing heroic-age heritage for themselves in order to raise their standing relative to Greek states with more illustrious pasts.[39]

AUTOCHTHONY

The Athenians' need to establish a special ancient history and heritage for themselves took another form that would be important in Pericles' day. Unlike most other Greeks, who often claimed descent from invaders or foreigners (the Thebans from Cadmus of Phoenicia, the Atreid family of Argos from Asia Minor, the ancient Peloponnesian Danaids from Egypt), the Athenians claimed to have always lived in the region of Attica. They were autochthonous, or descended from ancestors "sprung from the very soil."[40]

Hints and more, to be sure, remained even in the Athenians' own traditions that they had in fact expelled an earlier, perhaps pre-Greek population from Attica. Herodotus tells a fantastic and violent tale about the ancient Pelasgians and the way the Athenians drove them out of Attica, only to have the Pelasgians take bloody vengeance on the Athenians by abducting and then murdering Athenian women and the children those women bore them.[41]

The story, of course, reminds us (as the Greeks themselves believed) that the Hellenes were not native to the region that came to be called "Hellas" after them. (The name "Hellenes" itself is relatively late, as Homer does not refer to the Greeks by the term, a fact that Thucydides recognizes.[42]) As we have seen, stories of the migrations of the peoples eventually known as Greeks are commonplaces in the heroic tradition. Even the descendants of Herakles – the Herakleidai, including Dorian Sparta's ancestors – "returned" to the Peloponnese after being driven out.[43]

Thus the Athenians' insistence on their perpetual residence in Attica stands out as a very unusual claim for an ancient Greek people.[44] What, we might ask, did the Athenians stand to gain by such a claim?[45] Certainly it seems that the Athenians in the fifth century eventually used their claim to autochthony as a way to (attempt to) justify things like the Athenian empire or Athens' unusual government.[46] But why seize on the notion of auto-chthony, which (again) had no particular resonance in Hellas at large? The difficult answer to this question suggests another possibility: that the tradition rests on some kind of historical basis. It is at least possible that a good portion of the pre-Greek population of Attica (Herodotus's tale about the Pelasgians notwithstanding) remained there after the Greeks arrived. There is, in fact, little question that many non-Greek names and surely also people survived the invasion of the southern Balkans by Greek speakers (whenever that occurred: there is no scholarly consensus, though it must have hap-pened before about 1700 BC).[47] In this case, the legend of the Pelasgians' expulsion from Attica could have developed to counter claims that the ancient pre-Greeks had in fact remained and become "Athenians." Indeed, Herodotus at one point states baldly that the Athenians were Pelasgic in origin rather than Hellenic.[48]

The idea that the Athenians were not originally Greek certainly could have provided later Athenians with an incentive to explain their heritage in some way. But we should also consider the possibility that the Athenians, lacking any tradition of descent from heroic foreigners and desirous of some way to make themselves distinctive in a Greek world dominated by tales of the greatness and heritage of Sparta, Argos, Thebes, and other states, simply seized on an aspect no other major Greek power claimed: that of auto-chthony. The claim had the particular benefit of attracting no jealous attempts to disprove it, since other Greeks were happy enough with their foreign heritage. Moreover, even if one wished to debunk the Athenian claim, how could it possibly be done? In fact, the other Greeks appeared to have been perfectly satisfied to let the Athenians go on calling themselves "autochthonous" throughout the classical period.[49]

By the time of Pericles, however, the claim of autochthony seems to have produced a certain feeling of something like Athenian purity and superiority.[50] As we shall see, the Athenians of Pericles' day would restrict citizenship to those with both an Athenian father and an Athenian mother (whereas typically Greek citizenship passed through the male line). Other factors (beyond the idea of "real Athenians") clearly encouraged this action, but the Athenians' long-standing view of themselves as a people "sprung from the very soil" (or "always inhabiting the same land") surely made the restriction of the citizen privileges to a narrow group all the more attractive.

IONIAN VERSUS DORIAN

One might doubt that the Athenians of Pericles' day actually felt any discomfort about their hero Theseus, but there is little doubt that they felt uneasy about another aspect of their heritage. Athens, by ancient tradition, served as the mother country of the Greeks who called themselves Ionians. Today we think of this as a linguistic distinction – Ionic versus other dialects of Greek, such as Doric or Aeolic – but to the ancient Greeks "Ionian" stood for an ethnic or descent group.[51]

Most Ionian Greeks lived in Asia Minor or the Aegean islands, where (legend had it) they had fled after leaving Attica.[52] On the mainland, the Athenians thus found themselves surrounded by Greeks with a different ethnic heritage, especially the Dorians of Megara, Corinth, and Aegina, all of whom would be longtime enemies of Athens and all of whom would be aligned with the premier Dorian power, Sparta.

The Athenians of Pericles' day faced a problem: their status as the mother country of Ionians could be politically advantageous to them when they dealt with the islands or other Ionian states. On the other hand, Ionian Greeks had the reputation (to other Greeks) of luxury and effeminacy, a fact that Herodotus (who hailed from Dorian Halicarnassus in Asia Minor, near Ionian strongholds) in particular brings out, calling the Ionians of the fifth century BC "thrice conquered" – once by Lydia and twice by Persia.[53]

At some point before the classical period Athenian men had stopped adorning their hair with golden grasshoppers (after the fashion of Ionians) and adopted the more conservative style of attire favored by Dorians.[54] This may seem a small or insignificant action, but it suggests an attempt by the Athenian men to distance themselves from their Ionian relations and assimilate themselves to their more Dorian surroundings. Many Athenians (like other Greeks) admired the Dorian Spartans in particular, and even during and after the great wars between Athens and Sparta in the fifth century, some Athenians associated themselves with Sparta and Spartan culture by means of fashions (like wearing their hair long in Spartan style) or giving their children Spartan or Spartophilic names (for example, Pericles' rival Kimon named one of his sons Lakedaimonios: "The Spartan").[55]

Athens' unusual relationship with Sparta (which forms one of the great love-hate stories in all of antiquity) must be examined closely when we discuss Pericles' foreign policy, but we should at least notice here that the Athenians did feel a powerful attraction to non-Ionian styles and manners and that they did just as much to distance themselves from their Ionian heritage (in the context of their domestic life) as they did to emphasize it (in their foreign relations with Ionian powers).

SUPPLIANTS

The Athenians took great pride in their ancient reputation as the protector of suppliants—those who sought sacred protection from others by placing themselves at the mercy of an individual or power. This tradition of protecting the weak played, one may speculate, an increasing role after the Persian Wars, when the Athenians could make an at least partially sincere claim to acting as guardians of smaller powers against Persian encroachment. Nevertheless, the tradition of Athens' welcoming suppliants was unquestionably ancient, and Athens plays this role in several legends from the heroic age.[56] Indeed, Athens in these traditions acts as a kind of staging area for major actions by non-Athenians, whether it is the return of the descendants of Herakles to the Peloponnese or the departure of Ionians for the islands and Asia Minor.[57]

Geographically and historically, this tradition makes a good deal of sense. Attica lies between the Peloponnese and central Greece and between all of southern Greece and the islands. The region therefore acted as a natural conduit for travel north and south (via land) and east and west (via sea). With an extensive coastline that faced both east and west, and an adequate natural harbor (Phaleron), Athens offered obvious attractions for invaders, refugees, travelers, and traders. These facts, combined with the strong tradition of Athenian protection of suppliants, suggests that Athens did in fact play an important role in assisting and perhaps protecting others moving about Greece in the archaic period and before. Whatever the precise truth of the claims, the Athenians proudly trumpeted this heritage, and it played a role in the Athenians' presentation of themselves throughout the age of Pericles and beyond. Pericles himself apparently drew on these traditions in his portrait of Athenian greatness.[58]

THE GODS

All Greek city-states claimed a special relationship with one or more gods, and for the Athenians, of course, their protective deity was the goddess Athena, from whom the city took its name. Many of Athens' citizens also had a special relationship with the goddesses Demeter and Kore, who were worshipped in special mysteries celebrated at Eleusis, to the north and west of Athens proper in Attica.[59] Indeed, Greeks eventually came from around the Mediterranean to experience the sacred rites of Eleusis, but in the early period that concerns us, the mysteries remained a largely Athenian affair.[60]

Like other aspects of Athens' weak heroic-age heritage, the city itself (despite its special claim on a relationship with Zeus's daughter, Athena) does not appear to have held a special significance in Greek religion before the historical period. This should not surprise us, given the fact that the Greeks' most ancient sacred sites (Olympos, Delphi, Olympia, Dodona) were located in relative backwaters. Still, Athens was distant from these sites and claimed no special relationship with any of them (as, for example, the Spartans claimed with Delphi). These facts, along with the higher profile of states like Sparta, Argos, and Thebes in heroic tales of Greece's past, again gave Athens something of an apparent disadvantage when it came to propitiation of the gods.

By the sixth century (and perhaps before this) the Athenians had sought to raise the city's sacred profile by attempting to make the annual celebration of Athena and Athens (the Panathenaia) into an international Greek festival along the lines of festivals held in Olympia, Corinth, Delphi, and elsewhere.[61] In the fifth century, when the Athenians ruled a very large Greek empire, they eventually required their allies (now in fact subjects who made annual payments to Athens) to play the part of Athenian "colonists" and attend Athenian festivals laden with gifts for Athens' gods.[62] By that time Athens had become the most cosmopolitan and culturally elite city in Hellas, so many Greeks also attended these festivals for the sheer spectacle and entertainment rather than under compulsion.

Nevertheless, by the time Pericles achieved political dominance, the Athenians may have begun to attempt to foster or compel the worship of their goddess Athena outside of Athens and Attica. Certainly lands seized in other Greek states were dedicated to Athena, and rents were paid to her treasury from these properties.[63] When the Athenians collected tribute payments from their Greek subjects, they donated 1/60th of these funds to Athena off the top every year, and deposited much larger sums in her treasury (thereby making them available for Athenian projects like military operations and buildings).[64] As we shall see, under Pericles' guidance they also constructed the most elaborate temples yet attempted in the Greek world, especially the fantastically expensive temple on the acropolis dedicated to Athena Parthenos (the "maiden").[65]

With their remarkably humanistic approach to propitiating the gods, the Greeks built temples that surely glorified the builders as much as the honored deities, eating the choicest cuts of beef themselves after sacrificing the animals and burning the thighbones wrapped in fat for the gods. The Athenians' special relationship with Athena allowed or encouraged them to identify the goddess with the city, or rather with themselves. Was the Panathenaia festival "all Athena" or "all Athens" or "all Athenian"?[66] To the Athenians, the question probably did not much matter. It is clear, however, that as soon as the Athenians were able to do so, they forced other Greeks to grant to themselves and their tutelary goddess Athena a kind of sacred status that the city had never before possessed. This serves as an excellent reminder to us that the term "religion" today connotes an area of life distinct from the "secular" and that modern, Western culture (beyond Islam) has often strived to keep these spheres separate. Such an idea of separate spheres remained wholly alien to the ancient Greeks, who began everything from political meetings and dramatic contests to drinking parties with prayers and libations to the gods. In short, Athens' religious policy, if we can use an anachronistic term, reflected simply one part of a unified attempt to glorify Athens and Athenians as a whole (through Athena and other gods and their associated rites). This constituted no debasement of religion or the sacred, but rather continued a long tradition in which the religious, political, social, economic, and private spheres had no separate existence in theory or in practice.[67]

We should also note that the Athenians sought a special relationship with Apollo as he was worshipped on the small, central Aegean island of Delos, a place sacred to the Ionian Greeks, as we have seen. The tyrant Peisistratus had carried out or simply sponsored a "purification" of the island, suggesting that already in the sixth century some Athenians sought to portray themselves as the benefactors and protectors of Ionian Greeks as a whole.[68] A special connection with Delian Apollo could also balance the Dorian Spartans' close relations with Apollo at Delphi.[69] In the 470s BC, when the Athenians founded the new league against Persia that would swiftly become the Athenian empire, they made Delos the official capital of this alliance (hence the name Delian League, which moderns apply to what the ancients called "the Athenians and their allies"). The moneys collected from other Greek states rested on the island of Delos – admittedly managed by Athenian officials called euphemistically "Treasurers of the Greeks" (Hellenotamiai).[70] The allies met in the temple of Apollo on the sacred island, probably until the mid-450s, when the Athenians moved the moneys collected and stored on Delos to Athens and dedicated a good portion of them to Athena.[71] If the moneys had previously been dedicated to Apollo (as they may or may not have been), this fact apparently caused the Athenians little pause. As much as they wished to appear to be Apollo's and the Ionians' benefactors, the Athenians valued their relationship with Athena – a goddess whose worship came near to self-idolization – beyond any other connection with the divine.

TO BE AN ATHENIAN

Several factors combined to give the Athenians a unique profile and heritage in the centuries before Pericles' career. But what, one may ask, about those things *we* most closely associate with Athens – drama and other literature, philosophy, mastery of the material arts, and especially democracy? To be sure, the Athenians of Pericles' day made Athens into the cultural and intellectual capital of Hellas and therefore of the world in the fifth century BC.[72] However, to claim that Athens was special because of these things and then attempt to analyze them obscures a fundamental question: What was it about Athens and the Athenians that *produced* the fifth-century revolution in politics, literature, art, and thought? The response cannot be "fifth-century Athens." The answers (complex as they must be) rest in the period before these developments. This method of analyzing the past constitutes a radical theory – one all too rarely noticed in today's academy, where other kinds of theories (deriving from the social sciences or literary theory) hold sway. My friend and fellow historian Brendan McConville sarcastically calls this radical theory "chronology." To understand the Athenians of Pericles' day, we must attempt to understand what they had inherited and who they were *before* the epochal events – such as the Persian Wars and the creation of democracy – that obviously had a major impact on Athenian life and culture. We must attempt to understand upon what Athenian stuff these other later factors acted. The Athenians, after all, were not the only state to fight and defeat the Persians or to cast votes to make state policy.

So can we sum up what Pericles and his contemporaries inherited from their ancestors? In brief, all the factors we have described (and undoubtedly others) combined to provide the Athenians of Pericles' day with a complex and perhaps even contradictory view of themselves. Athens had a tradition of aggression and expansion in the archaic period but a dubious reputation from the heroic age. Both factors would play a role in fifth-century Athenian history, when Athens would finally establish a firm military reputation. Analysis of Pericles' Funeral Oration in Thucydides, other funeral speeches and orations given in classical Athens, and additional evidence like the Athenians' building policy and the uses to which they put their surplus revenues demonstrate that the Athenians of Pericles' day placed greater emphasis on their military prowess (and, perhaps, on their supposed role as a protector of suppliants) than on their cultural or political advances.[73] We are now better positioned to understand why this might be so. While tales about Theseus and far-flung Athenian adventures in the northeast Aegean demonstrate the city's early aspirations as a military power, the defeat of the Persians – first at Marathon and then at Salamis, Plataea, and Eurymedon (490 to ca. 466 BC) – finally provided the Athenians with the evidence to advance claims that could not previously have been easily supported through accounts of their earlier relations with neighboring Greeks. After these fifth-century victories, the Athenians could at last claim to be a first-rate power in Hellas. As we shall see, Athens' subsequent employment of naval forces – funded by Attica's highly unusual silver mines and created to defeat the Persians – in order to reduce their former Greek allies to servitude placed a seal on the Athenians' martial prowess. The Athenians, who had for ages past seen themselves as somehow different, and not always in completely comfortable ways, found something beyond the dubious claims of autochthony and spawning the Ionians on which to base their ever-increasing pride. In this environment, Pericles' message of Athenian superiority and his hyper-nationalist agenda would take root and bear prodigious fruit.

Beyond the Athenians' history and tradition of aggression, perhaps the inherited factor that most influenced Pericles and his contemporaries was the successful tyranny of the Peisistratids. Remarkable parallels exist between Athens' actions and policies under Peisistratus and his sons and those under Periclean and democratic leadership. Pericles' Athens would, in effect, have the same friends and enemies as Peisistratid Athens and seek to dominate or influence the same areas of the Aegean basin. Perhaps even more striking (as we shall see in the next chapter), the Peisistratid tyranny exposed and aggravated a weakness in the Athenian aristocracy and a latent power in the Athenian populace at large. The common Athenians apparently supported the tyrants until the Spartans intervened and overthrew the regime. The aristocrats who resisted the Peisistratids (as opposed to those who assisted them) possessed insufficient power or support to end the tyranny by themselves. And once the tyrants had been expelled, the Athenian people supported a new regime created by a former ally and marriage relation of the Peisistratids. This man, Cleisthenes, who received credit for founding Athenian *demokratia*, stemmed from the family of the Alkmeonids, the clan that also produced Pericles' mother.[74]

At least some Athenians recognized how much they owed to the period of Peisistratid rule. Nevertheless, a strong antityrant tradition, doubtless fostered by the aristocratic families whom the tyrants had disadvantaged, arose soon after the tyranny's collapse and gained strength throughout the fifth century. In a remarkable and probably unintentional act of historical legerdemain, the aristocrats who had (it was maintained) unsuccessfully attempted to overthrow the tyranny became heroes of democratic Athens.[75] What in the sixth century had been an opposition (from the aristocrats' point of view) between aristocratic or "free" government and tyrannic or "unfree" regimes, had by the middle of the fifth century become an opposition between democratic "free" government and "unfree" tyrannic or aristocratic/oligarchic regimes. The irony, of course, lay in the fact that the tyrannic regime had actually championed and empowered the middle- and lower-class Athenians at the expense of the wealthier citizens. For anyone, especially Athenians of the fifth century, to lump tyrants and aristocrats/oligarchs together as enemies of freedom or democracy represents (then and now) a deep misunderstanding of the sixth-century political environment.

But that misunderstanding provided Pericles and other democratic leaders with a superb tool for exploiting the populace's fear of any regime that could be painted as limiting their advantages and freedoms. It allowed Pericles to adopt certain techniques of the tyrants while defending himself against any accusations of tyranny. Such accusations clearly occurred. Even the Athenian lawgiver Solon had been accused of attempting to set himself up as a tyrant, and some Athenians claimed that Pericles bore a striking resemblance to Peisistratus, especially in his voice.[76]

The voice proved to be crucial. It was the tool used by Pericles to inspire and provoke the Athenian people. That people had inherited a past many knew fell short of that of their neighbors and Ionian relations, who even the Athenians believed to be effete and easily conquered. Pericles addressed an Athenian people with the motive, resources, and will to change Athens' relationship with other Greeks and to establish – at long last – a heritage for the Athenian people that no other Greek state could match.

Few Athenians after Pericles' day would feel any discomfort about Theseus, Homer's songs of Greek (but little Athenian) greatness, or weak Ionian relatives. Pericles would promise and deliver to Athens a new heritage, a new history on which future Athenians could pride themselves and at which other Greeks could only wonder. In this way, Pericles would seek to conquer both the Athenians' past and their future.

TWO

Curses, Tyrants, and Persians
(ca. 500–479)

Analysis of Pericles' career demands attention to his family background as well as the periods just before and after his birth. Pericles' ancestors on his mother's side had incurred a religious curse in the late seventh century BC but then enjoyed (and suffered from) close relations with the tyrant family of the Peisistratrids, who ruled Athens from about 546 to 510 BC. Pericles' maternal family also produced the reformer Cleisthenes, who around 507 passed the measures establishing Athenian democratic government – a more liberalized form of Greek polis government, which typically embraced popular sovereignty. This family, however, fell out of favor with the Athenians, and Pericles' father was ostracized (exiled for ten years) by the Athenians when Pericles was a youth, returning only in the general recall of exiles before the great war with Persia in 480–479. Pericles' father Xanthippus went on to play a leading role in that war, but Pericles inherited a checkered family history and, through that history, complicated relations with his fellow aristocrats, Sparta, Persia, and the Athenian people.

A few years after the glorious Athenian victory over the invading Persians at Marathon (490 BC), the young Pericles – perhaps in his early to mid-teens – learned that the Athenians had voted to ostracize his father, Xanthippus (485/4). Such a vote meant that his father, and undoubtedly Pericles and his mother, would have to leave their home and remain outside of Athens and Attica for the next ten years. Between 485/4 and 481/0, when the Athenians recalled those who had been ostracized, Xanthippus and his family lived as exiles in parts unknown.[1]

III. *Ostrakon* with the name of Pericles. This *ostrakon* was used by an Athenian to cast a vote against Pericles son of Xanthippus ("Perikles Xsanthippo"). Thousands of such *ostraka* bearing the names of Athenian leaders have been discovered in excavations at Athens. Although the Athenians never banished Pericles, they did vote to ostracize his father Xanthippus (485/4) and his political rivals Kimon (462/1) and Thucydides son of Melesias (444/3). Photo: Getty Images.

We should recall that it was not "the government" that forced Xanthippus to flee his homeland. Athenian ostracism occurred because a majority of the regular Athenian citizens meeting in a special assembly voted that an individual should be forced to leave. The Athenians voting in favor of ostracism needed no reason for the expulsion beyond suspicion, jealousy, or mere distaste. At this assembly each Athenian wrote a name on an *ostrakon* (the piece of broken pottery that gives ostracism its name: see Figure III), and occasionally the voters would add a word or two to suggest their personal motivation for the expulsion ("the accursed," "the Mede," etc.). More frequently they did not bother to provide any explanation for their choice. Our ancient sources associate the origins of ostracism with the idea of preventing another tyranny or simply restraining individuals who had gained too much authority, but whatever the institution's original purpose, no restrictions prevented an Athenian from voting to ostracize anyone against whom he felt a grudge. Indeed, a review of the Athenians ostracized or receiving significant numbers of votes for ostracism in the fifth century produces the names of many powerful politicians but only a few potential tyrants.[2]

One need not have studied psychology to understand the possible effects of this event on the young Pericles. His fellow citizens had exiled his father, a prominent figure who, after his return from ostracism, would serve with great distinction as one of Athens' elected generals.[3] Xanthippus had married into one of the most illustrious, if infamous, families in Athens. Indeed, this marriage is likely to have provided the primary cause for Xanthippus's ostracism.

Xanthippus's wife (and Pericles' mother) Agariste stemmed from the Athenian family known as the Alkmeonids. The family had been very prominent in Athenian history, holding the office of archon (chief magistrate) as early as the seventh century BC, before the reforms of the lawgivers Drakon and Solon. Yet sometime around 632 BC or so the family suffered a major setback, from which it would never completely recover. When an Athenian named Kylon attempted to make himself tyrant of Athens (with the support of his father-in-law, who was tyrant of nearby Megara), the people of Athens resisted and surrounded the would-be tyrant's supporters on the acropolis. Kylon's embattled allies sought the protection of a sacred altar, making themselves suppliants and thus gaining the protection of divine law: a Greek could not lawfully harm a suppliant after offering him protection. Despite this fact, some Athenian magistrates had Kylon's supporters executed after promising that the suppliants would not be harmed, and the Athenians believed that those performing this sacrilegious act had incurred a curse. Whatever the truth of the actual events, blame for this impiety came to rest on one family – the Alkmeonids. The Athenians subsequently expelled the Alkmeonid family from Athens and had the city ritually purified.[4]

The Alkmeonid family secured their return to Athens by around 590 BC and maintained a high profile in Greece at large. Megacles, the son of Alkmeon, gained an advantageous alliance by marrying Agariste, the daughter of Cleisthenes, the tyrant of Sicyon.[5] (Both the names Agariste and Cleisthenes would be adopted into the Alkmeonid family in subsequent generations.) Yet the stain of the curse remained with the Alkmeonids and continued to affect events in Athens throughout the sixth and fifth centuries BC, even as the family played a prominent role in Athenian politics. Indeed, when Peisistratus at one point needed an ally to regain the tyranny, he married an Alkmeonid woman in order to secure the support of her father, Megacles.[6] Later, in 525/4, during the tyranny of Peisistratus's son Hippias, Megacles' son Cleisthenes held the archonship (chief magistracy) in Athens. Since it seems clear that at that time the Peisistratids controlled this office, we may presume that some kind of alliance between the two families continued until at least that point.[7]

Nevertheless, after the tyrants were overthrown in 511/0, the Athenians began to rewrite the history of their relationship with the Peisistratids. At that point the Alkmeonid family found itself in need of a defense against the charge of collaboration with the tyrants. They could not deny the marriage of Peisistratus to Megacles' daughter, but they (or someone with similar interests) invented or retold a tale that Peisistratus had relations with his Alkmeonid wife in an abnormal fashion in order to prevent fathering a child from the cursed line. (Such a tale gained plausibility in that Peisistratus already had grown sons by a previous marriage and thus might wish to protect their inheritance.) In another attempt to scrub the record, the Alkmeonids, who had been expelled from Athens again after the murder of the Peisistratid Hippias's brother Hipparchus in 514, also eventually claimed that they had been outside of Athens for the whole period of the tyranny. This, however, constituted a patently false claim (as Cleisthenes' archonship in 525/4 shows) and reflects the Alkmeonid family's desperation to separate themselves from this aspect of their history.[8]

All this had happened before Pericles' birth, ca. 500–495 BC.[9] Sometime before those years, Pericles' father Xanthippus had married the Alkmeonid Agariste (a granddaughter of the Megacles who had given his daughter in marriage to Peisistratus). The marriage is likely to have occurred before 507, because around that year or shortly thereafter the Alkmeonid family suffered another disaster. Megacles' son Cleisthenes had proposed a series of political reforms that would radically reshape the Athenian regime, granting more power to the common Athenian through a new council of state comprising 500 members to be chosen by lot from the citizen body. Cleisthenes, the historian Herodotus tells us, made the common Athenians his political allies (*hetairoi*, "comrades"), thereby defeating his rivals and taking on the role of the people's champion.[10] The Spartans subsequently objected to this new regime, instituted by a marriage relation of the former tyrant Peisistratus and by a man (Cleisthenes) who was himself the homonymous grandson of another tyrant (Cleisthenes of Sicyon). This new government seemed to place this man Cleisthenes (with his tyrannical connections) in the position of the champion and protector of the demos (the common people) against the aristocrats. The Spartans surely saw this regime, eventually to be known as *demokratia*, as nothing other than a new tyranny, a form of government they opposed and sometimes used military force to overthrow.

In any case, upon the invitation of Cleisthenes' political rival Isagoras, the Spartans marched to Attica and demanded that that Athenians "drive out the accursed" (that is, the Alkmeonids). They thereby secured Cleisthenes' and the Alkmeonids' removal when the Athenians complied. But the Athenians balked when the Spartans sought to install a narrow oligarchic regime in place of the newly created council. Having resisted this in force, after the Spartan army returned home the Athenians recalled their exiled champion.[11] What happened next remains imperfectly understood, but it seems that Cleisthenes or his supporters soon after this sought an alliance with Persia as a way to protect Athens (and the Alkmeonids) from future Spartan interference. Cleisthenes, it appears, did not anticipate the Athenians' extremely hostile reaction to this potential relationship with Persia.[12] The fact that he or his allies did not foresee this reaction tells us something interesting: it was apparently possible ca. 507 to believe that the majority of Athenians would not oppose an alliance with Persia, even though the Persians had provided a haven for the exiled Peisistratid tyrant. Yet the belief proved to be unfounded, perhaps because attitudes toward the Athenian tyrants were growing increasingly negative. In the event, the people of Athens rejected the Persian alliance and Cleisthenes was apparently swept from power; thereafter he disappears from Athenian history.[13] By this time (ca. 507, or perhaps a few years later) we should probably assume that Cleisthenes' niece and Pericles' future mother, Agariste, was already married to Xanthippus. Such a marriage was less likely to have occurred in the years just after Cleisthenes' fall from grace.

Xanthippus's close connection with the once again tainted Alkmeonid clan must have made life in these early years of marriage somewhat uncomfortable. We know nothing of Xanthippus's political career at this time, but his ostracism in 485/4 suggests that he managed to overcome the disability of his marriage and achieve some notability – enough, at any rate, to warrant the negative attention of an ostracism. Since Xanthippus was swiftly elected general upon his return to Athens after 481, it is fair to assume he had already established a military career and probably served as general before his ostracism in 485/4.[14] He is likely to have been well over thirty years old (the minimum age for Athenian generals) by this time, since he had apparently already established a political reputation and since (as we have seen) his marriage to Agariste likely predated 507. Moreover, since Xanthippus was almost certainly over twenty years old by the time of his marriage, and perhaps thirty or more, we may put his date of birth no later than ca. 527 BC, while he could have been born as early as ca. 545.[15]

Returning to the young Pericles, we can see that he possessed quite an unusual heritage, one that was both illustrious and problematic. To understand just how problematic, we must examine the events surrounding the famous battle of Marathon in 490 BC and its aftermath. The Athenians, of course, won the battle in northeast Attica and saved Greece (for the first time) from Persian domination. The Persians had arrived at Marathon accompanied and guided by Hippias, the former Peisistratid tyrant of Athens, whom they clearly wished to establish in a puppet regime.[16]

This union of the tyrant family and the Persian menace surely encouraged even more Athenians to adopt a negative interpretation of the Peisistratid tyrants than had hitherto done so. Whatever one had thought about the Peisistratids before Marathon, there could be no justification for one of them collaborating with a Persian attempt to deprive Athens of its freedom and independence. The event also caused some to question the loyalty of other Athenians who were known to have had connections with the Peisistratids, including the Alkmeonids, whose leader Cleisthenes (we must remember) had apparently fallen from power after attempting an alliance with Persia.

These feelings culminated in a charge of treason leveled at the Alkmeonid clan in the years after the battle of Marathon. It was claimed that someone had attempted to assist the invading Persians by flashing a signal to them from a hilltop using a burnished shield.[17] The truth of this tale eludes us, but subsequent events show that many Athenians believed that the Alkmeonids had in fact attempted to betray Athens to Persia.[18] For this reason the Athenians in the early and mid-480s ostracized a series of leading citizens associated with the Peisistratids and Alkmeonids, including Pericles' father, Xanthippus,[19] and his uncle, Megacles.[20] The contemporary poet Pindar commemorated Megacles' victory in the chariot races at Delphi in the same year as his exile (486), while lamenting the Athenian feelings that had led to the Alkmeonid's expulsion.

Athens the might city!
For the strong house of the Alkmaionidai
This is the finest prelude
To lay as foundation stone
Of my chariot-song.
For in what country, what clan, would you dwell
And have more magnificent renown
For Hellas to hear?

For in every city the story runs
Of the citizens of Erechtheus,
Who built in shining Pytho
Thy porch, Apollo, marvelous to behold.[21]
There call to me also
Five victories at the Isthmos
And one paramount at God's Olympia
And two by Krisa,

Megakles, yours and your fathers'!
And in this last happy fortune
Some pleasure I have; but sorrow as well
At envy requiting your fine deeds.
– Thus always, they say,
Happiness, flowering and constant,
Brings after it
One thing with another.[22]

The young Pericles, therefore, grew up in a truly famous and infamous family that enjoyed the praise of Pindar's poetry but was tainted by both a religious curse and accusations of treason. Pericles' fellow Athenians had formally ostracized his father and uncle and the youth spent some of his formative years as a figurative (and probably a literal) outcast. The family's wealth undoubtedly prevented these years from creating actual economic hardship for Pericles and his parents, but surely we are justified in concluding that the experience left the young Athenian with (at best) an ambivalent attitude toward his fellow citizens and toward the whims of the majority in Athenian politics. Since it had been the Spartans who forced the Athenians to drive the Alkmeonids from Athens, we may imagine that Pericles also felt few warm feelings toward the most powerful state in Hellas.

It remains true that many ostracized Athenians returned to Athens and to political prominence (as did Pericles' father). One should admit, therefore, that ostracism by itself did not represent an indelible political stain.[23]

However, in the case of Pericles' family we are dealing not only with ostracism but also with accusations of treason, collaboration with tyrants, and the stain of a religious curse.

Some have speculated that the curse itself may have affected Pericles' own religious attitudes and beliefs, about which we know much less than we would like.[24] Growing up in a family that was considered cursed surely would tend to sharpen one's attitude toward such alleged "pollution." Pericles may have come to consider such matters mere superstition, either from adopting a convenient stance or from succumbing to the influence of increasingly rationalist views of the world, or both. And yet, apart from the relative paucity of religious references in his speeches in Thucydides, no evidence suggests that Pericles (at least publicly) adopted rationalist views. Certainly his sponsorship of the building program on the acropolis, a program that honored the Athenians' gods as much as the Athenians themselves, does not suggest that Pericles' public stance was anything other than that of a faithful practitioner of traditional religion. Had Pericles assumed a different position, we could reasonably expect some trace of attacks on his radical religious views in the often hostile sources that form our tradition. As we shall see, friends or acquaintances of Pericles incurred attacks based on supposedly radical views, but Pericles himself apparently never suffered from the suspicion of heterodox beliefs or actions where the gods were concerned.[25]

We therefore have little grounds on which to conclude that Pericles had unusual personal religious views, beyond noting that it would have been understandable and convenient for him to adopt a skeptical attitude toward matters like family curses and to note that he maintained relationships with those who had unorthodox opinions (as well as with others whose views were more conventional). Surely, however, Pericles' situation – the curse, the accusations of treason, and the ostracisms – created distance between himself and other young members of leading families. It may therefore have played a role in the aloof disposition Pericles displayed in later years.[26] Plutarch reports that Pericles was notorious in his unwillingness to attend social events. Pericles had very few close friends and, as we shall see, even those closest to him found him sometimes distant and seemingly oblivious.[27]

We can say almost nothing specific about the years before the battle of Marathon, when Pericles was a young boy. No sources provide us with even a hint of information about his childhood proper.[28] His class and family assure us that he received the best available education, which would have included training in music, poetry, and gymnastics, as well as (of course) reading, writing, and speaking. Wealthy Athenians entrusted such education to slaves known as *paidonomoi* ("trainers of boys"), paid instructors, or private schools, and Pericles undoubtedly spent considerable time under such instruction.[29] His later fame as a speaker suggests that he was an extremely able student of language and his interest in Athenian finance (Thuc. 2.13) and acquaintance with leading philosophical and scientific figures perhaps suggest he was also a capable student of mathematics and the sciences (such as they were).

Athens in the years from about 500 to 490 BC had not yet become the glistening center of Greek architecture, literature, philosophy, and culture it would be by the middle and late fifth century. A relatively new temple to the goddess Athena stood in the center of the acropolis atop the city;[30] in the lower city, construction had begun under the tyrants on a temple to Zeus that would remain unfinished until the time of the Roman emperor Hadrian. In general, the Peisistratids had given the city center of Athens a richer appearance, displaying their wealth and power in a way that rulers have employed from the times of the most ancient Near Eastern kingdoms. Yet young Pericles still confronted an Athens very different from the one he would help rebuild after the Persian Wars. It is likely that the Athenians of his day still employed the broad, sandy shore of Phaleron as their primary harbor, although at some point in this period the Athenians constructed and fortified more modern facilities at Peiraeus.[31] Temples and other public buildings were, of course, constructed in the archaic, sixth-century style: less elaborate, more stolid, and less ethereal than the forms of architecture that would take hold in Greece and especially Athens by the mid-fifth century.[32] The statuary in particular still possessed a stiffness and an air of the East that would hardly survive the Persian Wars (see Figure IV). Indeed, it seems to have been those very encounters with the Persians that encouraged the Greeks to define and represent themselves in ways that contrasted with the luxuries and traditions of the East.

Of course, the Athenians' own Ionian relations inhabited Aegean islands and parts of the western coast of Asia Minor, thus placing

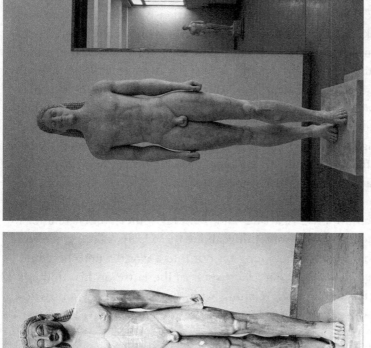
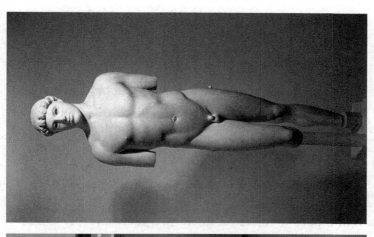
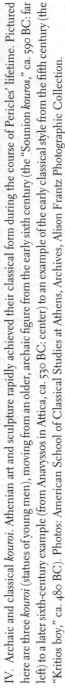

IV. Archaic and classical *kouroi*. Athenian art and sculpture rapidly achieved their classical form during the course of Pericles' lifetime. Pictured here are three *kouroi* (statues of young men), moving from an older, archaic figure from the early sixth century (the "Sounion *kouros*," ca. 590 BC: far left) to a later sixth-century example (from Anavyssos in Attica, ca. 530 BC: center) to an example of the early classical style from the fifth century (the "Kritios boy," ca. 480 BC). Photos: American School of Classical Studies at Athens, Archives, Alison Frantz Photographic Collection.

them in much closer contact with Lydia, Persia, and other eastern powers. By Pericles' childhood, many of those eastern Greeks had been paying tribute to Lydian and then Persian overlords for two generations. This fact may have contributed to the Athenian men abandoning some of their Ionian manners and adopting the more conservative style of dress of their Dorian neighbors on the mainland. Perhaps Pericles himself met older Athenian men who had refused to alter their fashion and continued to adorn their hair with golden pins shaped like grasshoppers. If so, he must have asked his father or mother what was the reason for this style. Or perhaps he asked why his father did not adorn himself in this way.

What did Xanthippus or Pericles' uncle Megacles the Alkmeonid tell the young boy about the Athenians' Ionian relations? About the Spartans and Thebans? About the great Persian Empire just to the east of the Greek lands in Anatolia, an empire to which once-free Greeks now made annual tribute payments? And what did they tell the young boy about the Peisistratid tyrants, who now lived as Persian dependents after their expulsion from Athens and who had helped the Persians attack Greece at Marathon? When Pericles asked his father who had built the great temple of Athena on the acropolis or relatively new buildings in the agora, did Xanthippus mention the tyrants without telling the boy about his mother's connection by marriage with the Peisistratid family? And what about the curse on his mother's clan?

Surely Xanthippus, Agariste, and Pericles' other, older relations must have told the boy something about these parts of his ancestry. One could hardly send the youngster out into a world where he could be confronted with unpleasant facts such as the curse on his mother's family and the Alkmeonids' relations with the Peisistratid tyrants without arming him with an explanation or defense of his ancestors' actions.

We should assume, therefore, that Xanthippus and Agariste told Pericles something about the Peisistratids and something about the curse on the Alkmeonids. There can be little doubt that once Pericles went out into the world, he heard versions of these stories from his young friends that were far less flattering to his family than the versions he heard at home. Can there be any doubt that Pericles heard the taunts of other boys, who would have surely mocked him for his mother's curse or his family's alleged treason? Can there be any doubt that such taunts had some effect on the young Athenian?

One would love to know what the young Pericles liked to read. What texts were available to him at home? What forms of literature did he encounter outside the home? We must recall that he lived in the days before Aeschylus's first tragedy had appeared on the stage. Whatever kind of drama was produced in the young Pericles' day was therefore an archaic form that had yet to see the second actor added to the production. A single actor interacted with a chorus in a performance that must have seemed dramatic only by comparison with a choral song or monody, a song by a single voice. Lyric verse (like Archilochus's famous account of throwing away his shield or his laments over his lost love), elegies that could range from epitaphs to longer narrative verse, and short poems celebrating aristocrats' victories (such as those in the Olympic games) perhaps formed the "hits" of Pericles' youth.[33] It was this latter type of poem that Pericles' older contemporary Pindar would master in the first half of the fifth century, composing (as we have seen) one such poem in honor of Pericles' Alkmeonid uncle Megacles. One must admit that such victory odes (if not Archilochus's lyrics) are relatively somber affairs when compared with the heart-wrenching tragedies and raucous comedies performed on the stage by multiple actors in later fifth-century Athens. Pericles, to put it in modern terms, grew up in a black-and-white world and then lived through the development of color, surround sound, and special effects. Athenian entertainment in his senior years must have seemed fantastic compared with the forms of drama and verse he experienced as a youth.

Of course, there was always Homer. There can be little doubt that Pericles and his young friends found the epic cycle of poems describing the Trojan War and the adventures of its heroes the most exciting entertainment they could experience. Perhaps they were not so enthralled by the long speeches and subtle themes of reciprocity that play such a prominent role in Homeric verse, but surely the tales of Achilles' duel with Hector or Odysseus's encounters with one-eyed monsters and seductive goddesses captured the boy's imagination. Indeed, in a world that had not yet seen even two actors on a stage together (much less the sensory-overloading forms of entertainment we experience today), Homeric poetry undoubtedly played a seminal role in shaping the attitudes, hopes, and aspirations of Greek boys like the young Pericles.[34]

I believe we can identify one Homeric lesson in particular that Pericles would learn well and that would inform his policies in Athens. Homer's heroes seek to display their *arete* ("excellence," especially in battle and in speech) in order to earn *time* ("honor" in its physical and abstract forms, enjoyed in the present day) and *kleos* ("fame or renown," including that enjoyed when those in the future look back on the *arete* and *time* of past figures). Perhaps most famously, Achilles eventually accepts that he will not survive the Trojan War but will leave behind him a great name to be honored in the future: his great exploits in a short life would ensure that his fame would be eternal (*kleos aphthiton*).

> For my mother Thetis the goddess of the silver feet tells me
> I carry two sorts of destiny toward the day of my death. Either,
> if I stay here and fight beside the city of the Trojans,
> my return home is gone, but my glory shall be everlasting;
> but if I return home to the beloved land of my fathers,
> the excellence of my glory is gone, but there will be a long life
> left for me, and my end in death will not come to me quickly.[35]

After his friend Patroklos's death, Achilles indeed returns to battle and, of course, eventually dies at Troy, ensuring his eternal glory. This heroic idea, as we shall see, became a fundamental part of Pericles' vision for Athens.[36]

At eighteen, Pericles probably became formally eligible to serve in the Athenian military. In the fourth century BC Athens created the group of *epheboi* (the "youth corps"), young men from middle-class families and above who served as home guards of the city before becoming full-fledged members of the militia at the age of twenty.[37] Although this institution long postdated Pericles' early life, it is likely that young Athenian men in their late teens were already providing a kind of informal home guard in the earlier period.[38] Indeed, the need for the Athenian infantry to be as large as possible at the battle of Marathon in 490 undoubtedly encouraged the use of young but fully grown Athenians in the infantry.

In this period, service as an Athenian infantryman (a Greek "hoplite," named for the circular *hoplon* shield he carried) probably still required that the soldier be able to supply his own gear. Thus the hoplites were drawn from the classes with enough wealth to afford a shield, spear, and defensive armor – generally speaking, this meant the middle class (independent farmers or moderately successful businessmen or perhaps even tradesmen).[39] Pericles could have entered this service in the troubled years between the battle of Marathon (490) and the invasion of Greece by the Persian Great King Xerxes (480) or just after this period. However, these were also the years when his mother's family and his father suffered ostracism because of supposed connections with the tyrants or suspicions of treason. It is therefore likely that Pericles was out of Athens at the very time when he should have joined the informal group that would eventually become *epheboi*. If he was not away from Athens, it would seem likely that the young Athenian endured some ribbing (at least) from the other young hoplites due to his connection with the cursed and allegedly treasonous family.

Wherever he spent the duration of his father's ostracism, Pericles had certainly returned to Athens by 481 when his father was recalled from exile, and since he was in his teens and perhaps even near twenty by that time, it is possible that he served in the Athenian army or navy during the Persian Wars of 480–479.[40] Given the desperate situation of the Greek allies against Persia, Pericles might have served wherever he was needed during these years. Yet because his father was a general (*strategos*) who at least sometimes commanded a contingent of the Athenian fleet and because most Athenians in this campaign served in the navy, Pericles (assuming he was old enough) is likely to have done military service in these years aboard an Athenian trireme. These warships (Figure V) with three banks of oars constituted the principal weapon of both the Greek and Persian navies, and by 480 Athens possessed a very large fleet of some 200 or more ships. With a complement of about 200 men per ship (170 rowers and 30 officers and marines), it required at least 40,000 sailors to man Athens' fleet in 480.[41]

Athens possessed the largest fleet in the Greek world by 480, having determined in 483/2 at the suggestion of Themistocles to use surplus revenues from the silver mines to construct warships.[42] The ships – although perhaps initially constructed to assist in a war with the nearby island of Aegina – proved to be crucial in the war against

V. Athenian trireme. Athens' imperial power depended on hundreds of warships called triremes. These vessels could be propelled by sails (usually lowered or completely removed during battle) or by three banks of rowers (from which the ship took its name). When attacking, the trireme attempted to use the bronze ram on its prow to damage enemy vessels. Photo: Courtesy of the Trireme Trust.

Persia in 480–479. Just as crucial as these ships, however, was the Athenians' decision to man them and resist the Persians even after Athens itself had been sacked. The historian Herodotus recounts the dramatic scene when Themistocles interpreted an ambiguous oracle from Delphi about a "wooden wall" that would save the Athenians and their children as an encouragement to fight the Persians at sea: the "wooden wall," in his view, was the Athenians' fleet of warships.[43] Themistocles apparently believed that a polis consisted of a group of citizens rather than a site or location, an idea that appears in his response to a Corinthian's taunt that he was a man without a city (after Athens' destruction) and later in a speech that Thucydides attributes to the Athenian general Nikias.[44] As we shall see, Themistocles' insistence on the importance of the fleet and of Athens as a notional group of human beings rather than as a physical location would prove crucial in Pericles' political and strategic beliefs. The Athenians' reaction to the Persian invasion of 480 and the Greeks' victory at Salamis, made possible by the Athenian fleet and the moral resolve of the Athenian people to abandon their homes and man Athens' warships, may very well have been the most important formative experiences in the young Pericles' life.

If we assume that Pericles was indeed old enough to serve with his father in these years, then he spent part of his time during the war along the coast of Asia Minor, where Xanthippus led the Athenian naval contingent in the campaign of 479.[45] That action culminated in the Greek allies' victory over the Persians at the battle of Mycale, traditionally believed to have been fought on the same day as the Greeks' victory over the Persians at Plataea in mainland Greece (summer 479). At Mycale, located on the coast of southeastern Asia Minor, some of the Greeks who had been fighting (under compulsion) for the Persians deserted the Persian ranks and joined the Greek allies, providing them with a claim (if a late one) of having fought for and earned their freedom.[46]

We must lament our lack of information about this campaign. However, it seems fair to assume that Pericles, whether he was at Mycale with his father or not, would have come to learn a great deal about Asia Minor and the Ionian (and other) Greeks who lived there from his own and/or his father's experiences in this war. This information undoubtedly played an important role in later years, when Pericles would be deeply involved with the Athenians' efforts to influence and control the eastern Greek states that became part of Athens' empire. Whatever views Pericles had or developed about Ionian Greeks surely rested in part on his early experiences in, or knowledge of, this war, when so many Ionians had fought alongside the Persians (even if under compulsion) before finally joining their Greek brothers against the great empire.

We may speculate that another important relationship in Pericles' life had its origins in this period. Just before war with Sparta broke out in 431, Pericles apparently feared that his formal friendship (*xenia*) with the king of Sparta (Archidamus) could cause him public relations problems when Sparta attacked. If the Spartan king, for example, ravaged the farms of other Athenians but left Pericles' estate untouched, this was likely to arouse negative feelings against the statesman. Pericles therefore renounced his lands before the Spartan invasion of Attica and made his estates public property, hoping thereby to forestall any accusation that he was not suffering the same fate as other Athenian landowners during the war.[47]

Thucydides, who gives us this information, does not provide any history of the relationship between Pericles and Archidamus. However, it seems probable that their *xenia* – a formal relationship between people of different states that was as much diplomatic as personal – stemmed from Xanthippus's service under the Spartan commander of the campaign at Mycale in Asia Minor in 479. The Spartans, as is sometimes forgotten, commanded the Greek forces on both land and sea in 480–479, despite the fact that they had virtually no fleet or experience of naval warfare: such was the respect that other Greeks had for the Spartans in the early fifth century. The commander of the Greek fleet operating in the eastern Aegean in 479 was the later Spartan king Archidamus's grandfather, Leotychides. We may reasonably assume that he and the Athenian commander Xanthippus developed a relationship of *xenia* that was passed down to their descendants (as was typically the case with this kind of friendship) and that this accounted for Pericles' worries about Archidamus in 431.[48]

After the Persians were defeated at Mycale, the Greek allies sailed to the Hellespont in order to break down the floating bridges the Persian king Xerxes had constructed there to allow his army to invade Europe. Finding the bridges destroyed by a storm, the Spartans returned to their Peloponnesian homes. The Athenian fleet under Xanthippus, however, remained in the Hellespont region, campaigning to expel remaining Persians and regain Athenian control in this crucial area.[49] As we have seen, the Athenians had interests on both sides of the Hellespont that stretched well back into the sixth century and even predated the Peisistratid tyranny. The grain supplies provided by the Black Sea and the other trade flowing through the straits made influence in this region a fundamental aspect of Athenian foreign policy for over 250 years, up until the wars with Macedon in the mid- and late fourth century BC. In the winter of 479/8, Xanthippus, perhaps Pericles, and the Athenian forces sought to force recalcitrant Persians from Sestos on the Chersonese and reestablish Athenian influence in the region. The Athenian family of the Kimonids had served as tyrants in the Chersonese in the late sixth century, but their leader Miltiades had been forced to return to Athens in 493. In the intervening years we have no evidence of Athenian activities in the Chersonese on the northern side of the Hellespont. The events of 479 offered the Athenians both a convenient motive and an opportunity to regain a foothold in this crucial region. They also potentially gave Pericles the opportunity to acquaint himself with this area, which had been and would remain so vital to Athenian foreign policy interests. Pericles himself would later campaign to establish Athenian settlements in this region, which he may very well have first visited in the winter of 479/8.

Aspects of Pericles' military strategy and his attitude toward Athens may also have taken shape in these years. In the year 480 and in 479, the Athenian people abandoned their homes in Athens and took to their ships in the face of the Persian invasion of Attica. The Persians sacked the city of Athens both years, but the Athenian people survived and contin-ued to fight, eventually gaining victory over the invading forces.[50] Some fifty years later, Pericles would suggest to the Athenians that they should readily sacrifice their lands and homes in the effort to defeat the invading Spartans. Thucydides reports that Pericles suggested that the Athenians should treat their city as if it were an island, recognizing that their power rested entirely in their fleet and the income they derived from their imperial possessions. Thucydides tells us that Pericles went so far as to say, "If I could, I would persuade you to go out and destroy your own lands in order to show our enemies that you will not submit on account of those possessions."[51]

This strategy that valued the fleet above the ancestral farms and land of Attica emerged originally as an act of necessity during the Persian invasion of 480. The young Pericles at that time saw an Athenian people who were willing to see their ancestral homes destroyed in order fight another day. The difference between the situations in 480 and 431, of course, was that the Athenians might have reached a negotiated peace with Sparta in 431 while retaining their independence, whereas the Persians demanded complete sub-mission and the payment of annual tribute to the Great King. In 490, moreover, the Persians had planned to install a puppet tyrant in Athens, and it seems unlikely that in 480 Xerxes would have allowed the Athenians to retain their independent, democratic government. However that may be, Pericles' strategy of treating the Athenian fleet as Athens' most important asset and his view that the Athenians must be willing to sacrifice their own property in the service of a greater goal surely derived in part from his experience of the Persian Wars.[52]

By the time the Persian Wars ended in 479 (though no Greek could have been certain at that point that they were indeed over), Pericles may have reached the age of twenty or more. He had probably seen and perhaps fought in one of the greatest military campaigns in Western history. At the very least he learned of these events from his father: the Greeks had staved off the Persian conquest of Athens and the rest of Hellas through a remarkable series of victories and, one must remember, perhaps the most inspiring defeat ever suffered, when 300 Spartans died defending the pass at Thermopylae in 480. The Greeks who emerged victorious from these wars, especially the citizens of Sparta, Athens, and Corinth – who had provided the bulk of the forces against Persia – undoubtedly experienced a level of confidence and pride never before seen in Hellas. These relatively small states had become "world powers" in a way that was inconceivable before 479. The mighty Persian juggernaut had met its match in the form of a relatively small and disorganized band of allied Greeks.[53]

We must recall, however, that most Greeks had not fought against the Persians. Indeed, only thirty-one city-states took the field to oppose this invasion.[54] The Ionian Greeks, once their own revolt from Persia was quashed in 494 BC, had been compelled to serve under their Persian overlords in the invasion of their ancestral home in mainland Hellas. The vast majority of other Greek states either remained neutral in the conflict or gave over "earth and water" – the formal symbols of Persian control of one's territory – to the invaders.

One could understand if Pericles and other Athenians felt less than warm toward those Greeks who had either collaborated with the Persians or simply not resisted them. Among this group were Argos and Thebes as well as certain elements in Thessaly, all of which would figure prominently in Periclean foreign policy in the later fifth century, although not always as one might expect on the basis of their historical relations with Athens or Persia. In the years just before and after 479, the Athenians did take action against a few states that had assisted the Persians, as (it would seem) did Sparta.[55] Yet this policy would change quickly into something quite different, and by 477 (as we shall see) the Athenians were drawing no formal distinction between the states that had fought for freedom and those that had not.[56]

Many Greeks understandably saw the Persians as barbarous invaders, although the best Greek literature of the fifth century displays a remarkably unbigoted (if not sympathetic) view of these foreigners.[57] Yet it is also more than possible that Pericles and others developed something like admiration or respect for the empire-building Persians. Certainly he does not seem to have developed a deep heat where Persia was concerned (as, perhaps, did his rival Kimon, whose family history probably made him particularly sensitive to any charge of going easy on the Persians[58]). We shall see that Pericles eventually supported ending the war with Persia and concentrating Athenian efforts on ruling other Greeks.[59] At the very least, it seems Pericles' experiences in or knowledge of the Persian wars predisposed him more toward an imperial attitude regarding other Greeks rather than an undying hostility toward Persia. Was this because the Greeks the Athenians encountered in Ionia and elsewhere had sometimes supinely accepted Persian rule, fought alongside their conquerors, or failed in whatever revolts they attempted? In such an environment it would have been understandable if Pericles did develop a certain respect for the imperialist Persians and thus eventually found it easier to imitate them in ruling the Ionians than to continue aggressive operations against the Great King.[60]

In terms of his domestic attitudes, Pericles' youth and heritage seem to have made him into something of an outsider. His mother's family's troubled history and especially the rumored associations with tyrants, traitors, and Persians undoubtedly created discomfort for the young Athenian. He saw his father and uncle literally ostracized by their fellow citizens and knew that he could easily suffer the same fate. Although a member of the Athenian elite and an undoubted aspirant to a political career such as his father and other relatives had enjoyed, he saw that the path to success was not perfectly straightforward. Someone with his heritage and connections ran definite risks in pursuing a public career. As we shall see in the next chapter, Pericles adopted a very conservative approach in the early years of his political life, seeking to minimize the opportunity for enemies to use the tools against him that had been employed against his relatives.

The Athenians who knew Pericles well in 479 must have thought of him as a young man with obvious political potential who also carried serious handicaps. They could hardly have imagined that he would become the single most important, influential, and powerful leader Athens would ever produce.[61]

❋ THREE ❋

Early Career: The Dominance of Kimon (ca. 479–462/1)

Our sources provide very little evidence about Pericles' early career. Yet the historical context of these years provides crucial insight into the statesman Pericles became in later life. Between 480 and about 462/1, Athens was allied with Sparta (against Persia) and Pericles' marriage relation Kimon – a pro-Spartan conservative – served as Athens' most important leader. During these years Kimon and his supporters created the Athenian empire, converting what had been an alliance against Persia into a tool for bringing Athens' long-standing ambitions in the Aegean to fruition by planting Athenian settlements and by collecting revenues from increasingly recalcitrant allies. Pericles undoubtedly served in the Athenian military in these years and may have been elected general, but his first certain appearance as a political figure appears in a (failed) prosecution of Kimon, an event that provides us with an opportunity to explore the Athenian people's eagerness for expansion as well as the extremely complicated relations between Kimon's and Pericles' families. Kimon's fall from political power and his exile from Athens in 462/1 opened the door for Pericles and the more progressive faction (or, rather, signaled that they had already asserted themselves).

T he end of the Persian Wars created two superstars in Greece. In Sparta, the regent Pausanias, acting as one of Sparta's two kings in the place of his underaged cousin, had gained unprecedented prestige after his victory over the Persians at Plataea (just north of Attica) in 479. The Athenians and Spartans alike recognized Athens' general Themistocles as a hero of the war against the invaders, since he was credited with the naval strategy that led to the Persians' defeat at Salamis just off the cost of Attica in 480.[1]

53

In 479 any observer would have predicted that Pausanias and Themistocles were likely to influence the political scenes in Sparta and Athens respectively for the foreseeable future. However, this was not to be. Although Pausanias continued to command the Greek allies in their mopping-up efforts against any remaining Persian outposts in the Aegean (and as far away as Cyprus) in the year 478, by the next year he had been replaced. It is likely that he had come under suspicion for treason: some believed Pausanias had undertaken illicit negotiations with the Persian Great King and eventually some alleged that he had offered to help the Persians bring Greece under his control.[2] Although these early accusations produced no conviction, Pausanias never again commanded Spartan forces. A few years later, probably in the late 470s, he was once more accused of treason, and this time the Spartans convinced themselves of his guilt. Sparta's leaders executed their former regent by starving him to death in the temple where he had sought protection as a suppliant. By this impious action the Spartans incurred a curse on themselves.[3]

The downfall of the great Pausanias brought trouble for Themistocles. Thucydides tells us that certain evidence suggesting treasonous actions on his part came to light during the investigations of the Spartan regent. Although prominent in the Persian Wars' immediate aftermath, Themistocles played no major role in Athenian politics and military actions in the years after 477.[4] It may be that he had already fallen out of favor with the Athenian people for reasons we can no longer recover. Plutarch writes that the Athenians' jealousy over Themistocles' fame, and his erection of a temple in Athens that seemed designed to glorify him as much as the goddess (Artemis) to whom it was dedicated, made them willing to listen to those wishing to slander him. (Themistocles had also made enemies outside of Athens by high-handed treatment of the allies.[5]) But Plutarch's resort to "jealousy" suggests that he in fact had no firm idea about the motive for the Athenians' actions.[6] In any case, in the late 470s the Athenians first ostracized their former hero and then sought to bring him to book for his alleged treason.[7]

The truth behind these allegations remains beyond recovery. Themistocles had apparently sent messages to the Persian king Xerxes during the campaigns of 480 – or at least many believed he had sent such messages.[8] Whether they were intended to trick and entrap Xerxes or to provide him with some apparent advantage (and thus put Themistocles in his good graces) or both, the belief in their existence apparently encouraged accusations of treason.[9] Fleeing his Athenian and Spartan accusers, Themistocles sought refuge with the Spartans' ancient enemy Argos before leading his would-be captors on a harrowing chase through northern Greece and across the Aegean, until he finally found protection with none other than the Persian Great King. Whatever the truth of the earlier charges against Themistocles, he died as a Persian retainer and thus provided evidence for those who claimed he had betrayed Greece before this. As a traitor, his body could not legally be buried in Attic soil, though one version of the tale maintains that his family found a way to circumvent this legal provision and bury Themistocles secretly in his homeland.[10]

KIMON'S FAMILY AND BACKGROUND

The ultimate beneficiary of Themistocles' misfortune was the Athenian leader Kimon, whose father Miltiades had been the tyrant of the Chersonese in the late sixth century and (more famously) a triumphant general in Athens' victory over the Persians at Marathon in 490.[11] Miltiades had nonetheless died in disgrace in 489, after a campaign of reprisal he proposed and led. This attack on the island of Paros, which had provided the Persians with one ship in the Marathon campaign, failed to produce any revenue or booty for the Athenian besiegers. Gravely injured during the campaign, Miltiades stood trial upon his return to Athens, was convicted, and reportedly was fined the huge sum of fifty talents. Dying of his wounds, he left the massive fine to be paid by his son, Kimon.[12]

Kimon would become Pericles' greatest rival and, in many ways, his greatest influence. Careful attention to his background and situation will elucidate his relationship with Pericles and the ways in which they resembled, and differed from, one another as Athenian leaders. Kimon's family were perhaps known in antiquity as the Philaids (an aristocratic Athenian clan claiming descent from Philaeus, a son of Ajax of Salamis) but are often called Kimonids by modern scholars because of the uncertain relationships between Kimon's direct ancestors (beginning with his grandfather, Kimon Koalemos) and the Philaid house.[13] In any case, Kimon's ancestors had played an important role as supporters of the Peisistratid tyrants in the sixth century, just as had

Pericles' mother's family (the Alkmeonids). The Kimonids (as I shall normally call them) had ruled the Chersonese with the assent (at least) and finally with the support of the Peisistratid tyrants of Athens. In 524/3 the Peisistratids ensured that Miltiades served as eponymous archon,[14] the important Athenian official who each year gave his name to the Athenian calendar (thus 524/3 was "the year of Miltiades"). In the position of archon Miltiades followed Cleisthenes, the scion of the Alkmeonid family who had held the position in 525/4. Both houses, there should be little doubt, supported the Peisistratids in this period, and both families found this embarrassing fact extremely inconvenient in the fifth century BC. Herodotus's reports of the families' activities bear the mark of their attempts to defend themselves against the charge of having supported the tyrants.[15]

Indeed, while the young Pericles suffered from his mother's family's curse, the young Kimon undoubtedly found his own family's recent history problematic. Beyond the association with the Peisistratids, the Kimonid family incurred suspicion of collaborating with Persia before and during the Ionian Greeks' revolt from the great Persian Empire. In about the year 513, when the Persian king Darius the Great led an invasion of Europe across the Bosporus, several Greek tyrants chose to cooperate with him in the face of Persian power.[16] Among them was Miltiades, who controlled the Chersonese and thus played a crucial role in Darius's plans. When Darius's army had launched an attack northward across the Danube River in order to subdue the warlike and seminomadic Scythians, he left certain Greek tyrants and their forces in charge of guarding the Danube bridge. He did this, we should note, because he trusted these Greeks to cover his route of return or retreat. In the event, Darius's campaign against the Scythians was something of a failure, and he ultimately returned across the Danube bridge into Thrace.

Herodotus tells us that while Darius and his forces remained north of the Danube, Miltiades supported a suggestion made by the Scythians that the Greeks destroy the bridge over the river and thus strand Darius and free Ionia from his control. The Greeks rejected this plan and decided instead only to give the appearance of going along with the Scythians' request.[17] Despite the failure of Miltiades' supposed efforts, this story apparently remained a key element in the Kimonid family's defense against the charge of collaboration with the Persians. To the charge that Miltiades had guarded Darius's bridge with the other Greek tyrants and thus collaborated with the Persians, the family could respond, "Actually, Miltiades was in favor of destroying the bridge and stranding Darius."

Yet, upon examination, this defense rings hollow. Darius's bridge was not in fact completely destroyed, the Greek tyrants remained on guard at the Danube and assisted the Persian ruler's return, and the Great King took no actions against Miltiades afterward. He obviously believed the Athenian tyrant had remained a loyal servant. Indeed, Miltiades did not leave the Chersonese until two decades later in 493, after the Persians had crushed the Ionian Greeks' revolt from their empire. Upon his return to Athens, Miltiades stood trial on the (patently merited) charge of tyranny. He was acquitted, and we are surely justified in seeing glimmers of the family's defense against the charges of tyranny and cozy relations with Persia in Herodotus's account of their history. The Kimonids' control of the Chersonese had been established or at the very least maintained with the help of the Peisistratid tyrants and then accepted by the Persians, to whom the deposed Peisistratids had fled. Miltiades' defense against the charge of tyranny (a charge available after the overthrow of Athens' tyrants and one that gained credence via the family's association with the Peisistratids and Persians) surely contained convenient elements precisely like this tale of Miltiades' unfulfilled plan to destroy the bridge over the Danube.[18]

The Kimonids' involvement with the Persians and the tyrants clearly led, at the very least, to a major problem in public relations. And the problems did not end with Miltiades' stewardship of the Danube bridge: when the Athenian fled from the Chersonese in 493, his son Metiochos (Kimon's half brother) was "captured," as Herodotus has it, by the Persians. Now if Miltiades or his family had done the Persians some great wrong, one might have suspected them to take out their vengeance on Metiochos. Yet, as Herodotus notes, the Persian Great King in fact welcomed the son of Miltiades, giving him a Persian wife by whom he had children "that were accounted Persians."[19]

Kimon thus found himself in awkward circumstances in the early 480s, when he was probably in his twenties (born ca. 510 BC, no doubt not in Athens but in the Chersonese).[20] His ancestors had close relations with the Peisistratid tyrants and his father had been accused of tyranny and suspected of Persian collaboration. His father, although a great hero at Marathon, had nonetheless died in disgrace and in terrible debt. His half-brother was living as a Persian with a Persian wife and children. If Pericles and Kimon met, as they undoubtedly did, during the mid-480s when Pericles' relatives began to be ostracized due to their own relations to the tyrants and suspicions of treason after Marathon, the two young aristocrats would have found it easy to compare their respective plights. Both had pedigrees and connections at once illustrious and extremely problematic.

Kimon confronted his own difficult circumstances in interesting ways. We are told he paid off the fine (on his father) of fifty talents, a stupendous sum by any standard. A single talent represented 6,000 drachmas, and one drachma was more than a good day's wage for a laborer in the fifth century. Miltiades himself apparently did not possess sufficient wealth to discharge this debt – perhaps a good deal of his holdings consisted of lands or revenues from them in the Chersonese. Still, although the family had very large estates in Attica, as our ancient sources testify, such assets did not produce a ready supply of cash.[21] It is, of course, also possible that he died too quickly to discharge the debt himself. A cash sum so great as fifty talents is unlikely to have been readily available to any but the most wealthy Athenian aristocrats and tyrants. Perhaps it is no surprise, therefore, that Kimon's sister Elpinike married a certain Kallias, by repute the richest man in Athens. The marriage suggests that Kallias played at least some role in discharging Kimon's inherited debt, as indeed Plutarch reports.[22]

Interestingly, when Kimon himself married his second wife sometime before 463 (see later discussion), he married a relation of Pericles, an Alkmeonid woman named Isodike.[23] Pericles (again, as we shall see) eventually and apparently amicably gave up his own first wife to a member of the Athenian aristocrat Kallias's family. The three families – Alkmeonid, Kimonid, and Kerykes/Kalliad[24] – thus formed a very close network in the early to mid-fifth century (see Figure VI). And although the evidence for this is somewhat speculative, the Kallias family apparently had connections with the Peisistratid tyrants in the sixth century, as did the other two families.[25]

Some scholars have seen consistent hostility between the families of Pericles and Kimon stretching back at least to the early fifth century, a hypothesis that relies in part on the clear later rivalry between the two greatest statesmen of Athenian history. The hard evidence for this hostility supposedly comes in the form of Pericles' father Xanthippus's prosecution of Miltiades in the trial of 489, after the disaster at Paros.[26] About twenty-five

The Family of Pericles

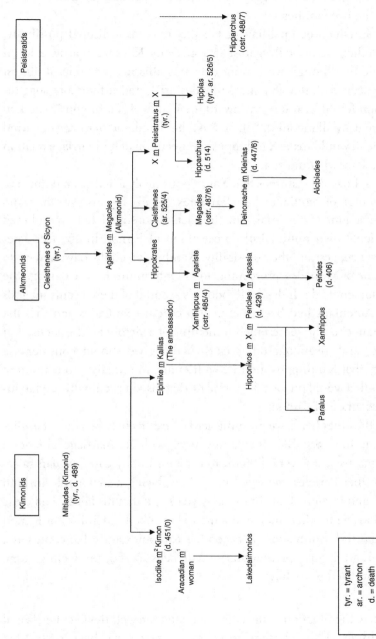

VI. Pericles' family and important relations. The families of the Kimonids, Kerykes (the family of Kallias), Alkmeonids, and Peisistratids were closely connected in the sixth and fifth centuries BC. Pericles was descended from the accursed Alkmeonid family on his mother's side and related to several other leading families by marriage. Stemma design: Peter Michelli.

or so years later (in 463), Pericles would prosecute Miltiades' son Kimon, and so the parallel could suggest continued competition (at the very least) between the two families.

Such sustained competition or hostility remains a distinct possibility. And yet other factors tell against it, especially Kimon's marriage to an Alkmeonid.[27] Although we cannot date this alliance precisely, it almost certainly occurred after 489 and Miltiades' trial, and it therefore suggests that Kimon felt little animosity toward the family of Xanthippus (who had also married an Alkmeonid).[28] If, on the other hand, the marriage occurred before 489, it would make Xanthippus's prosecution of his marriage relation Miltiades somewhat unusual.[29]

All this, however, assumes that Xanthippus really acted as an enthusiastic prosecutor of Miltiades, as Herodotus (6.136) reports. We have no detailed account of the trial, but the facts as outlined here, combined with Pericles' own minimalistic prosecution of Kimon in 463 (see later discussion) suggest another possibility. Xanthippus could have agreed to serve as one of Miltiades' prosecutors in order to minimize the damage the prosecution could do. Indeed, Herodotus's account of these events suggests that the Athenians had been inclined to execute Miltiades and that the punishment of a fine represented something of a victory for the accused. If this is so, and given our other facts, perhaps we should consider the possibility that Xanthippus mounted a friendly, minimalist prosecution of Miltiades that would provide the template that his son eventually used in his own prosecution of Kimon.

If, on the other hand, we presume actual hostility between these families as early as the 480s BC, the family tree (with its marriage alliances) confronting us seems very difficult to explain. In any case, we can safely conclude that Pericles witnessed his father playing a major role in both domestic and foreign affairs in his early years and that his family had close connections with other, major Athenian elites like the families of Kimon and Kallias. If hostility arose between the Kimonids and Alkmeonids as a result of Xanthippus's prosecution of Miltiades in 489, the feelings were either short-lived or shallow.

* * * * *

To return to the situation in the early 470s, after the victories over Persia and the expulsion of the Persian army from Greece, we have noted that

Themistocles found it impossible to convert his fame into actual, sustained political influence in Athens. As far as our sources allow us to gauge, after the early 470s Themistocles made virtually no important impression on Athenian history (up until the time of his ostracism and exile). No evidence suggests that the Athenians elected him general in these years. Instead, Miltiades' son Kimon became the most important Athenian political and military figure of the 470s and 460s BC. In this period, Kimon would achieve a sustained preeminence never before seen in democratic Athens. And he would provide numerous examples for Pericles to emulate (or reject) in his own leadership of the city-state.

The tool Kimon used to build his power and reputation was the Athenian navy, the force Themistocles had done so much to augment in the 480s. Both the navy and Athens' infantry were commanded by annually elected Athenian officials called *strategoi* (usually translated as "generals"). These commanders served for one year, but they could – unlike Athenian archons (who since 487 had been selected by lot) – return to office year after year if the Athenians chose to reelect them. The opportunity to hold the position repeatedly and Athens' belligerent profile helped the generalship become the most important political as well as military office in fifth-century Athens. As one of Athens' ten elected generals virtually every year over (it would seem) a period of some fifteen years, Kimon used Athens' fleet to establish control over crucial parts of the Aegean and to build an unprecedented reputation for himself.

To understand how this happened and how these events would set the stage for Pericles' rise to prominence, we must trace the events that occurred just after the Persian Wars ended in 479. As we have noted, by 477 Pausanias apparently had come under some level of suspicion. Herodotus and Thucydides tell us, moreover, that the Athenians used dissatisfaction with Pausanias as an excuse to take over leadership of the Greek alliance against Persia.[30] In fact, by the spring of 477 the Athenians and many of the Greeks of Ionia and the islands had formed a new organization – a league of primarily Ionian Greek states designed (ostensibly) to punish the Great King for his outrages against Hellas. This federation, which moderns call the Delian League (because the Greeks chose the Ionians' sacred island of Delos as their headquarters), comprised Greeks who had fought both against and with the Persians in the great war. The Spartans, quite interestingly, made no apparent objection to this new league. The individual they sent out in 477 to take over command of the Greek alliance (in place of Pausanias), upon discovering the new organization, simply sailed back to the Peloponnese. Thucydides tells us that the land-loving Spartans were quite satisfied to allow the Athenians to take over continued operations against Persia and more than happy to be able to stay at home.[31]

The nature of this new alliance has spawned masses of historical analysis.[32] We possess very little hard evidence about the organization beyond the brief account of Thucydides and the much later description in the Aristotelian *Constitution of Athens* (written in the 320s BC). For our purpose, it will be enough to note that the allies agreed to make annual payments or to provide ships in order to supply the alliance with a fleet that could be used against Persian interests. The Athenians would supervise the funds themselves on the island of Delos, and an Athenian (Aristides "the Just") was responsible for determining how much tribute each member of the alliance should pay annually. We see, therefore, that Athens played a special role in this alliance from the beginning. Since the Athenian fleet formed the bulk of the allied force, this was entirely natural.

However, if the ostensible purpose of this alliance was "to ravage the [Persian] king's land," as Thucydides tells us, then the first few years of the alliance fell far short of this goal. All of the league's military actions about which we know anything in this period occurred in the northern or western Aegean, not on the eastern or "Persian" side. Only land in Asia could be called (by Greeks) "the king's," and thus it seems difficult to see how the allied Greeks were living up to the stated purpose of the organization.

Instead, the Athenians and their allies under their general Kimon attacked Eion, a Greek city in the northern Aegean where a Persian garrison remained, taking the city and enslaving the population.[33] Somewhat later, the allies under Kimon took the island of Skyros in the western Aegean, claiming that the island provided a base for piracy. Enslaving the native population, the Athenians colonized the island themselves. Shortly thereafter, they made war on the city of Karystos, on the southern tip of the island of Euboea in the western Aegean, when the city refused to enter the league voluntarily.[34]

Some historians have attempted to justify these actions as somehow in accord with the professed purposes of the league.[35] However, the fact that they are all on the wrong side of the Aegean (and usually against other Greeks) should surely give us pause. More important, analysis of Athenian foreign policy before and after this period shows that these areas all fell into zones Athens had long considered (and would continue to consider) vital for its economic well-being. Eion commanded routes to mining revenues and timber supplies in the north, while Skyros and Karystos completed a chain of island stops for vessels traveling between Athens and the Hellespont begun by Kimon's own father Miltiades.[36] Are we to believe that Athenian actions in this period only coincidentally mirrored long-standing Athenian foreign policy interests?

At least some Greeks came to a different conclusion. Sometime around the year 470 the great island of Naxos announced that it intended to withdraw from the Delian League.[37] This decision tells us a great deal about the situation and about the Athenians' reputation even this early in the alliance: because Naxos lies in the southern Aegean, it was quite exposed to any new Persian threat. Indeed, the Persians had attacked Naxos in about 500 BC (unsuccessfully) and then sacked it in 490 on their way to Marathon.[38] The Naxians' decision to leave the alliance therefore illustrates their willingness to risk further attacks from Persia once they lost the protection of the Delian League. In effect, the Naxians had decided that they preferred the risk of Persian domination to the reality of Athenian control. This action shows us, therefore, that some Greeks had already concluded that the Athenians' desire to exploit them differed little from the Persians'.[39]

Athens' reaction to Naxos's announcement did nothing if it did not confirm the Naxians' view that the league had become a tool of Athenian domination. Refusing to allow Naxos to withdraw, the Athenians and their allies besieged the island and forced it to remain in the alliance, now as a tribute-paying member rather than an independent ally providing ships.[40] The participation of Athens' other allies in this action may have derived from a fear of similar treatment if they joined Naxos in rebellion, sympathy with the idea of "keeping the alliance together," or mere indifference to the fate of the Naxians. In any case, the historian Thucydides clearly marks this as the moment when the Athenians "violated the agreement" between the Greeks, effectively turning their alliance into an *arche* – an empire.[41]

By the early 460s at the latest, the onetime alliance of mainly Ionian Greek states against the Persians had become an Athenian empire, from which once-autonomous states were no longer free to withdraw. Kimon had been the principal Athenian military and political figure in this period, and, especially given his father's involvement in expanding Athenian territory and control, we should conclude that he fully supported Athens' efforts to impose its will on other Greek states.

Kimon gained very tangible political advantages from his leadership in converting the Delian League into an empire. In the first place, he expanded the opportunities for poorer Athenians to achieve economic independence. When lower-class Athenians settled conquered lands (such as those in Eion or Skyros), they achieved a status that life in Athens itself could not provide them. In effect, a poor Athenian could join the middling hoplite class—working his own farm and making enough surplus wealth to purchase the gear needed for service in the state militia. Such service in most Greek poleis qualified citizens for other privileges, including holding certain offices, and made an individual respectable in Greek society.[42]

Service in the Athenian military or navy also probably provided opportunities for the acquisition of individual wealth in the form of booty. Kimon and his men clearly benefited from their campaigns, as several anecdotes suggest,[43] but we have little evidence of Athenian commanders or soldiers benefiting as directly as (say) Roman soldiers in the republic.[44] Kimon himself apparently amassed quite a fortune from his successful military adventures. With the debt he inherited from his father paid off, he was able to employ this wealth to other ends. Most famously, Kimon sponsored building and beautification programs in several areas of Athens, including in the marketplace (the agora) and in the Academy (which subsequently became a garden spot in Athens).[45] He sponsored the building of a new wall for the acropolis and the erection of a special, sacred enclosure for the bones of the Athenian hero Theseus, relics that he claimed to have recovered from Skyros and brought back to Athens.[46]

This Kimonian building program, although little discussed today, clearly followed in a tradition established by the Peisistratids and set a precedent for the later (and much more famous) construction efforts of Pericles' day.[47] Kimon also provided a model for his somewhat younger contemporary in another way: Kimon distributed largesse to the poorer citizens by making his private estates open for their use and hosting a meal for his poorer neighbors (his demesmen) every day. When he walked through town, Kimon would ask his wealthy young retainers to hand out clothing to those who needed it.[48] In short, Kimon used the empire and the wealth he gained from it to benefit economically challenged Athenians and to ensure his own influence in the city.

Pericles must have watched Kimon go from strength to strength in the 470s and early 460s with great interest and some envy. He certainly noticed how Kimon converted his military achievements into political success. For the relatively conservative Kimon, this political influence served to provide support for the status quo. Aristotle tells us that in these years the Council of the Areopagus – a conservative political organ consisting of former Athenian archons serving for life – dominated Athenian politics.[49] It is likely that Aristotle had no actual evidence for this statement and that he drew this conclusion from the absence of any obvious, domestic political issues in this period and from the overthrow of the Areopagus council's powers in the great revolution of 462/1 (see the next chapter). Aristotle may simply have concluded that, since the later reformer Ephialtes had felt the need to limit the Areopagus's powers in some ways, the council's powers must have been significant in the earlier period.[50]

In any case, what activities occupied Pericles in the 470s and early 460s, while his marriage relation Kimon dominated the political scene? Plutarch tells us that Pericles delayed his entry into politics because he feared ostracism, an attitude that would have been perfectly reasonable given the experiences of Pericles' father and uncle. Plutarch also tells us that some older Athenians commented on the resemblance between Pericles and Peisistratus. His voice, in particular, resembled that of the great tyrant. (It is more than possible, however, that this similarity was only noticed later in Pericles' career. Indeed, sometime later, Pericles and his supporters would be known as the "new Peisistratids," an appellation that reflected the power and influence Pericles and his associates wielded in the mid-fifth century.[51])

If any Athenians actually did note (or claim) that Pericles resembled Peisistratus, this formed a particularly devastating claim to the young Athenian. As we have seen, Pericles' great aunt (the sister of Cleisthenes) had been married to Peisistratus. Moreover, our evidence suggests that some Athenians believed there had been a child of this union. This conclusion derives from the nature of the Alkmeonids' defense against the charge that they had been (literally) "sleeping with" the tyrants. Herodotus tells us that the Alkmeonid family had fallen out with Peisistratus after the tyrant refused to have intercourse with his (cursed) Alkmeonid wife in a way that would produce children.[52] As we have seen, the actual evidence shows the families remaining in alliance until well after Peisistratus's death in 527. In any case, this extremely intimate story makes the most sense if some Athenians had claimed that Peisistratus *did* father a child on his Alkmeonid wife. The response, "Impossible. Let us tell you what he really did. There were sexual irregularities . . . ," had the advantage of painting Peisistratus in a very negative light and making a child from the marriage impossible.[53]

One can understand, therefore, why the accusation of looking or sounding like Peisistratus could do real damage to Pericles. However, it remains possible that Plutarch had no good source for his assertion that fears of ostracism kept Pericles out of politics in the 470s and 460s. The biographer may simply have reached a very reasonable conclusion given the absence of any facts suggesting that Pericles had taken an active role in Athenian political life in these years.

We can assume that Pericles served in Athenian military campaigns (as a hoplite, ship commander, or cavalryman) in this period and he almost certainly, therefore, participated in some of the operations by which Kimon established Athenian dominance in the Aegean and his own preeminence in Athens. Indeed, Plutarch reports that in these early years Pericles devoted himself to military matters (although this may be no more than reasonable speculation).[54] Beyond this, we have only one secure datum about Pericles' activities. We know that in 472 he served as the *choregos* (financial producer) for Aeschylus's play *The Persians*.[55]

This fact deserves our careful attention. It has often been used to provide the latest possible date for Pericles' birth, because it is sometimes assumed that one must have been twenty (or thirty) years old to serve as a *choregos*, though there is little ancient support for this notion.[56] In any case, it is likely enough on other grounds that Pericles was already in his mid-twenties (at least) by 472, so his service as *choregos* does little more than confirm our suspicion that he was born (at least) before 492. His service as *choregos* could suggest that his father Xanthippus was already dead and that Pericles was acting as the head of his own household. Again, however, this conclusion is uncertain, and no evidence ensures that a young man with a living father could not serve as *choregos*.

Still, Pericles' connection with Aeschylus as early as 472 – we shall see that there was a later connection – and with the play *The Persians* in particular suggests some interesting possibilities. Aeschylus's play stands out among the surviving tragedies from the fifth century because it depicts historical events of the recent past. Most extant tragedies and the lost works we know about featured tales of the distant, mythical, or heroic past, often from the period before, during, or after the Trojan War. Aeschylus's unusual decision to depict recent events suggests that the play had purposes that were as political as they were aesthetic. Scholars have long noted that the play focuses on the role of the Athenian fleet in the defeat of the Persian invasion. The drama, after all, treats not the final victories over the Persians in 479 that ensured the Greeks' victory (Plataea and Mycale) but rather the battle fought the year before at Salamis.[57] Given the date of the play and the credit Themistocles had received for masterminding the Athenian naval victory at Salamis, some have suggested that Aeschylus composed his play in part in order to remind the Athenians how much they owed to Themistocles, who by the year 472 may have already come under the suspicions that would eventually lead to his exile, if he had not in fact already fled Athens.[58]

In agreeing to act as the producer (and thus partial financier) of this play, Pericles therefore attached himself to a potentially controversial project, both in terms of its purely dramatic content (as a play about the recent past) and in terms of its political ramifications (potentially seen as support for Themistocles). It may be, therefore, that Pericles' choice to back this play represents his first, perhaps rather tentative, entrance into the Athenian political scene. And we should notice that he stepped on the stage, if one will pardon the metaphor, in an alliance with the more progressive (rather than the more traditional) elements.

We have already seen that Pericles would eventually adopt Themistocles' policy of treating the fleet as Athens' most important asset, stressing the need to see the actual territory and ancestral farms of Attica as expendable. Indeed, Pericles' emphasis on naval power and "island Athens" stands as the logical culmination of Themistocles' early-fifth-century focus on building up Athens' fleet, fortifying the harbor, and treating the land of Attica as irrelevant to Athens' real power.[59] Themistocles also began the process of using Athens' fleet to force smaller states to make payments to Athens, a policy the Delian League/Athenian empire would institutionalize under Kimon and Pericles.[60] In addition, Themistocles also suffered from the suspicion of having treated with the Persians: whether this accusation had merit or not, no one could deny he ended his life as an exile and retainer of the Persian king.

Pericles ultimately adopted Themistoclean policies and, as we shall see, also ended active hostilities between Athens and Persia.[61] We may reasonably conclude that his association with Aeschylus's play in 472 reflected a significant and deliberate political choice by the young Athenian.[62] Pericles sought to align himself with those elements in Athens that supported Themistocles and wished to see that leader and the Athenian fleet – and the common Athenians who often rowed in it – receive the lion's share of the credit for the defeat of Persia.

Aeschylus's own political views form a vexed question to which scholars have given various answers. However, we shall see that he clearly took the side of the progressive faction by the year 458, when he staged his play *Eumenides*. Given this fact, his association with Pericles, and his apparent support of Themistocles, surely we are justified in aligning Aeschylus with the less conservative strain of Athenian politics. Such a conclusion need not suggest that Aeschylus composed his tragedies in the first instance in order to influence Athenian domestic policy, but we should remain alive to the fact that his dramas can operate on multiple levels at once and that one of those levels is topical and political.[63] Whatever else he intended to do, Aeschylus probably hoped to help Themistocles in 472 and (as we shall see) Pericles in 458.

Pericles' personal life in this period presents us with an opaque image. We can assume that he married his first wife sometime in the 470s or early 460s, given that his older sons were grown men by the time the Peloponnesian War broke out in 431.[64] However, we know almost nothing of this first wife – indeed, even her name is lost to us. We may assume she came from a well-to-do Athenian family, both by her ability to marry into the household of Xanthippus/Pericles and by her marriage into the family of Kallias (marrying his son Hipponikos after the dissolution of her marriage with Pericles).[65] Given the connections between the Alkmeonid, Kimonid, and Kalliad families, it is an attractive possibility that Pericles' first wife came from Kimonid or Kalliad stock, while more than one scholar has speculated that she may herself have been an Alkmeonid. However, the fact that our tradition has not retained the woman's name tells against these possibilities: surely the name of a woman from one of the other families so closely connected with Pericles' family and other famous Athenians would have survived.[66]

Whatever her family and whatever her name, Pericles' first wife would bear him at least two children, the sons Xanthippus and Paralus. One of these sons (Xanthippus), we should note, would himself go on to marry into the Kimonid family,[67] again showing that the families' connections that stretched back to the sixth century were not severed even by the very open rivalry between Pericles and Kimon in later years.

While Pericles apparently lived a relatively quiet life into the mid-460s, Kimon's public profile grew ever more imposing. Around the year 466 he led the Athenians and their allies in one of the greatest campaigns in Athens' military history. About that year the Athenians (finally) sent a great fleet to attack Persian forces on the eastern side of the Aegean. The allied Greeks met the Persian/Phoenician fleet along the coast of southern Asia Minor, near the river Eurymedon (see Figure VII). Here Kimon won both a land and a sea victory, effectively ending any Persian threat in the Aegean for the foreseeable future. Unfortunately, neither Herodotus nor Thucydides, our contemporary fifth-century historians, provides a full account of this campaign.[68] For details, we are reliant on later and suspect reports. Yet enough information survives to show that at the Eurymedon Kimon won a victory with few rivals in Athenian history. Fathers named their sons "Eurymedon," and Athenians painted pots that graphically and obscenely illustrated what the Greeks had metaphorically done to the Persians in this famous battle (see Figure VIII).[69]

The victory at the Eurymedon plays an important role in Pericles' career, as it set in motion factors that would lead to his first political act – his prosecution of Kimon in 463. To understand the context of this trial, we must trace events after the Athenians defeated the Persians in southern Asia Minor. That victory might have led to the dissolution of the Delian League. After all, one could reasonably argue after the Eurymedon that the need for a perpetual allied fleet prepared to fight the Persians in the Aegean and relying on annual tribute payments by the allies no longer remained pressing.[70] The revolt of Naxos only a few years before Eurymedon had already shown that some allies felt that the league had become a tool of Athenian domination. Yet no source indicates that the Athenians considered even for a moment releasing their grip on the allies in the Delian League. Indeed, quite the contrary.

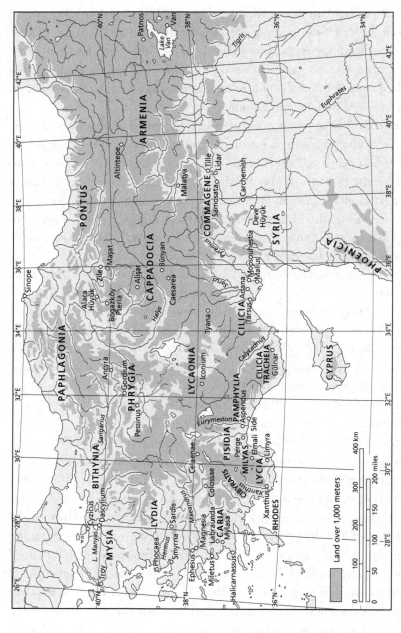

VII. Asia Minor and the northeastern Mediterranean. Athenian operations in the Mediterranean during Pericles' career extended all the way east to Cyprus and (briefly) Phoenicia, as well as south to Egypt.

VIII. The Eurymedon vase (Hamburg 1981.173). In the most likely interpretation of this famous Attic vase, a figure representing an eastern, "Persian" type is prepared to be sexually violated by a "Greek" figure. An inscription on the vase apparently identifies the submissive figure as "Eurymedon," the location in southern Asia Minor where the Athenian general Kimon won a great victory on land and sea over the Persians ca. 466 BC. The vase thus seems to illustrate the Athenian victory over the "barbarian" Persians in extremely graphic terms. Photos: Museum für Kunst und Gewerbe, Hamburg.

Shortly after the battle of the Eurymedon, in 465 Athens went to war against the large island of Thasos in the northern Aegean. Thucydides tells us that the Athenians and the Thasians disputed over "the mines and the markets" controlled by the Thasians on their island and on the mainland opposite the island. Thucydides does not detail the nature of this dispute, but that is hardly problematic. The only way a dispute between Athens and Thasos over the Thasians' mines and markets could occur would be if the Athenians had made some claim on them or their revenues. The citizens of Thasos undoubtedly responded that Athens should mind its own business and the Athenians voted to send their fleet to the island in order to ensure that the matter went in a way most advantageous to themselves.[71]

VIII. (cont.)

We must keep in mind that Thasos commanded a region in the northern Aegean that was crucial to Athenian interests. The mines on the mainland provided one of the only sources of precious metals in the entire Aegean. The timber supplies of the region, as we have seen, also figured prominently in the supply and maintenance of the Athenian fleet. Other evidence demonstrates that Athens' interests in Thasos reflected the island's strategic importance: about the same time as the Athenians sent their fleet to Thasos, they attempted to colonize land on the mainland just to the west of the island. This spot, as its name Ennea Hodoi (Nine Ways/Roads) suggests, served as critical conduit for trade and travel in this region. The Athenians' colonization attempt met with disaster, as the local Thracian population attacked and destroyed the colonists, whom they clearly did not consider welcome neighbors.[72] The Athenians, however, did not give up their interests in this location, and about a generation later (in 437/6) they would successfully found the colony of Amphipolis in the same region.[73]

The failed colonization attempt may have encouraged the Athenians to be even more aggressive in their treatment of Thasos, whose territory now provided Athens with a potential foothold in the region that it had been unable to acquire at Ennea Hodoi. In any case, the Athenians refused to take "no" for an answer. In 465 Kimon brought the fleet to bear on the island, whose citizens (amazingly) determined to stand up against this massive force. Naxos had fallen before the same fleet only a few years earlier, and the Thasians can have had little hope of successful resistance. Their determination not to submit in such unfavorable circumstances underscores once again the very strong feelings about independence motivating many Greek city-states.

Kimon besieged the island of Thasos, which ultimately capitulated two years later (463). The Spartans, who Thucydides tells us had promised to assist Thasos, were hindered from fulfilling their commitment of invading Attica by an earthquake in their territory.[74] The Athenians seized the island's fleet and destroyed its walls, compelling the Thasians to make annual tribute payments to Athens.[75] Once more victorious, Kimon returned to Athens. Yet, instead of collecting accolades, Kimon found himself accused of treason. He would face charges brought by a board of prosecutors that included Pericles, the son of the man (Xanthippus) who had prosecuted Kimon's own father, Miltiades.[76]

The nature of the charge against Kimon illustrates the incredibly aggressive nature of Athenian foreign policy in this period. No one accused Kimon of failing to carry out his mission where Thasos was concerned. Rather, Plutarch reports that the charges against Kimon maintained that he had accepted a bribe in order *not* to attack Macedon. Let us consider this accusation. The Athenians, it seems, believed that Kimon could have used the great fleet at his disposal to the advantage of Athens not only by reducing Thasos, but also by attacking the kingdom of Macedon. A bribe had allegedly forestalled an action that might have led to further Athenian expansion in the northern Aegean. One might object that the tale offers no clear picture of what an Athenian general and fleet could accomplish in Macedon. Such an objection, which is fair enough if we wish to consider the actual military/strategic situation, remains largely irrelevant to the political environment that could spawn these events: the charge seemingly reflects an attempt to bring Kimon down, and it reflects an Athenian belief – justified and realistic or not – that Athens could "do something" in Macedon.

The charge against Kimon, one must emphasize, relies on a historical environment in which (a) the idea that Athens could launch an unprovoked attack on Macedon was believable, and (b) the idea would have been acceptable to the Athenians. An Athenian commander, it would seem, was expected to "use his initiative" in such situations, a tradition of which Kimon had undoubtedly taken advantage in his earlier campaigns. Yet some Athenians believed he had let the Macedonians off easy when he might have seized the opportunity his fleet offered. To some Athenians the explanation for this must have been bribery.[77]

Kimon's trial presents us with a dramatic picture: Athens' greatest military hero facing accusers who included the son of his father's prosecutor.[78] The Athenians themselves obviously enjoyed stories about the spectacle. Most famously, some claimed that Kimon's sister Elpinike had offered herself to Pericles in exchange for him going easy on her brother. Pericles, so the story went, responded to Elpinike, "You are far too old to accomplish your mission."[79] This kind of tale, which Plutarch records for us, tends to persist in the tradition because it reflects poorly on both parties and because it reflects popular views of everyone involved. Kimon and Elpinike had such a close relationship that some joked that they lived as husband and wife instead of brother and sister.[80] The Athenians apparently considered Elpinike far too outspoken for an Athenian woman, and this added to or inspired suspicions about her character.[81] On the other side, Pericles, it would seem, had a reputation as a womanizer and wielded a somewhat sharp tongue.[82] All in all, this story about the trial fit the public images of the players beautifully.

However, the story might never have stuck without an additional fact: Pericles apparently did go easy on Kimon at the trial of 463, and thus some Athenians felt an explanation for this strange occurrence was needed.[83] Plutarch informs us that when the time came for Pericles to speak, he merely rose and made the briefest possible statement.[84] This report has elicited various explanations. It is possible, of course, that the as-yet-unestablished Pericles did not want to alienate the most powerful man in Athens or the eminent Kimon's friends. However, the close connections between the two families (connections that continued after Xanthippus's prosecution of Miltiades and Pericles' prosecution of Kimon) suggest the possibility that Pericles genuinely did not wish to do harm to Kimon. The later rivalry between the two leaders then led to the retrospective reinterpretation of this act and, perhaps, the need for a story attempting to explain it (hence Elpinike's failed visit).[85]

Yet Pericles' decision to act as one of the prosecutors in the case demands some kind of explanation. Certainly Athenian leaders often found themselves pressured into accepting roles they did not relish: Athenian generals could oppose a particular campaign and nevertheless find themselves sent as commanders (as the general Nikias was dispatched to Sicily in 415 BC).[86] Athenian prosecutions, however, at least usually relied on voluntary litigants. Athens did not elect individuals to bring cases against suspected criminals, and, if they were elected in special circumstances, they almost certainly could resign or refuse the office.[87] Pericles, therefore, apparently chose to join or accepted a role in the prosecution of Kimon, and this suggests one of two possibilities. Either Pericles intended to prosecute Kimon vigorously and then thought better of that decision (perhaps due to a perception that Kimon remained too powerful or the evidence against him too weak) or Pericles never intended to harm Kimon: that is, he planned to act as a "friendly prosecutor."[88]

Whatever his intentions, Pericles' approach to the case – doing the least he could possibly do – made an impression on the Athenians and perhaps contributed to Kimon's acquittal. The forces in Athens that wished to undermine Kimon's political position in Athens had, it would seem, overplayed their hand. After all, a man with Kimon's military reputation could hardly be believed to have missed an opportunity for advancing his own and Athens' martial agenda had such an opportunity actually presented itself. Kimon was already extremely wealthy and hardly needed the bribe of a Macedonian king. In short, whatever the truth of the charges (about which we can say virtually nothing), the story itself ultimately strained credulity, and this factor may also have influenced the young Pericles' decision to restrain himself.

Surveying the Athenian political landscape at the end of 463, Pericles could have reasonably predicted continued dominance by Kimon and his associates. Athens' formal alliance and other ties with Sparta remained strong:[89] Kimon had named one of his sons Lakedaimonios ("Spartan"), and Plutarch tells us that the general openly boasted of his close connections with the Dorians and belittled Athens' Ionian relations. Indeed, during his trial in 463, Kimon reportedly had said:

> that he was not, like some Athenians, the paid representative of rich Ionians or Thessalians, to be courted and rewarded for his services: if he were to represent anybody's interests it would be [those of] the Spartans, whose simplicity and moderation he was glad to imitate.[90]

At other times, Kimon liked to advise his fellow Athenians by simply stating, "That's not what the Spartans would do."[91]

The challenge to Kimon's power in the form of a public prosecution had failed, and subsequent events show that Kimon retained tremendous influence in the Athenian assembly. Yet the following year, 462/1, would prove that Kimon's position suffered from two fatal flaws. The general apparently overestimated the Athenians' willingness to share hegemony in Greece with Sparta and underestimated the desires of poorer Athenians to share in the political and economic glory that the empire had brought to Athens. Pericles' later career shows that he – unlike Kimon – was alive to both factors, and the unproven statesman would soon tap into these reservoirs of potential power, catapulting himself and Athens to unprecedented dominance.[92]

FOUR

The Democratic Revolution
(ca. 462/1–444/3)

The Athenians voted to ostracize Kimon in 462/1, and in the following decade Pericles and his associates remade Athenian democracy, removing authority from older and more conservative elements in the regime and distributing that power to common Athenians sitting on juries or serving in the Athenian council (which was chosen by lot). Pericles seems to have assumed leadership of the progressive faction soon after 462/1, since Aeschylus's Eumenides suggests that by 459/8 his supporters were seeking to distance him from the curse his family had inherited.

Probably during this period and in perhaps the most significant political maneuver of his career, Pericles proposed that Athenians should be paid for their service on the very large juries in Athens' courts. Once established, the principle of payment for public service became fundamental to Athenian democracy, tying the profits of Athens' empire directly to the political system. This practice arguably corrupted the Athenian political process, rendering proposals to reduce or restrict public expenditures stillborn as well as aggravating preexistent Athenian nationalism.

In 451/0 the Athenians voted – on Pericles' recommendation – to restrict the benefits of citizenship to those who had both an Athenian mother and an Athenian father. Around the same time, the Athenians decided to use the moneys collected from their Greek allies to adorn the city of Athens, beginning construction of the Parthenon and numerous other expensive public buildings. Pericles' central role in most (if not all) of these events illustrates one of the defining principles of his career: a willingness to foster policies that exploited non-Athenians in an effort to raise Athens to new heights.

77

Our sources suggest Pericles encountered a major obstacle in these years in the person of Kimon's relative and political heir, Thucydides son of Melesias. Analysis of Pericles' victory in this conflict shows that the statesman had mastered democratic politics and the Athenians' complex psychology, leaving his rivals frustrated in the face of his popular nationalistic policies.

In many ways 462/1 stands as one of the most important years in Athens' history. In that year the Athenians reversed their alliances in Greece and voted to radicalize their democratic government, providing significantly more power to the poorer elements of society. Yet the relative paucity of information about these momentous events has led to a palpable frustration among historians. Unfortunately, no fifth-century source describes these events in any detail. Thucydides gives us only the barest outline of the foreign policy angle while ignoring the domestic situation entirely. The fourth-century account by Aristotle or one of his students (*The Constitution of Athens*) provides only a dim picture of the constitutional changes. Later sources, especially Plutarch, provide a few tantalizing but often dubious details. Perhaps most important for our purposes, Pericles' alleged role in these events remains highly controversial.[1]

Nevertheless, one can hardly overemphasize the epochal nature of the changes Athens underwent in 462/1. Modern historians in recent years have provided a welcome corrective to the once-popular view that Athenian democracy more or less reached its identifiable, classical form not long after the reforms proposed by Pericles' great-uncle Cleisthenes in 507 BC. Scholars such as Peter Rhodes and Kurt Raaflaub have argued that the reforms of 462/1 provided significantly more power to poorer Athenians than they had enjoyed under the government of Cleisthenes.[2] Let us first examine what we know about the circumstances of these reforms and the reforms themselves, and then turn to the question of Pericles' supposed involvement in them. In this chapter we will focus on the domestic policy side of the equation, while recognizing that this cannot be separated in fact from the changes the Athenians made in their foreign policy at the same time.

Indeed, the major constitutional changes occurring in 462/1 apparently grew out of Athens' relations with the most powerful state in Greece. Sparta had long relied on a class of serfs (called "helots") who worked the land for their Spartan lords under compulsion and provided them with the surplus wealth that permitted them to focus on training for warfare rather than farming. Full Spartan citizens, unlike other Greeks, typically did not work their own land (assisted by slaves) but rather enjoyed an income provided by the forced labor of these helots.

Around the year 465/4, an earthquake in the Peloponnese led to a helot revolt in and around Sparta. Many of the enserfed class sought to break away from Spartan control. The revolt culminated in a siege: the Spartans surrounded the fortress mountain Ithome, where the helots and some other Peloponnesians supporting them had holed up. Inexperienced in siege warfare, the Spartans requested assistance from some of their Greek allies, including the Athenians.[3]

Perhaps some readers may find the idea of the democratic Athenians assisting the oligarchic Spartans in suppressing a helot revolt disturbing. The Athenians – who, we should remember, held thousands of chattel slaves – had no such feelings. Or, rather, the objections some Athenians voiced had nothing to do with supporting the idea of "freedom" for the helots. Instead, our sources tell us, some Athenians simply opposed the idea of helping the Spartans.[4] Here, they could argue, an opportunity for Athenian advantage had presented itself. Why help the Spartans when a strong Sparta prevented Athens from achieving real preeminence in Greece? A weakened Sparta meant a more powerful Athens.[5]

Our tradition associates the name of Ephialtes with this argument against assisting the Spartans. This Athenian leader, who would also receive credit for the democratic reforms of 462/1, features prominently only in the history of this year. We know virtually nothing about his career or his family. In his first appearance on the historical stage we find him opposing Kimon, the most powerful man in Athens, who supported sending assistance to the Spartans. As we have seen, Kimon had allegedly claimed (in the context of his trial in 463) that he preferred to be a friend and imitator of the Dorian Spartans rather than a paid representative of Ionians. In the debate over aiding Sparta in 462/1 he argued that the Athenians could not allow Greece to become "lame," meaning that Spartan and Athenian power were the two legs upon which Greece stood.[6] The implication, of course, is that the Persians or some other power might return someday, and only a strong Sparta and Athens working together could provide any real security for Greece as a whole.

Kimon's views carried the day, and an Athenian force of several thousand hoplites marched west and south into the Peloponnese in order to help the Spartan overlords re-enserf their helots. However, upon the arrival of this force, something quite unusual and unexpected happened. Thucydides tells us that the Spartans had a change of heart: the Athenians, they suddenly recalled, were not Dorians, and were given to doing "new things," the implication being that they would be a dangerous force to have in the vicinity of revolted helots. The Spartans therefore sent Kimon and the Athenian force back home. The insulted Athenians, upon their return, broke off their alliance with Sparta against the Persians and made alliances with the Thessalians and Argives, both peoples tainted with not opposing Persia and the latter serving as Sparta's bitterest enemies.[7]

Historians have sought to explain this bizarre story in various ways. The most likely explanation is that the Spartans, who obviously knew about the Athenians' ethnic background and tendency to do "new things" before Sparta ever summoned them to the Peloponnese, had become suspicious of the Athenians for some other reason after their arrival. The reason for the Spartans' change of heart is likely to have been political events that occurred in Athens after Kimon and his soldiers departed for Sparta.[8]

Ephialtes and his supporters, it would seem, seized on the opportunity presented by Kimon's absence (along with that of many of the hoplites and Kimon's supporters) to pass legislation through the Athenian assembly, an organ that operated based simply on majority rule. No constitutional restriction prevented the Athenians from holding an assembly and voting while a very large number of the citizens were away on a military campaign. Indeed, such votes were frequently necessary during the fifth century BC, when Athens was at war more years than it was at peace.

On the other hand, how could such revolutionary events happen in Athens and word reach the Spartans, causing them to react by sending the Athenians home? It seems likely that the foreign policy aspect of Ephialtes' revolution – the new alliances with Argos and Thessaly – played an important role here. Such alliances did not happen overnight, especially when Athens was (at the moment) in a long-standing alliance with Sparta against the Persians. Embassies must have been sent to or from Argos (for example), and it is quite likely that the Spartans got wind of such an embassy.[9] The prospect of an Athenian-Argive alliance undoubtedly created great discomfort in Sparta, as Argos had been Sparta's longtime enemy and rival for power in the Peloponnese. Perhaps, upon learning of such embassies, the Spartans went to Kimon and suggested he return to Athens to attempt to forestall or reverse this change in Athenian policy. Kimon would undoubtedly have been eager to do so.[10]

Upon his return to Athens, Kimon found that the political environment had changed dramatically. Whatever the truth about the Spartans' feelings and Kimon's reasons to return, Ephialtes and his political enemies undoubtedly claimed that the Spartans had insulted Athens by sending away its forces. What is more, the reforms Ephialtes had proposed and perhaps already passed through the Athenian assembly had proved sufficiently popular to turn a critical mass of Athenians against the conservative Kimon. Perhaps because Kimon opposed the popular changes in Athens' government and because of the ostensible or alleged insult his expedition to Sparta had received, the Athenians voted to ostracize Kimon. Kimon, Athens' greatest general and leader in the first half of the fifth century, therefore left Attica and played no role in Athenian politics for the next decade.

What precisely had Ephialtes done to so alter the political picture in Athens? Aristotle, our best source, tells us only that Ephialtes removed "additional powers" from the ancient Areopagus council.[11] Scholars have been forced to reconstruct Ephialtes' reforms by examining Athenian history from the period before and after the legislation. The technicalities of this debate should not concern us here. The general picture is relatively clear and uncontroversial. Ephialtes removed certain powers from the conservative Areopagus – which consisted of former Athenian magistrates (called archons and chosen from the wealthier classes of citizens) – and transferred them to other political organs of the Athenian state – organs that were controlled by regular Athenian citizens rather than by the former magistrates (and members of the elite) who sat on the ancient council of the Areopagus.[12]

It appears that before 462/1 the Areopagus council exercised fairly broad supervisory powers in Athenian government. In particular, the council probably carried out the vetting process that some Athenian officials went through before entering office and the audit of their actions after leaving office. In later Athenian history these processes (*dokimasia* and *euthynai*, respectively) occurred in large courts before jurors drawn by lot from regular Athenian citizens. In addition, it seems that certain types of legal cases (beyond those involving murder and impurity) after Ephialtes' reforms were transferred from the purview of the Areopagus to other

Athenian judicial organs, again controlled not by the wealthiest Athenians (as was the Areopagus) but rather by predominantly middle-class citizens.[13]

These changes essentially put most judicial functions in Athens in the hands of common citizens serving as jurors on Athenian courts or sitting as members (chosen by lot) of the Council of 500 created by Cleisthenes' legislation ca. 507. Although such a change may seem less than momentous to us, the ancient Greeks apparently felt differently. Aristotle, for example, treats popular control of the courts as one of the most important elements in democracy.[14] Elections and voting did not define democracy, in Aristotle's view: after all, nearly every Greek polis (including Sparta, for example) held elections and took votes on issues like war and peace. Elections, Aristotle maintained, in fact led to the rule of the rich.[15] On the other hand, when the common people serve as jurors in most legal cases, they gain real control over the state. The *demos* (the people collectively) exercises real *kratos* (power), the basis of *demokratia*. After Ephialtes' reforms, Athenian democracy assumed its classical form, with most judicial and legislative affairs in the hands of average Athenian citizens. Later Athenian reforms (apart from two oligarchical revolutions) consisted of minor modifications to the Ephialtean system or (at times) sometimes restricted the people's (the demos's) authority or freedom of action.[16]

The popularity of Ephialtes' proposals suggests that many Athenians resented the power the elites had previously exercised through the Areopagus. Despite Kimon's military successes and the material advantages they had brought to rich and poor Athenians alike, some citizens apparently believed that the political privileges they enjoyed did not reflect sufficient respect for the poorer majority. Some scholars have suggested that, ironically enough, it was precisely Kimon's successes – which depended on a fleet of warships often rowed by economically disadvantaged Athenians – that led to this revolution and Kimon's downfall. The sailors who rowed the Athenian warships had come to see that they played this crucial part in Athens' success. It only made sense if their privileges reflected their seminal role in making Athens the dominant power in the Aegean.[17]

With Kimon ostracized, it must have seemed that Ephialtes stood to wield significant political influence in Athens during the foreseeable future. However, shortly after these events Ephialtes was murdered by a man from Tanagra (a city in Boeotia, north of Attica) in circumstances we cannot reconstruct.[18] A very weak later tradition connected the murder with an envious Pericles, but authorities from Plutarch forward have rightly dismissed this.[19] The story of Pericles' jealousy over Ephialtes' political success almost certainly represents a desperate attempt to explain an event about which we know virtually nothing, and it illustrates just how little reliable material about Ephialtes, his reforms, and his demise has survived antiquity. To be fair, our ancient authorities were little better informed about the matter. Since Ephialtes was a relative unknown, sources like Aristotle sought to connect his reforms with other, more famous Athenians, including Themistocles (who was not even in Athens and may not even have been alive in 462/1) and Pericles (who had yet to make a political name for himself). Analysis has shown that these traditions rest on no sound basis other than the ancients' ignorance about Ephialtes and consequent desire to provide him with a famous colleague. Ephialtes himself should receive credit for these reforms.[20]

We may certainly infer from Pericles' later political actions that he supported Ephialtes' reforms and that he welcomed the political opportunity presented by Kimon's ostracism. The latter event opened the field for Pericles and others to attain political prominence in Athens without even risking the anger of the pro-Kimonian forces (a reaction that might have stemmed from a vigorous prosecution of the general in 463). The subsequent death of Ephialtes could hardly have been more politically convenient for the young Pericles, and this fact undoubtedly suggested the speculation that he must have been behind the murder.

Nevertheless, no ancient evidence describes Pericles immediately taking advantage of this situation. Reason does exist, however, to conclude that by 458 Pericles had assumed an important, if not dominant, role in what we might call the progressive faction in Athens. In the spring of that year, the dramatist Aeschylus produced his play *Eumenides*, the third part of the poet's famous *Oresteia* trilogy. This strange tragedy in its final section depicts the foundation of the Areopagus council in Athens. Critics have sometimes noted the uneasy way this bit of constitutional history sits in the story of a young man (Orestes) who had murdered his mother (Clytemnestra, who had killed her husband and Orestes' father, Agamemnon) and now sought expiation for this heinous crime.[21] Other features mark the drama as unusual. In the tragedy Aeschylus changes the story's traditional place of action from Mycenae to Argos and invents and then praises a mythical ancient alliance between Argos and Athens – this at a time when Athens had recently rejected its alliance with Sparta and made an agreement with the Argives, a people tainted with their failure to oppose the Persians in the great war and the Spartans' bitter enemies.[22] The play also makes an unusual argument about the irrelevance of the mother's blood in a man's biological inheritance, a position that benefited Orestes (the matricide) in the play and Pericles (the son of a cursed Alkmeonid mother) in the audience.[23]

Taken together with other factors identified by scholars, it seems likely that Aeschylus's play (beyond its larger aesthetic and dramatic purposes) was intended to provide support for Athens' political revolution in 462/1 and the new alliance with Argos, while providing a mythical argument that made Pericles' personal situation (the inherited curse) seem less important.[24] Such a conclusion need not imply that Aeschylus chose his subject and then composed the play simply "to help Pericles": it means only that Aeschylus adapted his story in a way that – along with its larger themes, including reconciliation between older gods like the avenging Furies and newer Olympians like Apollo and Athena – tended to diminish the apparent importance of the curse on Pericles' maternal family and blunt criticism of the recent alliance with Argos and the reform of the Areopagus. Since Aeschylus went so far out of his way to accomplish this – changing the location of the story and importing the unwieldy Areopagus council into the tale while also urging the Athenians to avoid civil strife and turn their energies outward – it appears that by 458 Pericles had become an important enough political figure to have attracted criticism and thus warrant such a defense. By 458, it seems, Pericles had achieved some political prominence in Athens.

* * * * *

Plutarch famously separates Pericles' political career into two parts: at first, Pericles played to the crowd and sought power through tactics typical of a demagogue. Later, according to Plutarch, he became a true statesman, willing to oppose the popular will and "lead [the people] more than being led by them" (as Thucydides puts it).[25] This view of the first part of Pericles' career reflects a negative construction placed on the statesman's politics quite early in our tradition – a view that Plutarch attempts to reconcile with the more positive Thucydidean summary (in 2.65) by positing a change in Pericles over time. While Pericles still lived, Athenian comic poets and others were attacking him for his oratorical style, demagoguery, oversized head, scandalous relations with women, and aggressive foreign policy.[26] By the early fourth century, Plato treated Pericles as a typical demagogue, who misled and corrupted the people and bought their support with public money.[27] To understand these negative views of Pericles, and to test Plutarch's hypothesis of an early "demagogic phase" in the statesman's career, we must examine the events of the 450s and early 440s.[28]

We have no firm record of Pericles serving as one of Athens' ten elected generals before the mid-450s, but after that period he seems to have served in that office frequently. This position combined military and political influence, a practice well illustrated by Kimon's dominance in the 470s and 460s, although the conservative Kimon had no new political agenda to put forward. Fifth-century Athenian generals often advised the Athenian people in the assembly, and their views on domestic as well as external affairs carried special weight. We will examine the foreign policy aspects of Pericles' early career in the next chapter, but here we should note that military campaigns undoubtedly helped Pericles achieve prominence in the 450s.[29] Again, Kimon had provided the example. Athenians expected to benefit in tangible ways at home from Athens' aggressive foreign policy, and Pericles (as we shall see) understood this.

Moreover, it was Athens' foreign policy and the income from its empire that helped make Pericles' domestic activities in this period possible. Perhaps the statesman's most important political innovation occurred sometime in this period, probably in the late 450s, when Pericles proposed that Athenians should be paid to serve as jurors in Athens' large courts.[30] Again, in a world inured to the idea of state funds distributed to individual citizens for various purposes – from welfare payments to farm subsidies and the like – the idea that the Athenians would pay their jurors may seem utterly innocuous and unremarkable. Yet the proposal stands as one of the most radical and influential in the history of democratic government, as it forever altered the relationships among the political leader, the state, and the citizenry.[31] The event therefore requires our careful attention.

Athenian juries present an odd image for moderns accustomed to courts with only a few (often twelve) jurors. Athens' courts relied on juries of hundreds or more jurors (*dikastai*). In the mid-fifth century, they were chosen more or less daily on a first-come, first-serve basis, but by the fourth century the process became quite elaborate, involving a daily lottery for service.[32] The introduction of payments to jurors in Athens thus had the potential to affect a very large number of citizens and a much larger percentage of the citizen body than would such a procedure in a modern democratic court system. The Athenians ultimately selected by lot 6,000 citizens to serve as a jury pool each year, and while only perhaps 1,500 to 2,000 of those might actually serve as jurors on any given day, this still represents a high percentage of the total Athenian citizen population, which was probably no more than 50,000 to 60,000 citizens at its height. A full 10 percent or more of Athens' citizens potentially served as jurors in any given year.[33]

By the mid-450s Athens had become extremely wealthy. In 454/3 the Athenians apparently brought the treasury of the Delian League, which contained thousands of talents collected from Athens' allies for the protection of Greece against Persia, to Athens and deposited a huge part of the funds it contained in their goddess Athena's treasury. This repository served as Athens' most important treasury in the mid-fifth century, and from it the citizens could fund everything from public buildings to military campaigns. Athens already possessed significant income from the silver mines, and that money had been put to public uses like building warships since 483. Athens' allies also paid annual tribute that would now flow directly to a treasury located in Athens. In short, by the late 450s the Athenians possessed public wealth that dwarfed that of other city-states and made them the richest citizen body in Greece.[34]

Perhaps it should not surprise us that Pericles and others determined to put some of this money to work. Probably around the late 450s, perhaps about the time Athens seized the league's treasury, Pericles made his proposal that Athenian jurors should be paid.[35] Since Athenian juries were very large affairs, with as many as 500 to 2,000 volunteers hearing cases most days of the year, payment of jurors would therefore not represent an inexpensive proposition.[36] Some prudent Athenians must have asked, "Can we afford this?" Or, perhaps, "We may be able to afford this now, but will we be able to afford it in the future? What if the empire is lost or the silver mines dry up?" Our meager tradition tells us nothing about such speculation or about any of the motives various Athenians could have had to support this policy. Did some argue that *demokratia* required the service and participation of poorer citizens and only payments would allow this? Any such theoretical considerations make no impact on our sources. The fact that it appears that payments accrued only to jurors – and not, initially, to other Athenian officials, such as members of the Council of 500 – perhaps suggests that the movement to pay *dikastai* represented an ad hoc rather than a philosophically democratic idea. In any case, we only know that the Athenian citizens voted to begin to pay themselves when they served as jurors. The precedent of voting themselves an income would have a debilitating effects on future Athenian public policy, since Athenians would necessarily thereafter take foreign policy and other financial decisions in light of their effect on public payments.[37]

Aristotle relates an interesting anecdote about these events. According to him, Pericles lamented to his friend (the philosopher and musician) Damon that he was not wealthy enough to compete with Kimon's famous largesse.[38] "Well," Damon responded, "why not give the people their own money?" This story presents us with several dubious aspects. First, Pericles was actually quite wealthy, and, if not as rich as Kimon, he certainly possessed the resources necessary for a political life in Athens. Second, the story suggests that Kimon and Pericles were active competitors at the time of the event described, and the only period fitting that description is (potentially) the short time after Kimon returned from ostracism in the late 450s.[39]

In short, this tale is more likely to reflect the kinds of anecdotes that circulated about Pericles than an actual event. Some time later, after the specific context of Pericles' proposal to institute jury pay had been forgotten but when people talked about how this had happened, someone invented or embellished a tale that centered on the ideas that (a) Pericles spent time with intellectuals (like Damon), who must have given him advice, and (b) Pericles had been a rival of the wealthy and famously generous Kimon. The story pretty clearly originated in, or was spread by, elements hostile to Pericles, who is the least impressive actor in the tale: the anecdote represents Kimon as philanthropic, Damon as clever, and Pericles as an opportunist and penny-pincher. The most significant thing the tale tells us is that some Athenians eventually treated Pericles' proposal as a cynical attempt to win influence with the mass of poorer Athenians.[40]

Were Pericles' critics right about him? Perhaps it is not even a fair question to ask whether Pericles' proposal was in fact cynical, in the sense that he had little real interest in justice or in bettering the lives of the average Athenian but instead merely sought to place himself in an advantageous political position. And yet the fact that Pericles' career, taken as a whole, exhibits remarkably little sympathy for the typical, individual Athenian citizen makes the question necessary.[41] Pericles introduced and supported policies that sent thousands of Athenians to their deaths in the service of an ideal of Athenian greatness and future fame. Should we imagine that such a man found the relative poverty and inability to partici-pate in the judicial process of the average Athenian sufficient motivations for such a radical and expensive action as proposing the use of public money to pay jurors?

Pericles perhaps did not foresee that the institution of jury pay would soon encourage payment for all manner of public activities in Athens. By the 420s, the Athenians had voted to pay virtually all public officials from state funds. The political argument in Athens became not whether such public payments were prudent or justified, but how much and how often Athenians should pay themselves. To that extent, Pericles' proposal for jury pay opened a floodgate that perhaps could not be readily closed by any peaceful, political means. Only short-lived oligarchic revolutions in Athens managed to end (temporarily) the practice of public payments, which featured as a defining feature of Athenian democracy from the mid-450s forward and which weakened Athens militarily in the fourth century, when the Athenians for too long refused to vote to move funds from the treasury for public payments to the military chest in order to take aggressive action in the face of Philip of Macedon.[42]

Perhaps we may attack the problem of Pericles' motivation for jury pay via another angle. In 451/0 he proposed another piece of legislation that would allow Athenian citizenship to be conferred only on those having two Athenian parents: previously, only the father needed to be Athenian for citizenship to be passed from parent to child.[43] Now, an Athenian mother was also required for the transfer of citizenship status. This legislation had the effect of limiting citizenship and shrinking the pool of potential wives for Athenian men (if they wished to pass their citizenship down to their sons). It came at a time when Athens was attracting numerous foreigners, who came to the city as artisans to ply their trades in the economic hotbed of imperial Athens or simply sought greater economic opportunities. Such a situation was bound to raise questions about Athenians' relations with, and status relative to, non-Athenians in the city.[44] Scholars have offered various explanations for the action – from punishing aristocratic elites who often married into wealthy families outside of Athens (as, for example, Kimon's father had done) to encouraging the idea of a special, psychologically ennobled citizenry.[45] Pericles, I believe we can conclude, saw numerous potential benefits in this legislation – including encouraging Athenians of the lower classes to think of themselves as the equals in some ways of the wealthier citizens – but among them must have been the simple but powerful idea that the benefits of Athenian citizenship should accrue to a limited number of "real Athenians."[46] In addition, by circumscribing the marital options of Athenian men, Pericles also limited the type of international family connections that might make foreign policy and diplomatic decisions for Athens complicated. Athenian history from time immemorial had offered examples of foreign entanglements that had led to problematic ends or suggested potential dynastic ambitions: the would-be tyrant Kylon had tried to seize power through the help of his Megarian father-in-law. Peisistratus had married an Argive woman before the allegedly troubled marriage to an Athenian (and Alkmeonid). Of course, the Alkmeonids themselves had contracted a marriage alliance with the tyrant Cleisthenes of Sicyon. Miltiades (Kimon's father), the tyrant of the Chersonese, had married the daughter of a Thracian king.[47]

In short, whatever else Pericles' legislation did, it certainly prevented the most elite families from continuing the practice of marrying into foreign dynastic families. It therefore had the potential to clear the field, as it were, of any familial obligations that could impinge on Athenian interests. From the popular viewpoint, it probably looked more like punishment of the wealthy and powerful than any particular benefit to the common Athenians, who had precious little opportunity to attract rich and aristocratic foreign wives, though even poorer Athenians could marry into wealthier metic families or find non-Athenian wives in the empire.[48] (We may note, however, that the law could have had a somewhat positive impact on Athenian families with daughters, who became more attractive by virtue of their now unique ability to confer citizenship on their children.) At the same time, the legislation cast a shadow on current Athenian leaders (including Kimon) whose parents were not both Athenian. Obviously the law was not retroactive, but it placed current leaders with non-Athenian mothers or wives in an awkward position.[49]

Recent study has attempted to put a less nationalistic spin on this citizenship law.[50] But surely we must admit that whatever else the legislation's effects or intent, this measure drew a figurative line between "real Athenians" and the rest of Greece. Athenian benefits would be enjoyed only by those with two Athenian parents. "Athenianness," as it were, had been marked off as something valuable and precious. Other Greek city-states could hardly have seen the action as anything other than an obnoxious statement of Athenian superiority, especially as the practice of marrying outside of one's polis had a long-standing tradition among aristocrats in Greece (beyond, perhaps, Sparta[51]).

With the proposal for jury pay and his new citizenship law, by 450 Pericles had certainly achieved the status of a leading figure in Athenian politics. We may pause to ask: Who figured as his primary rivals for power in this period? Again, we are woefully ignorant about Athenian politics between the primary years of interest for the historians Herodotus (480– 479) and Thucydides (431–411). Aristotle's *Constitution* provides us with a meager account of this period, suggesting he was little better informed than are we. We know the names of a few other generals in this period, but we can do little more with the names like Tolmides or Myronides than to connect them with some specific campaigns.[52]

Kimon remained in exile until 452/1, or possibly a bit earlier than that, if the story that the Athenians recalled him early rests on any good authority.[53] If the great statesman did return early, he made very little impact on our sources. It is perhaps better to accept that Kimon finished (or nearly finished) his ten-year period of exile than to imagine he came back to Athens and left no evidence of this in our record. We can be certain of his return by 451/0, when he negotiated a five-year peace treaty with Sparta (see the next chapter), an action that suggests Kimon's return coincided with renewed influence due to his pro-Spartan political stance.[54]

The swiftness with which Kimon brought Athenian foreign policy from a footing of war to peace where Sparta was concerned suggests that Pericles in 451/0 was not then the politically predominant force he was to become in the mid-440s, assuming (as we should in the absence of any other evidence) that Pericles had already adopted a relatively hostile stance toward Sparta. An occasion ca. 447 when he lost a debate over whether to send an army to central Greece confirms the conclusion of Pericles' less than dominant influence at this point.[55] He apparently also did not win election as general every year in the late 450s and early 440s. Of course, it is possible that Pericles' relationship with Kimon was not completely hostile upon the latter's return. Plutarch tells us that the two statesmen secretly agreed to divide Athenian political power, with Pericles dominating domestic and Kimon foreign policy.[56] Yet this conspiracy theory – suspiciously making Kimon's infamous sister Elpinike the intermediary – likely reflects an inference by Plutarch (or more likely one of his sources) rather than firm information. It may stem, for example, from nothing more than the fact that upon Kimon's return he secured peace between Athens and Sparta and then sailed off at the head of a great expedition against the Persians in the east while Pericles passed his citizenship law. These actions looked like major successes for each in the foreign and domestic spheres. In any case, subsequent historical events and the persistent rumors that Elpinike had approached Pericles with an earlier offer in 463,[57] combined with Pericles' success with the citizenship law and jury pay, probably suggested the appearance (if not the reality) of such a conspiracy concerning a division of power ca. 451/0.

Kimon died on this expedition against Persian interests in Cyprus (probably in 450) and soon after this a new rival for Pericles emerged – a relative of Kimon named Thucydides, son of Melesias. The precise relationship between this Thucydides and Kimon is unclear. They could have been cousins, relations by marriage, or both.[58] Whatever their precise connection, Thucydides Melesiou took on the leadership of the more conservative and pro-Spartan Athenians who had previously backed Kimon. And yet Thucydides did not have Kimon's illustrious military accomplishments on which to rest political influence. Thucydides, so far as we can tell, fought it out with Pericles in the assembly via Athenian electoral politics.[59] Plutarch even tells us that he made it a habit to have his supporters gather together in a particular spot in the assembly (presumably to emphasize their numbers or coherence, or perhaps to encourage one another in their opposition to Periclean policies).[60]

We should imagine that Kimon's supporters, and later those of Thucydides Melesiou, objected to such Periclean proposals as jury pay and the citizenship law, both of which could weaken more conservative, aristocratic leaders (if by no other means than by making Pericles and those who supported him more popular with the masses). Yet the only evidence we possess of a direct and sustained political battle between Pericles and Thucydides came not over either of these issues, but rather over the great Periclean building program in Athens that began in the years just after 450.

Kimon, as we have seen, also fostered a public building program in the 470s and 460s. However, the moneys used for those buildings apparently came principally from booty seized in Athenian campaigns. By the early 440s, Athens had taken possession of the moneys paid by its allies for the protection of Greece, formerly stored on the island of Delos but now kept in an Athenian treasury or treasuries. Research has shown that the Athenians began to use these funds to defray expenses previously met from purely Athenian sources, and fragments of the building accounts of the Parthenon show that some imperial moneys were used to pay directly for the Parthenon (others came from the goddess Athena's treasury, which had almost certainly received a large transfer from the allied moneys just before this period).[61]

The intricacies of the financial machinations in this period need not concern us, because it is perfectly clear that the moneys collected from the allies for the protection of Greece and now stored in Athens served as a resource for Athenian projects for the next two decades. Beyond the institution of jury pay and the maintenance of a very expensive and aggressive foreign policy, the Athenians in these years undertook to build some of the most fantastic structures ever erected in Hellas.

The temple to Athena Parthenos ("the maiden") atop the acropolis in Athens stands as the symbol for this building program, though in fact it represented only a fraction of the total work undertaken after about 448.[62] Construction of another huge temple (probably dedicated to the god Hephaistos) below the acropolis probably began in this period.[63] The Athenians also built a new center for music and the arts (the Odeion) below the acropolis, modeled on a Persian construction and probably meant to symbolize Athens' defeat of the invaders.[64] Expensive new gates (the Propylaia) to the acropolis would house an art gallery and provide an elaborate and impressive entrance to the sacred ground atop the citadel. Between the Propylaia and the Parthenon stood a huge bronze statue of Athena Promachos ("champion" or "warrior"), which apparently predated the Periclean construction and may have been funded from Kimon's victories.[65] Beyond it on the acropolis stood the grand new temple of Athena Parthenos, which would become the most famous example of architecture from all of classical antiquity. Inside the temple stood a giant statue of Athena, adorned with gold and ivory and holding the image of Victory (Nike) in her hand (see Figure IX).[66]

IX. Athena Parthenos with Nike in hand. The Parthenon on the acropolis housed a huge gold and ivory statue of Athena Parthenos ("the maiden"), who held a small statue of Nike ("Victory") in her hand. This modern re-creation (by Alan LeQuire) is based on ancient evidence for the original's appearance and stands in the replica of the Athenian Parthenon constructed in Nashville, Tennessee. The image was commissioned in 1982: Alan LeQuire, *Athena Parthenos*, The Parthenon, Nashville, Tennessee, photo by Gary Layda.

Nor did the Athenians restrict themselves to construction on and around the acropolis in this period. Expensive construction was carried on elsewhere in Attica, including to the northwest at Eleusis and on the peninsula's southern tip at Sounion, where a new temple to Poseidon was constructed.[67] And beyond the temples, public constructions such as

X. Pericles of Athens. Marble bust from Tivoli, Italy. Second-century BC Roman copy of Greek original. Now in the British Museum. Photo: Art Resource.

another wall to the Peiraeus harbor (walls built in the early 450s had already linked the city to the harbor) and new or restored fountains in Athens made life in the city more pleasant and demonstrated the city's amazing wealth to visitors.[68] The building program as a whole certainly focused on "public sanctuaries," but a significant fraction of the work addressed buildings with less sacral associations.[69]

Plutarch famously treats the building program associated with Pericles like some kind of ancient public works project, imagining the numbers of Athenian laborers and craftsmen who drew salaries from this endeavor.[70] Though this picture is exaggerated and overemphasizes (or invents) the socioeconomic motive for the program, Plutarch was surely right to conclude that many groups of Athenians benefited in very tangible ways from this massive project. The money doled out to artisans, stonemasons, day laborers, transporters, and others would also have entered the larger Athenian economy through purchases of food, lodging, goods, and entertainment.[71] The Athenian marketplace (agora) must have become an even more bustling center of commerce and communication in this period. Those with goods to sell would know that even the poorer classes in Athens had ready money – for those not engaged in the building program could serve as rowers in the Athenian fleet. Meanwhile the elderly or infirm could serve as jurors for pay in the Athenian courts. A citizen of Athens in the 440s found himself with numerous ways to earn at least a little money via public service.

When we examine the environment in this way, the economic and political impact of Pericles' support of this program becomes clear. The use of public funds offered the Athenian statesman an avenue for achieving preeminence previously outlined by Kimon and the Peisistratids. True, the popular votes in the assembly necessary to use public funds previously collected for, or dedicated to, other purposes (imperial, civic, or sacral) and the sheer scope of operations differentiated the Periclean program from those of the aristocrat and tyrants. It may, in fact, have been the involvement of the common Athenians via the vote and the clear impact the program had on Pericles' popularity that led Thucydides Melesiou and his supporters to oppose this construction.[72] Plutarch reports the story of their opposition, and, although its veracity has been questioned, no compelling grounds exist for discrediting the tradition, especially as it centers around the only known, serious rival for Pericles in midcentury and it provides reasonable context for Thucydides' subsequent downfall and Pericles' rise to the position of unquestioned "first man" in Athens.[73] Though neither Herodotus nor Thucydides (the historian, who was almost certainly a relation of Thucydides Melesiou) reports these events, they possibly came down through another fifth-century source, a certain Stesimbrotus of Thasos, who wrote a pamphlet called *On Themistocles, Thucydides* (son of Melesias), *and Pericles*. We know that Plutarch used this apparently scurrilous work in his biography of Pericles, and it is hardly likely that an author treating both Pericles and Thucydides Melesiou would fail to recount an event that involved both as the featured actors.[74]

Plutarch's account from his life of Pericles deserves quotation:

[12] But there was one measure above all which at once gave the greatest pleasure to the Athenians, adorned their city and created amazement among the rest of mankind, and which is today the sole testimony that the tales of the ancient power and glory of Greece are no mere fables. By this I mean his construction of temples and public buildings; and yet it was this, more than any other action of his, which his enemies slandered and misrepresented. They cried out in the Assembly that Athens had lost her good name and disgraced herself by transferring from

Delos into her own keeping the funds that had been contributed by the rest of Greece, and that now the most plausible excuse for this action, namely, that the money had been removed for fear of the barbarians and was being guarded in a safe place, had been demolished by Pericles himself. (2) "The Greeks must be outraged," they cried. "They must consider this an act of bare-faced tyranny, when they see that with their own contributions, extorted from them by force for the war against the Persians, we are gilding and beautifying our city, as if it were some vain woman decking herself out with costly stones and statues and temples worth millions of money."

(3) Pericles' answer to the people was that the Athenians were not obliged to give the allies any account of how their money was spent, provided that they carried on the war for them and kept the Persians away. "They do not give us a single horse, nor a soldier, nor a ship. All they supply is money," he told the Athenians, "and this belongs not to the people who give it, but to those who receive it, so long as they provide the services they are paid for. (4) It is no more than fair that after Athens has been equipped with all she needs to carry on the war, she should apply the surplus to public works, which, once completed, will bring her glory for all time,[75] and while they are being built will convert that surplus to immediate use. In this way all kinds of enterprises and demands will be created which will provide inspiration for every art, find employment for every hand, and transform the whole people into wage-earners, so that the city will decorate and maintain herself at the same time from her own resources." . . .

[14] Thucydides [son of Melesias] and the other members of his party were constantly denouncing Pericles for squandering public money and letting the national revenue run to waste, and so Pericles appealed to the people in the Assembly to declare whether in their opinion he had spent too much. "Far too much," was their reply, whereupon Pericles retorted, "Very well then, do not let it be charged to the public account but to my own, and I will dedicate all the public buildings in my name."[76] (2) It may have been that the people admired such a gesture in the grand manner, or else that they were just as ambitious as Pericles to have a share in the glory of his works. At any rate they raised an uproar and told him to draw freely on the public funds and spare no expense in his outlay. (3) Finally, Pericles ventured to put matters to the test of an ostracism, and the result was that he secured his rival's banishment and the dissolution of the party which had been organized against him.

[15] From this point political opposition was at an end, the parties had merged themselves into one, and the city presented a single and unbroken front. . . .

We may note that the context for this debate springs from events well after the beginning of construction. The Parthenon (and other buildings) were already under way when Thucydides and his supporters attacked Pericles for wasting money collected for the defense of Greeks and bedecking Athens like a vain woman. In addition, we should note that Pericles' critics apparently made no claim that the Athenian empire itself was unjust or should be dismantled or that tribute collection should cease: rather, they complained that Pericles had stolen the Athenians' *excuse* for the collection of such revenue. This attitude comports with everything we know about fifth-century Athenian ideas of justice in foreign policy from the period before and after Periclean domination.

Kimon, for example, showed no concern for the injustice of punishing all Dolopians on the island of Skyros for the actions of a few pirates or compelling recalcitrant states like Naxos or Thasos to do Athens' bidding. Likewise, the later conservative Athenian leader Nikias, as much as he favored peace with Sparta and a less forward foreign policy, participated fully in Athens' exploitation of other Greek states to the Athenians' own benefit. No sliver of evidence suggests Nikias opposed the empire, as much as he wished the Athenians would adopt a policy more favorable to the Spartans.[77] It is most unlikely, therefore, that Kimon's relative Thucydides made any argument in the 440s that rested on the "injustice" of the Athenians ruling other Greeks and collecting and utilizing revenues that primarily benefited Athens, and this conclusion should bolster our confidence in the general authenticity of the account, since no hint of such a view has influenced the report. That is, the story seems to reflect authentic fifth-century Athenian attitudes rather than retrospective assumptions.[78]

A minority view that the empire was, in fact, unjust did exist, as Pericles admits in his last speech in Thucydides (see p. 169), but it apparently gained no political traction in Athens until intellectual movements (and perhaps the oligarchic revolutions of 411 and 404/3) spawned a different and more philosophical conception of international justice, one that treated wars between Greeks as less justifiable than those against barbarians.[79] Such a view can be seen in Plato's *Republic* and elsewhere, but it never became a mainstream position in Athenian politics even in the fourth-century Athens, which tended to be almost as aggressive – if less successful and less well financed – as the fifth-century city.[80]

Instead of attacking the empire as unjust, Thucydides Melesiou and his supporters apparently accused Pericles of wasting funds best employed for other purposes and of flaunting Athens' dominance in the face of the allies. Little reason existed, they thought, to add insult to injury where the allies were concerned. Yet our other evidence shows that even this position did not reflect the attitudes of most Athenians, who apparently had little trouble with throwing Athens' predominance in the allies' faces. Let us take two examples. In 454/3 when the Athenians transferred the allied treasury from Delos to Athens, they began to pay one-sixtieth of the annual tribute payments made by the allies off the top to the goddess Athena. They erected a huge monolith on the acropolis (over three meters tall) and each year they inscribed on it in small letters the names of all the tribute-paying cities and the amounts of their payments siphoned off for Athena. The first year's list occupied a tiny fraction of the monolith's surface at the top of the stone. The rest of the huge block remained empty, announcing quite brazenly to anyone who viewed the stone that the Athenians intended to collect tribute in perpetuity.[81]

Perhaps even more garish was the annual display of the tribute payments of the allies that occurred during the Athenian festival of the Dionysia. At this celebration of the god Dionysus, attended by Greeks from all over Hellas, including Athens' tribute-paying allies, the Athenians marched the tribute payments into the theater one talent at a time, underscoring Athens' power and wealth and the Athenians' desire to broadcast both to the whole Greek world.[82] No, the Athenians of the fifth century were hardly shy about their dominance, and one wonders, again, how much of this attitude can be traced to a long-standing feeling that Athens had been overlooked for too long as a true power in Hellas. Such a feeling clearly existed in the sixth century, when the Athenians began to make the Panathenaia into an "international" Greek celebration and through such means (and through their expansionist foreign policy) to suggest that Athens now deserved a place in the first rank of Greek powers.

In short, Pericles' building program fits nicely into a series of attempts by Athens to increase its power and then to project that increased power to the Greek world. What differentiated the Athenians' efforts here were the scope, the peculiar means of funding the program, the direct involvement of the citizenry via their votes, and the opportunities the building program gave to a statesman like Pericles to make himself popular through proposals in the assembly.

We may surely conclude that Thucydides Melesiou opposed the program for the political advantage it gave Pericles, because it undercut the Athenians' excuse for usurping the allied treasury, and because he believed it had taken Athens' self-aggrandizement in the face of the allies (who provided the bulk of the funds) just a bit too far. The Athenian domestic political context surely played a prominent role. Probably in the late 450s, and not long before the building program debate (which might have occurred ca. 445), Pericles had made his proposals about jury pay and about Athenian citizenship. Pericles, therefore, had already created a kind of clientele for himself among the common Athenians, who must have seen him as a champion who brought payments to Athenians as Athenians – someone who made it possible for even those who remained in Athens and did not row a warship or join in an Athenian settlement abroad to profit from Athens' empire.[83]

Again, no ancient evidence tells us that Thucydides Melesiou or anyone else opposed the institution of jury pay, but I think we must conclude that such opposition occurred, even if it was short-lived and ineffective. Such a massive change in Athenian policy surely provoked opposition, and Thucydides and Kimon (if the introduction of jury pay occurred before his death ca. 450) obviously stand as the most likely Athenians to have led any effort to thwart the proposal.

Those of us inured to modern democratic politics may perhaps sympathize somewhat with the awkward position of those who opposed Pericles' introduction of public payments or his support of the massive building program. How, after all, does a politician in a democratic environment oppose a rival who promises pay to his supporters? We have seen, for example, the effects of a political environment in which liberal politicians propose the expansion of government benefits while conservatives promise lower taxes or economic advantages. Both groups emphasize the economic benefits to their supporters, and few if any modern American politicians campaign successfully on the idea that it will cost voters more (one way or the other) to do the right thing for the larger economy or for our descendants.

Pericles' opponents must have quickly discovered this conundrum. They could not oppose Pericles' proposals without appearing to want to take bread out of the mouths of the voters. Could an argument from prudence or justice succeed in such an environment? Modern experience suggests the answer to this question is in the negative, and Athens' history in the years after Pericles' introduction of public pay shows that any serious, successful opposition to Pericles would come not from the right (as it were), but from the left.[84] Later politicians wishing to rival Pericles would propose higher public payments or the expansion of payments to other offices. Pericles, we may surmise, by that time could be painted as overly conservative or cautious more easily than he could be tarred as imprudently or unjustly spending money that was not his own (or even the Athenians'). Pericles himself from time to time may have concluded that he had created a monster where the hunger and will of the demos were concerned.

Understanding the new political environment created by the institution of jury pay may help us comprehend the Athenians' extreme reaction to Thucydides Melesiou's opposition to the building program, a reaction that led to his formal banishment. Here was this Thucydides character once more opposing a program that led directly to more money in the voters' hands! And this Thucydides, although a relative of the great Kimon, had to his credit no military victories that had enriched Athenians or gained lands for them to colonize. What had he ever done for the common Athenian voters?! Hadn't he and his friends, after all, attempted to prevent jury pay?![85]

Plutarch's report of Pericles' defense of his use of imperial moneys for the building program seems all too believable given the Athenian context: as we have seen, Pericles argued that moneys collected belong not to the giver but to the collector, who can do what he wants with the funds.[86] Given that Pericles proposed paying Athenian voters – jurors, sailors, builders, and workers – with the funds, the success of this argument hardly surprises us. One might, of course, suspect that this argument stems from a hostile source such as Stesimbrotus, who does not seem to have been a fan of Pericles, and perhaps it does. Yet it in no way conflicts with the Pericles we find in Thucydides' speeches (as we shall see), which portray a leader who never hesitated to explain how what could seem unjust from one perspective in fact satisfied Greek traditions (conveniently interpreted) of *arete* (excellence), *time* (honor), and *doxa* (reputation) while also directly benefiting the Athenians.

The issue of Athens' reputation and standing may very well have contributed to this debate. That is, by opposing the use of imperial moneys for Athens' adornment, Thucydides Melesiou and his supporters were not just preventing a direct economic advantage to Athenians; they were also hampering Athens' attempt to establish itself as the clearly preeminent state in fifth-century Hellas. Personal and public motives may therefore have combined in influencing Athenians to choose to support either the

Periclean or the Thucydidean vision of Athens. And in mid-fifth-century Athens, the Athenians possessed the mechanism of ostracism, which allowed them to choose not only to prefer one policy or vision, but also effectively to *silence* the opposition by banishing the leader of one faction from Athens and thereby intimidating his supporters.

The Athenian people spoke. Probably in 444/3 they voted to ostracize Thucydides Melesiou, just as they had ostracized his relative Kimon.[87] Thucydides was compelled to leave Athens for ten years. The Athenians thus sent a very strong signal to any would-be leader who wished to succeed in Athenian politics: do not oppose payments to the voters or the use of imperial funds for Athenian ends or attempt to restrain Athens' aggrandizement. Such opposition policies were nonstarters in democratic Athens after 444/3. It would take disasters in Athenian foreign policy (the defeat in Sicily in 413 and the fall of Athens in 404) and oligarchic revolutions to suspend (temporarily) the principle of public pay in Athens. Under normal democratic government, the Athenians would never vote to give up their payments after the ostracism of Thucydides Melesiou, nor would any Athenian politician openly propose such a policy until the threat of Philip of Macedon made the idea thinkable (if still unacceptable).[88]

Thucydides Melesiou probably spent part of his ostracism with friends in Sparta, where his relative Thucydides the historian also spent time after his exile from Athens in 424/3. Relatives of Kimon, it seems, were very welcome among the Lakedaimonians.[89] An anecdote reported by Plutarch (again, perhaps from Stesimbrotus) well illustrates the political situation in Athens by 444/3. The Spartans apparently asked Thucydides, who hailed from an aristocratic family famous for its wrestling talent, how Pericles was able to defeat him politically. "When I throw him to the ground," said Thucydides, "he gets up and claims 'I was never down.' And he's able to make the people watching believe him!"[90]

The tale suggests that by ca. 444/3 Pericles had already earned a reputation as the greatest orator in Athens, one able to convince the Athenians that reality differs from what they perceive with their own eyes. It is possible that the story anticipates the fact, although we have evidence that by 439 the Athenians saw Pericles as a great public speaker. In that year they selected him to give the funeral oration over the Athenians who had died in the year's campaigning.[91] In any case, Thucydides' wrestling story expresses the frustration that Pericles' opponents must have felt by the mid-440s and that they would continue to feel in subsequent years. How does one oppose a leader who promises tangible economic and intangible psychological advantages to the voters and who possesses the greatest ability to defend his policy in speech? How can one oppose a leader who is able to deny plain fact ("I was never down") and make the people believe him? How can one oppose a leader who tells the people what they most want to hear and believe?[92]

Pericles' opponents ultimately found no answers to these questions: for the next fifteen years in a row, the people of Athens elected Pericles to the office of general.

FIVE

A Greek Empire (ca. 460–445)

The 450s saw the Athenians vote to pay themselves (on a motion of Pericles) and also elect to begin a war with Sparta and its allies. At about the same time as this war began, the Athenians (ca. 460/59) dispatched a large invasion force to Egypt, ostensibly to assist in a revolt from Persia but almost certainly also in an effort to exploit the power vacuum that would result from the Persians' departure. Pericles' political career thus developed in an environment of Athenian aggressiveness that would not be equaled until Athens' invasion of Sicily in 415. The disaster suffered by the fleet in Egypt in 454 and eventual problems with Athens' subject states ultimately provoked a period of retrenchment. About the year 449 the Athenians, almost certainly with Pericles' encouragement, negotiated an agreement of an informal type with the Persian Great King. With Persia's threat nullified, in immediately subsequent years Athens and Pericles would turn their attention to consolidating the Athenians' Greek empire. Pericles' ability to convince the Athenians to expand and exploit their Greek empire while agreeing to end hostilities with the hated Persians stands as a remarkable testimony to his own rhetorical powers and his vision of Athenian dominance in Hellas.

Pericles and his political opponents apparently shared the belief that Athens deserved to rule other Greeks, although they seem to have differed on attitudes toward Persia and Sparta. During the years from about 461 to 446/5, the Athenians would reverse their foreign policy toward the Spartans, engaging in a long, desultory conflict that historians call the First Peloponnesian War (to differentiate it from the great Peloponnesian War beginning in 431). During the same period, the Athenians launched a major offensive into Persian-controlled Egypt, only to retrench after a disaster there. A few years later (and after another anti-Persian expedition), the Athenians sought some kind of accommodation or treaty with their former Persian enemies. In the early 440s, other Greeks thus witnessed or suspected the anomaly of an Athens making war on the allies who had helped the Greeks fight Persia while negotiating for peace with the Persians themselves. This situation provoked a crisis in the Athenian empire and led to even harsher measures of reprisal and control by the Athenians. Pericles played a crucial role in these years, though our picture at times remains cloudy and we must reconstruct Pericles' own policies and actions with some care and considerable uncertainty.

We have seen that upon the return of Kimon from Sparta in 462/1 the Athenians voted to ostracize the great leader and to adopt a hostile stance toward Sparta and its ally Corinth while making alliances with Argos and Thessaly, states tainted with "medism" (helping the Medes and Persians) during the Persian Wars. Certain events had created an opportunity for breaking with Sparta and attempting to make Athens the unquestionably dominant power in Greece (instead of a partner in rule, as Kimon had envisioned). The earthquake in the Peloponnese ca. 465 had weakened Sparta and its control over other Peloponnesian cities. Megara, a Dorian polis located to the west of Athens on the isthmus between Attica and Corinth, broke away from its Spartan alliance and made a treaty with Athens around 460. Disagreements between neighboring Corinth and Megara apparently precipitated the change of heart by the Megarians, who had hardly been the Athenians' friends previously and with whom Athens had contended for control of the island of Salamis in the early sixth century.[1]

The Athenians readily seized the opportunity, moving troops into Megara and building long walls from the city to its harbor on the Saronic Gulf, effectively giving the Megarian-Athenian alliance control of all land traffic between southern and central Greece.[2] Since Megara had ports on both the northern (Gulf of Corinth) and southern (Saronic Gulf) side of the isthmus, Athens had also gained direct access to locations of strategic value for its fleet. Corinth, which provided the Spartans with the naval arm of their military, reacted immediately to this direct threat to its economic and political power, and by 460 or so Athens and Corinth were engaged in open hostilities.[3]

Meanwhile, the Athenians learned that a Libyan ruler had launched a revolt in Egypt, which Persia had controlled since the 520s. The Athenians voted to send a huge fleet of 200 warships to Egypt in order to support this revolt and (probably) to exploit the power vacuum that would result from the expulsion of Persian authority from the rich Egyptian territory.[4] The image of an Athenian populace willing to vote to take on the Corinthians (and by extension their Spartan allies) at the same time as they fought the Persian Empire has received far too little attention by modern historians, a fact partially explained by the meager account we have of these events in Thucydides, our most reliable source. Yet we must pause to consider the ramifications of this policy of taking on two major wars in distantly separated theaters of operation at one time. Any Athenian fleet operating in Egypt would need to be almost completely self-sufficient. Communications with, and resupply from, Athens would be virtually impossible. Moreover, 200 warships probably represented some two-thirds or more of Athens' effective fleet in this period. The Athenians never seem to have been able to field a total fleet of more than 300 triremes at any one time in the fifth century, though these years may offer us the best possibility of an active fleet that reached upwards of 400 ships.[5] The Athenians thus voted to fight a war in mainland Hellas against the Corinthians while diminishing the size of their (or, rather, the allied) navy by 200 ships. Even if they were able with the help of their allies to field a fleet of an additional 100 to 200 ships in Greece itself, such a fleet hardly offered an overwhelming force against the combined forces of the Peloponnese: such a navy would include not only the ships of Corinth but also those of Athens' old Dorian enemy Aegina.

Perhaps the outlandish nature of this two-front war explains the hint in our tradition that some Athenians, perhaps including Pericles, opposed the expedition to Egypt. Plutarch reports that Pericles opposed sending forces to Egypt in a context that could indicate the reinforcement of the expedition there in the mid-450s or a later expedition ca. 450.[6] By the time of the outbreak of the great Peloponnesian War against Sparta in 431, Pericles had adopted a policy of limiting Athens to one major war at a time, and it is certainly possible that he had developed such a view even as early as ca. 460.[7] In any case, surely some Athenians questioned the wisdom of dispatching such a huge portion of Athens' available fleet to far-flung Egypt at the same time as the Athenians faced a war with the Peloponnesians at home. The fact that such an argument failed presents us with clear evidence of the Athenians' extremely aggressive stance in the middle of the fifth century. Whatever Pericles' own feelings were about the operation, the majority of Athenians who voted in the assembly readily accepted the danger associated with wars with both the Peloponnesians in Hellas and the Persians in Egypt.

While the Athenian fleet campaigned in Egypt, at home Athens faced a war that threatened to extend over all of southern Hellas. Open hostilities with Corinth led to a direct confrontation with Sparta, probably in the year 458/7.[8] The Spartans had launched an expedition into central Greece in support of the region of Doris, from which the Dorians claimed to have sprung. Their return route took them through Boeotia north of Attica, a region dominated by the Spartans' allies (and the Athenians' enemies) in Thebes. In yet another sign of Athens' hyper-martial character in this period, the Athenians voted to send their infantry north to take on the combined Spartan/Theban forces. The two sides met at a place called Tanagra (in Boeotia), where the Spartans and Thebans defeated the Athenian army, allowing the Spartan forces to make their return to the Peloponnese via the land route. The Athenians, apparently unchastened by their defeat, returned to Boeotia two months later and defeated the Theban infantry in a battle at Oinophyta. By means of this battle Athens added much of central Greece (Boeotia and perhaps the region of Phokis) to its empire.[9]

Actions in and around the Peloponnese in these years also added significant territory to the region of Athenian hegemony. The Athenians gained control of several cities in northeastern Peloponnese and probably in 456 they defeated the great island of Aegina and added it to the Athenian empire, compelling the Aeginetans to pay an annual tribute of 30 talents to Athens. No subject state ever paid a higher amount into Athens' imperial treasury.[10] Aegina was a major Greek power, more prosperous, as Russell Meiggs noted, than Athens in the seventh century and at least Athens' equal in the sixth. Pericles, probably ca. 431, would famously refer to this island as "the pus in Peiraeus' eye," and encourage the Athenians to clean out the infection.[11] The reduction of this important Dorian island to the status of a tributary subject of Athens "marks an epoch in classical Greek history."[12]

The Athenians also made raids on other parts of the Peloponnese. Pericles himself, in his first securely attested military command, led an Athenian attack on the city of Sicyon just to the west of Corinth (probably in

455/4 or 454/3).[13] The location may have been significant in terms of Pericles' personal history and political career. His Alkmeonid ancestors on his mother's side had married into the family of Cleisthenes of Sicyon, one of the most famous Greek tyrants of the sixth century. Pericles' mother Agariste bore the name of the tyrant Cleisthenes' daughter. It is possible that Pericles looked upon his command in this attack as a way to undercut any notion that he might favor Sicyon due to his family's connection with the state. In any case, we can state with certainty that by the mid-450s Pericles had begun to establish a military career for himself.

By ca. 454 Athens seemed poised to achieve a predominance never seen before in Hellas. Although Sparta still controlled or influenced most of the Peloponnese, Athens had gained a foothold there while spreading its hegemony across the Aegean and into central, mainland Greece. The sea power of old rival Dorian Aegina had been nullified. If the expedition in Egypt succeeded, Athens stood to benefit from the wealth of that great region, at least through opportunities for trade, by improving grain supplies, and perhaps through more direct forms of influence or exploitation, including the establishment of colonies or cleruchies.[14]

We may pause to emphasize how close the Athenians had come by 454 to dominating the Greek world, a truly remarkable achievement for a city that had been in the second tier of Greek powers until the Persian Wars just a few decades before. Only Sparta offered any serious resistance to Athenian power at this moment, and the Spartans were weakened by their long helot revolt (which probably had only just ended by 455), the loss of Megara, and the Athenians' defeat of the Spartans' allies Thebes and Aegina. A Sparta bereft of all these allies offered the Athenians the prospect of gaining control of other parts of the Peloponnese and thereby isolating Sparta as a largely irrelevant, land-based, military power.

Prospects such as these undoubtedly influenced the rising politician Pericles and other members of the Athenian faction who were not so favorably disposed toward Sparta as were the supporters of Kimon. In these heady times, some such Athenians surely now laughed at Kimon's old formula of Athens and Sparta sharing control of Hellas. The moment had come, at least a few must have argued, for Athens to reign as the unquestionably dominant city-state in Greece.

And yet none of it was to be. In 454 the Athenian fleet in Egypt met with disaster. Historians have debated whether the entire force of over 200 vessels could have been lost, but the best account we have (that of Thucydides) certainly implies that this was the case.[15] Since each ship carried a complement of 200 men, some 40,000 sailors and soldiers – Athenians and allies – may have met their deaths, been enslaved, or found themselves stranded very far from their Greek homes. More conservative estimates, based on the conclusion that the Athenians must have withdrawn a good portion of the fleet before the final disaster, still place Greek losses at 14,000 to 20,000 souls, with the number of Athenians killed or captured in a range from 5,000 to 9,000 men.[16]

No source describes the scene in Athens when word of the disaster in Egypt arrived, but one can envision the devastation such news brought. With a force of this size, even if the majority of the sailors were non-Athenians, virtually no Athenian family could have been untouched by the disaster. Even the more conservative modern estimates place the loss of Athenian citizens in this action as high as some 10 to 15 percent of the total citizen population. Political recriminations almost certainly followed, as we can see by analogy with other Athenian military and diplomatic disasters in earlier periods (Miltiades' failed expedition to Paros) and later (e.g., Philocrates' disastrous peace with Philip of Macedon in 347/6).[17] The fact that no source reports that Pericles suffered from this catastrophe could suggest that he was not associated with the initial decision ca. 460 to invade Egypt, that he truly opposed the decision, or that he managed to convince the Athenians that he had not supported the failed operation (whatever the truth of the matter).

A period of retrenchment apparently followed the Athenian failure in Egypt. We know of no large-scale Athenian military operations in the years just after 454/3. We do possess evidence that in that year the Athenians brought the treasury of the Delian League from Delos to Athens, and it has been reasonably suggested by many scholars that this decision reflected the environment after the Egyptian disaster.[18] Some Greeks may have actually feared Persian reprisal operations in the Aegean, but in any case the Athenians must have seized the opportunity provided by such fears to bring the funds to Athens, perhaps attempting to make a virtue of necessity. Pericles probably served as general in this year (454/3), and while his election to the post does not assure us that he approved of the measure, his later policies that rested on the use of the moneys (collected from the allies) for Athenian purposes allows us to conclude that Pericles supported the treasury's transfer to Athens.[19]

What of Sparta in these years? The fact that the Spartans apparently made no attempt to capitalize on Athens' failure in Egypt underscores just how much events of the last decade had weakened the Spartans' control of the Peloponnese. This fact also illustrates how close Athens had come ca. 455 to making herself the sole superpower in the Greek world. Had events in Egypt gone differently, we are justified in concluding that the whole history of the Greek world in the fifth and fourth centuries could have looked quite different. Victorious in Egypt and with its fleet intact, Athens might not have wished to end the war with Sparta by truce in 451/0. Athens might have won the First Peloponnesian War outright,[20] perhaps forestalling the later war with Sparta that would result in the loss of the Athenian empire. We may wonder whether a preeminent Athens in the fourth century, still possessed of its fifth-century empire, would have allowed Philip of Macedon to achieve the power that allowed him to conquer southern Greece. An Athens that dominated all of Greece might have forestalled Philip and thus Alexander, and thereby have prevented or radically altered the spread of Greek culture and ideals that produced the Hellenistic world. In short, the potential effects of the Athenian disaster in Egypt can hardly be overstated.

Not that long ago, in the 1930s, so imminent a Greek historian as H. T. Wade-Gery lamented Athens' disasters in Egypt and later in Sicily (413) in graphic terms. For Wade-Gery, this constituted "sheer disaster: it means the failure of Athens, the failure of the fifth century, the failure of Greece as a world power."[21] For Wade-Gery an Athenian empire ruling Greece on land and sea would have meant success. Perhaps, however, we may be permitted to imagine the potentially negative as well as the positive effects of Athenian domination of Hellas and to appreciate the spread of Greek culture that followed the rise of Macedon and Alexander's conquest of the Persian Empire. Moreover, unlike the later Roman empire, Athens had moved already by 451/0 to restrict citizenship rather than to incorporate non-Athenians into the Athenian polity. Such an attitude arguably prevented Athens from building a great empire in the Mediterranean and limited the (especially human) resources on which it could rely. In the end, we are hardly in a position to assert that a Greece dominated by Athens would have represented a long-lived or beneficial development.[22]

Although we cannot reconstruct the political environment in Athens in this period in any detail, one fact does permit us to draw some conclusions.

In 452/1 Kimon apparently returned from ostracism and, it would seem, immediately reestablished himself as a major force on the Athenian political scene. This inference flows from the peace treaty that he negotiated with Sparta soon after his return (and the subsequent campaign in Cyprus that Kimon led). In 451/0 Athens and Sparta made an agreement that would prevent war for five years (often called the Five Years Truce).[23] The goodwill the Spartans felt toward Kimon undoubtedly encouraged this agreement, which also suggests that Kimon bore the Spartans no ill will (thus making the story of their alleged "insult" to him in 462/1 at Ithome all the more unlikely). The Athenian people, it would seem, readily embraced Kimon and his policies upon his return, again suggesting that some of them felt something like chagrin over their earlier ostracism of the arguably greatest military leader in Athens' history.

Although Athens' power reached an unprecedented peak in 455 or so, just before the disaster in Egypt, and the city seems to have pulled back in the next several years to lick its proverbial wounds and consolidate power while rebuilding the fleet, the Five Years Truce in 451/0 in many ways marks the high-water mark of Athenian control in Greece. In that year, the Spartans formally recognized Athens' impressive gains in the previous two decades, including its control over central Greece, Megara, Aegina, and even parts of the Peloponnese. Although Athens may have possessed more real power in 455, in 451/0 the Athenians arguably compelled the Spartans to recognize their position as the dominant power in Greece. Certainly the treaty showed that the Spartans recognized Athens as Sparta's equal in terms of sheer power; we may imagine that Kimon's long-standing good relations with Sparta made this treaty palatable, if not ideal, to the Spartans.

We have seen that one tradition suggests that Pericles did not oppose Kimon upon his recall and that the two may have even cooperated, or at least agreed to operate in different spheres of influence, at this time. It is, therefore, perhaps unsurprising that Pericles' famous legislation about citizenship (451/0) came just after Kimon's return and that his introduction of jury pay very likely belongs to the same time period. Kimon, on the other hand, intended to restart his military career, and probably in the year 450, under Kimon's leadership as elected general, the Athenians launched a new campaign against Persian interests in Cyprus.[24]

Let us once more notice the extremely aggressive stance of the Athenians. Although they had suffered a devastating loss to the Persians in

Egypt just a few years before, in 450 they voted to risk a full-scale war with Persia once again by operating in the eastern Mediterranean around Cyprus and even sending a force back to Egypt (!) in order to assist anti-Persian forces operating there.[25] Surely we are justified in seeing the Athenians here wishing to recover their honor and make a statement about their continued viability as an international power.

No source suggests that Pericles opposed this campaign to Cyprus, nor does any suggest he participated. Perhaps he was not elected general in 451/0, a year in which Kimon's supporters are likely to have benefited in the elections from their leader's return and diplomatic success in Sparta. The expedition would nevertheless prove to be crucial in Pericles' career, because it led both to Kimon's death and to some kind of arrangement with Persia that ended hostilities between the Persian Empire and Athens.

We need not expend too much time on the Cyprus expedition itself. Suffice it to say that Kimon's forces won great land and sea battles against the Persian forces there, although Kimon himself died before the final, crucial victories. The Athenians reestablished themselves as a credible anti-Persian force in the eastern Mediterranean and returned to Athens. What followed this campaign in some of our sources – a treaty between Athens and Persia usually called the "Peace of Kallias" after the Athenian who supposedly negotiated it – remains the most vexed question in all of fifth-century Greek history.[26] The event plays an important role in any evaluation of Pericles' career and thought, so we must examine it in some detail.

The essential facts about the Peace of Kallias are as follows. No fifth-century source mentions the treaty, although Herodotus tells us that the Athenian Kallias visited the Persian capital of Susa as an ambassador sometime in the mid-fifth century.[27] The first Greek source to mention the treaty is the fourth-century Athenian intellectual and orator Isocrates, who around 380 criticizes the recent Spartan treaty with the Persians (387/6) by comparing it with the ostensibly more glorious treaty the Athenians had (supposedly) made in the previous century.[28] The first-century BC Greek historian Diodorus Siculus gives us a fulsome account of the alleged treaty's negotiation, and his treatment may be based on the fourth-century BC historian Ephorus.[29] What sources Ephorus himself could have consulted and how reliable his account would have been are disputed issues. Other fourth-century and later authorities provide conflicting accounts of the terms, date, and even authenticity of the alleged treaty.[30] Beyond the information in these sources, we may note that the Athenians engaged in no hostilities with the Persians for many years after about 449, although in the year 440 they apparently feared that Persia might send a fleet to assist the island of Samos (which was in revolt from Athens). It has also been argued that the revolts of some Athenian allies in the early 440s suggest that a peace treaty between Athens and Persia ca. 449 had led to disaffection in the league.[31]

The state of our sources and other evidence perhaps makes impossible a compelling answer to the question of whether the Athenians made a treaty with the Persians ca. 449. Yet the issue has featured prominently in discussions of Athenian imperialism. Some historians have built their conception of the rise of the Athenian empire on the notion that the Peace of Kallias marked the moment when Athens became openly imperialistic and no longer made any pretensions that it was leading an alliance of independent states.[32] I have argued elsewhere that this (once orthodox) view of the Athenian empire is misguided and fails to appreciate that the Athenians had become open imperialists at least as early as the early 460s, when they forced the island of Naxos to remain in the league.[33] The Peace of Kallias, to put it bluntly, is irrelevant to the birth of Athenian imperialism. The peace fundamentally affects only our view of Athens' relations with Persia, although certainly the end of hostilities with Persia would have given Athens the ability to concentrate more fully on the control of the Greek states in the Aegean.[34]

Yet the supposed treaty – or at least the events that spawned the belief in such a treaty – may remain important for our evaluation of Pericles' career and policies. Without, therefore, providing another detailed treatment of the peace, I must admit that I no longer believe that the Athenians and Persians reached a formal peace agreement ca. 449 BC.[35] My reasons for this change of mind are relatively simple: our contemporary sources make no mention of such a treaty, which would have been a momentous event, and I cannot see that it was in either Athens' or the Persian Great King's interest to make such an agreement. For Athens, a formal treaty gave the lie to any pretensions of "defending Hellas" from potential Persian aggression, while for the Great King a formal agreement looked like a humiliating admission of his inability to avenge his father's defeats at Greek hands and a concession of a "Greek sphere of influence" on his western frontier. These considerations, combined with the fourth-century sources' confusion about the supposed event and the ample motives and opportunities to invent the agreement, make the existence of a formal treaty between Athens and Persia in the mid-fifth century unlikely.

But what of Herodotus's report that the Athenian Kallias was in the Persian capital of Susa sometime in the mid-fifth century "on another matter" (as Herodotus puts it)? This detail, which Herodotus provides in passing while telling the story of Argos's relations and negotiations with Persia, deserves our credence for the very reason that it serves no purpose in the narrative. Unlike many tales about Athenians in Herodotus, this report does not bear the mark of a defense peddled by a prominent Athenian family or its supporters. A family, for example, that wished to defend its member Kallias from negotiating with the Persians would wish to show that Kallias never visited Persia, not that he was there "on another matter" while the Argives were discussing their relations with the Great King. On the other hand, a source that wished to impugn Kallias or the Athenians for such negotiations would wish to make it clear that Kallias visited Susa precisely in order to carry out peace talks with the Great King.[36]

It seems we must conclude that Kallias did in fact visit Susa (or, to be more precise, that Herodotus had been given a report that Kallias visited Susa). Other scholars have noted that, if Kallias was in Susa while Athens and Persia were still technically at war, the only reasonable explanation is that he was there to negotiate on Athens' behalf.[37] Apart from the highly unusual nature of an Athenian visiting the Persian capital during a time of formal hostilities, another factor suggests that negotiations occurred: Kallias was a kind of diplomat employed by Athens for important missions in the mid-fifth century.[38] We may presume, therefore, that Kallias went to Susa in order to accomplish something diplomatic with the Persians.[39]

It will be worthwhile to examine this Kallias and his family, which had important relations with Pericles and other leading Athenians. The Kerykes, as the larger clan was called, were notoriously wealthy and held an important ancestral priesthood at Eleusis.[40] We have seen that the family was probably part of the aristocratic group with ties to (if not providing direct support of) the Peisistratid tyrants.[41] Through these ties the Kerykes are likely to have had close relations with the Alkmeonid and Kimonid families at least back to the sixth century.[42] In the fifth century, as we have seen, the three families were related by marriage, with Kimon's sister Elpinike marrying the wealthy Kallias and the latter's son Hipponikos marrying the former wife of Pericles (see Figure VI).[43] In short, Kallias the ambassador had very close connections to both Kimon and Pericles.

Kimon had died at Cyprus ca. 450, perhaps leaving something of a leadership vacuum among the more conservative Athenians (which Thucydides son of Melesias would ultimately, if less than successfully, fill).[44] It is not impossible to imagine that Kimon's brother-in-law Kallias (married to Kimon's sister Elpinike) would have undertaken a mission of which Kimon himself would have disapproved, but perhaps we may safely conclude that the Kimonid faction would (at least) not have opposed the mission: after all, forcing the Great King into some kind of peace agreement could have been touted (in Athens) as an unprecedented success.[45] Pericles and those who supported him probably approved of the mission, if we may draw any conclusion from his subsequent policy of expanding and consolidating the Athenians' rule over other Greeks without taking provocative actions toward Persia. Peace with Persia would allow Athens to focus its efforts on ruling a Greek empire without constantly looking over its shoulder.

Compelling the Persian Great King to make a treaty could, therefore, have seemed like a kind of victory to Athenians of either a Kimonian or a Periclean stripe, and we should remember that both groups supported the creation and exploitation of a Greek empire to benefit Athenians. Athens' allies, on the other hand, probably would not have looked so kindly on such an agreement. Why, after all, would the Athenians continue to collect tribute if they had made a formal peace treaty with Persia? Would it not seem to such allies that Athens had conveniently put aside the war with Persia in order to collect tribute from Greek states without any worry of spending the sums collected on the defense of Greece? Could not the anti-Athenian faction of any polis now attempt to paint the Athenians themselves as the "medizers"?

All these factors taken together, combined with Thucydides' silence on the subject and the first account of a formal treaty between Athens and Persia appearing quite late – in the 380s, after Sparta had made an ignominious treaty with the Persians – suggest to me that Kallias visited Susa to negotiate with the Persians but that no formal treaty emerged from those talks. Indeed, would it not have been better from the perspectives of the Athenians and the Persians to keep any kind of arrangement as informal as possible? Spheres of influence there could certainly be, but why tie either party to a public, formal agreement that would embarrass both? Kallias, the brother-in-law of Kimon and the associate of Pericles,[46] could speak with authority about Athenian political and foreign policy concerns. Perhaps no one was better positioned to parley with the Great King and his ministers about an arrangement that could be useful to both sides, with the Persian (say) giving up no formal claims to control of Greeks in Asia Minor and the Athenians giving up no formal claims to defending Greece from Persian control.

It is fair to object that such an arrangement has little precedent in Athenian history. Are we, for example, to imagine a vote of the Athenian assembly to "send Kallias to make an informal agreement with the Great King"? Such a vote seems most unlikely. However, the idea that the Athenians voted to send Kallias on a diplomatic mission to Persia and that leading Athenians (like Pericles and Kallias) determined that the best outcome of such a mission was an informal, rather than a formal arrangement, seems both possible and consistent with the evidence as we have it.[47]

Another problematic piece of evidence involving Pericles suggests that this scenario is likely if not certain. Plutarch reports that Pericles sent out an invitation to the Greek states to a "congress" in order to discuss the "free sailing" of the Aegean and other subjects of mutual interest. The Spartans, Plutarch informs us, refused to participate in such a congress, a perfectly understandable reaction given their landlocked status and usual disinterest in matters maritime as well as their lack of interest in bolstering Athens' current position in Greece. However, once the Spartans balked, the other Greeks did so as well, and Pericles' "Congress Decree" failed to bring about the proposed meeting.[48] In the once-orthodox reconstruction of Athenian history, this failed decree became the formal excuse for the Athenians to take the moneys paid by the other Greek states for defense against Persia and use them for such projects as the Parthenon and other buildings. Pericles and the Athenians, so the argument goes, seized the opportunity of the failed Congress Decree (if they did not contrive it) to justify Athens' usurpation of the allies' funds.[49]

Like the Peace of Kallias, the Congress Decree appears in no contemporary fifth-century report. Although some scholars have detected the glimmer of an epigraphic record behind the account, Plutarch's rather fulsome report of the event may derive from the fourth-century historian Ephorus or even later sources, and scholars have justifiably questioned its veracity.[50] However, whether or not Pericles actually issued the invitation to a congress, the report of these events accurately reflects the situation that prevailed in Greece after about 449. The Athenians had defeated the Persians in Cyprus and once again effectively ended (at least for a time) the threat of Persian operations in the Aegean. The Athenians had pushed further east with greater success against the Persians than any previous Greek force, perhaps sending forces as far as Phoenicia.[51] Yet Athens had not ended tribute payments or made any move to dismantle the organization formed for (at least) the defense of Greece or (at most) offensive operations against Persian holdings. Surely, some Greeks would argue, the Athenians should either stop collecting tribute or continue pressing their advantage against the Persians. If tribute payments were not to be ended, surely they should at least be adjusted to reflect changing conditions.

In fact, none of these things happened. The Athenians continued to collect tribute and some allies apparently resented this fact.[52] Our evidence suggests that some allies became recalcitrant in the early 440s and attempted to leave the league. Some states paid the tribute reluctantly or irregularly.[53] Meanwhile, by 447 Athens had begun to build the Parthenon and was expending hundreds of talents on other buildings and on jury pay for Athenian citizens. As we have seen, the moneys collected for operations against Persia and brought to Athens ca. 454 encouraged these expenditures. Whatever the truth about the Congress Decree, Pericles and others are quite likely to have defended these actions on the grounds that Athens had borne the brunt of the fighting against Persia and continued to protect Greece from any Persian advances, and that some allies had proven to be less than reliable. Athens, they could argue, could justifiably do whatever it chose with the tribute paid, and the other Greeks would simply have to live with it.

In short, what occurred in the years from about 451 (when Kimon returned and made peace with Sparta) to about 447 (when the Athenians began massive expenditures on the Parthenon) was not – as was once believed – the creation or development of "the Athenian empire." That entity had already existed for twenty years, from the time the Athenians forced formerly independent and sovereign states to remain in an alliance that they wished to leave. Rather, in the years around midcentury a series of events illustrated Athenian imperialism in very explicit terms. Any non-

Athenians around the Aegean who, in previous years, had been inclined to excuse the Athenians for this or that reason would find it much more difficult to do so credibly after this period. Indeed, we may profitably speculate on the (different) attitudes inside and outside Athens in the years between (say) 470 and 447. No evidence suggests that any political faction in Athens opposed the reduction of Greek allies (like Naxos) or others as far back as the first decade of the Delian League. Nor does any evidence suggest that Thucydides Melesiou or his supporters criticized Pericles in the early 440s for the empire or for exploitation of the allies *per se.* In short, there is simply no reason whatsoever to conclude that the vast majority of Athenians of whatever political stripe opposed Athenian imperialism.

But Greeks outside of Athens surely had widely differing views on the subject. The citizens of Naxos after the island's reduction ca. 470 are hardly likely to have shared the same views as most of those from Chios, an island that continued to provide ships for the allied fleet and (probably) continued to benefit from the seizure of booty in Athenian actions throughout the mid-fifth century. In poleis that had yet to feel Athens' direct intervention, views undoubtedly remained mixed. Those who paid the taxes that supported the annual tribute payments may have been more inclined to criticize the Athenians than the poorest residents, some of whom could find employment as rowers in the Athenian fleet. As late as the early 450s many non-Athenians may have found reason to praise Athens' power in the Aegean. Yet the Athenians' actions between 454 and 447 or so made it increasingly hard for any remaining apologists outside of Athens to justify the Athenians' actions to their fellow citizens. The Athenians, it had become increasingly clear, dominated Greece primarily with an eye toward Athenian interests, and their supposed protection of Greece from Persia had become a convenient excuse rather than a reasonable justification.

Indeed, by the middle of the fifth century Athens had developed numerous techniques for the exploitation of its former allies (now subjects), as the evidence of Athenian inscriptions concerning the management of the empire shows. Beyond continuing to collect tribute, the Athenians forcibly installed democratic governments and placed troops in certain cities.[54] Elsewhere (as we shall examine later) Athens issued special privileges compromising the tax revenue base of conquered cities and required locals to swear oaths of allegiance to Athens.[55] It expelled the residents of some states and replaced them with Athenian colonists while taking prime lands in other cities and handing them over to Athenian "cleruchs" (lot holders: that is, Athenian citizens who held property seized in other states); this also, of course, reduced the property-tax base of the conquered state.[56] In Ionia the Athenians apparently ordered certain cities to pull down their fortifications, and they regularly ordered this of cities that revolted from Athenian control.[57] Beyond the regular annual tribute collection, Athens also occasionally ordered additional payments.[58] Athenian officials (*episkopoi*: "inspectors") were dispatched to monitor local activities, while some locals became official friends (*proxenoi*) of Athens, incurring enough dislike from their fellow citizens that the Athenians passed legislation protecting them from assassination.[59]

In Plutarch, Pericles infamously defends the Athenians against the charge of misusing the allies' tribute payments by claiming that money collected belonged to the collectors and not to the payers: the Athenians had the right to do whatever they liked with the allies' tribute payments.[60] In inscriptions recording Athenian laws or decrees from this period, we glimpse the same Athenian attitude. Recent attempts to make the tone of these documents seem less harsh fail to convince.[61] We can readily admit that the Athenians were sensitive enough to public relations that they used different language among themselves than they did when speaking "diplomatically." Yet the Athenians' idea of diplomatic language betrays the citizens' very stark idea of diplomacy.

Let us examine one document, which is especially relevant because of Pericles' direct involvement. During the somewhat troubled early 440s, when some of Athens' allies apparently attempted to leave the league or short the Athenians on tribute payments, trouble also broke out in central Greece. Facing the threat of losing their control of Boeotia, the Athenians sent an expedition northward in 447. At Koroneia in Boeotia, the Boeotians and certain exiles from nearby regions defeated the Athenians and freed central Greece from Athenian control.[62] (Alcibiades' father Kleinias died in this battle, and the young Alcibiades came to live with his relative Pericles as a result.[63]) Pericles, we should note, apparently opposed this expedition and thereby earned a reputation for foresight and prudence.[64] Pericles' failure to convince the assembly here demonstrates that his foreign policy influence in the mid-440s fell short of its later height in the 430s.[65] In the following year (446), when the Five Years Truce between Athens and Sparta lapsed, the Spartans sent an army

toward Attica, and the Athenians' subjects on the island of Euboea to the
east revolted. Faced with war on two fronts, Pericles apparently negotiated
some kind of arrangement with the Spartans – perhaps including a bribe
of a Spartan king – and quickly took the army to Euboea, where he
defeated the revolting city-states.[66] The Athenians subsequently expelled
the citizens of the Euboean city of Histiaia (who had killed the crew of an
Athenian ship[67]) and imposed treaties on Chalkis and Eretria, the two
most important city-states in Euboea. A document describing part of the
regulations Athens imposed on Chalkis has survived relatively unscathed
and provides very interesting testimony to the Athenians' management of
the empire ca. 446.[68]

Resolved by the council and the people, Antiochis held the pry-
tany, Drakontides presided, Diognetos made the motion:
On the following terms an oath shall be sworn by the Athenian
council and jurors: "I shall not expel Chalkidians from Chalkis, nor the city (of Chalkis) shall 5
I move (or, destroy), nor any private citizen shall I deprive
of his citizen rights nor shall I punish (him) by exile nor seize
(him) nor slay (him) nor (his) property shall I take
away without trial, without (the approval of) the people of the Athenians, nor shall I put (anything) to a vote against a party 10
    that has not been summoned to trial,
either against the government or against any private citizen
whatever, and an embassy arriving I shall lead before
the council and people within ten days whenever
I am one of the *prytaneis*,[69] to the best of my ability. And these things I shall
establish firmly for the Chalkidians (if they are) obedient to the 15
people of the Athenians." The oath shall be administered by an embassy
coming from Chalkis along with the oath commissioners
to the Athenians, and they shall list (the names of) those swearing
the oath. That all swear the oath shall be the responsibility of the generals. [empty space] 20
On the following terms the Chalkidians shall swear: "I shall not revolt from the people of the Athenians by any arti-
fice or any contrivance at all, neither by word nor
by deed, nor shall I be persuaded by anyone in revolt,
and if anyone revolts I shall denounce him to the Athenians, 25
and I shall pay the tribute to the Athenians, which
I may persuade the Athenians (to assess?), and an ally shall I
be, the best and most just possible,
and the people of the Athenians I shall assist

and defend, if anyone does an injustice to the people of the   30
Athenians; and I shall be obedient to the people of the Athenians." This oath shall be taken by the Chalkidian adults,
all of them. Whoever does not swear the oath, (his) citizen rights
shall be lost and his property become public and
a sacred tithe to Olympian Zeus   35
shall be (paid) from this property. The oath shall be administered by an
    embassy of Athenians coming to Chalkis with
the oath-commissioners in Chalkis, and they shall list
(the names of) the Chalkidians who swear.
[empty line]
Antikles made the motion: With good fortune for the Athenians   40
shall the oath be made by the Athenians and the Chal-
kidians, just as for the Eretrians it was decreed
by the people of the Athenians. That as swiftly as possible it may happen will be the responsibility of the generals.
(As) those who shall administer the oath after arriving in   45
Chalkis, the people shall elect five men
immediately. And concerning the hostages, let there be an
answer given to the Chalkidians, that at present the Athenians are resolved to allow matters (to remain) as voted.
And whenever it seems good, having taken counsel there shall be made   50
an agreement, just as it may seem suitable
to the Athenians and Chalkidians. And (as for) the
foreigners in Chalkis, except for however many dwelling (there)
pay taxes in Athens, and any to whom has been given
immunity from taxes by the people of the Athenians, the others   55
shall pay taxes in Chalkis, just as the other
Chalkidians. And this decree and the
oath shall be inscribed at Athens by the secretary of the council on a stone tablet and (he) shall
place (the tablet) on the acropolis at the expense of the Chalkidians;   60
and in Chalkis, in the temple of Zeus the
Olympian the council of the Chalkidians having inscribed (the same things)
shall place (the tablet). These things were decreed for the Chalkidians. [empty spaces] And the sacrifices (required by) the oracles
for defense of Euboea shall be made as swiftly as possible by   65
Hierokles with three men who may be elected by
the council from its own (members). That as swiftly as possible the sacrifices may occur shall be the joint responsibility of the generals and
the silver (payment) for them they (the generals) shall furnish. [empty spaces]
Archestratos made the motion: The other matters (shall be) just as   70
Antikles (moved). But the *euthynai*[70] for the Chalkidians, among
themselves in Chalkis shall be (carried out), just as in Ath-

ens for Athenians, except (in cases involving) exile, death,
and loss of citizen rights. Concerning these (cases) the appeal shall be
in Athens in the *heliaia* of the *thesmoth-*   75
etai,[71] in accordance with the decree of the people. And concerning the
guard of Euboea the generals shall have the responsi-
bility, to the best of their ability, that it be
the best possible for the Athenians.
                    (THE) OATH[72]   80

This inscription describing the regulations for the reduced city of Chalkis
(after its revolt) consists in the main of two oaths to be sworn by the
Athenians and the Chalkidians respectively. The Athenians swear that
they will not exile or execute any Chalkidian, or deprive him of his property
or political rights ... without due process in Athenian courts or the
Athenian assembly (4–11). The Athenians promise to uphold their oath so
long as the Chalkidians obey them (14–16). For their part, the Chalkidians
swear that they will not revolt from Athens or persuade others to revolt, and
they swear to be obedient to the Athenians (21–32). Later, in an additional
motion moved by Antikles (lines 40ff.), the Athenians give "chilly answers to
Chalkidian pleas for concessions."[73] Although a few scholars have sought to
paint this inscription as less than harsh, the imperial tone remains quite
striking.[74] It is almost the same tone we find the Athenians adopting in
Thucydides' account of negotiations just before the Peloponnesian War
(ca. 432), when the Athenians claim (before the Spartans and Corinthians)
that their empire should be judged on a relative scale. Compared to other
rulers, the Athenians assert, Athens' empire looks pretty good. The Spartans
would be at least as unpopular as the Athenians if they were in Athens'
shoes. In particular, the Athenians maintain, people blame us for holding
trials in Athens that involve Athenians and subjects, when the fact is that we
could simply take what we want instead of holding trials at all.[75]

The regulations for Chalkis portray this Athenian attitude in graphic
terms. The Athenians expressly swear not to do anything violent unless they
vote to do so (!). They promise to keep their oaths so long as the Chalkidians
obey Athens' dictates. The Athenians undoubtedly justified the asymmetric
nature of the relationship based on the Chalkidians' revolt. As punitive
measures, they could assert, these arrangements should be seen as rather
mild (never mind that the revolt had stemmed from a former independent
ally's desire to regain lost sovereignty). Later in the inscription the

Athenians even concede – graciously, they no doubt claimed – that foreigners living in Chalkis should pay taxes to Chalkis, unless (of course) the Athenians had made special exceptions for anyone (lines 52–57). As for the ominous reference to (clearly Chalkidian) "hostages" under Athenian control, we can say little more than that the Chalkidians had apparently made some request about them and the Athenians had voted to retain the status quo for the time being (lines 47–49).

Certainly Athenians like Pericles had a point when they argued that Athens might have been much harsher to its subjects. On the other hand, Athens' opponents could justifiably argue that Athens was asserting its will over formerly free and sovereign Greek states that should have the right to separate themselves from an alliance or league when they chose to do so, just as the Athenians had chosen to leave their alliance with Sparta against Persia in 462/1. On what grounds could the Athenians, who had abandoned the alliance with Sparta and then accepted Sparta's ally Megara into alliance (c. 460), reasonably assert that any alliance "against the Mede" must be permanent?

The Athenians' treatment of former allies like Chalkis also reminds us of Pericles' supposed claim that moneys collected belonged to the collector and not to the payer. The Athenian principle at work here is expressed this way by Athenians in Thucydides: "Justice is only a question between equals."[76] Or, as the Athenians again explain to the Melians in 416, "The strong do what they can, and the weak suffer what they must."[77] The Athenians could, as they did, claim that their empire was less harsh than others, but their formerly independent allies were not likely to have found much solace in this, or in the fact that the actual language employed in the decree was somewhat more diplomatic than Thucydides' sometimes stark formulations of the reality.

We must remember that the attitudes expressed in this document had not just emerged in Athens in the 440s. In 463 the Athenians reduced Thasos in order to gain control over the city's mines and markets and in the 470s they had seized Skyros and colonized the place themselves. In the late sixth century Athenian agents held a tyranny in the Chersonese (from which they seized the formerly independent island of Lemnos), and in the early sixth century Athens had seized Sigeion on the other side of the Hellespont and the island of Salamis. At some point before this Athens had absorbed all the towns and villages in Attica, at times violently. In short, the Athenians had long before the age of Pericles determined that they would exercise their power wherever they were able to do so. It just so happens that by the mid-fifth century the Athenians were pursuing this goal in more places, and at the same time we begin to have contemporary documents describing these actions (and the imperial bureaucracy Athens had developed) in graphic terms.

Pericles had led the Athenian forces that reduced Chalkis and imposed this "settlement" on the ancient city. A longtime Greek power, Chalkis had launched colonies all over the Mediterranean and fought a great war with its neighbor Eretria long before Athens had become an international force.[78] The Chalkidians also hailed from the same Ionian stock as the Athenians. Nevertheless, as soon as they were able, the Athenians imposed their will on the Chalkidians and other cities on the island of Euboea. In Chalkis and in other formerly independent cities, Pericles and the Athenians established a paradigm of Athenian dominance spreading far beyond the ancient zones of Athenian vital interests (especially the Hellespont and northern Aegean). How far would such dominance spread?[79]

Although the Athenians succeeded in reestablishing control over Euboea, the events of 447 and 446 had resulted in the loss of central Greece. The regions of Boeotia and Phokis had regained their independence.[80] Moreover, Athens had lost Megara and thereby control over the isthmus and the land route to the Peloponnese. Athens thus made a new peace treaty with Sparta in 446/5. This treaty, negotiated by the Athenian diplomatic specialist Kallias,[81] established terms under which Athens and the Spartan alliance would remain at peace for thirty years. We do not possess a text of this Thirty Years Peace treaty, but we are able to reconstruct some of its terms from Thucydides' account of events leading up to the Peloponnesian War of 431.

The Thirty Years Peace treaty apparently stipulated that no city allied with Athens or Sparta could leave that alliance in order to join the other side. Disputes between Athens and Sparta were to be submitted to arbitration. Athens was compelled to give back the places in the Peloponnese it had seized during the First Peloponnesian War, and the Athenians were to allow the island of Aegina to be autonomous. Boeotia and Phokis would remain independent, and Megara would return to the Peloponnesian League. In short, by the terms of this truce Athens ceded most of the gains it had made during the years 460 to 451/0. The Spartans, whom the earthquake and helot revolt had so weakened, reasserted themselves as the premier power in southern Greece, maintaining varying levels of influence and control throughout most of the Peloponnese and demonstrating that they could even restrain the Athenians when necessary. True, the Spartans in effect recognized Athens' right to deal with its allies/subjects as it pleased, but Sparta had never objected to such actions since the Delian League's foundation.[82]

The conclusion of this treaty, which ended the First Peloponnesian War but marked a decline in Athenian power, apparently had little if any negative impact on Pericles' career. We have already seen that shortly after this, probably in 444/3, Pericles secured the ostracism of his chief rival Thucydides Melesiou. Indeed, so far as we can discern, Pericles' military reputation had been enhanced during this war through his recapture of Euboea and (perhaps) through his deft handling of the abortive Spartan invasion of Attica in 446. Yet his ability to avoid any apparent blame for Athens' ultimate disappointment in this war deserves our attention. Pericles and others like him had certainly supported this war with the Peloponnesians. In Thucydides Pericles would later claim that he always had one policy: "no concessions to the Peloponnesians"; and the historian himself confirms that this was Pericles' policy.[83] Even if Pericles had actually opposed opening up a second front in Egypt, we have every reason to believe that he supported Athens' first war with Sparta.

This war had led thousands of Athenians and other Greeks to their deaths and had resulted in the loss of considerable Athenian power. Athens was forced to accept an embarrassing treaty that detailed the reduction of its powers in central and southern Greece, while admittedly doing nothing to prevent it from continuing to profit from the exploitation of its subjects in the Aegean. And here, perhaps, we find one of the reasons Pericles emerged from the disappointing end of the First Peloponnesian War politically unscathed. As much as Athenians may have connected Pericles, his political supporters or associates, or the faction[84] he led with the war against Sparta and Corinth, they apparently associated the statesman most closely with the naval empire Athens maintained in the Aegean.[85] Pericles had secured this association through measures like the introduction of jury pay and the sponsorship of the building program. Both actions depended to some degree on the wealth Athens continued to collect in the form of annual tribute payments from other Greeks. By the early 440s Pericles had positioned himself as the chief proponent of using those funds to benefit common Athenians. Such a position had apparently given him a kind of political capital that even the failure of the First Peloponnesian War could not exhaust. Pericles must have believed that, as long as Athens continued to collect hundreds of talents a year from its former allies, his political position would remain strong.

Indeed, the cultivation of Athens' imperial resources seems to have been the primary concern of Pericles and the Athenians in the years just after 446/5. However, we shall see in the next chapter that by the 430s (at the latest), Pericles had apparently embraced a renewed version of Athenian ambitions in the 450s: Athens should not be content to hold merely an equal (much less the second) place in Greece. The central Mediterranean offered opportunities to expand Athens' power once more. Other Greek naval powers, including the Spartans' allies in Corinth, would be forced to accept the spread of Athenian influence into zones where it had not previously reached. Pericles apparently concluded that the central and southern mainland in Greece could not be conquered by conventional means. Athens' superiority would have to be established in other ways. And like Pompey the Great, Pericles' Athens could brook no equal.[86]

❧ SIX ❧

Pericles and Sparta: The Outbreak of the Great War (444/3–431)

The Periclean policy of "no concessions to the Peloponnesians" and the related efforts to make Athens predominant in and around the Aegean resulted in the outbreak of the great Peloponnesian War in 431. A careful analysis of our sources shows that Pericles deserves the chief credit (or blame) for convincing the Athenians that the dream of dominance and a place in history justified a protracted war with Sparta. Pericles' relationship (probably marriage) with the notorious Aspasia of Miletus came to figure prominently in popular discussions of the war's causes, but our evidence suggests that attacks on this relationship and on other supporters of Pericles stemmed largely from his political enemies' inability to thwart the statesman directly. Pericles' speeches in Thucydides present us with a baldly nationalistic and statist vision that encouraged war with Sparta and that apparently resonated deeply with the Athenian people.

G reeks had lived in the central Mediterranean from at least the eighth century BC. Cities like Chalkis, Eretria, Corinth, and even Sparta established colonies in southern Italy (which the Romans would eventually call "great Greece": *magna Graecia*) and Sicily.[1] Yet Athens played no role in this early Hellenic expansion to the west. The Athenians, as we have seen, apparently spent the eighth and seventh centuries consolidating their unusual, direct control of the large territory of Attica. Although the Athenians would ultimately claim that Athens had launched the Ionian Greeks on their ancient colonization of the islands and Asia Minor, the early Athenians could claim to be metropolis ("mother city") of no Greek state founded in historical times.

By the mid-fifth century this situation had changed. In the 440s Athens played the leading role in the foundation of the colony of Thurii in southern Italy. The colony was unusual. A number of cities provided colonists, and the settlement was to occupy the site of the ancient Greek city of Sybaris, infamous for its luxurious lifestyle (giving us the term "sybaritic") and torn by factional battles that had led to the city's destruction. The Greek intellectual and town planner Hippodamus of Miletus apparently played a role in designing the layout of the new settlement (as he had apparently designed the Athenians' Peiraeus harbor).[2] A late authority reports that the philosopher Protagoras made laws for the new city.[3] The historian Herodotus is sometimes thought to have joined the colonists of Thurii at its foundation ca. 444/3, but no credible evidence ensures that he went there so early and it is far more likely he spent his later years there (after his experience of Periclean Athens and the gathering of material for his history there). In any case, we may say that Thurii represented an atypical kind of colony, where Greeks from various parts of the Hellenic world met.[4]

Pericles has sometimes been associated with Thurii's foundation but the direct evidence for his actual involvement is slight.[5] However, since the colony's foundation occurred about the time Pericles began his unbroken run of fifteen years as elected Athenian general and about the time of the ostracism of his political rival Thucydides Melesiou, we may perhaps conclude that Pericles (at worst) did not oppose the colony. Of course, Pericles' repeated election to the position of *strategos* does not ensure that he never took unpopular positions – as, indeed, Thucydides claims he did (2.65 and see later discussion). But his consistent electoral success over this long stretch combined with the influence we shall see him wield in the mid- to late 430s suggests that Pericles was usually in tune with Athenian wishes.

One wonders, however, why the Athenians did not establish the colony themselves as a proper Athenian settlement. In 437/6 Athens would establish another multinational colony at Amphipolis in a strategic location in the Thraceward region to the north. While the majority of settlers at Amphipolis may have been Athenian, many were not, and the colony would ultimately choose the Spartan side in the Peloponnesian War.[6] Whatever the reasons for Athens' reluctance to establish a purely Athenian colony in this period – and the reasons may have been as simple as a shortage of available colonists from Athens – the foundation of Thurii suggests growing Athenian interest in the far-flung central Mediterranean, where Athens' rivals (like Corinth) and its subjects (like Chalkis) already had major colonies.[7]

Corinth's interests in the west figure prominently in the run-up to the Peloponnesian War in 431. Corinth was the mother city of Syracuse, the most powerful and important city in Sicily and already an international power by the early fifth century.[8] The Syracusans exercised a great deal of influence in Sicily as a whole and in the mid-fifth century the city – like Athens – was governed by an often-aggressive democratic government.[9] We should imagine, therefore, that they took an interest when the great eastern naval power Athens participated in the founding of Thurii and, especially, when the Athenians made alliances with the cities of Rhegion (in southern Italy) and Leontinoi in Sicily. The original date of these alliances remains unknown: we can only state with certainty that they already existed in 433/2, when the Athenians renewed the alliances (as our inscriptional record shows).[10]

Though we can say little specifically about the Athenians' new interest in the central Mediterranean, a picture of Athens' and Pericles' policies in this period begins to emerge as we examine other areas of Athenian activity. Probably in the 430s Pericles led an expedition into the Black Sea, where Athens had long-standing interests due to its need for a large and regular grain supply. The Athenians sent 600 settlers to occupy lands at Sinope, on the southern coast of the Black Sea, and perhaps locations elsewhere in the region.[11] It is possible that about this time Athens also placed some cleruchs (settlers) in the Chersonese, another strategically vital location for Athens since at least the early sixth century BC, although this may have occurred somewhat earlier.[12] This demonstration of Athenian power and influence to the (far) north and east, when added to Athens' growing interests in the distant west, suggests that the Athenians in the 430s saw their own policy in terms of a very wide field. Could Athens in fact play an influential role in the Mediterranean world from the Black Sea to Sicily? It would seem the Athenians believed so, and so far from avoiding entanglements that could require the dispatch of a large fleet to so distant a region as Sicily, Athens' colonization of Thurii and the alliance in Sicily suggest that the citizens welcomed the opportunities to expand the city's diplomatic and military horizons.[13]

We may note, however, that Athens' actions in this period remain quite distant from the Peloponnese and central Greece. In the late 440s and early

430s Athens attempted no new conquests that would require a great infantry expedition or risk a direct provocation of Sparta or Thebes. Already employing a new policy later associated directly with Pericles, Athens' actions relied almost entirely on its large and extremely well-funded fleet, supplied by the annual tribute payments of its imperial subjects.

The Athenians in this period continued to collect that tribute regularly, although our records suggest some interesting changes in their bookkeeping methods in the 430s and the likelihood that Athens at times collected more than the regular amount due.[14] By the late 440s, Athens had developed the imperial bureaucracy into a fairly complex operation, by which the Athenians attempted to ensure regular tribute payments and to manage the funds they collected in ways that benefited Athens.[15] The revolts of the early 440s seem to have subsided, perhaps in part because after the arrangement (of whatever kind) with the Persians the Athenians felt free to focus their powers on strict control of the allies. Most of the latter apparently soon realized that such resistance was doomed to failure.

Pericles' political stock had continued to rise in the late 440s. In his personal life, he entered into a relationship (and probably a marriage) with a woman from Miletus in Asia Minor, the infamous Aspasia, who would figure prominently in stories surrounding the Athenian statesman.[16] Indeed, Aspasia attracted the attention of the comic poets during her lifetime, when she was often compared with Hera, Deianeira, Helen, or other mythical females with powers over their male consorts. After Pericles' death, she became a comic cause of the statesman's intransigence and hostility toward Sparta.[17] In later years, she became a figure in philosophical dialogues, where her alleged intelligence perhaps served as a way to diminish Pericles' genius.[18] Aspasia's hometown Miletus played a crucial role in Athens' war with Samos, the most important military action in the period between the Thirty Years Peace (446/5) and the outbreak of the Peloponnesian War (432/1). Athens' conflict with Samos in the years 440–39 also played an important role in Pericles' military and political career.

Sometime before 441 Samos, a large island just off the southwestern coast of Asia Minor, entered into a dispute with the great coastal city of Miletus.[19] The latter had been a center of Ionian Greek culture and power throughout the archaic age, producing the foremost intellectuals of the sixth century BC. However, after the Ionians' failed revolt from Persia ca. 499–494, the city had been sacked. Still, Miletus remained one of the most important cities in eastern Hellas, and the Milesians' dispute with Samos over a city (Priene) on the mainland that lay between the two powers represented a potentially serious diplomatic and/or military problem for Athens. Both Samos and Miletus were members of the Athenian empire, with Samos still counting itself as an independent ally because the island provided ships for the empire's fleet instead of making annual tribute payments, as did the Milesians.

The Athenians' reaction to this situation might have been to adopt the role of a truly neutral arbitrator. Instead, Athens took the side of the Milesians, ordering the Samians (who had gained the upper hand in the dispute) to stop fighting and then submit the matter to Athenian arbitration. Both Thucydides and Plutarch make it clear that the Milesians appealed to Athens for aid after they had been defeated by the Samians, who understandably now saw the Athenian order to cease and desist as an intervention on the bested Milesians' behalf and thus refused.[20] Since Pericles' wife (or paramour) Aspasia hailed from Miletus, some Athenians understandably concluded that she had played a role in convincing the statesman to back her homeland. Whatever the truth of this rumor, Athens' support of Miletus provoked the Samians to refuse to accept Athens' intervention. In response, Pericles led a force to the island, seized hostages from the Samians, and installed a democratic government there. The Athenians apparently assumed that a democratic regime would be more friendly to Athenian policy.

The Samians, however, did not accede to this situation. Samians hostile to Athens launched a successful plot to take back the island and free their hostages, applying to the Persian satrap (governor) in western Asia Minor for support. The Samians then turned over the captured Athenian garrison to the Persian governor. We therefore see here, once again, an Athenian ally that found the prospect of Persian influence in the homeland preferable to continued subjection to Athenian power.

The Athenians responded to this uprising by sending a substantial fleet to Samos, where Pericles won a major naval battle with the Samians and then besieged the island. Over the course of about nine months in 440–439 Pericles ultimately defeated the Samians and brought the island under direct Athenian control. The Athenians then imposed a huge indemnity payment on the Samians, who were thereby forced to cover the costs of the suppression of their own revolt.[21] Some ancient sources state that the

Athenians took particularly harsh measures after this revolt (such as publicly crucifying and then beating the Samian captives to death).[22] However, these reports remain dubious. It is far more likely that the Athenians simply executed the leaders of the Samian revolt and then left a sufficient number of observers (and perhaps some troops) on the island to discourage further Samian acts of independence.

Reaction in Athens to the Samian War was apparently mixed. Pericles obviously had sufficient support in the assembly to win a vote to make war on the Samians and impose a democracy there, but a number of Athenians still seem to have vehemently opposed the action. Kimon's infamous sister Elpinike is supposed to have upbraided Pericles publicly for making war on fellow Greeks instead of the Persians.[23] Scholars have reasonably suggested that comic poets of the period leveled attacks on Pericles or Athenian magistrates in general that led to a short-lived law (440/39–437/6) that may have prevented the abuse of politicians on the Athenian comic stage, though other explanations of this measure are possible.[24] It also seems likely that some of Pericles' associates suffered from real legal or mock-comic attacks in this period, including Aspasia and such Pericleans as the philosophers Damon and Anaxagoras and perhaps the sculptor and manager of the Parthenon project, Pheidias.[25]

Our historical sources from this period are particularly poor. It is possible that nothing more happened to some of Pericles' friends at this time than to be ridiculed by comedians for their association with the Athenian leader and for their supposedly radical views (e.g., Anaxagoras, a philosopher/scientist who questioned traditional views of the gods) or questionable morals (Aspasia's relationship with Pericles apparently scandalized the city).[26] Damon was almost certainly ostracized, and the sculptor Pheidias very likely was accused of financial impropriety and probably expelled or exiled from Athens sometime in the 430s, but the case against him may have had more to do with events leading up to the Peloponnesian War (see later discussion) than the Samian War.[27]

It nevertheless appears likely that some of the more conservative elements in Athenian public life (including at the very least some comic poets) seized on the opportunity provided by the Samian War to attempt to undermine Pericles and Pericleans in this period. It is equally clear that their efforts were utterly unsuccessful. Pericles continued his unbroken string of elected generalships throughout the 430s. Moreover, the

Athenians selected him to give the public funeral oration over the soldiers who had died in the Samian War.[28] In short, the fallout after Athens' reduction of Samos demonstrates quite clearly that, although a faction opposing Pericles existed in Athens during this period, this group possessed insufficient power to defeat him in elections or even to launch a frontal assault on him (as opposed to his associates) in the courts.

Some hints in our sources point to the reactions of other Greek powers to Athens' actions toward Samos. There can be little doubt that the Samians made some kind of appeal to Sparta and the Peloponnesian League for assistance against Athens. Indeed, in the diplomatic maneuvering just before the Peloponnesian War reported by Thucydides, the Corinthians remind the Athenians that they, Sparta's allies, made no effort to encourage Sparta to support Samos during the island's revolt. The Corinthians, they themselves maintain, considered the matter to be an internal Athenian affair.[29]

It is fascinating to imagine the debate that must have gone on between the Spartans and their allies as they watched Samos revolt from Athens and then saw the Athenians crush this rebellion. Samos possessed a significant fleet, of some sixty warships or more.[30] Such a fleet, combined with that of Corinth, would have presented a major difficulty for the Athenians. Had the Spartans themselves agreed to march on Attica while the Corinthians and Samians fought the Athenians at sea, Athens might have been forced (at least) to allow the Samians their independence. Indeed, in Thucydides' account one can almost sense the Corinthians' chagrin at the missed opportunity the Samian War had offered Athens' rivals in the Peloponnese.[31]

This war offers us other glimpses into Pericles' policies and career. During the revolt the Athenians dispatched a portion of their fleet to the east and south of Samos in order to counter any ships the Persians might send in support of the rebels.[32] This action, as well as the Persian governor's interference in the matter, suggests that no formal treaty existed between Athens and Persia ca. 440, helping confirm our earlier suspicions about the nature of the understanding the two powers probably reached ca. 449: any such agreement existed only so long as it remained advantageous for both parties involved. Pericles and the Athenians thought that the Persians might seize an opportunity to capitalize on Athenian weakness if any such chance occurred. Pericles clearly did not believe Athens had carte blanche to act in whatever way it pleased in the eastern Aegean without any possibility of Persian interference.

The decision to reduce Samos and the dispatch of the naval contingent to counter any Persian response thus show us that by ca. 440 Athens was willing to risk provoking renewed hostilities with Persia in order to establish control over the eastern Mediterranean and western Asia Minor. We must also remember the risk Athens ran in provoking Corinth and/or Sparta into action in support of Samos. In short, Athens' actions and posture during the Samian War suggest that Pericles and the Athenians felt sufficient confidence in their current military power to go to war with multiple major powers. It may be, too, that the Peloponnesians' failure to act in this matter encouraged Pericles to believe that he could push them even further in the future.

We know the names of some of the other elected Athenian generals who served during the Samian War. Perhaps most interesting to us (beyond a certain Thucydides, who is unlikely to have been either the historian or Pericles' rival the son of Melesias[33]) is the tragedian Sophocles.[34] We will examine his relationship with Pericles in a later chapter, but we may note here that Sophocles' election in these years and his presence in the Samian campaign may demonstrate the broad support that Pericles and Athens' reduction of Samos enjoyed with Athenians of various stripes.[35] Sophocles' political views remain controversial, but no one suggests that he favored a radical democracy. Kimon's demonstrated preference for Sophocles over Aeschylus in a dramatic competition may have reflected both aesthetic and political tastes.[36] Sophocles' later career shows that he had sympathies with the more conservative elements in Athens while he also saw their flaws.[37] The dramatist therefore probably did not support the most radical aspects of Pericles' public policies (like pay for public service), yet a difference of opinion about such matters did not prevent him from active involvement in Athens' aggressive foreign policy. As with Kimon and Thucydides Melesiou, Sophocles' career illustrates that the vast majority of Athenians of whatever domestic political views supported the extension of Athenian power over other Greeks.

Pericles weathered the political storms brought on by the Samian War and moved into the last decade of his life and career (439 to 429) holding a position of almost unprecedented authority under Athens' democratic government. Not since Kimon's dominance in the 470s and 460s had one Athenian wielded so much influence. Yet the conservative nature of Kimon's political views and foreign policy gives the appearance of relative calm to the period of his leadership (even if in reality Athens was accumulating significant power in the Aegean at this time). In contrast, Athens of the period after Kimon's ostracism took aggressive and unprecedented steps to grant more power and privileges to common Athenian citizens and lurched from an anti-Persian alliance with Sparta to alliance with Sparta's (but not Persia's) enemies (in Argos) while sending a huge force to support an anti-Persian revolt in Egypt only (finally) to come to some kind of understanding with the Persians ca. 449. Athens under the anti-Kimonians' influence appears extremely dynamic (to put the best possible construction on it) when compared with the state's policies when Kimon predominated.

The last decade of Pericles' career underscored a major difference between his own conception of Athenian leadership in Greece and that of his marriage relation and rival Kimon. In this decade, Athens would take steps that led to another (and greater) war with Sparta and its allies. Kimon's conception of a Greece protected (and ruled) by a team of Sparta and Athens could not survive in the face of Athenian impingement on Sparta's sphere of influence. In terms of our evaluation of Pericles, the 430s provide the clearest indication of the statesman's views about Athens' place in Greece and in history. The Athenians' actions in this period, combined with the speeches found in Thucydides, demonstrate that by the 430s at the very latest Pericles had adopted the view that Athens should strive for superiority in Hellas.[38]

A glance at a list of Athenian actions in the 430s, bracketed by the war with Samos (ending in 439) and the great war with Sparta (beginning in 431) might give the appearance of relative quiescence. Yet we have already seen that Athens founded a new colony in northern Greece in the critical Thraceward region at Amphipolis in 437/6 and that Pericles most probably led an Athenian expedition (and show of force) to the Black Sea, settling Athenians there, during this decade. The Athenians may also have placed new settlements in the Chersonese and elsewhere, as they certainly did in the 440s. Let us recall as well that by the 430s Athens had already entered into treaty agreements (which were renewed in 433/2) with Rhegion and Leontinoi in southern Italy and Sicily and founded the colony Thurii. Athens thus vastly extended its influence both to the east and to the west in the years just before and after the Samian War while continuing to demonstrate interest in controlling or influencing areas (especially the northern Aegean) that had long been vital to Athens' imperial foreign policy.

Relatively distant events in northwest Greece created the environment within which Pericles would lead Athens to war with Sparta at the end of this decade. Sometime around 435 the city of Epidamnus (on the mainland in far northwestern Hellas) expelled certain citizens after a civil war had erupted in the city.[39] The exiles made common cause with some non-Greeks in the area and attacked Epidamnus. The Epidamnians appealed to their mother city, Corcyra (a large island to their south), for assistance, but the Corcyreans refused to provide it. The Epidamnians then appealed to Corcyra's own mother city, Corinth, and the Corinthians agreed to provide help. Angered at the intervention of their metropolis, the Corcyreans responded by assisting the exiles from Epidamnus.[40]

Relations between the mother (Corinth) and daughter (Corcyra) poleis had been problematic since at least the time of Periander, the tyrant who ruled Corinth and whose son ruled Corcyra in the late seventh century BC. Both states had large navies and competed for influence in western Hellas and the central Mediterranean. Thucydides tells us that the Corcyreans did not pay the traditional honors to their mother city and this long-standing hostility between the two states undoubtedly influenced Corinth's decision to involve itself with Epidamnus and the Corcyreans' angry response to this intervention.[41]

Corcyra and Corinth fought a naval battle in 435 in which the daughter city defeated the mother. The Corinthians nursed their wounds and prepared for a great assault on the rebellious and ungrateful (they could argue) Corcyreans. The citizens of Corcyra, recognizing that Corinth would eventually attack again, sought an alliance with Athens, the greatest naval power in Hellas. The Corinthians, for their part, sent an embassy to Athens to request that the Athenians stay out of affairs that concerned the Corinthians and their proper sphere of influence.[42]

Thucydides begins his formal account of the Peloponnesian War's outbreak with a description of these events in and around Corcyra and Epidamnus. Because the Corinthians were Sparta's most important and powerful allies (providing the fleet Sparta lacked), the Athenians' reaction to Corcyra's request for an alliance threatened to upset the uneasy peace that existed between Sparta and Athens after 446/5 (the year of the Thirty Years Peace). Would Athens accept the Corcyreans' request and potentially enter into a war with Corinth (and thus Sparta)? This was the essential question when the Corcyrean and Corinthian embassies arrived at Athens in 433.

Pericles plays no apparent role in Thucydides' account of the Athenian debate on this subject. The historian, in fact, does not tell us the names of the Athenians who supported Athens' eventual alliance with Corcyra.[43] Subsequent events leave little doubt that Pericles and his supporters formed the core of the faction encouraging Athens to join Corcyra, but Thucydides apparently chose to hold back his introduction of Pericles as a historical actor in this drama until events after this initial decision. The Corcyrean ambassadors, according to Thucydides, argued that Athens should make an alliance with them since a war with Sparta was obviously coming and Athens would want Corcyra (and its fleet) on the Athenians' side in this conflict. Corcyra, moreover, provided the natural jumping-off point for Greeks sailing to Italy and Sicily, where the Athenians had interests. In short, Athens' self-interest compelled the city to join the Corcyrean camp.[44] The Corinthians, on the other hand, argued that it would be unjust for Athens to enter such an alliance since Corcyra fell within the Corinthian/ Peloponnesian sphere of influence. Corinth had not involved itself in Athens' war with Samos, nor should the Athenians intervene here. If the treaty did not formally prevent such an intervention, surely the spirit of the arrangement dictated that Athens remain neutral in this matter.[45]

That Pericles and other Athenians saw that their actions on this issue could lead to war with Sparta is suggested by the nature of the debate presented and by the assembly's vacillation on the question. At first, the Athenians were inclined to reject Corcyra's appeal for an alliance. The next day, however, they reversed themselves and agreed to make an alliance by terms of which they would help defend Corcyra from aggression, but would not join with the Corcyreans in any attack on Corinth.[46] This stipulation of a defensive alliance suggests several things. Some Athenians may have actually believed such a clause in the treaty would prevent the outbreak of open hostilities between Athens and the Peloponnesian League. Others, I would suggest, saw that the stipulation placed Athens in the best possible light diplomatically speaking (given that the citizens had voted to help Corcyra at all). The Athenians could claim, in short, that they had no intention of breaking the treaty of 446/5 even as they took actions that clearly strained the spirit if not the letter of that agreement. There was, after all, no real question of Corcyra attacking Corinth and thus of Athenian assistance in such an attack. The matter at issue was an expected Corinthian attack on Corcyra. Therefore the stipulation of a defensive alliance had no real effect, although it provided some potential cover for the Athenians if they wished to justify their actions before other Greeks.

To understand Pericles' position at this time, it is necessary to discuss briefly the other issues that separated Athens and Sparta in the years 433 and 432. Once Athens had sent a fleet to Corcyra and assisted the Corcyreans in a naval battle with Corinth in 433 at Sybota, where the Corinthians were defeated, the Athenians sent orders to the Corinthian colony of Poteidaia in northern Hellas, ordering the city to expel its Corinthian magistrates (Poteidaia was a colony of Corinth but a tribute-paying member of the Athenian empire).[47] Despite Thucydides' report that the Athenians feared that Corinth might persuade Poteidaia to revolt, this aggressive action against the Corinthian colony suggests that the faction in Athens supporting a war with the Peloponnesians had made gains: the preemptive order to expel Corinthian magistrates sent a clearly provocative message to the Peloponnesians and could hardly be justified on any diplomatic grounds.[48]

Meanwhile, the Dorian island of Aegina complained to Sparta that Athens had impinged on its political autonomy in some way. The Aeginetans had been compelled to pay Athens tribute since the 450s but were supposedly allowed to manage their own domestic political affairs since the treaty of 446/5.[49]

Finally, the Spartans' Dorian allies in Megara had their own complaints against Athens. Embroiled in a dispute over land lying between the two states, Athens (apparently on the motion of Pericles) had dispatched a herald to Megara, where the sacred and inviolate spokesman had allegedly been killed. In response, another Athenian (Charinos) proposed a measure banning the Megarians from all Athenian-controlled harbors in the Aegean (effectively meaning virtually every harbor) and from the Athenian market-place. For a state whose wealth depended largely on trade, this so-called Megarian Decree had a devastating economic effect. The Megarians appealed to the Spartans to compel Athens to lift the measure and allow Megarian trade in the empire once more.[50]

Sparta and its allies discussed these matters in the Peloponnese, and the Spartans ultimately decided that Athens had in fact broken the terms of the treaty of 446/5. Even so, the Spartans did not dispatch their army to Attica to force the Athenians into compliance. Rather, Sparta began almost a year of diplomatic efforts to avoid war with Athens.[51] These efforts and Athens' response to them must figure prominently in any attempt to understand Pericles' foreign policy and his vision for Athens.

The Spartans understood that Pericles presented the greatest obstacle to maintaining peace. Thucydides tells us that Pericles led Athens at this time and was "always urging Athens to war" with Sparta.[52] The Spartans therefore sent a message to Athens telling them to "drive out the accursed" in Athens: that is, the Spartans suggested that the Athenians should expel the cursed family of the Alkmeonids, as the Athenians had done once before under Spartan compulsion.[53] As we have seen, Pericles was tainted with this curse on his mother's side. It is unclear whether such an order for the Alkmeonids to leave Athens, had it been given by the Athenians, would have included Pericles himself, but that was not the issue. The Spartans wished to weaken Pericles' position by reminding the Athenians that their principal leader hailed from a family stained by religious impiety. In addition, we may imagine, reminding the Athenians of the Alkmeonids' checkered history probably brought other things to mind, including their connections with the Athenian tyrants and the belief that they had betrayed Athens after the battle of Marathon. In short, the Spartan order to "drive out the accursed" reflected an oblique and not unsubtle effort on the Spartans' part to undermine their greatest enemy in Athens.[54]

Yet this campaign came to nothing, as the Athenians merely responded that the Spartans should drive out their own "accursed," a reference to a curse incurred from the Spartans' impious execution of their leader Pausanias ca. 471 BC.[55] The Spartans therefore began a series of embassies to Athens attempting to gain concessions from the Athenians that could forestall war.[56] Scholars have sometimes painted these diplomatic efforts as insincere or as attempts to establish a pretext for war, but such conclusions do not comport with our evidence.[57] The Spartans, somewhat desperately, sought a way to prevent this war by showing their allies that the Athenians could be compelled to make at least some concession.[58]

Pericles' attitude at this time may be summed up in the first words out of his mouth in Thucydides' history: "I am always of the same opinion, Athenians: no concessions to the Peloponnesians." These words are striking not only because they provide a formal introduction to the figure of Pericles in Thucydides' history,[59] but also because they are so un-Thucydidean. The speeches in the history often begin with some kind of general or theoretical statement or principle. To have Pericles step onto the historical stage with such a bald and unsubtle pronouncement as "no concessions to the

Peloponnesians" makes a very strong statement about his position at the time and his role in bringing about this war.

We must pause to consider Pericles' speech to the Athenians (as presented by Thucydides) during the course of these diplomatic efforts by Sparta. We may profitably read the entire speech in the (adapted) translation of R. Crawley.

[140] There is one principle, Athenians, which I hold to through everything, and that is the principle of no concessions to the Peloponnesians. I know that the spirit which inspires men while they are being persuaded to make war is not always retained in action; that as circumstances change, resolutions change. Yet I see that now as before the same, almost literally the same, counsel is demanded of me; and I put it to those of you who are allowing yourselves to be persuaded, to support the national resolves even in the case of reverse, or to forfeit all credit for their wisdom in the event of success. For sometimes the course of things is as arbitrary as the plans of men; indeed this is why we usually blame chance for whatever does not happen as we expected. (2) Now it was clear before that Lacedaemon entertained designs against us; it is still more clear now. The treaty provides that we shall mutually submit our differences to legal settlement, and that we shall meanwhile each keep what we have. Yet the Lacedaemonians never yet made us any such offer, never yet would accept from us any such offer; on the contrary, they wish complaints to be settled by war instead of by negotiations; and in the end we find them here dropping the tone of request and adopting that of command. (3) They order us to raise the siege of Potidaea, to let Aegina be independent, and to revoke the Megarian decree; and they conclude with an ultimatum warning us to leave the Hellenes independent. (4) I hope that you will none of you think that we shall be going to war for a trifle if we refuse to revoke the Megarian decree, which appears in front of their complaints, and the revocation of which is to save us from war, or let any feeling of self-reproach linger in your minds, as if you went to war for slight cause. (5) Why, this trifle contains the whole seal of your resolution. If you give way, you will instantly have to meet some greater demand, as having been frightened into obedience in the first instance; but a firm refusal will make them clearly understand that they must treat you more as equals. [141] Make your decision therefore at once, either to submit before you are harmed, or if we are to go to war, as I for one think we ought, to do so without caring whether the ostensible cause be great or small, resolved against making concessions or consenting to a precarious tenure of our possessions. For all claims from an equal, urged upon a neighbor as commands, before any attempt at legal settlement, be they great or small, have only one meaning, and that is slavery.

(2) As to the war and the resources of either party, a detailed comparison will not show you the inferiority of Athens. (3) Personally engaged in the cultivation of their land, without funds either private or public, the

Peloponnesians are also without experience in long wars across sea, from the strict limit which poverty imposes on their attacks upon each other. (4) Powers of this description are quite incapable of often manning a fleet or often sending out an army: they cannot afford the absence from their homes, and the expenditure from their own funds; and besides, they have not command of the sea. (5) Surplus funds, it must be remembered, maintain a war more than forced contributions. Farmers are a class of men that are always more ready to serve in person than in purse. Confident that the former will survive their dangers, they are by no means so sure that the latter will not be prematurely exhausted, especially if the war last longer than they expect, which it very likely will. (6) In a single battle the Peloponnesians and their allies may be able to defy all Hellas, but they are incapacitated from carrying on a war against a power different in character from their own, by the want of the single council-chamber requisite to prompt and vigorous action, and the substitution of a diet composed of various tribes, in which every state possesses an equal vote, and each presses for its own ends, a condition of things which generally results in no action at all. (7) The great wish of some is to avenge themselves on some particular enemy, the great wish of others is to save their own pockets. Slow in assembling, they devote a very small fraction of the time to the consideration of any public object, most of it to the prosecution of their own objects. Meanwhile, each fancies that no harm will come of his neglect, that it is the business of somebody else to look after this or that for him; and so, by the same notion being entertained by all separately, the common cause imperceptibly decays.

[142] But the principal point is the hindrance that they will experience from want of money. The slowness with which it comes in will cause delay; but the opportunities of war wait for no man. (2) Again, we need not be alarmed either at the possibility of their raising fortifications in Attica, or at their navy. (3) It would be difficult for any system of fortifications to establish a rival city even in time of peace, much more, surely, in an enemy's country, with Athens just as fortified against it, as it against Athens; (4) and while a mere outpost might be able to do some harm to the country by incursions and by the facilities which it would afford for desertion, in can never prevent our sailing into their country and raising fortifications there, and making reprisals with our powerful fleet. (5) For our naval skill is of more use to us for service on land, than their skill as infantrymen is to them for service at sea. (6) Familiarity with the sea they will not find an easy acquisition. (7) If you who have been practicing at it ever since the Median invasion have not yet brought it to perfection, is there any chance of anything considerable being effected by an agricultural, unseafaring population, who will besides be prevented from practicing by the constant presence of strong squadrons of observation from Athens? (8) With a small squadron they might hazard an engagement, encouraging their ignorance by numbers; but the restraint of a strong force will prevent their moving, and through want of practice they will

grow more clumsy, and consequently more timid. (9) It must be kept in mind that seamanship, just like anything else, is a matter of art, and will not admit of being taken up occasionally as an occupation for times of leisure; on the contrary, it is so exacting as to leave leisure for nothing else.

[143] Even if they were to touch the money [in the sacred treasuries] at Olympia or Delphi, and try to seduce our foreign sailors by the temptation of higher pay, that would be a serious danger only if we could not still be a match for them by embarking our own citizens and the aliens resident among us. But in fact by this means we are always a match for them; and, best of all, we have a larger and higher class of helmsmen and officers among our own citizens than all the rest of Hellas. (2) And to say nothing of the danger of such a step, none of our foreign sailors would consent to become an outlaw from his country, and to take service with them and their hopes, for the sake of a few days' high pay.

(3) This, I think, is a tolerably fair account of the position of the Peloponnesians; that of Athens is free from the defects that I have criticized in them, and has other advantages of its own, which they can show nothing to equal. (4) If they march against our country we will sail against theirs, and it will then be found that the desolation of the whole of Attica is not the same as that of even a fraction of Peloponnese; for they will not be able to supply the deficiency except by a battle, while we have plenty of land both on the islands and the continent. (5) The rule of the sea is indeed a great matter. Consider for a moment. Suppose that we were islanders; can you conceive of a more impregnable position? Well, this in future should, as far as possible, be our conception of our position. Dismissing all thought of our land and houses, we must vigilantly guard the sea and the city. No irritation that we may feel for the former must provoke us to a battle with the numerical superiority of the Peloponnesians. A victory would only be succeeded by another battle against the same superiority: a reverse involves the loss of our allies, the source of our strength, who will not remain quiet a day after we become unable to proceed with forces against them. We must cry not over the loss of houses and land but of men's lives; for houses and land do not gain men, but men them. And if I had thought that I could persuade you, I would have bid you go out and lay them waste with your own hands, and show the Peloponnesians that this at any rate will not make you submit.

[144] I have many other reasons to hope for a favourable issue, if you can consent not to combine schemes of fresh conquest with the conduct of the war, and will abstain from willfully involving yourselves in other dangers; indeed, I am more afraid of our own blunders than of the enemy's devices. (2) But these matters shall be explained in another speech, as events require. For the present, dismiss these men with the answer that we will allow Megara the use of our market and harbours when the Lacedaemonians suspend their alien acts in favour of us and our allies, there being nothing in the treaty to prevent either one or the other; that we will leave the cities independent, if

independent we found them when we made the treaty, and when the Lacedaemonians grant to their cities an independence not involving subservience to Lacedaemonian interest, but such as each severally may desire; that we are willing to give the legal satisfaction which our agreements specify; and that we shall not commence hostilities, but shall resist those who do commence them. This is an answer agreeable at once to the rights and the dignity of Athens. (3) It must be thoroughly understood that war is a necessity, and that the more readily we accept it, the less will be the ardour of our opponents, and that out of the greatest dangers communities and individuals acquire the greatest honors. (4) Did not our fathers resist the Medes not only with resources far different from ours, but even when those resources had been abandoned? And more by wisdom than by fortune, more by daring than by strength, did not they beat off the barbarian and advance their affairs to their present height? We must not fall behind them, but must resist our enemies in any way and in every way, and attempt to hand down our power to our posterity unimpaired.

As a piece of rhetoric this speech is remarkable. We may note, for example, that Pericles lumps together the Spartans' various diplomatic offers in a group (140.3), as if they had all been demanded at once, only then to admit that renouncing the Megarian Decree by itself could actually prevent the war (140.4). Pericles' demands that the Athenians compel the Spartans to treat them as equals (140.5–141) and his comparison of conceding to any Spartan demand with "slavery" (*doulosis*: 141.1) both bespeak an Athenian feeling of inferiority, an attitude that the statesman believes he must confront directly ("a detailed comparison will not show you the inferiority of Athens": 141.2). Pericles then indeed moves to a detailed discussion of the strategic situation, emphasizing the weaknesses of a Peloponnesian force that must rely primarily on farmers – a strange claim in that it applied only to the Spartans' allies and not to the Spartans themselves, who had helots who worked the land for them[60] – and that has poor revenues and capital resources. Even here Pericles must admit the enemy's ability "to defy all Hellas" in a single battle (141.6), an amazing concession he nevertheless attempts to undercut by noting that the Peloponnesians must make decisions through a council consisting of the various powers in alliance with Sparta, all possessing an equal vote and each having its own interests. Pericles claims that this situation leads to military impotence, a remarkable argument to be made by the leader of a democracy, a form of government criticized since antiquity for the very weakness Pericles here applies to the war council of the Peloponnesians. It is surely true that Pericles means to emphasize that Athens does *not* have to consult its allies/subjects before taking any military actions, but this hardly lessens the irony of the fact that Athens itself took decisions in a council and assembly that comprised voters of equal power and often conflicting interests.

Following this, Pericles dilates on the issue of money and the Peloponnesians' difficulty in acquiring it and the naval skills that will be required to meet Athens at sea (142). He emphasizes the Athenians' superior skills as seamen and the supposed loyalty of the foreigners who row in Athens' fleet (142–43). He goes on to describe the advantages that control of the sea and virtual island status give Athens. The Athenians must recognize that the control of the sea is all to them and their lands must be seen as of little moment[61] – indeed, Pericles goes so far as to say he would encourage their destruction simply to show the Spartans that the Athenians will not compromise simply to save their property (143.5).

Pericles then tells the Athenians why they should hope for victory, especially if they realize the war is inevitable and enter it willingly without attempting to expand their empire while conducting it (144.1). He concludes not with the specific answers he urges the Athenians to give to the Spartan envoys, but rather with a reminder that Athens must be willing to accept great danger in order to achieve great honors (*timai*: the plural of *time*)[62] and thereby not to fall short of the standards set by their ancestors (144.3–4).

Pericles' assertion in this speech that revoking the Megarian Decree would prevent war with Sparta (1.140.3–5) has elicited considerable confusion. Scholars at one time tended to focus on this passage as an admission by Thucydides or Pericles that the Megarian Decree was "the real" or a crucial cause of the Peloponnesian War, or the factor most discussed in the relevant assemblies.[63] Such a view could derive support from Aristophanes' comedies, which more than once make jokes about the Megarian Decree as the "spark" that set off the blazes of war. For example, in *Acharnians* (425), Aristophanes has his protagonist Dikaiopolis ("Just city") proclaim

> But friends – for there are only friends here listening –
> why blame these things entirely on the Spartans?
> It was men of ours – I do not say our polis –
> but some badly-minded troublemaking creeps,
> some worthless counterfeit foreign currency,
> who started denouncing shirts from Megara
> and if they spotted a cucumber or a bunny
> or piglets, cloves of garlic, lumps of salt,

it was Megarian, grabbed, sold off that very day.
Now that was merely local; small potatoes.
But then some young crapshooters got to drinking
and went to Megara and stole the whore Simaetha.
And then the Megarians, garlic-stung with passion,
got even by stealing two whores from Aspasia.[64]
From this the origin of the war broke forth
on all the Greeks: from three sluts.
And then in wrath Olympian Pericles
did lighten and thunder and turn Greece upside-down,
establishing laws that read like drinking songs:
"Megarians shall be banned from land and markets
and banned from sea and also banned from shore."
Whereupon the Megarians, starving inch by inch,
appealed to Sparta to help make us repeal
the decree we passed in the matter of the whores.
But we refused although they repeatedly asked,
And then it came to a clashing of shields.[65]

A few years later (421), in his play *Peace*, Aristophanes provides the following exchange between characters and the chorus leader, tying the outbreak of the war to the Megarian Decree and Pheidias, Pericles' supposed friend and the artist most closely associated with the Parthenon's sculptures and decoration.[66]

CHORUS-LEADER [TO HERMES]: But where can this goddess [Peace] have been, to be away from us all this long time? Friendliest of gods, do explain this to us.

HERMES: "O indigent peasants, mark well my words," if you want to hear how it was that she vanished. What started it all in the first place was Pheidias getting into trouble. Then Pericles became frightened he might share in Pheidias' fate – for he was afraid of your character and your hard-biting temper – and before anything terrible could happen to him, he set the city ablaze by dropping into it a tiny spark of a Megarian decree and he fanned up so great a war that all the Greeks were in tears with the smoke, both those over there and those over here; and as soon as the first vine had

	reluctantly begun to crackle, and the first wine-jar received a knock and kicked out in vengeful anger at another jar, there was no longer anyone who could put a stop to it, and Peace was disappearing.
TRYGAEUS:	Well, by Apollo, I'd never been told that by anyone before, nor had I heard how she [Peace] was connected with Pheidias.[67]
CHORUS-LEADER:	No more had I, not till now. So that's why she's so fair of face – because she's a relation of his! There's a lot of things we don't realize.[68]

These passages in Aristophanes show, so the theory goes, that Thucydides either did not understand just how (economically and thus politically) important the Megarian Decree really was or that he attempted to cover up the importance of the measure in order to further his own hypothesis about the war's true origin (and perhaps to defend Pericles from criticism).[69] Aristophanes' emphasis on the decree's importance in these plays, this view holds, gives the lie to Thucydides' account.[70]

Such conclusions utterly misconceive the situation and Pericles' reaction to it. In his speech in Thucydides, Pericles expressly notes that the Megarian Decree is a small matter, but a small matter over which the Athenians should be willing to go to war. Any concession to the Spartans, no matter how small, represents an intolerable affront to Athenian sovereignty and independence and would suggest a weakness that would lead to further demands, according to Pericles. Aristophanes' humor, so far from somehow giving the lie to Thucydides' account, dovetails perfectly with it. The great joke, as Aristophanes shows, is that Athens really *could* have avoided war with Sparta precisely by rescinding the Megarian Decree. Pericles knew this and thus dealt directly with the issue. Years later Athenians looked back and laughed (bitterly, no doubt) because Aristophanes reminded them that they had *actually* gone to war over something as minor as the Megarian Decree. Surely something like that called for an explanation, and thus Aristophanes provides his comic explanations of the Megarian Decree itself.[71] But we must understand that the whole comedic context of the passages in Aristophanes and the historical context of Pericles' speech in Thucydides depend on the same fact: the Megarian Decree was a minor affair (to Athens), but the Athenians nevertheless refused to rescind it to avoid war with Sparta.[72]

What else can Pericles' first speech in Thucydides tell us about the leader? The oration is the only one of the three speeches made by Pericles in the history that treats the practical matters of war in any detail.[73] In particular, Pericles discusses the need for training and practice where naval warfare is concerned and the unlikelihood that a landlocked and monetarily strapped power like Sparta will be able to stand up to the well-trained and well-funded Athenian navy. He also warns against attempting to expand the empire during the course of the war. In general, the speech strikingly privileges the fleet and the concerns of the city (proper) of Athens over the concerns of farmers and the countryside. Since Pericles made this speech (or one like it) before the Athenians had been compelled to abandon their farms and move inside the city walls, the statesman apparently geared his address to an audience that consisted primarily of city dwellers. His later speeches in Thucydides do not display this bias in favor of the urban and seafaring population. In those addresses, Pericles spoke to an audience that included a greater proportion of those who dwelled in the country rather than the city.[74]

Pericles makes no grand ideological or philosophical claims about Athens in this first speech, as he will later do in his last two speeches in Thucydides' work. The more complex ideas here (for example, that people in a war do not always maintain the same spirit with which they entered it: 140.1) have nothing to do with ostensibly *Athenian* character traits or ideals. The statesman maintains that Athens' dignity and the accomplishments of the city's ancestors demand and justify the acceptance of this war, but he tells his audience nothing special about Athens or Athenians beyond the fact that they are particularly good sailors. Pericles appears here as a practical leader and politician who wishes to convince his audience that war with Sparta is necessary and that the prospects for victory in such a war are quite good. In a way, this reverses our natural (or, perhaps, our modern) expectations. Would not a leader such as Pericles make a grander pronouncement about the value and necessity of war before the outbreak of hostilities, explaining (for example) some significant differences between the Athenians and their enemies beyond the one's attachment to the sea and the other's to the land? The highest moral claim in the speech stems merely from the fact that Athens has offered arbitration and the Spartans have refused it. Was there really little more to say about Spartan aggression here than the fact that the Spartans had refused to treat the Athenians as equals? The paucity of such material in this speech suggests that Pericles did not believe he needed to work very hard in order to inflame the Athenians against Sparta. What he most needed to do, if Thucydides has given us a relatively accurate picture of the speech's themes, was to explain the practical advantages Athens faced in a war with Sparta.

Pericles does introduce subjects in this speech that he will echo and extend in his later addresses in Thucydides. In particular we should note his insistence that glory demands that states and individuals undergo dangers and that the Athenians must not allow the size of their empire to be reduced. These (minor) points in this address become major themes of Pericles' later speeches. In fact, as we shall see, his speeches in Thucydides become increasingly belligerent: it is not that in his first oration he appears conciliatory or less than enthusiastic about war with Sparta. Rather, it is that Pericles' speeches increasingly focus on the abstract and practical value of ruling others, the necessity of personal sacrifice for the good of the state, and the goal of making sure Athens achieves future fame for the power it exercises in this period. Pericles, if we may put it this way, becomes less interested in discussing the necessities or exigencies created by this particular war and more focused on the larger issue of Athenian predominance, one necessity of which was a war with Sparta.[75]

We should examine carefully one other particularly interesting passage of this speech. As we have seen, early in the address (1.140.5–141.1) Pericles asserts that the Spartans must learn to deal with the Athenians as equals, while the Athenians must appreciate that to give in to the demands of equals (here ironically using the Spartans' regular term for themselves: *homoioi*, "similars") is tantamount to slavery (*doulosis*). J. E. Lendon has rightly urged that issues of rank played a major role in bringing about wars between Greek city-states, and this passage suggests that Pericles was alive to this issue.[76] Indeed, the defensive tone of the passage is striking: as we have seen, Pericles recognizes that his audience *feels* insecure about their status as "Sparta's equals," and he faces the issue squarely.

In the Funeral Oration, Pericles returns to this theme, but there he begins to make the case not for equality with Sparta, but rather for Athenian superiority (based on the Athenian character and way of life). There is, it is true, still considerable defensiveness over the issue of

Athens' military reputation and power.[77] By the last speech in Thucydides, the statesman makes his bald case for Athenian superiority without a hint of defensiveness, claiming that Athens' resolution and power will establish its "perpetual reputation," as the state that "ruled more Greeks than any other Greek state." In short, in this first speech Pericles introduces a subject – the Athenians' self-image as compared with other Greeks – on which he will build a good portion of his case for Athens' resolution in the face of war with Sparta. Pericles' willingness to identify and exploit this aspect of the Athenian character figures prominently in his ability to persuade the Athenian people to undertake war with the greatest power in Greece.

Thucydides' account of events leading up to the beginning of the Peloponnesian War has elicited a great deal of controversy among historians, many of whom have focused on the historian's separation of the causes of the war (1.23.5–6) into "explanations and points of complaint" (*aitiai* and *diaphorai*) and what he calls the "truest cause" (*alethestate prophasis*), though least spoken about openly."[78] Thucydides in this passage claims that, although certain events (like the affair at Epidamnus and the Megarian Decree) created the environment for war, the "truest cause" stemmed from Athens' ever-increasing power, which "inspired fear in the Spartans and compelled them to go to war."[79] The thesis that increased Athenian power drove Sparta to war appears especially in Thucydides' account of the years between the Persian and Peloponnesian wars (1.89–117), where he illustrates his thesis that Athenian actions over these five decades had led to increasing Spartan concern about Athens' growing power (1.88, 118).[80] However, too few scholars have noticed that Thucydides' account of the war's outbreak taken as a whole in fact places clear emphasis on Pericles' personal role in provoking hostilities.[81]

Modern historians have often praised Thucydides' willingness to broaden his analysis of the war's causes to include things like Athens' growing power and the Spartan psychology this induced and have perhaps understandably therefore ignored or minimized the role the historian attributes to Pericles. Yet Thucydides presents the statesman, in effect, as the primary reason that war broke out in 432/1: Pericles, he notes, was the leading figure in Athens and always "urging the Athenians on to war" with Sparta. Pericles' first speech, as we have seen, begins with the bald statement "no concessions to the Spartans." After Pericles' speech, Thucydides reports that the Athenians acted as the statesman had suggested in their (hardly conciliatory) response to Sparta's diplomatic efforts.[82] Shortly after this, Thucydides tells us that Pericles prevented the Athenians even from listening to a Spartan peace embassy after the Spartan army had marched out from Lakedaimon.[83] Pericles then, according to Thucydides, delivered another speech (which the historian only summarizes) aimed at encouraging the Athenians in the face of the oncoming war by describing the ample financial and military resources Athens possessed.[84] Following this, we are told that Pericles prevented the Athenians from holding an assembly meeting (at which he apparently expected the Athenians to buckle before the Spartan invasion).[85] Beyond all this, Thucydides makes it clear (as we have seen) that the Spartans themselves considered Pericles to be the primary proponent of war in Athens.

Despite many efforts to undermine Thucydides' credibility or paint him as an apologist for Athens (or Sparta),[86] no scholar suggests that Thucydides invented the basic historical outline of events leading up to the Peloponnesian War. Certainly, many historians believe the speeches contained in this work are largely or wholly Thucydides' invention, but even scholars who maintain this view (and I am not among them) do not argue that Thucydides invented events such as the Megarian Decree, the Spartan peace embassies, or Aegina's complaints about Athens. Thucydides, after all, wrote about contemporary events for an audience who had experienced them. His position differed markedly from that of a modern historian attempting to re-create events in the distant past. Thucydides' audience's own knowledge of events and the public nature of Athenian decision making – as well as his belief that events of the past could act as a guide to the future (1.22.4) – acted as checks on the historian, compelling him to limit the amount of freedom in his presentation if he wished to persuade an audience familiar with these events (and to be true to his own professed principles).

Of course Thucydides was capable of making errors and capable of coloring events in a way that led the reader to a conclusion he desired (though I believe he was admirably restrained in this). Nevertheless, once we recognize the fact that Thucydides had little opportunity or motive to invent basic *facts* (or, for example, to change the actual order of events), then it becomes necessary to read his account of Pericles' involvement in the war's outbreak rather differently than scholars have usually done. Too often, debate over whether Pericles "really said" X or Y in the speeches of Thucydides has overshadowed a very basic historical datum that Thucydides cannot reasonably be accused of inventing: Pericles acted as the chief proponent of war with Sparta in 432/1, and he pursued a policy designed to drive Athens and Sparta into conflict if Sparta would not concede to Athens' increasing power and status. This conclusion follows not from the words of the speeches Pericles makes in Thucydides, but from the historian's report of the events and the environment in the run-up to the war.

In short, even the most skeptical historian should conclude that Pericles actually wanted Athens and Sparta to go to war – or, to be more precise, Pericles believed that the Athenians should make no concessions to Sparta, even reasonable concessions, that could prevent the war.[87] In adopting this position, Pericles may well have relied on a defensive Athenian attitude that bristled at the idea of Athens "taking orders" (any longer) from Sparta.[88] He also perhaps depended on a Spartan reluctance to engage in long or distant conflicts and a certain Spartan scrupulousness over treaties and religious obligations. Indeed, the Spartans eventually blamed themselves (Thuc. 7.18) for the war since they had refused arbitration and had been the technical aggressors (by invading Attica). Such factors allowed Pericles to adopt the position he did and to expect a favorable outcome from such intransigence. But this in no way minimizes Pericles' personal and direct involvement in encouraging this war.

Historians who wish to minimize Pericles' (or the Athenians') responsibility for bringing on this war with Sparta have often focused on the clause of the Thirty Years Peace (446/5) that apparently called for arbitration if Sparta and Athens reached an impasse over some issue.[89] Pericles, indeed, mentions this arbitration clause in his speech to the Athenians before the war, complaining that the Spartans had not been willing to go to arbitration even though the Athenians had offered to do so.[90] Do not the Spartans deserve primary blame for the war, the argument goes, since they would not submit to arbitration?

The problem with this view, as Pericles undoubtedly saw, is twofold: first, who would arbitrate in any conflict between Athens and Sparta? Where was the neutral Greek state, figure, or force to play this role?[91] More important, the Spartans had nothing with which to bargain in any arbitration. Everything on the table reflected a potential act of Athenian aggression (Corcyra, Poteidaia, Aegina, Megara). Any "arbitration" could only result in Sparta formally conceding the legitimacy of one or more of Athens' actions.[92] Expecting Sparta to go to arbitration with the Athenians in 432/1 is like expecting a property owner to go to arbitration with the man who robbed him: should the thief be allowed to keep the television if he gives back the silverware?

At the very least the facts compel us to try to consider the matter from the Spartans' point of view. Their allies had come to them with pleas for assistance to stop Athenian encroachment on their spheres of influence or sovereignty. The Spartans responded by sending a series of embassies that attempted to offer a way out for both Athens and Sparta. They sought, in effect, *some* concession from Athens that would allow them to save face in front of their allies and prevent the necessity of a full-scale war with Athens. Pericles' position of "no concessions" therefore virtually forced the issue of war on both states.

Pericles' biography and the historical events leading up to 432/1 perhaps help us understand why and how the statesman (and those who supported him) had come to this intransigent position. His rival Kimon had supported a policy that encouraged Spartan and Athenian alliance against Persia while each attempted to control its own sphere of influence in Hellas, with the Athenians dominating the Aegean and the Spartans the southern mainland. Under this arrangement, we should note, the Spartans made no formal attempts whatsoever to limit Athenian power in the Aegean. They made no complaints about Athens' reductions of Naxos or Thasos or the colonization of Skyros or (attempted at) Ennea Hodoi.[93] They made no efforts to prevent Athens from collecting tribute from other Greeks or increasing the size of its fleet. This policy of alliance and cooperation featured in the joint Spartan-Athenian pursuit of the disgraced Themistocles and culminated in an Athenian army marching to Sparta to assist in the suppression of a helot revolt in 462/1.

The reversal of foreign policy that spawned Kimon's ostracism had shattered this alliance and led immediately to war. In essence, the first war with Sparta and its allies thus developed from the Athenians' rejection of the Kimonian ideal of joint rule and influence in Hellas.[94] Athens determined that it would be the first power in Greece and that Athenians would exercise power not only in their own sphere (the Aegean) but also in mainland Greece, including the Peloponnese. In short, already by ca. 460 the Athenians had staked a claim to dominance in all of Hellas.

Whatever we conclude about Pericles' view of the Athenian adventure in Egypt in the 450s, there can be no real doubt that he supported the first war with the Peloponnesians and the attempt to extend Athenian power in Hellas. The return of Kimon from ostracism in 452/1 and the truce with Sparta he negotiated in 451/0, followed by the disastrous years 447 and 446 and the Thirty Years Peace of 446/5, represented major (but temporary) setbacks for the Athenians who sought to establish Athens as the dominant power in Greece.

We must recognize, therefore, that Pericles' actions in 431 reflect an ideal of Athenian power and predominance that stretched back at least 30 years.[95] Between 460 and 431 Athenian policy had wavered between war and peace with the Peloponnesians while the Athenians continued to expand and intensify their control over the empire. The issue for the Spartans had never been the Athenian empire itself, Athens' right to which they clearly and readily granted, or even the Athenians' establishment as a first-rank power in Hellas. The primary issue for Sparta was Athens' encroachment on the Spartan sphere of influence, a policy Athens had adopted ca. 461 when it allied with Megara (and Argos) and again in 433 when it made an agreement with Corcyra and ordered Poteidaia to expel its magistrates. In both cases Athens' actions led to war.

One wonders how much influence generational factors had in this situation. By 433, very few Athenians who had fought beside the Spartans against Persia remained alive. In the late 430s, many young Athenians (and Spartans), as Thucydides noted (2.8.1), had never experienced a major war, and most Athenian men of any age had never experienced a battle with Sparta. The only certain hoplite battle ever fought between Athens and Sparta had occurred ca. 457 at Tanagra, more than twenty-five years before Pericles' pushed his "no concessions" policy.[96] Athenians like Pericles could dismiss that battle by noting that the Spartans had the Thebans to support them at Tanagra. However, Sparta's reputation as an invincible land power apparently remained intact in the late 430s. It is striking that Pericles' speeches never suggest that the Athenians actually believed they could defeat the Spartans in a hoplite battle: indeed, Pericles concedes that the Spartans were likely to win any "single battle." Pericles' whole strategy, publicly stated, depended on avoiding an infantry encounter that he clearly believed the Athenians would lose.[97]

Between ca. 461 and 446/5 it seems that a sufficient number of Athenians still respected the Spartans and wished to avoid (or end) conflict with Sparta to make Kimon's brief return to prominence after his ostracism and the treaties of 451/0 and 446/5 possible. By terms of the latter treaty, we must recall, Athens ceded virtually all its previous gains from the Peloponnesians' sphere of influence.[98]

Surely these concessions in 446/5 rankled some Athenians over the next fifteen years. Over that course of time, the Athenians launched only one major military operation – the entirely successful reduction of the great island of Samos. This, of course, had been a largely naval affair with little need for hoplite operations. Again, by 432/1, perhaps no Athenian man younger than thirty-five had ever witnessed a full-scale hoplite battle, and the men in their twenties and thirties would form the bulk of any Athenian infantry force if Athens and Sparta went to war.

The success of Pericles' intransigent policy in 432/1 relied in part on the Athenians' recent inexperience in the field of hoplite warfare, on Athenian resentment over the terms of the peace treaty of 446/5, on a generational change that had removed many of Sparta's old allies in Athens, and on a general Athenian exuberance and lust for power that had been unchecked in the last fifteen or so years. We must add to this the great wealth Athens had amassed over these years, a factor necessary for successful warfare, as Pericles himself emphasized in a speech just before the outbreak of war.[99] The Athenians, Pericles must have seen, by 432/1 were ripe for the renewal of open hostilities with Sparta and for the final rejection of any notion of joint rule of Hellas. Pericles' message of Athenian superiority and no concessions to Sparta thus found rich soil for growth. In consequence, the Athenians voted to enter the greatest war in their history.[100]

SEVEN

Pericles and Athenian Nationalism:
The Conquest of History

At the urging of Pericles, Athens entered a war with Sparta in 431 BC. The statesman's strategy required the Athenians to refuse an infantry battle, withdrawing behind the city walls to watch the Spartans ravage their farms. Pericles' status allowed him to convince the Athenians to accept this plan, and he remained popular enough in the first year of the war to be chosen to deliver the annual funeral oration. In this speech Pericles laid out his vision of the Athenians' special qualities and their right to rule, as well as the need of individuals to sacrifice themselves in the service of their beloved Athens and of the city-state's current power and future glory.

As the war continued and a plague struck Athens, Pericles' popularity waned. In his final speech in Thucydides he makes a bald case for the glory and advantages of rule over other Greeks and the dangers of letting that rule slip away. The Athenians took out their frustrations on Pericles even as they continued to fight the war he had promoted. Thucydides' analysis of Pericles as a leader reflects the statesman's admirable qualities, the deficiencies of the leaders who followed him, and the criticisms of those who believed Pericles had corrupted the political process and led Athens into a disastrous war. Looking back on Pericles as an older man, Thucydides sought to defend the leader his own history had shown to be the principal cause of war in 431.

One wonders about the mood in Athens as the Spartans marched northeast toward Attica in the early summer of 431.[1] We know that the playwright Euripides produced his Medea in that spring, and its story of a mother driven to murder her own children might strike us as reflective of a particularly disturbing moment in Athenian history were the tale not a traditional feature of Greek mythology. Still, Euripides felt compelled to choose this story and present it in the way he did as Athens prepared for war with the other great power in Hellas. It is more than possible that some Athenians who watched the play in the spring that year felt a discomfort amplified both by the approaching war and by the cries of infuriated Medea.

Athens itself would have become a crowded and unpleasant place by the time the Spartan army arrived in Attica. Pericles' strategy for the war as outlined in Thucydides consisted of moving the Athenians from their farms and homes in the countryside into the walled city. The Spartans would be permitted to ravage the Athenians' land, a typical action used by a Greek army to provoke the landowners to come out and meet the invaders in battle. Despite the ignominy that Athens' citizens would feel at allowing such destruction, Pericles had convinced the Athenians to ignore this affront to their honor and damage to their real property.[2] Athens' power, he asserted, stemmed from its empire and fleet and the revenues these generated. As we have seen, Thucydides has Pericles go so far as to say he would like to see the Athenians ravage their own farmlands in order to show the invading Spartans that they would not submit over concern for their property.

No event in Pericles' life more clearly demonstrates his authority and standing with the Athenian people than his ability to convince them to abandon their ancestral lands and move into the city of Athens in 431.[3] Thucydides describes the painful process of Athenians gathering up their movable valuables and furniture and transferring them into an already crowded city. Athenians took up temporary residence in the space between the long walls leading from the city down to the fortified Peiraeus harbor, in temple precincts, and anywhere else they could improvise some kind of covering.[4] Sanitary conditions, not to mention the need for food and water, must have made this situation wretched and would soon encourage the outbreak of a devastating and deadly plague that would kill thousands of Athenians. Yet even before the plague struck, many Athenians must have asked whether a policy of "no concessions to the Peloponnesians" justified all this misery.

Still, this was a temporary affair. The Spartans stayed in Attica a few weeks and then returned to the Peloponnese, allowing the Athenians to disperse to their (often ravaged) farms.[5] While the Spartans had remained in Attica, the Athenians had used their cavalry to harass the Peloponnesians and provide some measure of protection for the area in the immediate vicinity of the city walls, but overall the Spartans had enjoyed free rein in Attica.[6] Meanwhile, operations continued in the north, where the Athenians' siege of Poteidaia and other actions had undoubtedly resulted in some casualties. The Athenians also sent a fleet to ravage the coast of the Peloponnese and another to Locris and Euboea in central Hellas.[7] Athens expelled the Aeginetans from their island (on the grounds that they had caused the war with Sparta) and colonized the island themselves.[8] In the late summer, Pericles himself led an assault on the territory of Megara.[9]

Overall, Athens' losses in the first season of war with Sparta had been light, and the Athenians must have breathed something like a sigh of relief that they had weathered the Spartans' first attack so easily. Pericles' strategy probably seemed sound: the homebody Spartans surely would not continue to march up to Attica every year. They would grow weary of such operations and Athens would "win," in that it would retain everything the city currently possessed without having had to meet the Spartans in a hoplite battle. Unable to force any concessions from Athens, Sparta would lose credibility with its allies, and Athens' position in Hellas would be materially and psychologically strengthened.[10]

That winter the Athenians voted to have Pericles give the annual funeral oration over the soldiers who had died in the war's first year, clearly a sign that a majority of those voting in the assembly continued to support his policy and the conflict with Sparta.[11] The speech that Pericles gave in the version presented by Thucydides stands as the most famous account of Athenian culture, society, and politics to survive antiquity. Its ideas and imagery continue to resonate in our own culture. I can remember hearing U.S. Supreme Court Justice Stephen Breyer quoting Pericles' words from the speech during an NPR interview as I drove home from Boston a few years ago.[12] Meanwhile, scholars and others continue to cite selective portions of Pericles' Funeral Oration as if it provides an accurate account of Athens' institutions, ideology, or ideals, and, most important for our purposes, as if these select portions of the speech reflect either Pericles' own views or (more usually) the views of the historian Thucydides. Scholars have often seen the speech as the historian's attempt to paint an idealized picture of Athens and/or Pericles.[13] Since the speech has figured so prominently in virtually all treatments of Athenian history and since it has the potential to illuminate Pericles' thought, we should examine it in full (again, in the translation of R. Crawley).

[2.35] Most of my predecessors in this place have commended him who made this speech part of the law, telling us that it is well that it should be delivered at the burial of those who fall in battle. For myself, I should have thought that the worth which had displayed itself in deeds, would be sufficiently rewarded by honors (*timai*) also shown by deeds, such as you now see in this funeral prepared at the people's cost. And I could have wished that the merits (*aretai*) of many brave men were not to be imperiled in the mouth of a single individual, to stand or fall according as he spoke well or ill. (2) For it is hard to speak properly upon a subject where it is even difficult to convince your hearers that you are speaking the truth. On the one hand, the friend who is familiar with every fact of the story may think that some point has not been set forth with that fullness which he wishes and knows it to deserve; on the other, he who is a stranger to the matter may be led by envy to suspect exaggeration if he hears anything above his own nature. For men can endure to hear others praised only so long as they can severally persuade themselves of their own ability to equal the actions recounted: when this point is passed, envy comes in and with it incredulity. (3) However, since our ancestors have stamped this custom with their approval, it becomes my duty to obey the law and to try to satisfy your several wishes and opinions as best I may.

[2.36] I shall begin with our ancestors: it is both just and proper that they should have the honour (*time*) of the first mention on an occasion like the present. They dwelt in the country without break in the succession from generation to generation,[14] and handed it down free to the present time by their valor (*arete*). (2) And if our more remote ancestors deserve praise, much more do our own fathers, who added to their inheritance the empire which we now possess, and spared no pains to be able to leave their acquisitions to us of the present generation. (3) Lastly, there are few parts of our dominions that have not been augmented by those of us here, who are still more or less in the vigor of life; and the mother country has been furnished by us with everything that can enable her to depend on her own resources whether for war or for peace. (4) That part of our history which tells of the military achievements which gave us our several possessions, or of the ready valour with which either we or our fathers stemmed the tide of Hellenic or foreign aggression, is a theme too familiar to my hearers for me to dilate on, and I shall therefore pass it by. But by what road we reached our position, under what form of government our greatness grew, out of what national habits it sprang – these are subjects which I may pursue before I proceed to my panegyric upon these men; for I think them to be themes upon which on the present occasion a speaker may properly dwell, and to which the whole assemblage, whether citizens or foreigners, may listen with advantage.

[2.37] Our constitution does not copy the laws of neighbouring states; we are rather a pattern to others than imitators ourselves. Its administration favours the many instead of the few; this is why it is called a democracy. However, if we look to the laws, they afford equal justice to all in their private differences; if to social standing, advancement in public life falls to reputation for capacity, class considerations not being allowed to interfere with merit (*arete*); nor again does poverty bar the way: if a man is able to serve the state, he is not hindered by the obscurity of his condition. (2) The freedom which we enjoy in our government extends also to our ordinary life. There, far from exercising a jealous surveillance over each other, we do not feel called upon to be angry with our neighbor for doing what he likes, or even to indulge in those injurious looks which cannot fail to be offensive, although they inflict no positive penalty. (3) But all this ease in our private relations does not make us lawless as citizens. Against this, fear is our chief safeguard, teaching us to obey the magistrates and the laws, particularly such as regard the protection of the injured, whether they are actually on the statute book, or belong to that code which, although unwritten, yet cannot be broken without acknowledged disgrace.[15]

[2.38] Further, we provide plenty of means for the mind to refresh itself from business. We celebrate games and sacrifices all the year round, and the elegance of our private establishments forms a daily source of pleasure and helps to banish our cares; (2) and the magnitude of our city draws the produce of the world into our harbour, so that to the Athenian the fruits of other countries are as familiar a luxury as those of his own.

[2.39] If we turn to our military policy, there also we differ from our antagonists. We throw open our city to the world, and never by special laws exclude foreigners from any opportunity of learning and observing, although the eyes of an enemy may occasionally profit by our liberality; we trust less in system and policy than in the native spirit of our citizens; and in education, where our rivals from their very cradles by a painful discipline seek after manliness, at Athens we live exactly as we please, and yet are just as ready to encounter every legitimate danger. (2) In proof of this it may be noticed that the Lacedaemonians do not invade our country alone, but bring with them all their confederates, while we Athenians advance unsupported into the territory of a neighbour, and fighting upon foreign soil usually vanquish with ease men who are defending their homes. (3) Our united force was never yet encountered by any enemy, because we have at once to attend to our naval affairs and to dispatch our citizens by land upon a hundred different services; thus wherever they engage with some such fraction of our strength, a success against a detachment is magnified into a victory over the nation, and a defeat into a reverse suffered at the hands of our entire people. (4) And yet if with the habits not of labour but of ease, and by dint of manly habits as much as by law, we are still willing to encounter danger, we have the double advantage of escaping the experience of hardships in anticipation and of facing them in the hour of need as fearlessly as those who are never free from them.

Nor are these the only points in which our city is worthy of admiration. [2.40] We cultivate refinement without extravagance and knowledge without effeminacy; wealth we employ more for use than for show, and place the real disgrace of poverty not in owning to the fact but in declining to struggle against it. (2) Our public men have, besides politics, their private affairs to attend to, and our ordinary citizens, though occupied in their own work, are still fair judges of public matters; for, unlike any other nation, regarding him who takes no part in these duties not as unambitious but as useless, we Athenians are able to judge at all events if we cannot originate, and instead of looking on discussion as a stumbling-block in the way of action, we think it an indispensable preliminary to any wise action at all. (3) Again, in our enterprises we present the singular spectacle of daring and deliberation, each carried to its highest point, and both united in the same persons, although usually decision is the fruit of ignorance, hesitation of reflection. But the palm of courage will surely be adjudged most justly to those who know best the difference between hardship and pleasure and yet are never tempted to shrink from danger. (4) In our excellence (*arete*) we are equally unique, acquiring our friends by conferring, not by receiving, favours. Yet, of course, the doer of the favour is the firmer friend of the two, in order by continued kindness to keep the recipient in his debt, while the debtor feels less keenly from the very consciousness that the return he makes will be a payment, not a free gift. (5) And it is only the Athenians who, fearless of consequences, confer their benefits less from calculations of expediency than in the confidence of liberality.

[2.41] In short, I say that as a city we are an education for Greece; and I doubt if the world can produce a man, who where he has only himself to depend upon, is equal to so many emergencies, and graced by so happy a versatility as the Athenian. (2) And that this is no mere boast thrown out for the occasion, but plain matter of fact, the power of the state acquired by these habits proves. (3) For Athens alone of her contemporaries is found when tested to be greater than her reputation, and alone gives no occasion to her assailants to blush at the antagonist by whom they have been worsted, or to her subjects to question her title by merit to rule. (4) Rather, the admiration of the present and succeeding ages will be ours, since we have not left our power without witness, but have shown it by mighty proofs; and far from needing a Homer for our panegyrist, or other of his craft whose verses might charm for the moment only for the impression which they gave to melt at the touch of fact, we have forced every sea and land to the highway of our daring, and everywhere, whether for evil or for good, have left imperishable monuments behind us. (5) Such is the Athens for which these men nobly fought and died; and well may every one of their survivors be ready to suffer in her cause.

[2.42] Indeed, if I have dwelt at some length upon the character of our country, it has been to show that our stake in the struggle is not the same as theirs who have no such blessings to lose, and also that the panegyric of the men over whom I am now speaking might be by definite proofs established. (2) That panegyric is now in a great measure complete; for the Athens that I have celebrated is only what the heroism (*aretai*) of these and their like have made her, men whose fame, unlike that of most Hellenes, will be found to be only commensurate with their deserts. And if a test of worth be wanted, it is to be found in their closing scene, and this not only in the cases in which it set the final seal upon their merit (*arete*), but also in those in which it gave the first intimation of their having any. (3) For there is justice in the claim that steadfastness in his country's battles should be as a cloak to cover a man's other imperfections; for the good action has blotted out the bad, and his merit as a citizen more than outweighed his demerits as an individual. (4) But none of these allowed either wealth with its prospect of future enjoyment to unnerve his spirit, or poverty with its hope of a day of freedom and riches to tempt him to shrink from danger. No, holding that vengeance upon their enemies was more to be desired than any personal blessings, and reckoning this to be the most glorious of hazards, they joyfully determined to accept the risk, and to make sure of their vengeance and to let their wishes wait; and while committing to hope the uncertainty of final success, in the business before them they thought fit to act boldly and trust in themselves. Thus choosing to die resisting, rather than to live submitting, they fled only from dishonour, but met danger face to face, and after one brief moment, while at the summit of their fortune, escaped not from their fear, but from their glory.

[2.43] So died these men as became Athenians. You, their survivors, must determine to have as unfaltering a resolution in the field, though you may pray that it may have a happier result. And not contented with ideas derived only from words of the advantages which are bound up with the defense of your country, though these would furnish a valuable text to a speaker even before an audience so alive to them as the present, you must yourselves realize the power of Athens, and feed your eyes upon her from day to day, till love of her fills your hearts; and then when all her greatness shall break upon you, you must reflect that it was by courage, sense of duty, and a keen feeling of honour in action that men were enabled to win all this, and that no personal failure in an enterprise could make them consent to deprive their country of their valour (*arete*), but they laid it at her feet as the most glorious contribution that they could offer. (2) For this offering of their lives made in common by them all they each of them individually received the praise which never grows old (*ageron epainon*), and for a sepulcher, not so much that in which their bones have been deposited, but that noblest of shrines wherein their glory is laid up to be eternally remembered upon every occasion on which deed or story shall call for its commemoration. (3) For heroes have the whole earth as their tomb; and in lands far from their own, where the public marker with its epitaph declares it, there is enshrined in every breast a record unwritten with no tablet to preserve it, except that of the heart. (4) These take as your model, and judging happiness to be the fruit of freedom and freedom of valour, never decline the dangers of war. (5) For it is not the miserable that would most justly be unsparing of their lives; these have nothing to hope for; it is rather they to whom continued life may bring reverses as yet unknown, and to whom a fall, if it came, would be most tremendous in its consequences. (6) And surely, to a man of spirit, the degradation of cowardice must be immeasurably more grievous than the unfelt death which strikes him in the midst of his strength and patriotism.

[2.44] Comfort, therefore, not condolence, is what I have to offer to the parents of the dead who may be here. Numberless are the chances to which, as they know, the life of man is subject; but fortunate indeed are they who draw for their lot a death so glorious as that which has caused your mourning, and to whom life has been so exactly measured as to terminate in the happiness in which it has been passed. (2) Still I know that this is a hard saying, especially when those are in question of whom you will constantly be reminded by seeing in the homes of others blessings of which once you also boasted: for grief is felt not so much for the want of what we have never known, as for the loss of that to which we have been long accustomed. (3) Yet you who are still of an age to beget children must bear up in the hope of having others in their stead; not only will they help you to forget those whom you have lost, but will be to the state at once a reinforcement and a security; for never can a fair or just policy be expected of the citizen who does not, like his fellows, bring to the decision the interests and apprehensions of a father. (4) And those of you who have passed your prime must congratulate yourselves with the thought that the best part of your life was fortunate, and that the brief span that remains will be cheered by the fame of the departed. For it is only the love of honour (*philotimon*) that never grows old; and honour it is, not gain, as some would have it, that rejoices the heart of age and helplessness.

[2.45] Turning to the sons or brothers of the dead, I see an arduous struggle before you. When a man is gone, all are wont to praise him, and should your merit (*arete*) be ever so transcendent, you will still find it difficult not merely to overtake, but even to approach their renown. The living have envy to contend with, while those who are no longer in our path are honoured with a goodwill into which rivalry does not enter. (2) On the other hand, if I must say something on the subject of female excellence (*arete*) to those of you who will now be in widowhood, it will be all comprised in this brief exhortation. Great will be your glory in not falling short of your natural character; and greatest will be hers who is least talked about among the men whether for good (*arete*) or for bad.[16]

[46] My task is now finished. I have performed it to the best of my ability, and in words, at least, the requirements of the law are now satisfied. If deeds be in question, those who are here interred have received part of

their honours already, and for the rest, their children will be brought up till manhood at the public expense; the state thus offers a valuable prize as the garland of victory in this race of valour, for the reward both of those who have fallen and their survivors. And where the rewards for merit (*arete*) are greatest, there are found the best citizens.

(2) And now that you have brought to a close your lamentations for your relatives, you may depart.

It would be interesting to know how many readers, confronting this speech for the first time, find it as attractive as have most modern historians. As noted, many scholars hold that this speech reflects Thucydides' own, idealized view of Athens or Pericles, but I believe this view is demonstrably mistaken: first, because Thucydides' work actually undermines many supposed Athenian ideals expressed in the Funeral Oration (and thus many of the views in it are unlikely to be Thucydides' own) and second because the picture of Pericles that emerges from the speech on a careful reading is hardly idealized.[17] In other words, to the extent that the speech presents an "idealized" picture, it is an idealization of Athens *by* Pericles rather than an idealization *of* Pericles (or of Athens) by Thucydides – and it is an idealization that contains numerous problematic or inaccurate features and that emphasizes certain uncomfortable facts about Athens and Pericles.[18]

We should also note that some scholars have recently argued that the speech fits its historical context admirably and is quite likely to reflect ideas and perhaps even some of the language Pericles actually employed on the occasion. A. B. Bosworth has stressed the large number of people that heard this address and the emphasis on the size of the audience in Thucydides' account. For this and for other reasons, Bosworth believes the speech as we have it contains a good deal of Periclean material.[19] I would only emphasize again that I do not treat the speech in Thucydides as anything like a verbatim account of Pericles' actual address, but rather approach it as the report of an interested and intelligent observer, who expressed his intentions to present speeches that did not do violence to the themes of the actual speeches given. We can and should, I believe, treat many of the fundamental ideas of this speech as Periclean, especially those that appear in his other speeches in Thucydides and that comport with our knowledge of Athens' – and Pericles' – history.[20]

In this oration Pericles argues that the highest form of *arete* (human excellence) consists of service to the state. Indeed, such service should shield a man from the criticism his personal failures would normally elicit (2.42).

Athens and its power should be the objects of passionate longing on the part of the citizens, who must fill their eyes and hearts with a love of the city that reflects that of suitors (*erastai*) for their would-be lovers (2.43.1). Athens' future reputation will not rest on the words of any Homer or other poet but rather on the actual deeds – good and bad – done by the Athenians all over the Greek world (2.41.1). In essence, Pericles suggests that the Athenians have become their own bards, composing a kind of self-praise through action that can never be destroyed or undermined as can the words of a poet.[21] This is a theme to which Pericles will return in even more explicit language in his last speech in Thucydides, again calling to mind the Homeric vision of *kleos* (fame that encompasses the future's memory of the past) and placing Athens clearly in the position of Achilles: like Achilles in Homer, the Athenians must choose glory in the future, even if it means a short life (or short-lived empire) now.[22]

These parts of the Funeral Oration draw significantly less attention than Pericles' account of the Athenians' democracy and open society. Yet those more famous passages contain a defensive statement of democracy's qualities: Pericles asserts that, despite the fact that the regime is democratic and thus geared toward the many rather than the few, equal justice and a respect for the advancement of merit prevail (2.37.1).[23] It is clear that Pericles expects the word *demokratia* to provoke a negative reaction in at least part of his audience; the term therefore needs a defense. Moreover, Pericles' praise of Athenian freedom rings somewhat hollow, since Athenian practice actually fell far short of the ideal he outlines (see later discussion). Indeed, it is the nationalistic and belligerent parts of the speech that tie it most clearly to the Athenians' actual qualities, a conclusion confirmed by Pericles' foreign policy and Athenian actions in the mid-fifth century and underscored by the other two speeches presented by the statesman in Thucydides.[24]

The Funeral Oration also connects the more practical concerns of Pericles' first speech in Thucydides (and the speech summarized in 2.13) to the outright statement of his abstract, nationalist vision in the last speech. Pericles in the Funeral Oration uses the moment of discussing Athenian soldiers' sacrifice to begin to lay out the principles that justify this sacrifice: domination over other Greeks, driven by the zeal to ensure that history remembers Athens' power above any other quality.

Although historians have often doubted that Pericles gave this speech in this precise form, they have just as often used Pericles'/Thucydides' words to characterize Athenian politics, culture, and history in the mid-fifth century.[25]

But even if we had a verbatim text of Pericles' oration over the Athenian war dead of 431, we could hardly treat such a speech as an accurate account of Athenian habits and institutions. The context of such a speech required that the statesman delivering it be alive to the political and social environment. No Athenian statesman standing before an audience consisting of the relatives of dead Athenians is likely to have given a speech that presented a historically accurate picture of Athens' society or government. The speech needed to justify the deaths of these Athenian men and Pericles chose to do this (according to Thucydides) not by focusing on alleged injustices committed by Athens' enemies (a subject strikingly not even addressed in the Funeral Oration) but rather by focusing on the putatively superior qualities of Athenians and Athens itself. The argument, in short, is that the Athenians' native superiority and customs compel the citizens to live up to the excellence of their city-state, to love it passionately, to sacrifice for it, and to die willingly for it. To do this ensures that their private failings will be overlooked and the future will look back on them as heroes – not so much as individuals, but as parts of a collective heroism and power embodied by Athens itself.

We must not be surprised, therefore, that Pericles paints a picture of an idealized Athenian society that hardly reflects reality. Athenians did not live however they liked ("we live exactly as we please"), free from the suspicion of their fellow citizens (2.37.2, 39.1), as Socrates and others who ran afoul of Athenian notions of piety or propriety and found themselves prosecuted or worse discovered.[26] The implied contrast with Sparta's more regimented lifestyle (Thuc. 2.38–40) was surely justified, but certainly overdrawn. Likewise, the Athenians' system of government hardly advanced individuals to leadership purely on the basis of merit, as Pericles claims (2.37.1). At the time Pericles gave this speech, so far as we can tell, the vast majority of Athenian political leaders stemmed from the wealthier, aristocratic families. As for the Athenians' attitudes toward wealth and luxury, Pericles' claims about the Athenians' restraint in this area (2.40.1) would hardly have been endorsed by any non-Athenian visiting the acropolis and seeing the monumental gold and ivory Athena (see Figure IX) ensconced in the hyper-ornamented and huge Parthenon. The building certainly impressed, but it hardly demonstrated Athens' restraint.

Pericles' claim that the Athenians "advance unsupported" (2.39.2) against their neighbors comes close to absurdity: while it may have been technically true that Athens' infantry consisted almost exclusively of Athenians, its fleet relied heavily on paid oarsmen from around Greece and on hundreds of talents of tribute paid every year by Athens' subjects.[27] In any case, to what military operations carried out by Athenians alone against any enemies like Sparta could Pericles point? In fact, we must note that the Greek here refers (strictly speaking) to Athens' neighbors (like Megara and perhaps Aegina or Euboea). Even Pericles does not claim that Athens advanced boldly and unsupported against Sparta.[28] Did Pericles really think the Athenians should take special pride in "usually" (!) being able to defeat neighbors such as the Megarians without the aid of their allies? In their last major military operation the Athenians had reduced the island of Samos with the help of the islands Chios and Lesbos. Beyond Megara, where had the Athenians in recent years advanced by themselves against a major enemy?[29] Pericles' argument that Athens' enemies had never met Athens' full (rather than divided) forces (2.39.2–3) applied just as well to the Peloponnesians, who typically marched out with some fraction of their total military force (e.g., two-thirds of the forces available in 431: Thuc. 2.10.2). In short, Pericles' distinction between the Spartans attacking Attica with "all their confederates" (2.39.2) and the Athenians' supposed practice of never fighting an enemy with their total forces is simply specious (if inspiring) rhetoric.

The irony of historians treating Pericles' Funeral Oration as a kind of encapsulation of actual Athenian history, society, democracy, or values in the mid-fifth century could hardly be deeper. The speech instead provides us with Thucydides' account of the kinds of things Pericles would have said in this highly charged and politically sensitive situation. It reflects the historian's view of Pericles as a speaker, thinker, and leader and the statesman's sensitivity to the political and historical context provided by a funeral oration over the war dead before an Athenian audience inclined to hear praise of themselves and of their professed values and to hear a justification of their sacrifices. To be sure, the speech can tell us much about what Thucydides wished us to conclude that Pericles and the Athenians believed or wished to believe, but that is a far cry from presenting us with anything like an accurate picture of Athens or Athenian life in 431. In short, if I may be blunt, the speech is likely to tell us far more about Thucydides and Pericles as thinkers and about the Athenians' self-image than about the function and structure of Athens as a society and political entity. And one thing the speech clearly tells us is that Pericles could and did play on the Athenians' self-image in his effort to encourage Athens to continue the war.

Thucydides' famously follows Pericles' somewhat grimly optimistic Funeral Oration[30] with his account of the plague that broke out in Athens during the spring of 430. No evidence suggests that Thucydides fudged the chronological order of these events to make a philosophical or literary statement, but he almost certainly juxtaposed them as closely as possible in the text in order to provide the reader with the same kind of jarring experience the Athenians themselves confronted after the first year of the war.[31] The situation in Athens changed drastically once the highly infectious and deadly (but still unidentified) plague began to spread through the city.[32]

Thucydides contracted the disease himself, and he provides a careful description of its physical horrors (extreme fever, open sores, dementia, loss of extremities or eyes, and usually death) and psychological impact: the worst thing about the plague, according to the historian (2.51), was that those who contracted it knew that they would almost certainly die. The Athenians heaped the bodies of the dead around the city as the corpses collected too fast for traditional disposal. Thucydides' vivid description of the scene has struck many readers as one of the most moving and pathetic in the entire history.

The plague struck virtually every family in Athens, including Pericles'. The statesman apparently lost his two older sons (by his first wife), Xanthippus and Paralus, to the horrible disease.[33] They were both grown men who probably had children of their own.[34] Pericles therefore saw the war he had encouraged and the plague that the war aggravated exact an incredible price. According to Plutarch, the famously reserved statesman maintained his equanimity until he finally broke down in tears at the death of his second son, a very rare expression of emotion in Pericles' life. Meanwhile, the war moved into its second year with another Spartan invasion of Attica and Athenian raids on the Peloponnese.[35] Forced once more into the now plague-infested city and seeing their farms ravaged again, many Athenians apparently began to complain that the war had become too costly and that Pericles' strategy of withdrawing inside the walls was unworkable. The comic poet Hermippus mocked Pericles and accused him (in sexually charged terms) of talking a big game about war but refusing to fight:

> Satyr King, how come you never
> wish to draw your sword, but brave
> words you brandish on the war?
> Yours is the spirit of a draft dodger.[36]

At one point during this period Pericles' influence declined to such a level that he was unable to prevent the Athenians from sending embassies to

Sparta seeking peace.[37] We know nothing about these diplomatic efforts: what, for example, did the Athenians offer the Spartans? We can only say that they were unsuccessful, surely in part because the Spartans now saw an Athens so weakened by the plague that they believed that a Peloponnesian victory in the war was virtually assured and that the Athenians deserved their sufferings.[38] Indeed, the plague had broken out even in Athens' forces besieging Poteidaia. It must have seemed in mid-430 that Athens could not hold out much longer in its war with Sparta.

In these adverse circumstances Pericles delivered the speech that represents the last such address recounted for us by Thucydides (2.60–64). The oration is striking in particular because of its aggressive and belligerent tone: Pericles makes virtually no effort to assuage the angry feelings of an Athenian populace that now faced a war and a plague. Perhaps even more striking is the thoroughly nationalistic and abstract message of the speech. The practical considerations that dominated his first address in Thucydides and the justifications for the Athenians' sacrifices on cultural grounds that figured in the Funeral Oration have both given way to a bald statement about power and the future's recognition of Athens' military greatness. The speech deserves to be read in full.[39]

> [2.60] I was not unprepared for the indignation of which I have been the object, as I know its causes; and I have called an assembly for the purpose of reminding you upon certain points, and of protesting against your being unreasonably irritated with me, or cowed by your sufferings. (2) I am of the opinion that national greatness is more for the advantage of private citizens, than any individual well-being coupled with public humiliation. (3) A man may be personally ever so well off, and yet if his country be ruined he must be ruined with it; whereas a flourishing commonwealth always affords chances of salvation to unfortunate individuals. (4) Since then a state can support the misfortunes of private citizens, while they cannot support hers, it is surely the duty of everyone to be forward in her defense, and not like you to be so confounded with your domestic afflictions as to give up all thoughts of the common safety, and to blame me for having counseled war and yourselves for having voted it. (5) And yet if you are angry with me, it is with one who, as I believe, is second to no man either in knowledge of the proper policy, or in the ability to expound it, and who is moreover not only a patriot but one who cannot be bribed. (6) A man possessing that knowledge without that faculty of exposition might as well have no idea at all on the matter: if he had both these gifts, but no love for his country, he would be but a cold advocate for her interests; and were his patriotism not proof against bribery, everything would go for a price. (7) So if you thought that I was even moderately distinguished for these qualities

when you took my advice and went to war, there is certainly no reason now why I should be charged with having done wrong.

[2.61] For those of course who have a free choice in the matter and whose fortunes are not at stake, war is the greatest of follies. But if the only choice was between submission with loss of independence,[40] and danger with the hope of preserving that independence – in such a case it is he who will not accept the risk that deserves blame, not he who will. (2) I am the same man and do not alter; it is you who change, since in fact you took my advice while unhurt, and waited for misfortune to repent of it; and the apparent error of my policy lies in the infirmity of your resolution, since the suffering that it entails is being felt by everyone among you, while its advantage is still remote and obscure to all, and a great and sudden reverse having befallen you, your minds are too much depressed to persevere in your resolves. (3) For what is sudden, unexpected, and least within calculation enslaves the spirit; and putting all else aside, the plague has certainly been an emergency of this kind. (4) Born, however, as you are, citizens of a great state, and brought up, as you have been, with habits equal to your birth, you should be ready to face the greatest disasters and still keep unimpaired the lustre of your name. For the judgement of mankind is as relentless to the weakness that falls short of a recognized renown, as it is jealous of the arrogance that aspires higher than its due. Cease then to grieve for your private afflictions, and address yourselves instead to the safety of the commonwealth.

[2.62] If you shrink before the exertions which the war makes necessary, and fear that after all they may not have a happy result, you know the reasons by which I have often demonstrated to you the groundlessness of your apprehension. If those are not enough, I will now reveal an advantage arising from the greatness of your dominion, which I think has never yet suggested itself to you, which I never mentioned in my previous speeches, and which has so bold a sound that I should scarce venture it now, were it not for the unnatural depression which I see around me. (2) You perhaps think that your empire extends only over your allies; I will declare to you the truth. The visible field of action has two parts, land and sea. In the whole of one of these you are completely supreme, not merely as far as you use it at present, but also to what further extent you may think fit: in fine, your naval resources are such that your vessels may go where they please, without the king [of Persia] or any other nation on earth being able to stop them.[41] (3) So that although you may think it a great privation to lose the use of your land and houses, still you must see that this power is something widely different; and instead of fretting on their account, you should really regard them in the light of the gardens and other accessories that embellish a great fortune, and as, in comparison, of little moment. You should know too that liberty preserved by your efforts will easily recover for us what we have lost, while, the knee once bowed, even what you have will pass from you. Your fathers, receiving these possessions not from others, but from themselves, did not let slip what their labor had acquired, but delivered them safe to you; and in this respect at least you must prove yourselves their equals, remembering that to lose what one has got is more disgraceful than to be balked in getting, and you must confront your enemies not merely with spirit but with disdain. (4) Confidence, indeed, a blissful ignorance can impart, even to a coward's breast, but disdain is the privilege of those who, like us, have been assured by reflection of their superiority to their adversary. (5) And where the chances are the same, knowledge fortifies courage by the contempt which is its consequence, its trust being placed, not in hope, which is the prop of the desperate, but in a judgment grounded upon existing resources, whose anticipations are more to be depended upon.

[2.63] Again, your country has a right to your services in sustaining the glories of her position. These are a common source of pride to you all, and you cannot decline the burdens of empire and still expect to share its honours (*timai*). You should remember also that what you are fighting against is not merely slavery (*douleia*) as an exchange for independence, but also loss of your empire and danger from the animosities incurred in its exercise. (2) Besides, to recede is no longer possible, if indeed any of you in the alarm of the moment has become enamoured of the honesty of such an unambitious part. For what you hold, is, to speak somewhat plainly, a tyranny; to take it perhaps was wrong, but to let it go is unsafe. (3) And men of these retiring views, making converts of others, would quickly ruin a state; indeed, the result would be the same if they could live independent by themselves; for the retiring and unambitious are never secure without vigorous protectors at their side; in fine, such qualities are useless to an imperial city, though they may help a subject state to play the part of a slave in safety.

[2.64] But you must not be seduced by citizens like these nor be angry with me – who, if I voted for the war, did only as you did yourselves – in spite of the enemy having invaded your country and done what you could be certain that he would do if you refused to comply with his demands, and although besides what we counted for, the plague has come upon us – the only point indeed at which our calculation has been at fault. It is this, I know, that has a large share in making me more unpopular than I should otherwise have been – quite undeservedly, unless you are also prepared to give me the credit of any success with which chance may present you. (2) But divine matters must be born with resignation, that of the enemy with fortitude; this was the old way at Athens, and do not you prevent it being so still. (3) Remember, too, that if your country has the greatest name in all the world, it is because she never bent before disaster, and because she has expended more lives and effort in war than any other city, and has won for herself a power greater than any hitherto known, the memory of which will descend to the latest posterity; even if now, in obedience to the general law of decay, we should ever be forced to yield, still it will be remembered that we held rule over more Hellenes than any other Hellenic state, that we sustained the greatest wars against their united or separate powers, and inhabited a city unrivalled by any other resources or magnitude. (4) These glories may incur the censure of the slow and unambitious; but in the breast of energy they will awake emulation, and in those who must remain without them an envious regret. (5) Hatred and unpopularity at the moment have fallen to the lot of all who have aspired to rule others; but where odium must be incurred, true wisdom incurs it for the highest objects. Hatred also is short-lived; but that which makes the splendor (*lamprotes*) of the present and the glory of the future remains forever unforgotten (*doxa aieimnestos*). (6) Make your decision, therefore, for glory then and honour now, and attain both objects by instant and zealous effort: do not send heralds to Lacedaemon, and do not betray any sign of being oppressed by your present sufferings, since they whose minds are least sensitive to calamity, and whose hands are most quick to meet it, are the greatest men and the greatest communities.

Thucydides followed his account of this speech with a kind of epitaph summarizing and explaining Pericles' career (2.65). In that passage he notes that Pericles never attempted to gain power by improper means and that he spoke frankly to the crowd instead of simply telling them what they wanted to hear. Indeed, no speech in Thucydides' history has less of the demagogue in it than this last speech of Pericles. The statesman upbraids the Athenians for changing their minds and (in essence) failing to see that he is both steadier and more knowledgeable than they are (2.60.5). Pericles tells the Athenians – who were suffering from the effects of a war and a plague – to stop complaining and focus on what they can do to help Athens (2.61.4). He assures his fellow citizens that Athens will be remembered, not for its art, literature, or culture, but rather for the power it exercised. Moreover, the Athenians should recognize that the empire will in all likelihood eventually pass away, but the future will know that they "held rule over more Greeks than any other Greek state" and that they were more ready to die to acquire power than other Greeks were (2.64.3). As if this abstract contemplation of Athens' downfall was not enough, Pericles goes on to emphasize that the best kind of people admire striving after power for its own sake, and it is the admiration of those individuals that Athens' current actions will ensure (2.64.4–6).

As we have noted, some scholars have recently begun to admit that the image of Pericles presented in some or all of the speeches in Thucydides, and especially in his last speech, is neither idealized nor representative of Thucydides' own views.[42] Indeed, taking Thucydides' work as a whole, it seems relatively clear that he could not have found Pericles' policy toward

Sparta or Periclean democracy "ideal." Thucydides preferred a more conservative form of government to radicalized democracy, saw Athenian imperialism as an understandable but lamentable force, and conceived of the war between Sparta and Athens as the kind of human tragedy that so dominated Greek history (recent and distant).[43] Such a war was tragic because men act in accordance with their acquisitive natures and all too often find themselves confronted with circumstances they cannot control. Man is morally responsible for his actions, but a rational analysis shows that, although human beings may display more noble sentiments during peace, "by taking away the daily necessities of life war acts as a violent teacher, and reduces most men's passions to the level of their circumstances" (3.82.2).[44] As A. W. Gomme said of this passage, the historian "appears here to be expressly dissociating himself from the cynical doctrine of force which he puts so often in the mouths of others."[45]

Thucydides did not endorse Pericles' abstract nationalism[46] – which contemplated a future admiration of Athenian superiority (even after Athens' downfall) on the basis of the fact that Athens had ruled more Greeks than other Hellenic states (2.64.3) – or the statesman's views that a man's service to the state defined his excellence, any more than the historian endorsed the Athenians' claim that "might makes right" during the famous Melian Dialogue. In that exchange with the small state (Melos) they were about to subjugate, the Athenians expand on the view that they had already expressed in book 1 of Thucydides' history: "About gods we believe and about men we know that by a law of their nature they use their power wherever they are able to do so" (5.105.2). Indeed, in his own voice, Thucydides expressly laments the plight of moderates in the midst of civil war, the sad fact that men are more likely to praise clever wickedness than honest simplicity, and the self-imposed doom of those who toss aside traditional protections offered by custom and law when they are empowered, only to find those protections absent when they themselves are weakened and in need (3.82–84). In this passage Thucydides confirms that men are indeed the naturally acquisitive and power-seeking creatures the Athenians describe in their public speech before the Spartans (1.73–78) and in their private address to the Melians (5.85–111). Thucydides, in essence, seeks to show us how man really *is*, but he does not argue that man *should* be this way, and in fact he illustrates the tragic aspect of the human condition as played out in war.

Pericles' abstract nationalism and belligerence in his speeches therefore hardly seem likely to have drawn Thucydides' approval, much less his idealization.[47] The Pericles who confronts us in Thucydides therefore does not act as a mouthpiece for the historian. Nor does Thucydides expect the reader to admire everything about the statesman. Additional support for this conclusion may be found in the epitaph Thucydides provides for Pericles immediately after the account of his last speech. This passage (2.65) arguably represents the single most important piece of evidence about Pericles' character and career, and stands as one of those rare places where Thucydides explicitly provides us with his personal views and analysis. Again, the passage deserves quotation in full.

[2.65] Such were the arguments by which Pericles tried to cure the Athenians of their anger against him and to divert their thoughts from their immediate afflictions. (2) As a community he succeeded in convincing them; they not only gave up all idea of sending to Lacedaemon, but applied themselves with increased energy to the war; still as private individuals they could not help smarting under their sufferings, the common people having been deprived of the little that they ever possessed, while the higher orders had lost fine properties with costly establishments and buildings in the country, and, worst of all, had war instead of peace. (3) In fact, the public feeling against him did not subside until he had been fined. (4) Not long afterwards, however, according to the way of the crowd, they again elected him general and committed all their affairs to his hands, having now become less sensitive to their private and domestic afflictions, and understanding that he was the best man of all for the public necessities. (5) For as long as he was at the head of the state during the peace, he led moderately and safely guarded the city; and in his time its greatness was at its height. When the war broke out, here also he seems to have rightly gauged the power of his country. (6) He outlived its commencement two years and six months, and the correctness of his previsions respecting it became better known by his death. (7) He told them to wait quietly, to pay attention to their sea power, to attempt no new conquests, and to expose the city to no hazards during the war, and doing this, promised them a favourable result.[48] What they did was the very contrary, allowing private ambitions and private interests, in matters apparently quite foreign to the war, to lead them into projects unjust both to themselves and to their allies – projects whose success would only conduce to the honour and advantage of private persons, and whose failure entailed certain disaster on the country in the war. (8) The causes of this are not far to seek. Pericles, indeed, by his rank, ability, and known integrity, was enabled to exercise an independent control over the multitude – in short, to lead them more than being led by them; for as he never sought power by improper means, he was never compelled to flatter them, but, on the contrary, enjoyed so high an estimation that he could afford to anger them by contradiction. (9) Whenever he saw them unseasonably and insolently elated, he would with a word reduce them to alarm; on the other hand, if they fell victims to a panic, he could at once restore them to confidence.[49] In short, what was in name a democracy became in his hands rule by the first citizen.

(10) With his successors it was different. More on a level with one another, and each grasping at supremacy, they ended by committing even the conduct of state affairs to the whims of the people. (11) This, as might have been expected in a great and sovereign state, produced a host of blunders, and amongst them the Sicilian expedition, though this failed not so much through a miscalculation of the power of those against whom it was sent, as through a fault in the senders in not taking the best measures afterwards to assist those who had gone out, but choosing rather to occupy themselves with private cabals for the leadership of the commons, by which they not only paralysed operations in the field, but also first introduced civil discord at home. (12) Yet after losing most of their fleet besides other forces in Sicily, and with faction already dominant in the city, they could still for three years make head against their original adversaries, joined not only by the Sicilians, but also by their own allies nearly all in revolt, and at last by the [Persian] king's son, Cyrus, who furnished the funds for the Peloponnesian navy. Nor did they finally succumb till they fell the victims of their own intestine disorders. (13) So superfluously abundant were the resources from which the genius of Pericles foresaw a very easy success in the war over the unaided forces of the Peloponnesians.

Scholars have long noticed certain problems this passage presents. Thucydides' reasons for the failure of the Athenian invasion of Sicily given here (2.65.11) differ from his own extensive account in books 6 and 7 of his history.[50] Perhaps more disturbing, his view that Athens would have very easily won the war with Sparta had the Athenians merely followed Pericles' strategy (2.65.13) seems overly optimistic if not downright absurd.[51] How could Athens have easily won (or even easily survived) any war in which the enemy annually ravaged the citizens' lands? Moreover, few historians have noticed that Thucydides' description of Pericles' foreign policy in this passage (as moderate and designed to keep the city safe: 2.65.5) contradicts the historian's presentation of events leading up to the outbreak of the war.[52] In his own account, Thucydides shows Pericles "always urging" the Athenians to war with Sparta and advocating a policy of "no concessions," not to mention contemplating the eventual collapse of their empire.[53] How could Thucydides call this policy moderate and safe?[54]

The answer to this question lies in the manner in which Thucydides put his (unfinished) history together.[55] Although the historian's text breaks off abruptly in the middle of his account of 411, his description of Pericles' career in 2.65 contains references to the end of the Peloponnesian War and thus was necessarily written or revised after 404 BC, when Athens had lost the war and lost its empire.[56] By that time Thucydides had seen leaders after Pericles (like Cleon and Alcibiades) whose policies actually made Pericles' actions look relatively moderate and safe in retrospect.[57] Pericles had advocated fighting "one war at a time" and not attempting to expand Athens' empire while the war with Sparta continued (1.144.1). After his death, the Athenians did "the very contrary" (as Thucydides somewhat exaggerates: 2.65.7) with expeditions to Sicily (in 427 as well as 415) and other adventures that violated Pericles' strategic vision of wearing the Spartans out through attrition. Pericles, perhaps Thucydides thought, might have accepted the Spartans' offer of peace in 425/4 that Cleon encouraged the Athenians to reject despite the fact that it would have placed Athens in an admirable and arguably superior position (retaining its gains against Peloponnesian interests and with Sparta as a grateful ally rather than an enemy).[58] In short, looking back on Pericles from the standpoint of Athens' fall in 404, Thucydides found himself admiring a type of restraint and foresight all too rare in the Athenian leaders who followed Pericles.

We may also note that Pericles' apparent policy of "one war at a time" could look moderate when compared with the Athenians' aggressive stance in the 450s, when they took on both Sparta and its allies as well as the Persian-backed forces in Egypt. Pericles may have advocated avoiding opening a major war on two fronts from the mid-440s on.[59] It certainly seems he had come to that view by the 430s. Yet because of Athens' earlier aggression and because of the Athenians' later war with both the Sicilians and the Spartans, even Pericles' enthusiasm in 432/1 for a war with Sparta (by itself) could appear moderate in retrospect.[60]

Thucydides provides "epitaphs" of a sort for four individuals in his history: Themistocles, Pericles, Nikias, and Antiphon.[61] In each of these cases Thucydides stops his narrative in order to tell us something about the man in question in close connection with the report of his death. In every case the historian paints a positive picture in this epitaph and in every case he has just recounted or is about to recount events that could naturally lead the reader to draw a negative conclusion about the individual in question. Themistocles had defected to the Persians and died as a Persian retainer, yet Thucydides praises him for his intelligence and ability to improvise solutions to any problem. Nikias took decisions that led to utter disaster and the deaths of thousands of Athenians in Sicily, yet Thucydides calls him "the man of all

Greeks in my day who least deserved such a fate, because he had directed his entire life toward what men call excellence (*arete*)." Antiphon served as the brains behind the oligarchic revolution that overthrew Athens' democratic government in 411, but Thucydides praises him for his intelligence and *arete* and says that he gave the best defense speech ever given in Athens.[62]

What of Pericles' epitaph? Although disproportionately long, I believe it performs the same function as other such passages in Thucydides' text. It is placed at 2.65, just after Pericles' last speech in the history and well before his actual death chronologically – which occurred the year after the speech was delivered, but which Thucydides nonetheless chooses to mention here – precisely because Thucydides wishes to counteract the effect of what the reader has just read. Just as with Themistocles, Nikias, and Antiphon, Thucydides understands that his history had painted a less than positive picture of this individual, and the historian wants to correct the impression his own account left and remind the reader of the excellent qualities of this man.[63] In short, the character and placement of this epitaph tell us that Thucydides did not expect his readers to admire unreservedly the last speech of Pericles (and that the historian did not use that speech to express his own views). Rather, Thucydides understood that the reader's natural reaction to this speech would have been at best ambivalent and at worst critical. This hyper-nationalist and belligerent oration paints the picture of a man willing to risk the defeat and destruction of his homeland on the chance that Athens might succeed and thereby earn the admiration of would-be imperialists throughout history. This was a statesman who openly admitted that Athens' empire was a virtual tyranny, which it may have been unjust to take but was now unsafe to release.[64] Justice, indeed, was not the issue. Even *arete* as Pericles had redefined it in the Funeral Oration – as service to the state – takes a backseat in his final speech. Power and the splendor (*lamprotes*)[65] that power would earn Athens in the present and in the future justified whatever actions the Athenians saw fit to take in their service.[66]

After this speech, therefore, Thucydides pauses to remind the reader that this Pericles was much more than a belligerent nationalist, and he expressly asks the reader to remember the context.[67] The historian reminds us that those who came after Pericles lacked both his foresight and his political integrity: whatever one might think about Pericles' policies, he could not be bought, and he did not simply play the demagogue and tell the Athenians what they wanted to hear. In fact, Thucydides holds, Pericles' military policy would actually have succeeded had the Athenians continued to follow his advice. As with his other epitaphs, Thucydides provides us with a positive summary that attempts to adjust the negative impression created by his own narrative.

Did the historian go too far in his attempt to show the other, positive side of Pericles? The answer to this question is arguably in the affirmative. Thucydides so rarely gives us personal opinions that when he does so historians understandably tend to allow them a disproportionate weight in their analysis.[68] In the case of Pericles, Thucydides' praise in 2.65 encouraged theories that Thucydides wrote the first part of his history as a defense of Pericles or that he had been a young admirer of Pericles who never changed his youthful view of the statesman.[69] Such views take their leave both from the extended praise of the statesman in 2.65 and from the misguided opinion that the Funeral Oration expresses Thucydides' own views or views that Thucydides especially admired and shared.

Should Thucydides' extremely positive analysis of Pericles in 2.65 lead us to treat the entire first two books of the history as an attempt to defend the statesman from the criticisms he received after the war's end and the empire's destruction in 404? I believe this conclusion is faulty, in large part because Thucydides' account in books 1 and 2 does not in fact defend Pericles or diminish in any way his or Athens' responsibility for the war. We have seen that the historian, in fact, underscores Pericles' personal responsibility for the conflict, and the speeches he gives the statesman repeatedly demonstrate his belligerence and nationalism. If Thucydides composed the first two books of his history in an effort to defend Pericles, then he arguably failed miserably.

I suggest instead that Thucydides composed his initial account of the events that occurred just before and early in the war, including Pericles' speeches, rather soon after those events. However, when he went back after 404 to revise his work, he realized his account of Pericles' actions in 432–430 provided ample evidence for anyone after 404 who wished to blame the war on Pericles. Thucydides thus composed (or revised) 2.65 to remind his readers that, once Pericles' actions are placed in context and he is compared with the demagogues and opportunists who succeeded him, the statesman's true virtues become apparent. This polemical and defensive nature of 2.65 strikes the reader immediately.[70] Nevertheless, despite writing or revising his epitaph and defense of the statesman, Thucydides did not allow himself to change his account of events in order to make Pericles seem more "moderate" or less responsible for the devastating war: instead, he argued in 2.65 that Pericles' strategy could have worked and that he had led Athens into war not because of personal ambition or private gain but because of honestly held convictions. Pericles' vision and political honesty separated him from those who followed, even if they seemed on the surface to advocate similar policies.[71]

We find ourselves confronted in current scholarship with a Thucydides who admires Pericles or one who seeks to demonstrate the deep flaws in his thinking. The truth is not in the middle: rather, both views are true. Thucydides' great admiration for Pericles developed in retrospect and in comparison with the demagogues who followed him. Far from a youthful admirer of Pericles, Thucydides only in his later years developed a deep appreciation for the popular leader based on his honesty and intelligence, while his unfinished text retains the historian's original view of Pericles' responsibility for a tragic war.[72]

Thucydides clearly recognized that his account of the war's outbreak and first years would leave the reader with the (accurate) impression that Pericles had urged Athens to war and done everything he could to prevent any diplomatic solution to the conflict. Pericles' actions and speeches in the history present us with the picture of a statesman driven by a desire for his homeland to achieve *lamprotes* and future fame: Pericles unabashedly claims that the Athenians' striving for power will leave behind them "imperishable monuments of bad actions and good" (*mnemeia kakon te kagathon aidia*: 2.41.4). Thucydides presents us, in short, with a Pericles who sees Athens as an Achillean figure, unwilling (until the very end, in Achilles' case) to compromise even when appealed to on the most human of terms and willing to live a short life in order to leave behind a glorious and perpetual memory.[73] This is precisely the formulation Pericles asks the Athenians to accept: even if their empire might be short, their fame will be perpetual (*doxa aieimnestos*: 2.64.5). And as Homer uses the last books of his *Iliad* to make Achilles a more human and sympathetic character, Thucydides reminds us in 2.65 that Pericles' good qualities stand in greater relief when we compare him to the kinds of leaders who followed him.

Pericles' speech in 430 did not satisfy the Athenians. Thucydides tells us that although they voted as Pericles wished and refused to make peace with Sparta, they fined the statesman. Many historians have concluded that the Athenians also temporarily removed Pericles from office in this year, as Plutarch maintains.[74] Thucydides only tells us that after they fined him they eventually elected him again (for the year 429/8) and "committed all their affairs to his hands."[75] It would seem, therefore, that in the last months of his life Pericles had reestablished himself as the political leader of Athens.

Pericles died in the fall of 429 BC, perhaps from complications brought on by the plague.[76] He was survived by his wife (or consort) Aspasia and their son, also called Pericles.[77] For her part, Aspasia married an aspiring demagogue (Lysicles) within six months of Pericles' death.[78] The marriage suggests that her relationship with Pericles had a political aspect and that at least one Athenian believed a relationship with the widow of Pericles could serve as an asset, despite the woman's questionable reputation and the sport made of her on the comic stage.[79]

When Pericles died, Athens had endured three campaigning seasons of the Peloponnesian War, which would eventually stretch to twenty-seven years. Although Thucydides praises Pericles' military foresight, Pericles' strategy of wearing Sparta out by forcing the Spartans into repeated offensives had not proved successful. Pericles had clearly believed that no more than a few years would be necessary for this policy to bring about Sparta's acquiescence to the status quo. The proof of this lies in the rate at which Athens spent the Athenians' war reserves in the first years of the war. By 428 the Athenians felt compelled to levy a property tax on themselves in order to finance continuing operations. Analysis has demonstrated that by that year they had already spent most of the 6,000 talents of coined money they had stored up before the war began.[80] Pericles' financial speech before the war, summarized by Thucydides (2.13), had been designed to encourage the Athenians by detailing this war chest and the 6,000 talents it contained, as well as the other resources the Athenians possessed. But four years of war drained even this massive reserve, and Pericles surely understood that the moneys Athens had on hand could not support the war efforts for more than a few years.

No statesman in the years after Pericles' death could hope to have encouraged the Athenians by summarizing their current financial condition (as Pericles had done in 431): facing the depletion of their war chest, the revolt of important allies like Mytilene on Lesbos (428/7), and now paying a healthy property tax, the Athenians after Pericles' death could not face the prospect of a continuing war with Sparta without expecting to feel the financial pinch in very real terms.

Pericles' successors, for all their faults in Thucydides' (and history's) eyes, did not enjoy the advantages of the full Athenian treasuries Pericles had known. If war were to continue, measures needed to be taken. Besides beginning to tax their own property in 428, in 425 the Athenians drastically raised the amount of tribute demanded from their subjects.[81] The fact that the Athenians agreed to tax themselves and increase the taxes on their allies to continue this war demonstrates that they had not undertaken this conflict simply for profit.[82] Pericles' attitudes about the need to cement Athens' place in history – to win power in the present and glory in the future – apparently continued to resonate after his death. The citizens therefore continued to show a willingness to make personal sacrifices to realize this vision of Athenian superiority, just as Pericles had urged.

Athens' leaders after Pericles would alter the statesman's vision by suggesting that the city could expand its empire at the same time as it was fighting Sparta. By 427 the Athenians had launched an expedition to Sicily, and they were soon after attempting major land operations in central and northern Greece.[83] Expansion of Athens' war aims led to a major success at Pylos in 425, when the Athenians captured 120 Spartiates and occupied a prime location in southwestern Peloponnese. Nevertheless, facing setbacks in virtually every other theater and a dangerously depleted treasury, the Athenians eventually came to terms with Sparta in 421.[84] Yet by 418 they had joined the Spartans' Argive enemies in a military adventure against Sparta in the Peloponnese itself.[85] And despite the resulting and devastating loss to the Spartans at Mantineia in that year, in 416 the Athenians voted to attack Sparta's ancient colony on the island of Melos and in 415 they determined to send a great armada against the city of Syracuse, Corinth's powerful (and democratic) colony in Sicily.[86] Athens in the years from 418 to 415 thus took aggressive actions that threatened to reopen full-scale hostilities with Sparta.

The Athenians by this time had, in short, doubled down on the Periclean vision of power and empire, but they had forgotten the statesman's message of restraint and taking on only one major enemy at a time: the Pericles of 431 would hardly have endorsed attacking powerful Syracuse in Sicily while taking on Sparta in mainland Hellas. True, the statesman had aggravated and amplified long-standing Athenian ambitions, tapping into Athens' ancient anxieties about its meager heroic and archaic accomplishments. He should, therefore, bear some responsibility for the Athenians' hyper-aggression after his death. Yet Pericles, as Thucydides emphasizes, was able to wield such a tool as the Athenians' collective psychology because he could both restrain and encourage the citizen body. Unlike him and like most democratic leaders throughout history, Pericles' successors rarely even attempted to restrain the populace, which they rather treated as an ineluctable force able to propel their careers by dint of its own will. One needed only to be willing to go wherever "the people" led instead of attempting to curb them in order to succeed. Such demagoguery, as Thucydides notes (and perhaps somewhat exaggerates), played a significant role in Athens' ultimate downfall.

We know only a little about the precise circumstances of Pericles' death or how he spent his final days. One anecdote suggests that as the end approached Pericles allowed those taking care of him to put an amulet designed to ward off illness around this neck, though he realized the absurdity of the action.[87] Plutarch tells us that not long before Pericles died he awoke to interrupt a discussion among his visitors about his greatest accomplishments, which Pericles' well-wishers considered to be his military victories. The biography reports that Pericles commented that he was most proud not of his martial success, but rather of the fact that "No Athenian has ever put on mourning because of me." Very few modern commentators have under-scored the bizarre nature of this claim. Pericles' policies in the form of his direct advocacy of wars against Sparta and the expansion of Athens' empire had certainly led to the deaths of thousands of Athenians and other Greeks. Pericles surely bears considerable responsibility for as many Greek and Athenian deaths as any Hellenic leader of the mid-fifth century.[88]

Philip Stadter comments that in this passage Plutarch "chooses to ignore the many deaths in military actions that might have been avoided by a different policy."[89] However, it is more disturbing that Pericles himself reportedly ignored these facts. What could the statesman possibly have meant by such a statement? That he had not personally killed another Athenian? Such a claim – in its literal sense – was hardly distinguishing. Stadter takes it to mean "that Pericles did not win power by violence or civil war" and that "no Athenian deaths could be attributed to [his] lack of care, self-control, or foresight." But, again, such a claim was unremarkable, unless Pericles actually meant to compare himself with the tyrants of Greece's (and Athens') past. Some time ago another scholar suggested that Pericles preened himself here on the fact that he had not engaged in the "arbitrary use of his power" to cause the death of a political opponent via execution or assassination (!).[90] Again, surely this would be an unremark-able claim for anyone beyond a tyrant. Did the dying Pericles, therefore, refer to his career as a prosecutor? Straightforward death sentences were hardly common in fifth-century Athenian courts, so far as we can tell, and why would Pericles have prided himself on never having played a role in the execution of a convicted criminal?

Since no Athenian is likely to have prided himself on playing no role in the deaths of criminals, we are forced to conclude that Pericles indeed referred to the deaths of innocent Athenian citizens. But how could the statesman possibly claim that no Athenian mother, wife, or daughter had put on mourning because of him? As we have seen, Pericles had sponsored and commanded numerous Athenian military actions and worked to prevent a diplomatic solution to the conflict with Sparta.

Pericles' comment, if we accept its historicity, leaves the reader with the impression of a man who has convinced himself of a lie. It suggests that Pericles in fact recognized the very crucial role he had played in the deaths of thousands of his fellow citizens – and it tells us that he could not face that reality. Rather, Pericles constructed a vision of himself in which he bore no responsibility for these deaths. He had, after all, never killed a fellow citizen. He had not risen to power by violence or civil war. And the decisions of the Athenian state to go to war with its enemies had been, after all, collective decisions for which he bore (he could argue) no more responsibility than any other leader or citizen. The deaths of Athenians that resulted from those votes could not be laid at his doorstep and, in any case, Athens' military losses under his leadership had arguably been lighter than in the two generations before him.[91]

Pericles, in short, asserted his innocence on a charge he apparently felt all too acutely.[92] Near the end of his life, Pericles perhaps recognized that the cost of the future glory he wanted so badly for Athens had been the deaths of many fellow citizens and two of his sons. In his speeches in Thucydides Pericles argues that this cost is not too great for the goal sought: indeed, he maintains that history will remember and reward the Athenians for their very willingness to run the greatest risks and to die on behalf of Athens' future reputation.

Pericles had earned a reputation for safety and prudence while sending many Athenians to their deaths. If the statesman did not actually speak the final words attributed to him in Plutarch, they were arguably put into his mouth by a source that wished to illustrate this ironic aspect of his career and life.[93] Perhaps to many the conclusion that the statement was invented will remain preferable to the uncomfortable alternative: in the last days of his life, having lost both his elder sons in a plague aggravated by the war he championed, did Pericles question whether the price of Athens' glory had in fact been too high?

EIGHT

Athenian Culture and the Intellectual Revolution: Pericles and the People

Wealth, democracy, empire, Athens' national character, and the intellectual heat of fifth-century Greece combined to make Pericles' environment unique. Both an exponent of and a catalyst for this fervor, Pericles' relations with other thinkers and artists of the fifth century demand our attention even as they frustrate our comprehension. Often portrayed as a friend of intellectuals like Anaxagoras, poets like Sophocles, or scholars like Herodotus, Pericles in fact represents a very different strain of thought from all three, one which renders the state or collective itself and the future opinions of men the most important factors in determining policy and making moral valuations. Pericles' precise philosophical and religious views cannot be recovered, but analysis of his career, his ideas in Thucydides, and the details Plutarch provides suggest that he combined orthodox religious practice with a certain skepticism about divine causation. Both a radical and a conservative, Pericles emphasized the need to respect society's norms even as he asked his fellow citizens to reshape those norms in the service of Athens' place in history. Pericles' most important intellectual, political, and perhaps even personal relationship proved to be that with the Athenian people.

The popular image of "Periclean Athens" evokes a picture of intellectual and cultural fervor in an aesthetic environment dominated by monuments like the Parthenon, Sophoclean masterpieces like *Ajax* and *Oedipus Rex*, and debates involving scientists and philosophers of the rank of Protagoras, Anaxagoras, and Socrates. Yet the reality of mid-fifth-century Athens probably struck the visitor as something closer to a Middle Eastern bazaar than the Greek antiquities exhibition at a modern museum – more a farmers' market than philosophical academy. Strolling through the city's Dipylon Gate along a route just north of the Sacred Way (which connected the city center with Eleusis to the northwest) and heading through the Kerameikos district toward the center of town, a visitor ca. 431 could see toward the southeast the acropolis and the massive and elaborate Parthenon temple surmounting it. The city itself boasted many other beautiful new buildings, some constructed while Kimon held sway in Athens but more deriving from the building program sponsored by Pericles: a new music hall beneath the acropolis, a new springhouse where water could be drawn, various temples, and other constructions. A new wall had been built to help secure access to the Peiraeus harbor about four miles from the city proper. Moving through the agora, our visitor finds the goods of the entire Hellenic and Mediterranean world for sale. Surely no marketplace in all of Greece could impress a visitor as could the Athenian agora, where one could find delicacies hardly imaginable in the surrounding countryside or in most cities of Hellas.

Notice, too, the number of non-Athenians and even non-Greeks about. Many foreigners have moved to Athens to enjoy the economic opportunities it provides. A shield maker like Cephalus has moved his business from Sicily to the place where the most shields are needed: Athenians, after all, go to war more than any other Greeks. Protagoras of Abdera and other thinkers come to Athens to sell their services as teachers, promising to make well-to-do young Athenians better speakers and thus more successful in politics and in the courts.[1] And there's that infamous Athenian layabout Socrates, talking to a group of wealthy young men about "justice" or "piety" but never seeming to reach a conclusion. Yes, Pericles' young ward and cousin Alcibiades is with Socrates again. He's the good-looking one with the lisp sitting next to the young Kallias, the richest man in Athens. Oh, and Nikias's son is with them: his father is extremely rich as well. He made his money renting out gangs of slaves to the Athenian silver miners. But come on, let's head up to the acropolis so you can see the buildings there.

We just have to head south past the agora and then turn toward the acropolis, keeping the Parthenon – looming ever larger – on our left. Now, come on. The path up the citadel moves eastward, through these amazing gates the Athenians call simply "the gates" (Propylaia). But notice, there's a kind of art gallery located inside. Have you ever seen such an elaborate entrance to anything? And don't forget that gorgeous little temple to Athena the Victor over there just before the Propylaia. Imagine how much that one small building cost! Athena Nike, "the Victor" indeed. Half of this stuff was paid for with money we paid to the Athenians to protect us from Persia. Well, nobody's seen a Persian warship in these parts for thirty years or more! Anyway, come on up. Let's look at the Parthenon. Yes, that is a huge statue of Athena in front of the temple. They call her Athena Promachos, "the warrior." Are you noticing a theme? Athena Victor, Athena Warrior. Yes, not too subtle, I agree.

Now, watch out, the whole upper acropolis is covered with these stone tablets. Yes, you can read them if you want. What does that one say? "It seemed best to the council and to the people of Athens that the allies bring tribute payments to Athens in the spring of every year at the time of the festival of Dionysus." Were you at the festival last year? Yes, I was. I brought the tribute from home and stayed for the plays. Absolutely amazing stuff. The new guy, Euripides, gave old Sophocles a run for his money, although Sophocles won the contest, of course. But these Athenians, they certainly aren't shy. Do you know that before the plays they had the tribute we all paid carried in talent by talent? Talk about garish. As if we don't know who had to pay for all this already! Anyway, here, look at this stone tablet that is so much bigger than all the others. This is where the Athenians inscribe the names of all the states that pay tribute to them every year. Let's find home. Uh, let's see. . . . Right! Here we are. And here. And here again. This tablet has about fifteen years of tribute payments on it. And once they filled it up, they put up another one (but not quite as big – I think they found it hard to find another tablet of this size). Yes, you're right. The same theme again: "We are Athens and you will pay us! Forever!"

Well, come on, let's look at the Parthenon closely. It's fully painted now. My father saw it when they were putting it up, and he said it was entirely white for several years! Can you imagine an entirely white marble temple? It must have looked naked and awful. Now it's covered in these beautiful blues, reds, and yellows. Amazing. Wait a minute, here's the thing I wanted to show you. Come up here inside the columns on the outside of the temple. Right. Look out for that cat over there. Scram, kitty! Okay, now can you crane your neck and look up at the outside of the building inside the final row of columns? Right, see that way up there. Yes, it's an elaborate frieze, a kind of low sculpture that runs all the way around the building. I know – you can hardly even see it! Crazy! Imagine the expense of that part of the building alone. I wondered what it depicted, too, but someone told me it's an image of the Athenians themselves! I know! No one does that: putting *themselves* on a temple. Right, right, back to the theme: "We're rich. We're powerful. We're wonderful. We're special. We're Athens." Yes, you're so right. That *does* sound like Pericles! Okay, had enough? Let's go back to the agora and get some of those Boeotian eels and some Egyptian beer. I'm starved. . . .[2]

* * * * *

Pericles' Athens undoubtedly shocked, seduced, outraged, and utterly impressed most of the city's visitors. By 431 there was no other place like it in the Greek world in terms of sheer wealth on display as well as cultural and intellectual dynamism. Yet the purely intellectual aspect of Athens' profile plays no role whatsoever in Pericles' description of the city in his Funeral Oration in Thucydides.[3] The beauty of the city, its wealth, religious festivals, and the opportunities it provides to common citizens figure prominently, but Pericles says not a word about drama or philosophy: the intellectual world, so far as one could gauge from Pericles' speeches in Thucydides, did not play a major role in the Athenians' image of themselves.[4]

Nor, more shockingly, did democracy. Although historians have sought to explain away, minimize, or deny this fact, the Athenians spent virtually no time analyzing or praising their form of government during the age of Pericles. "Democracy" *per se* does not emerge as a subject of interest until at least the 420s, and it remained a marginal topic until the oligarchic revolution of 411 apparently forced the issue, as it were: Athenians then needed to make an active choice between democratic and nondemocratic government. After the Athenians lost their democracy to reactionary revolutions (in 411 and again in 404/3), some Athenians became much more interested in what precisely *demokratia* was and how it could be differentiated from other forms of polis government. In the period before this, democracy provoked the attention of comedians but apparently few others, and Pericles' words about *demokratia* betray a defensiveness seemingly born out of the negative connotations of the word: *kratos* ("power") of the *demos* ("common people").[5]

In short, as far as we can tell, the Athenians of the 430s had not yet become obsessed with or even particularly self-conscious about their form of government, though they had begun to see their city as a marvel, at least in terms of its physical appearance and the types of luxuries and the lifestyle available there. Pericles notes the number of festivals the Athenians celebrate without even commenting on the dramas performed at some of them.[6] Perhaps Pericles realized that many Athenians treated the tragedies and comedies of the festivals and the intellectuals and their students cluttering up the agora primarily as interesting diversions (dramas) and minor annoyances (intellectuals). True, the dramas formed an important part of popular culture, and they and the sophists flocking to Athens increasingly featured in the Athenians' self-image. But for most, the crucial advantages to life in Athens probably consisted of the ability to buy whatever kind of fish or cheese or oil one might desire at a good price and the manifold festivals and beautiful parts of the city that one could enjoy. And the most important fact about Athens by the 430s was undoubtedly the military power and prestige it enjoyed.[7]

Pericles' Funeral Oration therefore should remind us that the typical Athenian probably treated the aspects of Athens that we find most interesting as minor or marginal. Asked "What makes life in Athens special?" most Athenians likely expatiated on the food, festivals, and funds rather than on the (admittedly) entertaining plays and the ability to hire a foreign intellectual to instruct one's children.

Most Athenians, we must recall, had little interest in or time for the kind of poring over Sophocles' latest play that modern academics find attractive. Much better to watch it in the theater while munching on some Cretan almonds and quaffing Boeotian wine. The best passages, characters, or plot points might be remembered, of course, and comedic playwrights could draw on this knowledge to make sport of tragic authors, a practice that itself demonstrates that the Athenians did not treat the dramas as sacrosanct. The average Athenian probably felt no need to take the side of Protagoras or Socrates in a debate about whether excellence/virtue (*arete*) could be taught. When the Athenian people met in assembly to vote about whether to attack this or that city or to raise tribute payments or to establish a colony on lands seized from other Greeks, they did not (it would seem) adduce the latest lesson taken from Sophocles' *Antigone* about the importance of divine (over human) law or Protagoras' view that justice (*dike*) had been given to all men.[8] Meetings of the Athenian people in the assembly or in the courts were not philosophical conventions in which the Athenians deployed the latest intellectual propositions in order to advance their causes. Practical matters and issues of advantage (to the individual and the state), including the gods' propitiation, dominated debates, a fact that should hardly surprise anyone who has experienced modern democratic government.[9]

In short, to focus on the "intellectual world" or aesthetic/artistic "revolution" in Athens during Pericles' career runs a great risk of grossly misrepresenting the experience of Athenians and other Greeks in this time and thus of painting a misleading picture of Pericles himself. Leaving the Athenians themselves aside for the moment, we must recognize that most other Greeks – unlike our imagined visitors at the beginning of this chapter – had never been to Athens or experienced a play of Euripides or listened to Anaxagoras or Socrates. They had never seen the Parthenon or Propylaia or the statue of Athena Promachos. The experience of "Athens" for most other Greeks undoubtedly consisted of encounters with Athenians in or near Athens' warships, which most often appeared when payments of tribute were due (or overdue).[10] If they had been asked, "What are Athenians like?" most other Greeks would probably have answered, "They are like rulers." Or, perhaps, "They are like tyrants."[11]

We must keep all this in mind when we ask questions about "Athenian thought" or "culture" in the Periclean age. Such questions privilege a very tiny fraction of the Athenian populace, essentially focusing us on a group of intellectuals, artists, and politicians that can never have been more than a few hundred individuals. Primarily these were members of wealthier Athenian families – like those of Kallias, Nikias, and Pericles himself – or richer visitors to Athens from cities all over Greece. The middle-class stonemason Socrates fit rather uncomfortably in this crowd: he was an outsider in more ways than his approach to questions about life.[12] But even Socrates apparently spent most of his time with wealthy Athenians and foreigners: they formed the audience for his type of speculation. In short, we must emphasize that the Athens reflected in Plato's dialogues or in encomiastic modern descriptions of Athenian architecture or drama represents a very different picture from the average (Athenian or foreign) Greek's experience of the city.[13]

The "typical" Athenian citizen of Pericles' day, if we can attempt to reconstruct him for a moment,[14] came in several flavors, with two perhaps predominating: (1) a farmer who spent most of his time in the countryside working his ten to twelve acres of land and who only rarely visited the city center proper, and (2) an urban resident of Athens, who was most likely to be relatively poor (or of the lower middle class), but who could also be one of the well-to-do aristocrats who kept a house in the city. Both the city dwellers and those in the countryside will almost certainly have served regularly in the Athenian military – the farmer as a hoplite in Athens' infantry and the poorer resident as a rower on an Athenian warship. Wealthier Athenians, we should note, often acted as "trierarchs," well-to-do citizens who paid for the upkeep of an Athenian warship (*trieres* or "trireme") for a year.[15] Ironically, therefore, the wealthier and the poorer Athenians were more likely to share significant experience with Athens' fleet than were the middle-class farmers. However, by 431 some of these hoplite-farmers will also have sailed aboard Athenian warships, either as members of the thirty or so marines and other nonrowers who typically manned each vessel or simply as passengers on their way to this or that Athenian military operation.[16]

Indeed, one thing virtually all Athenian citizens had in common in Pericles' day was their service in the Athenian military. The other thing that many, if not most, would have experienced was the great festivals held in Athens on an annual basis, especially the City Dionysia that occurred in the spring (roughly April) of each year. Pericles emphasizes these festivals in his description of Athens, and even Attica's farmers occasionally visited the city during these celebrations. During the festivals merchants must have made special wares and foods available for purchase due to the increased opportunities provided by additional visitors to the city. Still, one hardly expects that the farmers of Attica represented a particularly acquisitive or spendthrift lot. It may very well be that the average non-Athenian visitor presented a better opportunity for an Athenian merchant to profit than did the average hardscrabble Attic hoplite-farmer.

We have imagined the mind-set of a foreign visitor to Athens, but the experience of the middle-class Athenian who visited the city at most a few times a year is unlikely to have differed markedly. Despite economic, social, and political connections that tied countryside to city in Attica, a kind of psychological division separated farmer from city dweller.[17] Even after a year's service on the Council of 500, a body selected annually by lot and requiring its members to spend many days in the city during the year,[18] the city of Athens remained, to the farmer, somewhat alien, with an urban population that cared as little about farming as he cared about philosophy or pottery making or warships.

However, one fact clearly differentiated the Athenian citizen visiting Athens and hailing, say, from the village of Marathon, some 25 miles distant, from the non-Athenian who traveled to Athens from other, more distant locales: the Athenian understood Athens' government because he had taken part in it, and he understood that the wealth of the city and the opportunities for economic improvement created by Athens' empire benefited him and other Athenians in very direct ways. Whatever the average Athenian farmer may have thought of the poorer Athenians who rowed the triremes or the wealthier citizens who commanded them, he understood that these ships brought money to Athens and (probably more important for him) opened up lands elsewhere for Athenians to farm and markets where farmers' produce could be sold.[19] A son of a poorer Athenian farmer with multiple sons could join an Athenian colony or cleruchy and immediately transform himself into a respectable member of the middle class. Such opportunities provided an amazing safety valve, relieving socioeconomic pressures that would have necessarily built up after the Athenians had begun to exploit all the best farmland in Attica.[20]

The fact that no Athenian political faction before the last decade or so of the fifth century opposed Athens' acquisition and rule of a Greek empire therefore should hardly surprise us. Every class of Athenian – from hoplite farmer to urban poor to wealthy sophisticate – stood to profit from Athens' exercise of power in Greece. Beyond the lands available to rich and poor alike, money entered the Athenian economy through payments for rowing in the fleet and serving on juries, and for building triremes and temples. Pericles hardly needed to work hard to convince the Athenians that they should aspire to rule other Greeks because the empire made them richer and their lives more pleasant. Such a message found excellent traction and abundant proof in Athens, and it helps explain why Athenians so often voted to send themselves into life-threatening conflicts. It was Pericles' abstraction of the Athenians from their historical circumstances and his contemplation of the possibility that Athens could and eventually would lose its empire that made his message unusual. Pericles apparently attempted to convince the Athenians that they fought and sacrificed not so much for their own profit as for their city's reputation in history – for the brilliant fame that the future would award to Athens.

Perhaps we may now better understand why Pericles' speeches in Thucydides spend almost no time on philosophical justifications for

Athens' government or on the intellectual and cultural superiority Athens had achieved by the 430s BC. To put it bluntly, few Athenians cared very much about those things. Could Pericles have convinced the Athenians to go to war with Sparta because Athens had more or less created Greek drama or because the city attracted and produced the greatest philosophical minds in Hellas (while Sparta had become an intellectual and artistic backwater)? Surely not. Instead, Pericles apparently attempted to make a very subtle shift in the argument that empire simply was profitable and glorious and there-fore should be pursued. Pericles attempted to show the Athenians that the *time* – the honor and profit – that empire gained them came in different forms. The greatest form, for Pericles, rested in the admiration later ages would feel for Athens. And we must emphasize again that Pericles repeat-edly asserts in Thucydides that that admiration would rest almost entirely on Athens' *power* rather than on its cultural achievements. This attitude appears both in the Funeral Oration and (in an even starker form) in his final speech in Thucydides. We can, of course, never know whether Pericles actually believed this (though I personally have little doubt that he did), but we should at least conclude that he saw this argument as more effective with his Athenian audience than any claim to superiority or justification of rule based on intellectual or aesthetic (not to mention moral) grounds.

Therefore, to turn to the intellectual and aesthetic world of Pericles is, in effect, to turn away from the world that he considered most important in terms of his career and his goals for Athens. Once again, we must recognize that we therefore run the risk of skewing our image of Pericles, his work, and his world.[21] I therefore do not intend to attempt to show how Pericles exemplifies or embodies the intellectual or artistic spirit of his age. Quite the contrary. I wish to show how Pericles' life, work, and ideology contrasted with the principal philosophical and aesthetic movements of his times. In short, I hope to help explain how Pericles (Figure X) could be so popular with average Athenians. Later Athenian history and our own experience of popular politics suggest that Pericles' success as a statesman derived from nothing so little as any supposed involvement with an intellectual, philoso-phical, or artistic circle. If anything, such attachments are likely to have been – and in fact demonstrably were – political liabilities to Pericles, who apparently came under some popular suspicion for his involvement with such figures. The Athenians' obvious love of drama and festivals and the city's fame for attracting and (sometimes) producing intellectuals did not mean that the citizens wanted an intellectual as a leader. What we most need to understand is how Pericles appealed to those citizens who carried the day in the assembly, and to do that we must see how Pericles *differed* from the intellectuals of his day.

We may begin with the non-Athenian historian Herodotus, who visited Athens during the Periclean age and who some scholars believe sought to defend Athens (and by extension Pericles) from the unpopularity the Athenians were experiencing in the middle and later fifth century due to their rule of other Greeks.[22] The historian mentions Pericles only once in his history, when he relates that before giving birth Pericles' mother Agariste dreamed she bore a lion cub. This anecdote, as some have come to recognize, cut more than one way, as the lion was a symbol of dangerous and destructive power in Herodotus and Greek culture.[23] The passage therefore can hardly demonstrate Herodotus's admiration for Pericles or Periclean Athens.

Other scholars have pointed out that Herodotus's "religious" worldview, which emphasized the role the jealous gods play in punishing both overweening pride (*hybris*) and too much prosperity, must have been quite uncomfortable for Pericles.[24] Indeed, this discomfort stemmed not only from the stigma caused by the curse on Pericles' family, but also from Pericles' insistence (in his policies and in the speeches in Thucydides) that Athens strive for the very prosperity Herodotus's work so clearly warns against. For the historian, the gods cannot abide a man or a state that rises too far above others.[25] Herodotus's worldview suggested that Athens, in pursuing Pericles' policy of dominance in Hellas, called down the wrath of the gods on the city. A sensitive reader of Herodotus's work in the period from ca. 420 to 414 BC (the most likely time of his work's publication[26]) would have seen an ominous message for Athens: like Persia and so many other great powers, Athens will meet its nemesis. The Athenian disaster in Sicily in 413, when the entire invasion force of over 150 warships and their crews was lost, could hardly have fit the Herodotean model better.

Pericles could not have embraced the worldview of Herodotus, even if he appreciated the historian's praise of Athens' role in defending Greece from the Persians and his defense of Pericles' maternal ancestors (the Alkmeonids) against charges of treason and supporting tyranny.[27] True, Pericles' view of Athens' future, to judge from his speeches in

Thucydides, remained somewhat fatalistic: all this may pass away, as it is the nature of things to grow and then die. But Pericles did not expect divine forces to punish Athens for its pride, its success, or its pursuit of greatness. He did recognize the plague that struck Athens as an unexpected and divine force,[28] but Pericles would hardly have seen it as punishment for Athenian *hybris*. Nevertheless, many Greeks (and perhaps even Herodotus) must have thought such an interpretation all too powerful.

We imagine Herodotus's work to have been popular in part because it embraced a view of moral responsibility and divine reciprocity, vengeance, and jealousy similar to the view we see reflected in other fifth-century literature, including the tragedies of Sophocles and (to some degree) those of Aeschylus.[29] Herodotus's work, that is, broke new ground in terms of Greek literature but not in terms of Greek thought about the nature of the world. If anything, Herodotus could be dismissed by more progressive thinkers in the last decades of the fifth century as somewhat old-fashioned. Herodotus and Pericles probably met at some point during Herodotus's visit(s) to Athens, but it remains unlikely that the two could have been friends in any but the most superficial of senses.[30]

At the other end of the intellectual spectrum from Herodotus stood the philosopher Anaxagoras, who held notoriously heterodox views about the gods, even claiming that the sun was a physical rather than divine object.[31] Plutarch tells us that Anaxagoras and Pericles had been friends at one point, and such a friendship certainly suggests that Pericles had no fear of being seen among the freethinkers of his day.[32] Yet Plutarch's account also shows that the relationship between Pericles and Anaxagoras cooled in later years.[33] The statesman stopped visiting the philosopher/scientist, who grew old and had no one to take care of him. Eventually, after learning of his former friend's poverty and determination to starve himself, Pericles did visit the aged and poor Anaxagoras, expressing his desire that the philosopher continue living because Pericles needed him. Anaxagoras's humorous response, if we can believe Plutarch's account, emphasized that Pericles had done nothing to help Anaxagoras in his hour of need: "Even a lamp has oil put into it by those who use it." In other words, "I helped you out, Pericles. But where were you when I needed something to eat?!"

We may doubt the truth of the tale while recognizing its significance. The story depicts Pericles as someone with less than perfect human sympathy: he worries about Anaxagoras's death because of the effect it will have on himself, not because he has concern for the aging philosopher's plight. In the tale Pericles has not even considered that he might help the philosopher with his own wealth. The story tells us that many people envisioned Pericles as a somewhat cold and withdrawn individual, an image supported by several other anecdotes in Plutarch's account and thrown into relief by the few occasions when Pericles is said to have shown open emotion.[34] We may note in particular Pericles' stern encouragement of the audience in his Funeral Oration to produce more children to compensate for their losses, advice that seems unrealistic for many of the bereaved fathers and probably impossible for the middle-aged or older mothers present.[35]

Given the details that our tradition has retained about Pericles' and Anaxagoras's friendship, it remains striking that no source describes Pericles himself as suffering from attacks based on outlandish religious or scientific views. Anaxagoras's heterodox views were well known, and some political rivals apparently sought to harm Pericles through attacking the scientist.[36] However, no Athenian, so far as we can gauge, ever accused Pericles of thinking the sun was a rock rather than a deity or even of questioning conventional views about the Greek gods. No one accused Pericles of omitting to perform the customary sacrifices or of failing to give the gods their due in his public or private life.[37] Pericles associated with the well-known *mantis* (religious interpreter) Lampon as well as rationalist philosophers like Anaxagoras.[38] Pericles supervised or sponsored religious construction on and off the acropolis, including a statue of Athena "the healer," supposedly a thank offering after the goddess assisted him (through a dream) in healing an injured worker.[39] The Athenians chose him at least twice to deliver the orations over their fallen soldiers (ca. 440/39 and in 431/0), a position to which they were hardly likely to elect a person of patently unorthodox religious views.

Scholars have often noted that Pericles says almost nothing about the gods in his speeches in Thucydides, and all too often this has led to a view that either the statesman or Thucydides himself held heterodox religious opinions.[40] However, in this case an argument from the silence of our evidence is quite telling: we know that some Athenians criticized Pericles for his wife/concubine Aspasia, for his sexual adventures,[41] for his cold manner, for his friendships with odd public figures, and for his very physical appearance. If Pericles had ever suffered abuse for his supposed religious views, we can reasonably expect to have found evidence of this in our tradition. We may note, finally, that even Plutarch does not associate Anaxagoras's heterodox religious or philosophical positions with Pericles. For Plutarch, the most important thing that Anaxagoras gave Pericles was the statesman's "high-mindedness," followed by a rejection of superstition.[42] The vague nature of these claims assures us that Plutarch had no evidence whatsoever of particular Anaxagoran notions or other unorthodox religious views held by the Athenian statesman.

Though we can never recover Pericles' actual beliefs, we may conclude that the statesman took great care to ensure that his public speech and actions demonstrated no heterodox views about the gods. Again, he supported a building program that was, in large part, religious in nature and sponsored the building of an altar to Athena the Healer. He associated with the soothsayer Lampon as well as with famous sophists. Despite his early friendship with Anaxagoras, therefore, we cannot associate him with the philosopher's own radical views or draw any conclusions from this association about Pericles' own philosophical or religious notions beyond his apparent tendency to look for natural rather than supernatural explanations of events. Perhaps Thucydides' speeches should lead us to conclude that Pericles was not the type of demagogic leader who used the gods as a tool to get the populace on his side, a technique apparently used by other Athenian leaders such as Cleon.[43] Indeed, Thucydides' praise of Pericles' political honesty harmonizes well with the notion that he shunned such techniques (beyond the sponsorship of religious construction).[44] True, we have a report of Pericles referencing the gods in the funeral oration he delivered for those who died in the Samian War ca. 440/39. In that speech Pericles reportedly said that the dead Athenians had become immortal like gods: "For we cannot see the gods, but we believe them to be immortal from the honors we pay them and the blessings we receive from them."[45] One might argue that the passage was remembered precisely because it was unusual for Pericles, yet there is no indication of this in the tradition. Indeed, the conventional stance of the quotation aligns well with Pericles' other known activities, including his involvement with temple building and the prayer he reportedly offered before addressing any assembly (asking that he might speak suitably for the occasion).[46]

In short, the evidence taken together depicts Pericles as a man with conventional religious views, who was nonetheless open to and interested in the "scientific" ideas of his day. Such a position can hardly have been unusual in mid- to late fifth-century Athens. Pericles, it would seem, relied on other factors than Greek piety in his attempts to convince the Athenians to accept war with Sparta or to pay jurors for public service, but the states-man maintained the image of a perfectly orthodox Athenian when it came to the gods. Pericles, in short, did not belong to the camp of radical Greek intellectuals of the later fifth century who openly questioned traditional views of religion.[47]

* * * * *

The dramatist Sophocles occupied a dominant position among Athenian writers of the Periclean age. By 456 Aeschylus had died and Euripides would not emerge as a real rival of Sophocles until the 430s.[48] In the intervening period (and later), Sophocles achieved victory after victory in Athenian dramatic contests, which featured votes by spectator-judges to determine the victors. He had, indeed, rivaled if not dominated Aeschylus as early as the 460s and would overshadow Euripides in the period from ca. 441 to 405. Sophocles, in short, stands easily as the top-ranking literary figure of the fifth century, if we use the Greeks' own opinions as our gauge.[49]

Like Herodotus, Sophocles propounded a view of man's place in the world that reflected traditional Greek views.[50] Man was responsible for his actions, in Sophocles' works, but he all too easily ran afoul of powers that were greater than he. The nature of the gods, of man, and of the world around him formed a web of compulsion (Greek *anagke*, "necessity") within which men acted and were punished for their actions, even if those deeds seemed utterly constrained by circumstances, individual char-acter, or the gods' own will or actions. This "tragic" view of man's position in the world emphasized the role of *physis* (nature) over *nomos* (custom or law) and the importance of divine justice or will over human reason or aspiration.[51] This view also pretty clearly reflected what many if not most Greeks believed about the world in which they lived.

Sophocles served as a statesman and leader beyond (and perhaps in part because of) his work as a playwright, though he is the only leading dramatist known to have had a kind of political "career." Sophocles is the only Athenian in the fifth century known to have served as *strategos* (general), Hellenotamias (imperial treasurer), and Proboulos (one of the special commissioners chosen in 413 when Athens faced a dire situation after the destruction of the entire Athenian invasion force in Sicily). In the last position, Sophocles played some role in allowing a group of oligarchs to convince the Athenian populace to replace their democracy with a more conservative regime. In an anecdote recorded by Aristotle, Sophocles responds to the question of why he participated in this act by stating, "There was nothing better to be done."[52] The response implies a period in which democracy had been restored and Sophocles felt the need to justify his actions that led to the oligarchic regime. Apparently the Athenian people accepted the dramatist's explanation: no evidence suggests that Sophocles suffered any ill effects from his apparently indirect involvement with the oligarchic revolution of 411 BC.[53]

Even if one doubts the historicity of the anecdote reported by Aristotle, Sophocles' extant works provide sufficient evidence that the playwright was not a friend of radical democracy or of the newer attitudes toward man's relationship to the divine that percolated in mid-fifth-century Athens. As we have noted, political interpretations of Athenian tragedies remain controversial, but Sophocles almost certainly stood in the Kimonian ranks when it came to his politics.[54] In particular, several of his plays point to the difficulties created when a ruler runs afoul of traditional norms or the divine will. It does not take an overly inventive reading of Sophocles' *Antigone* or *Oedipus Rex*, for example, to see that the poet's portraits of the regent Creon and of the well-intentioned but doomed king Oedipus bear clearly on the position of a predominant statesman like Pericles.[55] Among many other lessons, *Antigone* warns against a view that equates justice with the will of the ruler or ignores the demands of divine justice (in this case by giving the dead their proper burial). Creon's argument that obedience to the state forms a man's (or woman's) chief obligation reminds us of Pericles' views in the speeches Thucydides provides for him. Pericles, however, seems to concede that there are moral obligations beyond service to the polis, noting (for example) that men must obey those "unwritten laws" that are shameful to break.[56] While the great classicist and historian A. W. Gomme argued that, for Pericles, these unwritten laws were apparently not divine – whereas Sophocles uses the term explicitly to refer to the divine ordinances that must guide proper conduct – it seems more likely that Pericles (if he actually used such a phrase) understood that many if not most of his audience would associate such unwritten laws with the divine.[57]

Sophocles' masterpiece *Ajax* (perhaps produced as early as the 450s) presents us with another vision that could hardly be called progressive or friendly to the philosophical and rhetorical movements emerging in mid-fifth-century Athens. His hero Ajax represents the old, Homeric world in which a man's excellence (*arete*) is determined primarily by his dominance on the field of battle. In return for his display of this *arete*, society grants him honor and prizes (*time*). The issue that spawns the action of the play stems from the vote of the Greek chiefs at Troy to award the armor of now-deceased Achilles to Odysseus instead of Ajax, who by common consent was the greatest warrior among the Greeks after Achilles. By making this decision about the armor ostensibly "democratic" and contrasting the wily rhetorician and trickster Odysseus (a master of speech and guile) with the straightforward, old-fashioned warrior Ajax, Sophocles invites the audience to compare an older style of leader with a type emerging in the mid-fifth century.[58] And though Ajax strikes the reader as an imperfectly sympathetic figure, he nonetheless offers a reproach to the (initial) figure and manner of Odysseus in the play and especially to the conniving brothers Agamemnon and Menelaus. In the play's denouement, a now-changed Odysseus argues in favor of granting Ajax the burial of a great warrior despite his attempted murder of the Greeks who he believed had dishonored him. In short, the play suggests that the age of Ajax has indeed passed, but that the world has thereby lost something precious. Men of speech and cunning and the votes of councils and assemblies now carry the day, but the time may come when men need another Ajax.[59]

Many scholars have seen the resonances of Sophocles' treatment of Oedipus in the career and circumstances of Pericles: like the Athenian statesman, Oedipus suffers from a curse and leads a town enduring a subsequent plague.[60] Few classicists today accept a bald analogy between Oedipus and Pericles in Sophocles' great *Oedipus Rex*, yet one can hardly deny that many members of an Athenian audience were likely to think of Pericles when they watched the drama.[61] If they did, once again Sophocles' work could hardly be seen as encouraging support for the Periclean program or approach to politics. Sophocles' Oedipus attracts sympathy but only limited admiration. He is a man pursued by a past he did not comprehend and whose own confidence and actions brought catastrophe upon his family and his city. Little matter that this was all unintended or that Oedipus took actions he believed would forestall the oracle that he would kill his father and marry his mother, only to have those very actions result in the oracle's fulfillment. Human intentions make no difference in a universe where divine forces seek their own purposes. Oedipus's famed intelligence rescued the city from the Sphinx, but it could not save him or his family from ultimate disaster.

Among other things, the play arguably asked Athenians to question the faith some may have been beginning to put in a certain kind of leader in the early 420s, the probable time of the play's production.[62] Statesmen who promise to solve problems through speech or thwart the gods' oracles will all too often lead one astray. Better to retain a measure of humility in the face of the divine, the mysterious, the unknowable. It is, after all, arguably Oedipus's own desire "to know the truth" that destroys him. Herodotus undoubtedly enjoyed Sophocles' dramas immensely: he would have seen in them encouragement for continued respect for the gods' power and caprice (if not reciprocity). If Sophocles' gods are not as jealous of man's success as are Herodotus's, their power and will nevertheless all too often result in the downfall of men who trusted too much in their own abilities and prosperity.[63]

Sophocles and Pericles served as generals together during the Samian War, and a fragment from a now-lost work of their contemporary Ion of Chios preserves a conversation they had over dinner during this campaign. Sophocles, the story goes, commented on the good looks of a young boy, and Pericles responded (essentially) that a general should keep his mind on his business.[64] This tale suggests a certain prickliness between the dramatist and the statesman: commenting on the handsomeness of a boy hardly strikes one as unusual for the elites of fifth-century Athens.[65] Pericles, perhaps, sought to distance himself by means of this comment from the pederasty that played a significant role (to judge from Plato and Aristophanes) among Athenian aristocrats in the fifth century. Indeed, no story in our tradition associates Pericles with any younger (or older) male lover or with any positive comment on the practice.[66] The manifold stories told about Pericles' sexual liaisons, so far as we can judge, depicted them as entirely heterosexual in nature. Whatever the reasons for this – personal or political or both – the exchange with Sophocles reflects a distance between the two men that our readings of Sophocles' plays and our knowledge of Pericles' thought and career render quite credible. Undoubtedly acquaintances and fellow generals, Pericles and Sophocles are unlikely to have been friends.[67]

We have seen explicit testimony that the Athenian philosopher and musician Damon had a friendly relationship with Pericles.[68] We know a little about Damon. He wrote technical works on harmony and poetic meter and "studied the effects of different types of music on individual behavior and character."[69] Nevertheless, the anecdote in which he advises Pericles to "give the people their own money" places him among the type of sophists who gave advice about success in politics and in life. Damon probably had his own philosophical views, but the tradition could apparently associate him (rightly or wrongly) with the kind of cynical philosophers who could argue any side of an issue.[70] In any case, the Damon story redounds to the credit of neither the philosopher nor the statesman and was presumably peddled by those wishing to blacken Pericles' reputation. It is perhaps telling that we have no other stories providing specific links between Pericles and Damon. Indeed, we can say nothing more about the alleged relationship between the two, although at least one scholar has speculated that Damon's (possible) ostracism may have stemmed from discomfort over Pericles' interest in his research about ways to influence the people.[71]

As we seek to understand the associates of Pericles in an attempt to round out our image of the statesman, we come now to the sculptor Pheidias, who executed the gold and ivory statue of Athena in the Parthenon and may have acted in some kind of supervisory role over the decoration of the edifice or even of the acropolis building project as whole.[72] Several anecdotes connect Pericles with the artist, who allegedly included an image of the statesman in one of the relief sculptures on the shield held by the statue of Athena in the great temple.[73] Pheidias apparently fell afoul of the Athenians at some point in the 430s, when he was accused of embezzlement and probably forced to leave Athens.[74] Gossip connected the embezzlement somehow with Pericles, and the stories that Pheidias had benefited inappropriately from the moneys spent on the temple's adornment and that he carved Pericles' image into the goddess's shield are probably related. Pericles, the argument apparently went, had looked the other way while his buddy Pheidias embezzled funds and the artist in return immortalized the Athenian leader in his sculpture.

We are in no position today to judge the guilt or innocence of Pheidias in this matter. We can only say that a sufficient number of Athenians believed this story to warrant his departure or exile from Athens and that an insufficient number of Athenians believed Pericles had anything to do with it to justify official action against the statesman. Pericles seems to have suffered no serious political effects from the Pheidias incident. In the 430s, so far as we can tell, Pericles enjoyed such continued popularity that his enemies found it impossible to make anything stick to the Athenian leader. Pheidias and probably Damon (and perhaps Anaxagoras) may have been prosecuted, ostracized, or exiled in part because of a relationship with Pericles, but the faction opposing the statesman found it impossible to bring their demolition tackle to bear successfully on Pericles himself. He had become, to use the modern term, a Teflon politician.

Can an examination of Pheidias's artwork on the Parthenon tell us anything about Pericles? We first must assume that Pericles played an active role in the design or approval of the temple's decoration, a view for which there is no good evidence, although modern scholars have often accepted the ancient view that Pericles exercised some kind of influence if not control over the acropolis building program (or at least the Parthenon's construction).[75] Let us accept, however, that the tradition of a relationship between Pheidias and Pericles is strong enough to support the conclusion that the artist would not have wished to decorate the building in a way Pericles would have found objectionable. We may reasonably infer that Pericles did not object to the Parthenon's adornment even if he did not suggest or formally approve it.

The themes presented by the artwork on the exterior and interior of the Parthenon center on Athens' history, power, and unique contemporary position.[76] Thus the two pediments detailed the origins of Athens and the city's special relationship with the goddess Athena (showing her birth on the east side and her contest with Poseidon to become patron of Athens on the west), while the metopes that adorned the exterior (between the top of the columns and the roof of the building) treated a series of stories that emphasized the victory of civilization over barbarism (for example, the Greek Lapiths fighting the centaurs or the Athenians defeating the barbarian Amazons). Inside the building stood the massive statue of Athena Parthenos, holding the image of Victory (Nike) in her hand (Figure IX).[77] On the exterior wall of the building (within the colonnade) ran the long frieze depicting (most probably) the Athenian people in procession presenting a special robe made for the image of the goddess Athena.

This frieze represented an unusual deviation from typical temple sculpture in that it apparently depicted contemporary human beings. The Athenians, that is, had placed their own images on the temple dedicated to their guardian goddess Athena.[78] The frieze therefore strikes the note of Athenian nationalism and exceptionalism seen in Pericles' Funeral Oration and his last speech in Thucydides. The frieze suggests, in short, that just as Athena and the other gods deserve special recognition in their roles as Athens' protectors, the Athenian citizens themselves occupy a special and exalted position as a people worthy of immortalization upon the temple's walls. As one scholar has written, "To say that the Athenians built the Parthenon to worship themselves would be an exaggeration, but not a great one."[79]

Pericles could not but have approved of the overall effect of the temple, in the way that it proclaimed Athenian greatness as well as that of Athens' tutelary deity. And beyond the message sent by the particular artwork adorning the temple, the sheer size and expense of the temple made a compelling argument about the wealth and power of Athens. In building the Parthenon, the Athenians announced their intention to dominate the Greek world aesthetically as well as militarily and their intention to use the moneys they collected from other Greeks in whatever way they saw fit. And let us recall that the temple stood near the massive stone tablet on which the Athenians carved the names of the cities that paid them tribute each year. The effect of all this was not subtle or understated: rather, like Pericles' Funeral Oration, the buildings and tablets on the acropolis made the case for Athenian superiority without apology or qualification.

Of the prominent artists and intellectuals in fifth-century Athens examined so far, only Pheidias appears a likely candidate to have been a close friend of Pericles – someone, that is, who shared the statesman's worldview. This conclusion, of course, assumes that Pheidias actually had personal views on these matters: he may just have easily have been a hired gun who executed the plan (with brilliance) that was presented to him. If so, Pericles must nonetheless have been quite pleased that the sculptor had embraced this vision of Athens so thoroughly and effectively.

Beyond Pheidias, one other thinker in fifth-century Athens may have been a kindred spirit or mind for Pericles. The philosopher Protagoras of Abdera spent considerable time in Athens during the mid-fifth century, although only a small amount of evidence connects him directly with Pericles.[80] A fragment attributed to Protagoras praises Pericles' stoic resolution in the face of his older son's death.[81] Plutarch (*Per.* 36.2–3) recounts the tale of Pericles and Protagoras debating what thing or person was truly responsible for the accidental death of a man killed by a javelin at athletic games: the javelin, the athlete who threw it, or the organizer of the contest. Plutarch tells us that Pericles' own son Xanthippus maliciously spread this story, wishing to make his father appear ridiculous. Beyond this tale, we are told that the Athenians appointed Protagoras to draw up laws for the colony at Thurii in 444/3, and Pericles' influence in Athens at that time suggests that the statesman, at the very least, had no objections to Protagoras' appointment.[82]

Indeed, certain views associated with Protagoras do harmonize well with Periclean ideals as often identified in (or extrapolated from) the speeches in Thucydides. Protagoras' views that "man is the measure of all things," that "justice is given to all men," and that "excellence (*arete*) can be taught" all undergird the democratic humanism for which Athens (and, by extension, Pericles) would become famous. In particular, the view that all men have access to justice[83] reminds us of Pericles' claim in the Funeral Oration that even the average Athenian was a good judge (a view that Plato directly challenges in his *Apology* of Socrates).[84] Would Pericles have agreed that *arete* can be taught? I believe we can assume so, given his redefinition of the term in the Funeral Oration: if, after all, the highest form of *arete* is service to the state and if this kind of excellence can compensate for a man's other failings, surely men can learn to practice this *arete*. Indeed, one could argue that Pericles has taken on the role of such a teacher of *arete* in the speech and in his career.[85]

Scholars continue to debate what precisely the Protagorean epigram "Man is the measure of all things" actually meant, but most conclude that the phrase comments on the relative nature of knowledge and the effect of individual perspective on the perception of all information.[86] Pericles, however, might have been more inclined to understand the phrase in a slightly different way, taking it to mean that men's praise sets the standard by which achievements are measured. Indeed, Pericles' words in the Funeral Oration and his last speech in Thucydides suggest that the Athenians' actions will be judged not by the gods but precisely by the *men* of the future. Their judgment – the fame they will bestow on the Athenians for their accomplishments – justifies the Athenians' current striving for power and their effort to rule "over more Greeks than any other Greek state." In that sense, man – and not an abstract or divine idea of justice – provided the measuring stick by which the Athenians and their city would be gauged.

The most radical, relativistic interpretations of Protagoras's apothegm – positing no such thing as absolute right or wrong – as well as his infamous dictum that he was unable to say whether the gods exist strike me as very un-Periclean.[87] As we have noted, Pericles propounded no unorthodox religious views so far we are able to tell. Neither in the speeches in Thucydides nor in any other reported words or actions did Pericles ever assert a kind of moral relativism. Such a conclusion may seem strange given that Thucydides has Pericles call Athens' empire "a tyranny" and to admit that "to take it perhaps was unjust, but to let it go is unsafe" (2.63.2). However, the very admission that the Athenians could reasonably be accused of injustice because of their empire shows that Pericles had no intention of claiming that justice did not exist or was merely relative. Instead, Pericles suggests that the claims of expedience and glory override the claims of justice. Men can judge what is "right," but in certain situations it may be imprudent or unambitious to follow the path of justice. And, in Pericles' view, when future men look back on Athens, they will judge the city not by some abstract or divine concept of justice but rather by the very human standards of power.

Here we see once more just how Pericles' ideas combined a radicalism that could set justice to the side (without pretending it did not exist) combined with an apparently fairly conventional view of the gods and unwritten laws that govern man ("that code which, although unwritten, yet cannot be broken without acknowledged disgrace" [2.37.3]). Here, too, we see the very spot in Pericles' worldview that men like Sophocles and Herodotus would have found most disturbing. In Pericles' willingness to strive for the high opinion of future men even at the expense of acting justly now and in his belief that only superior power could ensure that the future would grant Athens the fame he sought for it, Pericles (like Athens) ran the risk of suffering the fate of Sophocles' tragic figures and the great but doomed powers in Herodotus. The playwright and the historian asserted that too much confidence in man's intellect or in human achievement (including law and government) and too much prosperity lead inexorably to disaster. Pericles' speeches in Thucydides and the policy the Athenians pursued in the middle of the fifth century could not provide a more compelling example of the very processes Sophocles and Herodotus sought to identify and explore. Pericles and Pericles' Athens, it seems clear, not only provided an intellectual and cultural environment in which writers like Sophocles and Herodotus could develop their masterpieces, but also served as the very historical examples that underscored the themes of their works: mortals face their lives constrained by necessities that all too often lead to tragic ends, while the divine continues to exact a price from men who fail to respect and fear a power greater than human.

PERICLES AND THE PEOPLE

Despite his acquaintance and perhaps friendship with some of the leading intellectual figures of mid-fifth-century Athens, Pericles finds no comfortable home among either the rationalist philosophers who questioned the role of the divine in human life or the staunch traditionalists who focused on the gods' jealousy or man's tragic fate.[88] Pericles rather exhibits a confidence in men's – or, rather, the Athenians' – ability to make their own future by accomplishing feats at which their contemporaries and later generations will be compelled to marvel. His view thus combines the optimism of a humanistic vision with the resignation of a realist: as he states in his third speech in Thucydides, Athens' power is likely to pass away, since everything that grows must eventually die. Acts of gods and nature, like the great plague in Athens, simply must be endured. Pericles assigns no moral quality to this suffering: he neither explains it by Athens' violation of some divine or human code of justice nor expects that any particular Athenian actions are likely to forestall the disaster. For Pericles, forces beyond the human remain inscrutable, whereas for Sophocles and Herodotus they follow a predictable pattern if not logic.

A careful reading of Thucydides could suggest that he shared Pericles' view. The historian spends little time treating the religious aspects of the events he describes.[89] Some scholars have concluded that Thucydides held rationalist or heterodox religious views; however, the historian's work taken as a whole does not justify this stance.[90] Thucydides says little if anything that casts doubt on mainstream Greek religious views. Instead, he arguably puts into practice Herodotus's claim that "all men know equally little about the gods" (2.3). Thucydides apparently did not believe that the gods' involvement in human life was a subject a historian could control or manage. The subject remained outside the realm of possible investigation that Thucydides describes in his methodological chapters (1.20–22). Since man cannot see the gods in action or question their motives and interpretations of events, there was little reason to introduce the divine into a discussion of historical causation.[91]

It is, of course, possible that Thucydides has transferred his own views about the gods to Pericles and thus suppressed references to the gods in Pericles' speeches. Such references did, it would seem, at least occasionally appear in other Periclean speeches.[92] However, since the historian evidently did not share other opinions of Pericles (e.g., the statesman's attitudes about Sparta or his dream of Athenian fame through power), this assumption seems to me unwarranted. If the historian has done anything in the way of creating a literary figure in his account of Pericles, he is much more likely to have made the statesman into an avatar for mid-fifth-century Athens than for his own views about history, warfare, Sparta, or the gods, on some of which subjects he clearly differed from the great statesman.

An exploration of the "Pericles as avatar" hypothesis at first suggests the real possibility that the "character" called Pericles in Thucydides' history does represent a certain (dominant) strain of Athenian thought and policy in the period before the Peloponnesian War. The confidence and nationalism, the drive to hegemony and power over other Greeks, the willingness to sacrifice Greek (and Athenian) lives to achieve preeminence – all these features of Pericles' orations in Thucydides clearly reflect actual *Athenian* attributes and policies in the mid-fifth century.[93] Even the relatively small amount of time devoted to Athens' peculiar form of government in the speeches mirrors the relative lack of emphasis the Athenians of this period placed on "democracy" *per se*: as we have seen, Athenian art and literature in this period show little interest in *demokratia*.[94] Has Thucydides simply used these Athenian characteristics to create the "character" called Pericles, who stands in his work not so much as a historically accurate figure as a way to provide a picture of what it meant to be Athenian in this period?

Such a view holds great attraction, especially in that it absolves Pericles himself of the uglier aspects of the Athenian national character in the fifth century (while applying them to the Athenians at large!). Nevertheless, I believe the evidence necessitates a rejection of this conclusion. A very simple fact confronts us. Pericles enjoyed the most successful public career in the history of Athenian democracy, rising to prominence ca. 460 and dominating the political scene after about 444 BC, when he began a run of 15 years in which the Athenians repeatedly elected him to office. Are we to believe that during this period Pericles held or propounded views that differed significantly from those held by the majority of Athenians? This is not to say that Pericles did not oppose the majority from time to time and sometimes succeed in changing their minds, as Thucydides claims he did. Pericles, for example, might advise against invading Egypt or opening a second front during the war with Sparta in the face of popular opposition. He might convince the Athenians to move into the city and watch the Spartans ravage their lands. But surely we are bound to conclude that, when he took such positions, he bolstered his arguments by drawing precisely on the Athenian character that he understood so well. Pericles' policies, even where they sought to restrain the initial impulses of the Athenian people, did so by means and in the service of the very ideals and goals – especially the dream of Athenian power and predominance – he knew the Athenians understood and shared.

Yet Athenian history and the statesman's speeches in Thucydides suggest that Pericles tapped into a deeper vein of Athenian thought and the Athenian self-image than the agonistic, universal Greek desire to compete with and dominate rivals. Pericles seemingly gave the Athenians a greater version of their own desire for power and glory in the present. He promised the Athenians immediate splendor and a fame that would last through the ages, thus establishing Athens' power as a permanent standard at which later men might marvel and which they might aim to emulate.

Thucydides' accounts of Pericles' speeches therefore help us understand precisely how the statesman was able to dominate the political scene in Athens and "to lead [the people] more than being led by them." Pericles, indeed, reflected and utilized the acquisitive and aggressive strain in the Athenian character, but he sought to turn that tendency toward a goal that was prospective and abstract rather than simply immediate and profitable. Pericles offered the Athenians more than the conquest of Greece. He offered them the conquest of history.

Pericles' deep connection with the people of Athens stands as the most important personal relationship in his life. A man with very few close personal friends or ties on a one-to-one level, Pericles rather built a strong bond with the Athenians as a group. This would be a technique that later demagogues like Cleon would develop into a cynical "renouncing of friends," in which the politician would claim that only members of the Athenian demos had the status of his personal friends.[95] Aristophanes would parody this stance in his superb comedy *Knights* (424), produced only a few years after Pericles' death, in which rival demagogues compete for the love of Mr. Demos by giving him gifts.[96] Pericles' critics clearly made the same complaint about him: he had gained the people's favor by offering them pay for jury service, gaudy building programs, and new lands to settle or exploit. All true, of course. But Pericles had also asked the Athenian people to make real sacrifices (ultimately in the form of their lives) in order to secure something even more valuable than payments and land. Pericles asked the Athenians to share his dream of perpetual Athenian glory.

Pericles' greatest achievement had been to see that the Athenian character and circumstances in Hellas together created a moment in which Athens could establish for itself a reputation unequaled by any previous Greek city-state. To help the Athenians themselves see this, he needed only to draw on their own natural tendencies, desires, and beliefs. The brilliance in Pericles' political strategy therefore stemmed largely from the fact that it relied on a deep understanding of the Athenians' national character. Drawing on both Thucydides and Plato, Plutarch (*Per.* 15) puts it this way:

> [Pericles kept the people under control] most often by using the people's hopes and fears as if they were rudders, curbing them when they were arrogant and raising their hopes or comforting them when they were disheartened. In this way he proved that rhetoric, in Plato's phrase [*Phaedrus* 271c], is the art of working upon the souls of men by means of words, and that its chief business is the knowledge of men's characters and passions which are, so to speak, the strings and stops of the soul and require a most skillful and delicate touch.[97]

Pericles, in short, did not have to remake the Athenians after some image he had created. He only needed to encourage those parts of them that had already led to far-flung adventures in the Aegean 150 years or more before the Peloponnesian War. He only needed to show the Athenians that a concerted plan based on intelligent planning and funded by surplus wealth drawn from the empire[98] could ensure that they would actually acquire not only everything they wanted but also things for which they had not dared to hope. Denied a prominent place in the Hellenes' ancient history, in the Homeric poetry that every Greek boy learned by heart, in the myths that told of powerful gods and heroic mortals, the Athenians could now create their own future (where they could only partially recast their own past). The Athenians would become, in effect, their own Homer, composing an epic not of words but of action, in which they would forever figure as heroes.

Thucydides therefore presents us with a Pericles who is not an avatar for Athens, although Pericles must have shared the views of most Athenians when it came to issues like the empire and the building program in order to achieve the unprecedented political career he did. The historian rather presents us with a picture of a supremely intelligent and visionary leader – a man in the service of a great idea but nevertheless in tune with the populace he led. Thucydides' account of the statesman's actions and speeches shows us precisely how Pericles moved from the pragmatic tactics necessary to manage diplomacy or military operations (in his first speech), to the needs of justifying Athenian deaths in the service of the state and the ideal of future glory (in the Funeral Oration), to a bald statement of the abstract goal itself (in his final speech): a reputation that could never be forgotten (*doxa aieimnestos*).[99] Thucydides in these three speeches shows us the statesman employing the techniques of the general, the demagogue, and the visionary or prophet. He does not present us at any time with a perfect statesman, but rather with different aspects of a masterful and charismatic leader who very clearly understood his citizen body and was able to erect a powerful ideology and effective vision from the Athenians' own beliefs and hopes. The picture of Pericles is hardly universally flattering, however: indeed, the image ultimately remains sufficiently negative that the historian must pause after Pericles' last speech to provide his long epitaph reminding the reader that Pericles far outstripped the leaders who came after him in terms of intelligence, character, and vision. For all that he led Athens into a war that would ultimately destroy the Athenian empire and for all his intransigence and bellicosity, Pericles – Thucydides asserts – deserves our admiration.

What Thucydides could not foresee was that Pericles' vision of establishing Athens' place in history would succeed beyond the statesman's wildest dreams, if not for the reasons he had expected. Thucydides himself had forecast that the future would probably rate Athens more highly than it deserved because of its buildings and wealth (1.10). What neither the historian nor the statesman foresaw, however, was that the future would heap praise upon the Athenians not for their power over other Greeks (Pericles' vision) or even their buildings (Thucydides' prediction) but rather for the amazing literature and philosophy they produced and, in our own day, especially for the type of government practiced in Periclean Athens.

Surely one lesson we may take from the inaccuracy in Pericles' and Thucydides' prophecies is that many, if not most, Athenians conceived of themselves and their city in ways very different from the way we view them. The lens created by the modern idealization of democracy and our own tendency to see it as the culmination if not perfection of political and social development are too strong for most of us to resist. We therefore credit Athens and perpetuate its renown for reasons that the Athenians themselves did not anticipate and hardly could have understood.

Pericles' vision for Athens – spelled out in Athenian actions in the mid-fifth century and confirmed by Thucydides' reports of his speeches – depended in the first and last instance on Athens' power and the Athenians' willingness to sacrifice and die in the city's service. That vision of Athenian power and eternal glory, if often eclipsed by a modern discomfort with any frank statement of nationalist or belligerent goals, remains the single feature of Pericles' life that most closely ties him to the city and fellow citizens he led.

Epilogue: The Periclean Tradition

Pericles has figured prominently in condemnations of and hymns to Athens.
He has frequently been compared to great modern statesmen, and yet his
singular import remains virtually unparalleled in the history of popular
government. As a brilliant rhetorician, extreme nationalist, immensely
popular politician, and visionary focused on power and reputation, Pericles
continues to provide the prime example of what one man can achieve, for
good or ill, in a democracy.

Athens produced no other Pericles. No political figure in the century of
independent, democratic government after his death in 429 ever
approached the influence, impact, and reputation of Pericles son of
Xanthippus.[1] True, no Athenian statesman after Pericles' death possessed
the resources Athens enjoyed in the 440s and 430s BC. By 428 the
Athenians had expended most of the monetary reserves Pericles' policies
had socked away for future needs. So far as we can tell, Athens never
possessed more than a few thousand talents of reserves in the later fifth
century (and this only briefly, ca. 415), and its resources in the fourth
century were far reduced even from those levels.[2]

The Peloponnesian War ground to a halt in 404, when the Spartans cut
off Athens and starved its citizens into submission after destroying most of
the Athenian fleet in the previous year. Athens lost its empire and was
temporarily reduced to the status of a Spartan dependency. Many
Athenians in these years apparently took a dim view of Pericles' policies
and leadership. Thucydides composed his defense of the leader (2.65) in

part to answer all-too-common criticisms of Pericles' conduct in leading Athens into an ultimately disastrous war.

Subsequent Athenian leaders rarely called on Pericles' memory even as they attempted to revive some of his policies. True, the comic poet Eupolis brought Pericles onto the stage in 412 as an example of a great statesman who could help Athens face the Sicilian disaster of the previous year, when the entire Athenian invasion force had been destroyed.[3] But in 412 the war in Greece had not yet been lost. Once it had been, Thucydides began working to turn his shorter histories – his account of the Ten Years War (431–421) between Athens and Sparta and his history of Athens' invasion of Sicily and the reopening of hostilities with Sparta (415–413) – into one great masterpiece, living long enough to compose his answer to Pericles' contemporary critics but not long enough to write or revise the connecting and concluding sections that would have completed his account of the entire conflict (431–404).[4]

Athens' recovery in subsequent years was swift but not complete. By the 390s it was attempting to reestablish a kind of empire in the northern Aegean. By the 370s the Athenians had formed a new league of Greek states – less powerful and less profitable for Athens than the fifth-century Athenian empire, but clearly providing evidence that the Athenians had not given up their ambition to dominate other Greek states. Predictably enough, Athens' policy in this period centered on the Hellespont, the northern Aegean coast, and the islands. Athens' foreign policy interests hardly changed over three centuries of Athenian history, no matter who led the state or what form of government the Athenians practiced or endured.[5] Calls for them to give up their imperial dreams – such as that in Isocrates' *On the Peace* from the mid-fourth century – were rare and stillborn.

One might argue that the fourth-century Athenians enjoyed insufficient political space or resources to allow for the rise of a democratic leader of the status of Pericles. Indeed, southern and central Greece as a whole did not produce a leader of Pericles' stature after the fifth century BC. The Spartan general Agesilaus and the Theban Epaminondas enjoyed briefly spectacular military careers that neither could convert into long-lived preeminence for his state or himself. Later, arising in the north and building on the work of his father Philip, Alexander the Great of Macedon would thoroughly dominate the political scene in his lifetime and thereafter, as rulers sought to hold, conquer, or reconquer portions of his great empire. Athens and the other Greek poleis became political relics, often practicing a form of local self-government that hardly masked their subservience to greater powers.[6]

The dominant (historical) political figure in fourth-century Athens was the ancient lawgiver Solon. So powerful was his reputation and attraction that Athenians readily attributed their laws to the sixth-century figure even if the statutes had been passed within recent memory.[7] Although surrounded by the physical monuments of the Periclean age, it seems very few Athenian politicians invoked Pericles' name for either praise or blame.[8] Philip Stadter comments that the fourth-century orators have "relatively little to say about Pericles."[9] Certainly they have little of substance to say about him. Analysis of the references that exist shows that by the mid-fourth century the statesman had become a rather bloodless example of wise leadership from a bygone era.[10] (At least Plato earlier in the century had treated Pericles as one of the demagogues who misled the people!) Perhaps the most interesting of the fourth-century references to Pericles appears very early in the century in Lysias (*Andoc.* 10), who reports that Pericles encouraged the use of both written and unwritten laws against those who blasphemed. The reference suggests that the theme of "unwritten laws" (Thuc. 2.37.3) may have been remembered as important for Pericles and underscores our conclusion about his conventional religious stance.[11]

Why, though, do we not find substantive appeals to Periclean thought or policies in an age when Athens sought to rebuild its empire? One reason for this undoubtedly stems from the very fact that Athens had lost the war that Pericles championed. But another must surely be that the Periclean vision of actual military predominance in Greece had become simply too unrealistic. The pursuit of such a dream had cost the Athenians far too much. More important, perhaps, Pericles had demanded that the Athenians sacrifice themselves in the service of this dream. He had asked that they serve personally and frequently in the Athenian infantry and navy, asserting that death in the service of the city-state was the highest form of *arete*. Fourth-century Athenians apparently found such a suggestion less than compelling. By the middle of the century the Athenians relied on mercenaries for a good deal of their infantry actions, even though the state had fewer resources for the payment of such soldiers for hire than it had possessed in Pericles' day.[12] By the middle of the fourth century, Pericles' proposal of pay for jury service had proliferated into payment for virtually every major state office and payments to citizens for attending festivals and even for voting in the assembly.[13]

Whatever the motivations for jury pay itself, Pericles' vision of rewarding citizens for their service and sacrifice in the name of Athenian greatness eventually turned into a system that funded public payments before immediately pressing military operations. Although it appears to be true that Athens continued to spend a good deal more on military matters than on domestic expenses like pay for public service or theater subsidies,[14] it was the marginal expenditures – that is, increases in military spending and related, necessary reductions in social spending needed to face unexpected or immediate circumstances – that potentially made the difference. As Alexander's father Philip of Macedon rose to power, the Athenians repeatedly failed to take the dangerous and expensive, extra military steps needed to protect their own interests. The greatest orator of the age, Demosthenes, had neither the ancestry, nor military career, nor personal charisma, nor understanding of the Athenian psyche to convince the Athenians to make the personal and financial sacrifices necessary to thwart and defeat Philip.[15] Yet given the changes that had occurred in the Athenians and their environment by ca. 340 BC, one doubts that Pericles himself could have convinced them to go to war with Philip until it was too late.[16]

Thucydides emphasized that the political leaders who followed Pericles lacked his intelligence and character. They also lacked his vision. Only Pericles' young ward Alcibiades appears as a potential rival for Periclean-type influence in the later fifth century. But Alcibiades' actions seem never to have been based on principles – even a principle like the acquisition of Athenian power.[17] Alcibiades almost always did what was best for Alcibiades, repeatedly betraying Athens just as readily as he defended it.[18] Pericles surely would have found the career of his younger relation utterly repellent.[19] Gifted with wealth, intelligence, nobility, and good looks, Alcibiades squandered it all by betraying both his country and his heritage.

Both Alcibiades' talents and his weaknesses glimmer in a story related by Xenophon. The young Alcibiades debates the nature of law with Pericles, with the youngster taking the relativist position that law is merely the exercise of force.[20] (This sophistic proposition strikes one as all too believable given Alcibiades' career.) The response of the increasingly frustrated Pericles in the anecdote is to dismiss such debate as a young man's intellectual game of the type he too engaged in as a youth. This leads Alcibiades to quip, "I wish I had known you when you were at your best."

Pericles figures in this story as an older, conventional thinker.[21] To sophistic youths like Alcibiades or would-be oligarchs like Critias (both associates of Socrates), he probably seemed so. Yet Pericles, Socrates, and Sophocles had all held that there were unwritten rules of society that were "shameful to break";[22] for all that divided these Athenians, their respect for conventional morality and their loyalty to Athens made them all old-fashioned by the standards of relativists like Alcibiades or certain other sophists.[23]

If Pericles enjoyed a marginal political afterlife in Athens, his reputation certainly both waxed and waned outside of that environment. The statesman attracted only moderate historical interest in antiquity: the historians who specialized in histories of Athens (whose works are reflected in *The Constitution of Athens* often attributed to Aristotle) apparently tended to treat him as one in a series of regrettable popular leaders or demagogues.[24] Indeed, "no authoritative biography of Pericles was written in the Hellenistic or later periods."[25] Cicero could speak of Pericles as a great orator and statesman, and 150 years or so after Cicero the biographer Plutarch composed a biography that (often) praised the leader and the Athens he helped create.[26] Yet, as we have seen, the sometimes compromised Pericles of Plutarch is not exactly the Pericles of Thucydides.

Plutarch attempted to portray the statesman over time rather than drawing a static picture of the leader ca. 432–430 (as had Thucydides). Plutarch's Pericles possesses all-too-human personal flaws and foibles;[27] he rises to power as a demagogue and becomes a statesman only after the defeat of his greatest rival, Thucydides Melesiou. Indeed, one need only examine the Roman with whom Plutarch paired Pericles in his *Parallel Lives* to understand the relatively modest position to which he assigned the Athenian. Plutarch conjoins his biography of Pericles with that of Fabius Maximus, the Roman general who "saved Rome" by preventing another pitched battle with the Carthaginian invader Hannibal in the first period of the Second Punic War (218–201 BC). Plutarch primarily seized on Fabius, known as "the Delayer" (Cunctator) by the Romans, because of shared virtues (especially moderation and incorruptibility[28]), their "ability to endure the follies of their people and their colleagues in office," and because of the superficial similarity between Fabius's military strategy and that of Pericles, who sought to prevent the Athenians from fighting an infantry battle with Sparta that they would surely lose.[29] And like Pericles, Fabius was punished by a populace that found his approach maddening, only to have the people later realize that he had in fact adopted the best strategy for the time.

But Fabius Maximus Cunctator stands in the second rank (at best) of great Roman statesmen. To link Pericles with Fabius is to remove the Athenian from the list of greatest Greek leaders. Plutarch, it would seem, thought more of Epaminondas (paired with Scipio Africanus) or Agesilaus (paired with Pompey the Great), and perhaps thought just as much of Demosthenes (paired with Cicero) as he did of Pericles. Yet Pericles' great rival Kimon finds his parallel life in that of the Roman general Lucullus, also a second-tier figure in Roman political and military annals. One begins to wonder if Plutarch, springing from Boeotian Chaeronea, could not bring himself to praise Athens and Athenian leaders quite as enthusiastically as he might have.

To be fair, the figure of Alexander and the great Hellenistic monarchs who succeeded and imitated him (like Pyrrhus of Epirus, for example) and the image of the mighty Roman generals so dominated the later Greek historical mind that one can hardly blame Plutarch for placing the leaders of mere city-states (like Pericles and Kimon) in the second rank. From the ancient perspective, particularly within the environment of vast Roman imperial power, Plutarch's choice makes perfect sense. And it is understandable that Pericles continued to occupy this second- or third-tier position until the rehabilitation of democracy and direct popular government that began in the early nineteenth century. Even to the eighteenth-century American Founders Pericles was a problematic character. He sailed a bit too near the figure of a warmongering demagogue so often abused in Greek comedy and philosophy, while his Athens was a turbulent and short-lived state.[30] Better by far to create some constitutional restraints that could ensure a stable republic than to turn over the management of affairs to a direct vote of the populace in the Athenian style.

George Grote's twelve-volume history of Greece (1846–1856) reflected, if it did not actually create, changing attitudes in the English-speaking world.[31] Grote praised the demagogues of Athens as principled leaders who reflected and enacted the will of the people.[32] Meanwhile, the nineteenth century saw the rehabilitation of the term "democracy," which lost its connection with mob rule and began to be used as a term of approbation rather than condemnation in serious political discussions.[33] By the twentieth century, leaders could speak of "making the world safe for democracy," an idea that would hardly have appealed to any political theorist before the 1800s. We must note, of course, that this changed attitude rested on the altered definition of democracy, which became the normal term for what was once called republican or constitutional government and which lost its traditional connection with direct popular rule by majority vote.[34]

The rehabilitation of democracy helped bring Pericles to prominence once again.[35] Thucydides, who wrote that Athens under Pericles was "in name a democracy but in fact the rule of the first man," would surely have appreciated the irony. The historian took pains to explain that Pericles often sought to change the people's minds rather than simply to reflect their will, and his work shows a marked distaste for the fickleness of "the people." Viewing Pericles as an idealized example of democracy *per se*, therefore, hardly reflects Thucydides' presentation of the statesman. Still more ironic has been the tendency to downplay or ignore the facets of Pericles' ideology and policies that Thucydides emphasized, especially his nationalism and belligerence.[36] While scholars quote Pericles' few words on democracy in Thucydides far more than any other description of that form of government, the much longer passages on Athenian superiority and power are typically ignored or palliated. However, as we have seen, it was on this power – and not Athens' form of government – that Pericles rested his hopes for Athens' future reputation.

In short, it was not Thucydides but rather the modern world that turned Pericles into an avatar. Moderns admire Pericles as an ostensible spokesman for humanistic and democratic values while pushing the other aspects of his career aside.[37] The historical Pericles saw Athenian greatness primarily in terms of military power and the wealth and independence this ensured for the state. Even Pericles' policies that distributed greater power and privileges to common Athenians almost certainly had their primary motivation in the statesman's recognition that the mass of poorer Athenians represented a source of power for himself and for Athens. The payments to poorer Athenians from moneys provided by the empire acted as an engine driving Athens to more and greater conquests and to more thorough exploitation of the Greek world. Pericles encouraged *demokratia* in order to feed the Athenian empire and thus ensure Athens' place in history.[38]

Such thoughts disturb us because we have grown accustomed to viewing democracies as peaceful and Pericles as an enlightened spokesman for that form of regime. Neither view will stand close scrutiny, but both remain so comforting, so absolutely satisfying to modern tastes and professed values, that they are unlikely to be replaced.

In reducing Pericles to an avatar for democracy or for Athens' cultural brilliance, we fail to capture the qualities that did make Pericles unique in Athenian – and, indeed, in Greek – history. For more than two decades Pericles led the most powerful, wealthy, and culturally dynamic state in Hellas. He supported policies that delivered more power to the average Athenian and more power to the city-state of Athens, demanding in return a level of commitment that required frequent, dangerous service in Athens' army or fleet.[39] He fostered a vision of Athens as a special city inhabited by a special people, who could secure for themselves a place in history as the greatest ruling power in Greece if they would only accept the cost: their own and their fellow Athenians' lives. The Athenians who continued to live would enjoy the most pleasant life in all of Hellas; those who died in creating this life would enjoy the admiration and praise of their fellow Athenians and of all future generations.

As Plutarch and Thucydides suggest, Pericles' success depended primarily on one factor. The statesman understood the Athenian psyche: the spirit that guides decisions and creates character. Pericles recognized that the Athenians possessed reservoirs of insecurity, energy, and arrogance that, once tapped, could make Athens the greatest city-state in Greece. He also recognized just how much Athenians were willing to sacrifice. He rightly gauged that Athenians would die more readily than other Greeks in the service of power and greatness and that a message of future fame in return for present sacrifice, if joined with the tangible benefits of empire, would be received with enthusiasm.

Pericles, in short, acted as both a divining rod and an amplifier. He located and tapped the wells of Athenian aggression and acquisitiveness and provided the mechanism needed to broadcast the Athenian signal across Hellas and across time. Proving that he understood the Athenians better than they understood themselves, Pericles became a conduit through which the Athenians' highest aspirations of glory and their dreams of power, wealth, and perpetual fame could flow.

And he all but succeeded.

APPENDIX 1

Pericles' Military Career[1]

Sails into eastern Mediterranean	Before/after 462/1?	Plut. *Kimon* 13.4[2]
Attack on Sicyon and Peloponnese	ca. 454	Thuc. 1.111.2, Plut. *Per.* 19.2–3[3]
Expedition to Chersonese	ca. early 440s?	Plut. *Per.* 19.1[4]
General in Sacred War	ca. 447	Plut. *Per.* 21.2
General in Euboea/ Megara	446/5	Thuc. 1.114, Plut. *Per.* 22.1–2[5]
Elected general every year	443/2–429/8	Plut. *Per.* 16.3[6]
General in Samian War	440–439	Thuc. 1.116–17, Plut. *Per.* 25.2–28
Expedition to Black Sea	ca. 436	Plut. *Per.* 20.1[7]
Invasion of Megarid	431	Thuc. 2.31.1, Plut. *Per.* 34[8]
Attacks by sea on Peloponnese	430/29?	Plut. *Per.* 35[9]

APPENDIX 2

Pericles' Legislation[1]

Ephialtes' reforms[2]	462/1	Plut. *Per.* 9.3–5, *Ath. Pol.* 25, 27.1
Public pay for jurors	Late 450s (?)	*Ath. Pol.* 27.3–5[3]
Recall of Kimon (?)[4]	ca. 452 (?)	Plut. *Kim.* 17.8, *Per.* 10.5
Citizenship law	451/0	*Ath. Pol.* 26.4, Plut. *Per.* 37.3–4
Festival payments (?)[5]	ca. 440s?	Plut. *Per.* 9.1
Congress Decree (?)[6]	ca. 449?	Plut. *Per.* 17
Building third wall to Peiraeus	ca. 444	Plato *Gorgias* 455e, Plut. *Per.* 13.7
Musical contests at Panathenaia[7]	ca. 442?	Plut. *Per.* 13.11
Samian War	ca. 440	Plut. *Per.* 24–25.1
Decree re Sinope (Black Sea)	ca. 436	Plut. *Per.* 20.2
Decree on Megara	ca. 433	Plut. *Per.* 30.3
No Spartan embassy to be received	431	Thuc. 2.12.2
No assembly to be held[8]	431	Thuc. 2.22.1

APPENDIX 3

Athenian Government in the Time of Pericles

Knowledge of the basic structure of Athenian government is necessary for any understanding of Pericles' political career and policies. Sometime after the reforms of Cleisthenes (ca. 507), the Athenians began to refer to their government as *demokratia*, a word that combines the ideas of "the people" (*demos*) with "power" (*kratos*), and thus is parallel to words like *aristokratia* (power in the hands of the "best," or *aristoi*) and *oligarchia* ("rule," or *arche*, in the hands of the "few," or *oligoi*). Despite the fact that a Greek might refer to Athens' regime as *demokratia* and Sparta's as either *oligarchia* or *aristokratia* (since the Spartans restricted full citizenship to those who owned a certain amount of property), both city-states were ruled by assemblies of citizens. The citizen assembly (called the *ekklesia* in Athens) was the heart of any Greek polis and usually acted as the sovereign body, making decisions on issues like war and peace and often serving as a court for certain kinds of cases.

Athens' sovereign assembly was different because even Athenian men without property could attend the assembly and cast their ballots. In addition, by the middle of the fifth century (after the reforms of Ephialtes, in 462/1), Athenians with little (or perhaps no) property could serve on the Athenian Council of 500 (the *boule*). This important government organ set the agenda for assembly meetings and comprised 500 citizens chosen by lot who served for one year. (The use of the lottery to choose officials for important offices constituted another important difference between *demokratia* and the polis government practiced in some other Greek city-states.) This council could and did also serve as a court for certain issues.

Athens had another, older council – the so-called Areopagus, named for the "hill of Ares" on which it met. Although it apparently played a major role in predemocratic and early democratic government, after 462/1 it served primarily as a court for particular kinds of homicide cases. The members of the Areopagus were all former Athenian archons, the executive officers of the state, who were elected from wealthier families for yearly terms before 487 but chosen by lot thereafter. The Athenians selected nine archons (and a secretary for the board) every year, including the archon "eponymous" (because his name was used to designate the year: "the year of Themistocles" was 493/2), the polemarch ("war archon"), and a primarily religious official known simply as the basileus ("king" or "king archon"). The archons had various executive and judicial functions, and after their year of office they entered the Areopagus, where they served for life.

By the time Pericles began his political career, the archonship had lost considerable status owing to the fact that the officials were no longer elected but were chosen by lot (and after 457/6 even middle-class citizens were eligible for the office). The Athenians recognized that they could not (for example) allow their military forces to be commanded by an official chosen in this way, so by the early fifth century they had placed the military in the hands of ten elected generals (*strategoi*). This position quickly (if not immediately) became the most important political as well as military office in Athens. Athenian leaders from Themistocles to Kimon to Pericles used the generalship to increase their political power and influence, and by the second quarter of the fifth century the Athenians apparently accepted that their generals were also their chief political officials, advising the citizens in the assembly on policy outside the realm of military matters (although not all generals seem to have concerned themselves with domestic politics).

As noted, state policy in Athens was determined by the assembly of citizens, who voted on when to go to war and when to make peace, where to send the army, how to manage the state's finances, how to punish former allies or subjects who had revolted, what construction projects to undertake, when and what kind of religious festivals to hold, and a host of other matters. Business came before the assembly in two basic ways: the Council of 500 could make a specific proposal, or it could simply place an item for discussion on the agenda. Individual citizens were free to rise and speak on any subject before the assembly and to propose changes to any legislation. It seems that certain leading citizens and generals tended to speak more than others, and we may surmise that the assembly constituted the primary arena within which political battles were won and lost in fifth-century Athens.

The powers of the Athenian people in the assembly were not limited in any meaningful way until late in the fifth century (well after the death of Pericles). There was no written constitution determining the way the government ran or restricting the people from carrying out its will. The assembly could decide to do X on one day and Y on the next, as we know it did from time to time, but (remarkably enough) it appears to have been able to follow a fairly consistent policy in important areas over reasonable periods of time (with some notable and devastating exceptions).

The most important other arena of political action in Athens was the courts. By the middle of the fifth century most Athenian legal cases were heard by large courts, often with 500 or more citizen jurors, who after Pericles' proposal (probably in the 450s) were paid for their service. In the fourth century BC the courts became notorious for the political cases brought by various Athenian leaders against each other. The fifth century provides fewer examples of this kind of political trial, although the prosecutions of Miltiades and Kimon remind us that political trials occurred in the earlier period as well (even if neither of these cases may have been tried before a regular Athenian jury). Aristotle believed that control of the courts meant significant control of the state, and thus he maintained that popular courts (with citizen jurors instead of aristocratic magistrates or councils making judgments) constituted another important quality of *demokratia*.

The Athenians also had various officials or boards of officials (usually chosen by lot or elected for one year) that managed technical matters from the state treasuries to the keeping of records, but the assembly, council, courts, and generalship formed the primary avenues for the development and deployment of political power in Athens. In such a system, it will be obvious why the skills that Pericles and other Athenian statesmen needed centered on public speech and the ability to persuade their fellow citizens.[1] Athenian government rested on expressed opinions (by vote) of the Athenian citizens, and the ability to persuade – or lead – that citizen body constituted the most important skill any Athenian statesman of the fifth century could possess.

APPENDIX 4

Periclean Ideas?

I have argued that we should accept ideas that appear in Pericles' speeches in Thucydides as "Periclean" if they comport with our knowledge of Athenian history and Pericles' biography, and especially if Pericles is made to repeat these ideas in Thucydides' work. We should add to this potentially Periclean material those views or ideas that Thucydides attributes to Pericles in his narrative rather than in a speech. (For example, in 2.13 Thucydides tells us things that Pericles said in a speech, but he does not actually attempt to re-create the address. This passage thus provides a useful example of the kind of facts Thucydides might have gathered before reproducing a speech for one of the figures in his history.)

Utilizing this procedure, something like the following picture of Periclean ideas emerges:

War with Sparta is necessary and the best policy: 1.127.3 and all three speeches.
My (Pericles') policy has not changed: 1.140.1, 2.61.2; 3.38.1 (echoed by Cleon).
Any concession to Sparta is tantamount to slavery: 1.141.1, 2.61.1, 2.62.3, 2.63.1, 2.63.3; cf. 1.140.5–141.1 (even a small concession is problematic).
Peloponnesians are inferior to Athenians at sea: 1.141.4–5, 1.142.4–9, 1.143.2, 1.143.4–5, 2.62.2.
Great honor comes from great risk/danger: 1.144.3, 2.42.4, 2.43.5.
It is important to achieve undying praise/fame/reputation: 2.43.2–3, 2.64.3–6; cf. 2.45.2 (possibly relevant negative example concerning *kleos* of women).

Service to the state and the state itself are more important than individual well-being: 2.43.1, 2.60.2–4, 2.61.4, 2.63.1; cf. 2.42.3.

Athenians are special and deserve to rule: 2.39.4, 2.40.4–41.4, 2.61.4.

The future will remember Athens for its power: 2.41.2–4, 2.64.3 (cf. 1.144.4).

Athenians' land/farms/houses are not important; real power lies in the fleet/empire: 1.143.5, 2.13.2, 2.62.3; 3.46.3 (echoed by Diodotos).

Athens' financial resources are superior to Sparta's and sufficient for the war: 1.142.1, 1.143.1, 2.13.3–6, 2.65.13.

Athens' military resources are abundant and should encourage the Athenians to expect victory: first speech (1.143.3, etc.), 2.13.3–9, 2.65.13.

Wealth from sacred resources (treasuries, statues, etc.) is available for war but must be paid back: 2.13.3–6.[1]

Success in war depends on surplus funds: 1.141.3–5, 1.142.1, 2.13.2–6.

Success in war depends on thoughtful planning (*gnome*): 2.13.2, 2.62.5.

Present Athenians must not fall short of their ancestors: 1.144.4, 2.62.3.

Readily accepting danger/war is crucial to success/greatness: 1.144.3, 2.64.6.

Athens should attempt no new conquests during this war: 1.144.1, 2.65.7.

Sparta has laws expelling foreigners: 1.144.2, 2.39.1.

Athens deserves your (the Athenians') devotion: 2.43.1, 2.44.3, 2.61.4, 2.63.1.

"Do-nothing" thinking and people are harmful/dangerous: 2.40.2, 2.63.2–3, 2.64.4; 6.18.6 (echoed by Alcibiades).

Athenians are responsible for their own choices but blame their leaders: 2.60.4–7, 2.61.2, 2.64.1; 3.43.5 (echoed by Diodotos).

Beyond these cases, there are a few statements made only once by Pericles in the text but echoed by later speakers in the history in a way that could lead us to believe they are drawing on actual Periclean ideas or imagery:

Athens' empire is a tyranny: 2.63.2; 3.37.2 (echoed by Cleon).

Speech and deliberation are worthy precursors to action: 2.40.2; 3.42 (echoed by Diodotos).

Superiority garners envy and hatred in the present but glory/honor in the future: 2.64.5 (re the state); 6.16.5 (echoed by Alcibiades re individuals).

Our fathers established this empire: 2.36.2 (cf. 1.144.4); 6.17.7, 6.18.6 (echoed by Alcibiades).

This exercise produces some interesting results. We see that the ideas most likely to be "Periclean" primarily concern the war and Athenian or human qualities that relate most closely to the war. Among the most striking absences in this list of hypothetically Periclean material are any of the more universal statements made by Pericles and his description of Athenian democracy. The "historical kernel" of Pericles in Thucydides, if one can use that term, reflects his qualities as a political and (especially) as a military leader.

Did Pericles actually use the kind of generalizing statements that often appear in his speeches in Thucydides (for example, his thoughts about the way men find it difficult to accept the praise of others once it exceeds what they believe they themselves could accomplish: 2.35)? Since these kinds of generalizations are common to speeches in Thucydides, I would maintain that (a) some Greeks probably did often speak this way in the fifth century BC, but that (b) this is an area where we are most likely to find "Thucydidean" material. The historian almost always bases these generalizations on (or uses them to elucidate) the actual historical issues of the speech in question. They therefore do not detract from the themes of what the speakers "actually said," and may in fact represent part of what Thucydides thought was "necessary" (*ta deonta*) given these themes and ideas, and which he therefore felt free to provide.[2]

As for Pericles' words about *demokratia* in the Funeral Oration (2.37.1), I personally believe that the important placement of this passage early in the address and its relatively unphilosophical tone suggest that the statesman did indeed treat the subject in something like the form Thucydides presents. My confidence about this is not, however, equal to the confidence I feel about the matters that relate more directly to the war and that Thucydides associates with Pericles in several places in speeches and/or in the narrative.

Notes

INTRODUCTION   BIOGRAPHY AND HISTORY

1. Plut. *Alex.* 1; see also P. Stadter, *Commentary*, pp. xxiii–xxvii. Cf. Plut. *Kim.* 2: "a portrait which reveals a man's character and inner qualities possesses a greater beauty than one which merely reproduces the face and physical appearance" (all translations of Plutarch, I. Scott-Kilvert, sometimes adapted). Ed. Meyer, *Forsch.* II.65–71, esp. 70 with n. 1, argues that Plutarch depended on a well-developed biographical tradition, a view rightly rejected by Stadter, p. lviii n. 70.

2. Some scholars believe Ephorus's (now lost) work could greatly help us supplement the picture of fifth-century Athens and thus attribute special importance to the extant work of first-century BC historian Diodorus Siculus, who employed Ephorus as a source for at least some parts of his account of Periclean Athens. For reasons to distrust Diodorus, especially when his account conflicts with that of Thucydides, see W. K. Pritchett, *Thucydides' Pentekontaetia and Other Essays*. For a strident but unconvincing defense, see P. Green, *Diodorus Siculus*, pp. 1–47. Green to some degree erects a straw man – the scholar who maintains that Diodorus was a "virtual imbecile" (p. 29). That is not the view of most scholars who have found Diodorus's work problematic. Green, it should be noted, argues (pp. 25–29) that we cannot be certain how much Diodorus used Ephorus and how much the latter's work has influenced the former's. The use of Diodorus requires great care and healthy skepticism.

3. Plutarch's method of drawing on widely different types of sources from various periods means that each piece of information he provides must be evaluated independently. The historian must ask (especially) where Plutarch is likely to have derived the information he provides, what his source's source (or sources) might have been, and what reason any of the figures in this chain might have had for including such information or for presenting it in a particular way or

context. P. Stadter's excellent *Commentary* on Plutarch's life of Pericles seeks to make the biographer into a better artist (and thus thinker) than some others have claimed. See especially the criticisms of A. W. Gomme, *HCT* I.54–84, esp. 65–70. Yet Gomme's critique remains quite trenchant and his analysis of Plutarch's division of Pericles' career into two stages (demagogic and statesman-like: esp. pp. 65–68) retains its relevance (see pp. 84ff.). Gomme actually defends Plutarch against the charge of not understanding some of the chronological problems his narrative presents and acknowledges that Plutarch's goals, which were essentially different from those of a historian, make some of his "short-comings" matters of perspective and intention.

4. Since these are the problems that interest me in this volume, the reader will not find here – except in one or two cases – lengthy and polemical discussions of many of the important and controversial issues that intersect with Pericles' career. Two books that do take this approach are C. Schubert, *Perikles*, and A. J. Podlecki, *Perikles and His Circle*. Both books have great value for the specialist in Greek history, but neither seeks to answer systematically the questions about Pericles' development and ideas that I wish to examine. Another approach, taken by G. Lehmann in his recent book, *Perikles: Staatsmann und Stratege*, is to provide a detailed picture of Athens itself during the period of Pericles' career. Such an approach is sometimes necessary due to the gaps in our knowledge about Pericles himself. I have nevertheless attempted to keep discussions of Athens focused on issues that affected or derived from Pericles' development and practice as a statesman and leader. A. Azoulay's recent biography, *Pericles of Athens*, does focus on the personality and style (if not the politics) of the statesman but often (e.g., p. 110) glosses over or ignores relevant historical problems while seeking relentlessly to find the middle ground on issues involving Pericles. Too often his conclusions derive from erecting straw men or employing the fallacy of the false alternative: e.g., "Pericles was neither a hero nor a nobody" (p. 14; cf. pp. 1–4, 34–35, 67–68, 122, 137, etc.). Azoulay both denies that Pericles has any relevance for our world (p. 226) and claims to find limited relevance (pp. 2–3) in his career. A historian can, I believe, recognize the major differences between our own world and that of fifth-century Athens and still find important and relevant lessons for the present day. A further problem with Azoulay's biography is his willingness to assert confidently a knowledge of Pericles' thoughts or intentions where we have no evidence for either: see, e.g., pp. 14 ("he no doubt hoped in this way to ward off the many attackers"), 21, 48 ("cleverly delegating power in order to strengthen his own authority"), 71–72 ("above all determined not to be placed in the position of a debtor," "determined not to pass for a profiteer or even a monopolist"), 72 ("unfailing concern for the well-being of the people"). In this volume I will attempt to reconstruct Pericles' thought through his (and Athens') actions and through analysis of the ideas attributed to him.

5. Will, "Perikles," col. 571, notes that the idea of an "Age of Pericles" emerged long after antiquity. For the eighteenth-century origins and history of the term, see Azoulay, *Pericles*, pp. 194–202.

6. See J. T. Roberts, *Athens on Trial*, pp. 119–36, esp. pp. 122–23 for the influence of Pericles' Funeral Oration on Leonardo Bruni, and pp. 125–26 for Guicciardini's (not unbounded) praise of Pericles. Pietro Perugino portrayed Pericles as one of the ancient figures (along with Scipio and Cincinnatus) representing temperance (*temperantia*) in a fresco decorating the Collegio del Cambio, Perugia (1497–1500). Azoulay, *Pericles*, pp. 157–76, provides an extremely thorough and useful study of Pericles' reputation in the Renaissance and early modern period.

7. See p. 297 n. 30.

8. For the changing views of Pericles in German scholarship, which has shown a greater diversity of opinion than has Anglophone work (even including, at times, criticism for Pericles' role in bringing on the Peloponnesian War and praise for his imperialism and supposed management of Athens as a principate rather than a democracy), see Lehmann, *Perikles*, pp. 254–56, and Azoulay, *Pericles*, pp. 210–20.

9. For the problematic relationship between democracy and values like freedom, choice, and diversity, see Samons, *What's Wrong with Democracy?*, pp. 163–86, esp. pp. 181–86. For recent work on Thucydides and Pericles, see nn. 13–15 and pp. 162ff. with notes.

10. For Pericles' aristocratic ideals for democratic Athens, cf. Gomme, *HCT* II.126.

11. See, e.g., P. J. Rhodes, "After the Three-Bar Sigma Controversy."

12. Azoulay, *Pericles*, p. 8, rightly notes that the literary evidence – and not epigraphical or archaeological material – continues to provide our main source of information for evaluating Pericles.

13. The scholarly literature on Thucydides' speeches is vast. One of the most sensible accounts appears in Gomme, *HCT* I.140–48. For another view, see S. Hornblower, *Thucydides*, pp. 45–72. Although I do not agree with Hornblower's view of *ta deonta* or his view that Thucydides' professed procedure contained "opposite and inconsistent" aims (p. 71: contrasting "what was actually said" with "what was appropriate"), we agree that Thucydides' speeches cannot be used as evidence for the historian's own thought or opinions. Perhaps the strongest case against the historicity of Thucydides' speeches is made by H. Strasburger, "Thucydides and the Political Self-Portrait of the Athenians." Although I agree with Strasburger on several points of detail, I believe he overstates the degree to which Athenians employ unrealistically frank speech about their empire in Thucydides. Lehmann, *Perikles*, e.g., p. 16, believes Thucydides' account provides some authentic Periclean material, a view criticized by W. Will, "Review." Azoulay, *Pericles*, p. 42, believes the speeches were written long after the orations were delivered and that they "certainly do not bear authentic witness to Pericles' eloquence."

14. It has become fashionable to treat Thucydides' speeches as free compositions designed more for literary than historical purposes. A more reasonable (but, to my mind, still unsatisfactory) approach treats them as "retrospective commentaries on what was happening at the time" (Lendon, *Song of Wrath*, p. 421). I take Thucydides' statement of his method seriously, while recognizing that he may have sometimes fallen short of his own ideal. We should also admit that

Thucydides understandably may have felt greater freedom in "elaborating" on speeches for which he had inferior or fewer sources. However, the speeches of Pericles that Thucydides includes in his work were heard by thousands of Athenians.

15. M. Chambers, "Thucydides and Pericles," in a sober analysis of the problem, treats the Funeral Oration as "a mixture of Thucydidean and Periclean thought" but believes the speech contains what Thucydides "would have liked him to say" (p. 81). This is the point on which we would disagree: I do not think the speech or the image of Pericles in Thucydides is idealized (see pp. 162ff.).

16. For potentially "Periclean" ideas in the speeches, see Appendix 4.

17. For the "Pericles as avatar" hypothesis, see pp. 205–8. It could be argued that Thucydides has painted a relatively positive picture of Pericles in order to contrast him more sharply with the leaders who followed. However, I will attempt to show that Thucydides' view of the statesman changed over time and that both a relatively critical and a strongly positive picture remain in the historian's unfinished work.

ONE   TO BE AN ATHENIAN

1. For the ancient independence of Eleusis and later synoicism with Athens, see Hdt. 1.30, Thuc. 2.15.1–16; see also Plut. *Thes.* 24–25. Hornblower's view (*CT* I.261) that Hdt. 1.30 refers to a war in (as opposed to with) Eleusis is unfounded. For supposed Athenian relations with the non-Greek Pelasgians in Attica, see pp. 22–23. For continued if largely ceremonial acts of independence by the Marathonian Tetrapolis in northeastern Attica, see Parker, *Athenian Religion*, pp. 331–32. G. Anderson, "Alkmeonid 'Homelands,'" suggests that the incorporation of outlying portions of Attica into the Athenian state proper continued into the late sixth century and the reforms of Cleisthenes (ca. 507).

2. I write of "the Athenians" as a collective in this period, but it is quite possible that the impetus for such activities came from powerful families or individuals rather than from any formal, collective vote or action (see also at n. 17 with Frost, "The Athenian Military before Cleisthenes"). Since, however, my aim is to show the aggression of early *Athenians*, this makes little difference.

3. Chr. Meier, *Athens*, pp. 35–91, provides an interesting chapter on the Athenians' late rise to prominence in archaic Greece, noting that Athens did not participate in the great colonizing movement during the years after ca. 750 (p. 35) and played no role in the great (perhaps seventh-century BC) war on the nearby island of Euboea between the cities of Chalkis and Etretria (p. 36), a war that involved a number of states from around the Greek world: see Hdt. 5.99, Thuc. 1.15.3 with Hornblower, *CT* I.49.

4. Hdt. 5.94–95; Strabo 13.1.38–39. J. K. Davies, *CAH* V^2.301, reports doubts about Athens' need for an external grain supply, but it is clear that the Athenians in later periods believed they needed such imports. If grain supplies did not provide the

motive for the initial expansion into the Hellespont, the region still offered many opportunities for economic exploitation.

5. A. Eckstein, *Mediterranean Anarchy*, has usefully demonstrated that states in the ancient Mediterranean world (including Greece: chapter 3) faced a dangerous environment filled with other aggressive powers. It is precisely, therefore, the places where Athens does something unusual that should attract our interest. Athens' unique expansion of its territory to encompass all of Attica, its early interests in distant regions (without colonizing them), and its eventual establishment of an unprecedented Greek empire all arguably reflect both the dangerous and acquisitive environment and the Athenians' sometimes unusual answers to the problems this perilous Mediterranean environment created. While Eckstein's theory well explains why Athens and Thebes (or even Sparta) ultimately fought wars, it does not explain the reason for any particular war at a particular moment in time or the extraordinary measures the Athenians sometimes adopted to expand their power and influence.

6. See p. 238 n. 9.

7. Recently a few scholars have begun to notice that Athenian aggression and expansion predated the fifth century BC, as I began to argue in 2001: "Democracy, Empire, and the Search for the Athenian Character," p. 146. See Samons, *What's Wrong with Democracy?* pp. 101–5; id., "Athens – a Democratic Empire"; and, more recently, J. K. Davies, "Corridors, Cleruchies, Commodities, and Coins," and Kallet, "The Origins of the Athenian Economic *Arche*." Azoulay, *Pericles*, p. 51, suggests that Pericles inherited a preexisting "imperialist system."

8. Hdt. 1.59.4; Plut. *Solon* 8–10, 12.

9. Toepffer, *Attische Genealogie*, p. 274, suggests that Megara had a legitimate claim on Salamis and that this is reflected in the Athenians' tradition of Ajax having a Megarian mother.

10. Plut. *Solon* 10.

11. Lendon, *Song of Wrath*, p. 38, refers to Athens' "second-rate glory" in the "age of heroes" and notes the importance of the mythic past in the relative ranking of fifth-century Greek states (pp. 40–42, 64, 89–90). Athens' defensiveness about its meager role in the Trojan cycle may be seen at Hdt. 9.27 and Plut. *Kimon* 7; in such cases (as S. Mills, *Theseus*, p. 9 with n. 39, with other references, points out) the Persian Wars often serve as something of a substitute for Athens' minuscule Homeric glory.

12. Plut. *Solon* 8; Hdt. 1.59.4.

13. At some point after 507 Athens acquired the southern Boeotian territory of Oropus, but it is unclear if or when it was incorporated into the Athenian state proper. For Oropus's history, see Hornblower, *CT* I.279.

14. For tyranny, see pp. 17–20.

15. Hdt. 6.34–40, 103. For the families' cooperation, see Samons, *What's Wrong with Democracy?*, p. 102 with n. 6, "Periclean Imperialism," and "Herodotus and the Kimonids." M. Stahl, *Aristokraten und Tyrannen*, pp. 111–15, argues that the first Miltiades' settlement in the Chersonese was entirely independent of the Peisistratids, although he recognizes that the younger Miltiades' tyranny there enjoyed the Athenian tyrants' support.

232 | *Notes to pages 16–18*

16. Hdt. 6.137–40. Lewis, *CAH* IV².298, believes this event probably occurred during the Ionian Revolt from Persia (499–494 BC). Wade-Gery, *Essays*, p. 163 with n. 3 put the event in ca. 499–498 or ca. 510–508. For later Athenian control of Lemnos, see Hornblower, *CT* I.189.

17. For a skeptical treatment of Athens' military power and activities in this period, see F. Frost, "The Athenian Military before Cleisthenes," essentially arguing that no organized "national" force existed before the Cleisthenic reforms (ca. 507). Even if this were technically true, it would not change the facts that Athenians acted collectively (if informally) in the military adventures detailed here and that these actions set precedents for later Athenian action and policy.

18. Hdt. 1.61.4, 64.1–2.

19. Solon describes Athens as "the oldest of the Ionian states" (*Ath. Pol.* 5.2 = Solon fr. 4a, West). Rhodes, *CAAP*, p. 66, collects other ancient testimony.

20. For Peisistratus's foreign policy, see also p. 28.

21. Hdt. 5.66 notes that Athens was a military power even before the Spartans overthrew the tyranny of the Peisistratids. Cf. 5.78, where Herodotus attributes Athens' military prowess (when compared to its neighbors) to *isegorie*, "freedom" (in particular of speech) and thus to the removal of the tyrants. Meyer, "Herodots Geschichtswerk," p. 227 n. 3, rightly notes that Herodotus understates the Peisistratid state's power in the latter passage. The activities in the Hellespont and the Aegean testify to Athens' growing power well before the overthrow of the tyrants. We can nevertheless agree with Raaflaub ("Democracy, Power, and Imperialism," p. 116) that even at the end of the sixth century Athens' power and prestige were hardly a match for a first-tier Greek power like Sparta.

22. Hdt. 5.74–78.

23. It is interesting to note that later Athenians, when listing their great accomplishments, focused on events of the heroic age (when Athens had supposedly, for example, defeated the Amazons, helped the descendants of Herakles, and protected suppliant women) and then skipped over the whole archaic (historical) period until Marathon and the Persian Wars: Strasburger, "Thucydides and the Self-Portrait of the Athenians," p. 198. While the Athenians inherited an actual tradition of aggression that went back (at least) to the age of synoicism in the eighth century BC, they did not inherit a list of grand victories they could trumpet in later years. This hole in Athens' military history, along with Athens' meager status in Homeric poetry, arguably played a role in Pericles' ability to convince the Athenians to construct a new, glorious record at which the future would be forced to marvel.

24. For the problematic issue of the dates of Peisistratus's tyrannies, see Rhodes, *CAAP*, pp. 191–99.

25. Thuc. 6.54, Hdt. 1.59.6; see also *Ath. Pol.* 14.3, 16. R. Thomas, *Oral Tradition*, p. 115, recognizes that archonships under the Peisistratids implied (for later Athenians) collaboration with the tyrants.

26. Hdt. 1.62–63 describes the final "battle" by which Peisistratus became master of Athens ca. 546 and suggests there was little actual resistance to the tyrant's return. Subsequent events confirm this impression.

27. For competing aristocratic power, see Stahl, *Aristokraten und Tyrannen*; cf. R. Sealey, *Essays*, pp. 9–41, who emphasizes regional factors in such struggles in Attica.

28. For example, the Athenian tyrants also helped spur the development of the Athenian agora as a central marketplace. Shear, *"Isonomous,"* p. 231: "the tyrants gave initial impetus to the growth of the Agora."

29. Thuc. 6.54, *Ath. Pol.* 16.4. By "statist" I mean nothing more than policies that empower the government – or, in this case, the ruling family – while weakening individuals and the view that a strong regime is more important than strong individuals (or other nongovernmental nodes of power). It should be noted that privileging the state versus individuals can carry with it advantages to some previously disadvantaged segments of the population.

30. For example, the state apparently took over control of the silver mines, which the Peisistratids had undoubtedly usurped (or developed) after taking power: see the next section.

31. For a useful recent treatment of early mining in Attica, see Davis, "Mining Money in Late Archaic Athens," and cf. Mussche, "Thorikos during the Last Years of the Sixth Century B.C."

32. Samons, *Empire of the Owl*, pp. 202–4.

33. Hdt. 7. 144.

34. Even Thucydides, for example, treats the basic story of the Trojan War as historical: Thuc. 1.9–11; compare Herodotus (1.1–5 with 3.122), who expresses doubts about such ancient events.

35. I hope I may be forgiven for using the term *state* to describe early discrete and sovereign political entities while recognizing that they are not equivalent to modern states.

36. D. Boedeker, "Athenian Religion," p. 50, calls Theseus a "civilizing hero." On this theme see also Mills, *Theseus*, passim.

37. Kurt Raaflaub suggests to me that such tales are less about desperation than about an effort to find a distant legitimation of democracy (and empire), which would ultimately be associated with Theseus. I do not doubt this desire for legitimation, but I do not think it alters the fact that the vehicle Athenians employed for this (Theseus and his legends) and the often somewhat lame feats themselves underscore rather than obscure Athens' weak heroic-age heritage. For Theseus's "labors," see Plut. *Theseus* and S. Mills, *Theseus*, esp. pp. 6–25. Shapiro, "Religion and Politics in Democratic Athens," p. 126, notes that in the sixth century Theseus "had been a rather colorless, Archaic monster-slayer," whom the fifth-century Athenians "pressed into service as both hero and symbol of the Athenian state" (p. 125). Wade-Gery, *Essays*, p. 96 n. 1, writes, "Theseus' greatness is post-Solonian." The hero's popularity was growing by the end of the sixth century as an "Athenian contrast to the Dorian Heracles": Burkert, *CAH* V^2.259–60; see also Mills, pp. 19, 23, 27–29. On the development of the Theseus myth, see especially Walker, *Theseus and Athens*, pp. 9–81, who details the development of new aspects of the myth in the sixth century and the attempt by Athenians to set up Theseus as a rival to Dorian

Herakles, and Mills, pp. 1–42. For Theseus and Pericles, see Podlecki, *Perikles*, p. 90: "Theseus … is sometimes thought to have been a dramatic 'alter-ego' for Perikles" (see also his p. 174 for comic characterizations of Pericles as Theseus). For the possibility of Thucydides' implicit comparison of Theseus and Pericles (Thuc. 2.14–16), see Walker, pp. 195–99. For the development of Theseus as a founder of democracy in fourth-century oratory and histories of Athens, see Ruschenbusch, "Theseus."

38. See Eur. *Suppliants* 399–494 and Paus. 1.3 (Theseus founds democracy). For Theseus's importance in Athenian drama and in the Athenians' historical imagination, see Mills, *Theseus*, and Walker, *Theseus and Athens*, esp. pp. 39–81, 195–205. Meyer, "Herodots Geschichtswerk," p. 220, notes that the Athenians' funeral orations and dramas sought to introduce Athens and the Athenian hero Theseus into older tales in which the Athenians had originally played no part.

39. Plato's *Timaeus* (20e–25d) provides a story about Athens' supposed greatness in the far distant past before the current age. The tale (though Socrates asserts it is not *mythos* but a "true story": 26e) is interesting in that even it places Athens' alleged (pre)historical military prowess at the forefront of the city's reputation: 23c, 25b–c.

40. This idea clearly developed over a long period, with origins going back at least as far as *Iliad* 2.546–51, where the Athenians' ancestor/king/hero Erechtheus is described as born of the earth. (And even if that passage is a sixth-century Athenian insertion, as has been claimed, it reflects an idea that already existed by that time.) The literature on autochthony is extensive: see, e.g., S. Lape, *Race and Citizen Identity*, esp. pp. 17–19; J. Blok, "Perikles' Citizenship Law"; C. Pelling, "Bringing Autochthony Up-to-Date"; Cohen, *Athenian Nation*, pp. 79–103; Hornblower, *CT* I.12–13; H. A. Shapiro, "Autochthony and the Visual Arts in Fifth-Century Athens"; and V. Rosivach, "Autochthony and the Athenians," who maintains that the term means "always inhabiting the same land." See also Thuc. 1.2. Azoulay, *Pericles*, p. 112, maintains that the Athenians only "began to proclaim themselves to be born from the earth" in the period from 450 to 430. The autochthony myth (or myths, since it developed and changed over time) is older than that (e.g., Lape, op. cit., p. 17), but the evidence for extensive use and thorough development of the (earlier) idea appears in the early to mid-fifth century (Cohen, pp. 82–85). Nonetheless, Azoulay's speculation on the possible role of Hephaistos and the temple dedicated to him in Athens in this regard is instructive (pp. 113–15). Cohen's treatment is valuable, demonstrating that the myth of autochthony could and did exist within a nexus of other beliefs and historical facts (like significant immigration to Attica) that seemingly contradicted the story: "The Athenians could 'believe' both in the literal generation from the earth of their collective and individual ancestors and also in the interpretation of that claim as merely a mythically expressed formulation of the tradition that Athenians had inhabited Attika for a very long time and that Attika – unlike other regions of Hellas – had never, through invasion and conquest, experienced a cataclysmic demographic alteration once its Athenian identity had crystallized" (p. 90).

41. Hdt. 6.137–39. For the way Euripides' *Ion* "traumatizes Athenian norms" with regard to autochthony and Athenian origins, see Cohen, *Athenian Nation*, pp. 85–88; see

also Lape, *Race and Citizen Identity*, pp. 95–136, who argues that Euripides "rewrites the story of autochthony in the terms of Athenian racialism" (p. 99).

42. Thuc. 1.3.6.

43. E.g., Thuc. 1.12. For the possible relationship of this tradition to the so-called "Dorian invasion," see Hornblower, *CT* I.39–40.

44. The poverty-stricken Arcadians in the central Peloponnese were also apparently considered (at least) very ancient inhabitants of their region: Thuc. 1.2.4 with Hornblower, *CT* I.11. The Theban nobility claimed descent from the men sprung from the dragon's teeth sown by Cadmus (Plato *Laws* 663e; Shapiro, "Autochthony," p. 131). Cohen, *Athenian Nation*, p. 81, discusses the earlier "groups in Hellenic antiquity [that] credited the land itself with the literal creation of their founders," but it is a short list.

45. At Hdt. 7.161.3 an Athenian envoy makes a claim about Athens' right to a share in the command of Greek forces based on the Athenians never having changed their abode. The weak nature of this argument is emphasized by the speaker's linking it to Homer's (very few) words about Athens' martial prowess.

46. See Lape, *Race and Citizen Identity*, esp. pp. 18–19, who, I believe, somewhat overemphasizes the way autochthony (at least initially) served "as a rationale for *democratic* political equality (inter alia)" (p. 18: emphasis mine).

47. For the argument that the invasion was quite late, ca. 1700 BC, see R. Drews's stimulating and readable work, *The Coming of the Greeks*.

48. Hdt. 1.56–58. In a fascinating passage (2.51.2) Herodotus clearly implies that the Athenians became considered Greeks only at a certain point in their history (and that the Pelasgians gained Greek status by moving to Attica and living with the Athenians). In another passage (8.44), Herodotus states that the Athenians were Pelasgians who only later took the name "Athenians." On the traditions about the Pelasgians in general, see J. McInerney, "Pelasgians and Leleges." Strasburger, "Thucydides and the Self-Portrait of the Athenians," p. 198, suggests that the Athenians' emphasis on autochthony related to their reputation for justice (and protectors of suppliants and the weak), since the Athenians claimed that they had not had to expel others from the lands they settled.

49. Pelling, "Bringing Autochthony Up-to-Date," p. 474, points out that autochthony later became a more popular claim, a fact undoubtedly encouraged by *classical* Athens' fame.

50. Cf. Shapiro, "Autochthony," p. 131. Parker, *Athenian Religion*, p. 139 n. 67, notes that the autochthony myth could be used not only to differentiate Athens from other cities but also to differentiate Athenians from noncitizens within Athens. On this subject, see especially, Lape, *Race and Citizen Identity* (and, in contrast, Cohen, *Athenian Nation*, pp. 79–103).

51. For the issue of Greek ethnicity in general, see Jonathan Hall, *Ethnic Identity in Greek Antiquity*, with Samons, "Democracy, Empire, and the Search for the Athenian Character," p. 157 nn. 50–51.

52. Thuc. 1.12.4, 7.57.4, Hdt. 1.146, 8.46.2–3. The (Athenian) tradition treated this as an organized colonization but this is highly unlikely: Gomme *HCT* I.120; cf. Hornblower, *CT* I.40–41.

53. Hdt. 6.32; see also 4.142, 5.69, 6.11–12, and see Thuc. 6.76, 82, 7.57–58, 8.25, Plut. *Kimon* 14.4, D. Gillis, *Collaboration with the Persians*, pp. 1–7, and Fornara/ Samons, *Athens from Cleisthenes to Pericles*, pp. 106–9.
54. Thuc. 1.6.3; cf. Hdt. 5.87–88 for Athenian women making the opposite change. One may wonder when precisely the Ionians acquired their reputation for weakness. Certainly their failure in the Ionian revolt from Persia (ca. 499–494) and their subsequent (admittedly compulsory) participation in the invasion of Greece (in 480) aggravated any previous negative attitudes toward them. Thucydides' tale of the golden grasshoppers suggests, however, that these attitudes predated the fifth century.
55. Plut. *Kimon* 4, 15–16; for Spartophiles in fifth-century Athens, see L. Carter, *The Quiet Athenian*, pp. 44–49, 62–63, 70–73.
56. See Aesch. *Suppliants* and, for Athens playing this role in other dramas, Walker, *Theseus*, pp. 172–74, and on the theme in general, Strasburger, "Thucydides and the Self-Portrait of the Athenians," and S. Mills, *Theseus*, esp. pp. 43–86; cf. Thuc. 1.2.5– 6. Mills, who focuses on Theseus in Athenian tragedy and thus images of the mid- and later fifth century, to my mind (understandably) overemphasizes the impor- tance of Athenian culture and Athens as a "civilizing" force in the Athenian self- image. These themes almost certainly achieved their central status in the fifth century, whereas here we are concerned with the Athenian self-image during Pericles' youth and earlier. Her statement that "Athens' behavior in the Persian Wars confirmed rather than created the image of Athens as the city which always fights against oppression" (p. 54) seems something of an overstatement, though it probably represents what many Athenians later in the fifth century believed. For the Athenians' pride in their benevolence and hospitality, see also Plut. *Kimon* 10.6–7. On supplication in general, see Gould, "Hiketeia."
57. Thuc. 1.2.4–6, 12.3.
58. Thuc. 2.37, 40, with p. 158 with n. 15.
59. Just how far back these relationships went is unclear. For a somewhat skeptical account of early Athenian religion, see Parker, *Athenian Religion*, pp. 10–28. For Athens and the gods, see also Boedeker, "Athenian Religion," pp. 47–49. For Athena and Erechtheus, see Homer *Iliad* 2.546–49 (with n. 40) and *Odyssey* 7.78–81, with Parker, pp. 19–20. Both passages may be late (Athenian) interpolations.
60. See Parker, *Athenian Religion*, pp. 97–101, on the early history of rites at Eleusis. K. Clinton, "The Eleusinian Mysteries and Panhellenism in Democratic Athens," argues that the Athenians used "access to the sanctuary [at Eleusis] as a tool in international relations" (p. 163) and began to "promote the Mysteries among other Greek cities at least as early as the first part of the sixth century B.C." (p. 170). Perhaps this international aspect of the mysteries played a role in the actions of certain members of the Kerykes family, which held Eleusinian priesthoods, as ambassadors for Athens (see pp. 113–14 with notes).
61. Andrewes, *CAH* III².3.410–11. For the sixth-century innovations in Athenian reli- gion, see Parker, *Athenian Religion*, pp. 67–101.

62. See Parker, *Athenian Religion*, pp. 142–44, 221. The most important epigraphic evidence: *IG* I³ 14 = ML 40.3–5, *IG* I³ 34 = ML 46.41–42, *IG* I³ 46 = ML 49.11–13, *IG* I³ 71 = ML 69.56–58.

63. See Thuc. 3.50.2 with Parker, *Athenian Religion*, pp. 144–45 (doubting the propagation of Athenian cults) and Smarczyk, *Religionspolitik*, pp. 58–153.

64. Samons, *Empire of the Owl*, esp. pp. 107–63.

65. For Athens' later claims as a place of special religious significances, see Ar. *Clouds* 302–11, with Burkert *CAH* V².248.

66. The name apparently should mean "all-Athenian": see Parker, *Athenian Religion*, p. 91 with Pausanias 8.2.1.

67. Samons, *What's Wrong with Democracy?*, pp. 163–75.

68. Hdt. 1.64.2; cf. Parker, *Athenian Religion*, pp. 87–88, 149–50.

69. As suggested to me by Kurt Raaflaub.

70. Thuc. 1.96.

71. For the foundation of the league and its financial arrangements, see Samons, *Empire of the Owl*, pp. 84–106.

72. Athens had not achieved this status until the Periclean period: M. Ostwald, *CAH* V².306–7.

73. See Samons, "Democracy, Empire, and the Search for the Athenian Character." For particular emphasis on the Athenians' pride in their role as protectors of suppliants and the weak, see Strasburger, "Thucydides and the Self-Portrait of the Athenians." It should be noted, however, that Strasburger (understandably) relies heavily on fourth-century (and later) evidence.

74. For Cleisthenes, see Fornara/Samons, *Athens from Cleisthenes to Pericles*, pp. 37–58, and see pp. 35–37.

75. The aristocrats Harmodius and Aristogeiton assassinated the tyrant Hippias's brother Hipparchus in 514, an event that led not to Athenian freedom but to a harsh period of tyranny under Hippias. The Spartans overthrew Hippias a few years later (511/10) and *demokratia* was not instituted until (at least) 507. Nevertheless, the Athenians eventually equated Harmodius and Aristogeiton's action with the development of free government (and democracy) in Athens. See Hdt. 5.55–57, 62–65, Thuc. 1.20, 6.53–60. On the historical tradition, see, e.g., Davies, *APF*, 446–49; Fornara/Samons, *Athens from Cleisthenes to Pericles*, pp. 37–47; Thomas, *Oral Tradition*, pp. 238–82; and Hornblower, *CT* III.433–53 (for bibliography).

76. Solon's defensive statement that he did not act like a tyrant betrays the accusation that he had in fact done so: *Ath. Pol.* 12.3. No intelligent politician defends himself against charges that have yet to be made. For Pericles and Peisistratus, see pp. 65–66.

TWO CURSES, TYRANTS, AND PERSIANS (CA. 500–479)

1. Xanthippus ostracized: *Ath. Pol.* 22.6.

2. See *Ath. Pol.* 22.3–8 and cf. Thuc. 8.73.3. On the origin, purpose, and mechanism of ostracism, see Rhodes, *CAAP*, pp. 267–71. For the most recently published *ostraka*, including some aimed at Pericles' father, and references to the other scholarly literature on the subject, see J. P. Sickinger, "Ostraka."

3. For this service, see pp. 45–49.

4. For these events see Hdt. 5.71 and Thuc. 1.126.3–12, with Fornara/Samons, *Athens from Cleisthenes to Pericles*, pp. 4–6.

5. Hdt. 6.125–31.

6. Hdt. 1.60–61. Podlecki, *Perikles*, p. 8, speculates that the woman Peisistratus married may or may not have been the daughter of Agariste, the daughter of Cleisthenes of Sicyon and wife of Megacles. Beyond connections with Greek tyrants, the Alkmeonid family also had close relations with Lydian monarchs (Hdt. 6.125), as did the Kimonid Miltiades (Hdt. 6.37). The Alkmeonid family apparently traced its origins to Pylos, as did the Peisistratids: see Hdt. 5.65, Paus. 2.18.7 with Toepffer, *Attische Genealogie*, pp. 225–26, and Wade-Gery, *Essays*, pp. 107–8, although Herodotus (5.62.2, 6.125.1) does not seem aware of (or is defensive about) this fact. Rhodes, *CAAP*, pp. 186–87, doubts the truth of this tradition and accepts Davies' (*APF*, pp. 369–70) view that the Alkmeonid family rose to prominence fairly late in Athenian history. The more important question for the purpose of Pericles' biography is whether Athenians of his day knew the story of an ancient connection between the Peisistratids and the Alkmeonids (through their allegedly shared Pylian origins), but the state of the evidence makes an answer to this question difficult. Some scholars have thought that the idea of "Neleid" (from Pylos) Athenians was an invention of the Periclean age intended to shore up Athens' claim on Ionia (where tradition held Neleids had become important): on this, and on the general confusion of late sources about the Alkmeonids, see R. Cromey, "The Alkmeonidai in Late Tradition."

7. ML 6 with commentary; Thuc. 6.54.6; Dover, *HCT* IV.330–31. The alliance may have been broken for a time and then reestablished: see next note.

8. Hdt. 1.61 (abnormal relations), 6.123 (outside Athens during the tyranny). Podlecki, *Perikles*, p. 8, accepts an early exile of the Alkmeonids under Peisistratus and interprets the Alkmeonid Cleisthenes' archonship under the Peisistratids in 525/4 as the tyrants "offering some degree of power-sharing to their former opponents." D. Lewis, *CAH* IV².288 (cf. also Dover, *HCT* IV.330–31), considers it possible that the Alkmeonids had been expelled and then also returned to Athens under Peisistratus. The view that the Alkmeonids had been exiled early and then recalled before 525/4 (and then were expelled again) is less likely than the assumption that they had never been expelled before 514: see Fornara/Samons, *Athens from Cleisthenes to Pericles*, pp. 17–21. For an argument supporting Herodotus's report of the Alkmeonids' absence during the tyranny, see M. Dillon, "Was Kleisthenes or Pleisthenes Archon at Athens in 525 B.C.?" In any case, even an expulsion and then recall under the Peisistratids would illustrate the special relationship between the families.

9. Davies, *APF*, p. 457, places Pericles' birth at 498 at the earliest, but he could easily have been born earlier. We possess no firm data. Podlecki, *Perikles*, p. 1, places his birth "probably between 495 and 492." See p. 66 for Pericles' *choregia* in 473/2, by which time it is often assumed he must have been at least twenty years old and which is therefore sometimes used to provide a birthdate for Pericles ca. 494/3. This is the year accepted by Lehmann, *Perikles*, pp. 30, 273 n. 1 (though arguing on other grounds), and followed by Azoulay, *Pericles of Athens*, p. 5. Pericles' older brother Ariphron was apparently a candidate for ostracism in the 470s (see Lewis, "Megakles and Eretria," and Podlecki, pp. 2–3), and thus old enough by that time to have achieved some notoriety. This suggests a birthdate for him of ca. 500 BC or earlier, and Pericles, of course, may have been born within a year or two of his brother. Ariphron's son (and Pericles' nephew) Hippokrates was serving as a general by 426 (*IG* I³ 369) and was killed in 424 at the battle of Delion (Thuc. 4.101.2), but his age at that time is unknown.

10. Hdt. 5.66, 69, 131.

11. Hdt. 5.70–73.

12. Hdt. 5.73.

13. Fornara/Samons, *Athens from Cleisthenes to Pericles*, pp. 19–22.

14. Podlecki, *Perikles*, pp. 6–7, believes Xanthippus's generalship in 479–478 and his campaigns at Mycale and Sestos were responsible for his military reputation. Certainly these events cemented his status, but it seems likely that in the momentous years of 481 to 479 the Athenians usually chose generals who already had some experience as military leaders. Figueira, "Xanthippos," maintains that Xanthippus held an important position associated with the fleet in the early 480s and was involved in the campaign against Aegina in these years. His article should be consulted by anyone interested in Xanthippus's career, although I do not share all of its conclusions. Pausanias (1.25.1) mentions a statue of Xanthippus on the acropolis.

15. Cf. Davies, *APF*, pp. 455–56, who does not accept the relevance of Cleisthenes' fate to Xanthippus's marriage and thus places his birth ca. 535–520.

16. Hdt. 6.102–17 provides our best source for the battle of Marathon.

17. Hdt. 6.121–24.

18. Bicknell, *Studies*, p. 52, accepts that the Alkmeonids were in fact "in league with Hippias and the Persians" at the time of Marathon, but the evidence only allows us to conclude that many Athenians believed this.

19. *Ath. Pol.* 22.6 claims that Xanthippus was the first person ostracized who was not connected with the tyrants. Rhodes, *CAAP*, pp. 276–77, accepts this, and Figueira, "Xanthippos," also attempts to support *Ath. Pol.*'s claim, while nonetheless arguing that Xanthippus's father and Xanthippus himself (as a youth) were associated with the Peisistratids. Xanthippus's marriage to an Alkmeonid and his ostracism at a time when the Athenians were focusing their opprobrium on Alkmeonids and Peisistratids surely warrant the natural conclusion: Xanthippus was associated in the popular mind with the Peisistratids and their (sometime) allies the Alkmeonids. By the time *Ath. Pol.* was written,

Xanthippus's status as the father of Pericles had largely obscured his position as
the husband of the Alkmeonid Agariste, who was connected with the tyrants by
virtue of her family's history. *Ath. Pol.*'s assertion that Xanthippus had no
connection with the tyrants is both factually incorrect (as he was married to
an Alkmeonid, and that family was connected with the tyrants and suspected of
having helped them in 490) and demonstrably defensive in character.

20. *Ath. Pol.* 22.4–6. Podlecki, *Perikles*, p. 9, notes that this Megacles was most likely
Agariste's brother and the subject of Pindar *Pythian* 7. Megacles may have been
ostracized again (!) in the 470s: Rhodes, *CAAP*, p. 275, Lewis, "Megakles and
Eretria."

21. The Alkmeonids had provided funds for the building of a new temple for Apollo
at Delphi. Some eventually believed that they had also (or thereby) suborned the
religious officials there so that they gave oracles to the Spartans to "free the
Athenians" (from the Peisistratid tyranny): see Hdt. 5.62–63.

22. *Pythian* 7, trans. C. M. Bowra.

23. For Plutarch's view on ostracism, including the idea that it was not intended to do
irreparable harm to the ostracized leader, see Plut. *Arist.* 7.

24. Fornara/Samons, *Athens from Cleisthenes to Pericles*, p. 35; Foster, *Thucydides,
Pericles, and Periclean Imperialism*, p. 133.

25. See pp. 193–95.

26. However, we cannot say (with Azoulay, *Pericles*, p. 123) that the "inherited
pollution was clearly at the origin of all the accusations made in Athens against
the *strategos*." One must believe that Azoulay means only accusations made
just before the Peloponnesian War (see p. 138), but even this would be an
exaggeration.

27. For Pericles as a man "detached from society," see Fornara/Samons, *Athens from
Cleisthenes to Pericles*, p. 36, and cf. pp. 206–7.

28. The family did have a dog, which died tragically after swimming behind its master
Xanthippus's warship before the battle of Salamis in 480: Plut. *Them.* 10.

29. For Greek education in this period, see H. Marrou, *A History of Education in
Antiquity*, and M. Griffith, "Public and Private in Early Greek Institutions of
Education."

30. The date of the construction of this sixth-century temple to Athena on the acropolis
is much disputed: see, e.g., W. A. P. Childs, "The Date of the Old Temple of Athena
on the Athenian Acropolis," who dates the building to the period after 510, and
J. Hurwit, *The Athenian Acropolis*, pp. 105–29, who surveys the problem and also
opts for a post-Peisistratid date for this temple. Another temple was begun on the site
of the future Parthenon (south of the Old Temple) in the 480s but was never
completed: Hurwit, pp. 132–36.

31. Hornblower, *CT* I.138–39, accepts the notion that Themistocles fortified Piraeus
harbor during his year as eponymous archon (493/2). However, the passage in
Thucydides (1.93.3) on which this view depends most probably refers to another
office, which Themistocles held "yearly" (rather than "for one year"), as Gomme
(*HCT* I.261–62) suggested and others have supported: see M. Chambers,

"Themistocles and the Piraeus." Fortification of the harbor in the years just after 483/2 and Themistocles' proposal to use revenues from the Athenian silver mines for the fleet seems most likely.

32. The city's public buildings remained "unpretentious" well into the fifth century: R. E. Wycherley, *CAH* V².211, 213.

33. Epinician (victory) odes were popular in years after the Persian Wars, but declined rapidly after Peloponnesian War began: N. J. Richardson, *CAH* V².237–44. See also Ostwald, *CAH* V².326–27 (also noting the popularity of dithyrambs) for the period immediately after Salamis. V. Ehrenberg, *The People of Aristophanes*, p. 104, notes that youths of the mid- and later fifth century preferred more contemporary songs to the great lyrics of the seventh and sixth centuries BC.

34. On the importance of Homer in Athenian culture and education, see Goldhill, *Reading Greek Tragedy*, pp. 139–42: "The Homeric texts, then, were essential not only to the actual procedure of teaching but also to the fabric of Athenian social attitudes and understanding as a privileged source of and authority for knowledge, behavior, ethics" (p. 142).

35. *Iliad* 9.410–416, trans. Lattimore.

36. V. Ehrenberg, *The People of Aristophanes*, p. 302, writes that *kleos* as an individual ideal was waning in the later fifth century but that it lived on "as a quality of the State to which the citizens might contribute" (citing Thuc. 1.25.4, 2.64.3, *IG* I² 943.95, 945.13). As we shall see, Pericles' speeches in Thucydides reflect this new view of future renown. S. Scully, *Homer and the Sacred City*, pp. 54–55, usefully points out differences between Periclean and Homeric motivation for warfare, but we shall see that in his emphasis on a reputation that would be everlasting, Pericles asks the Athenians to embrace something of the outlook of Homer's heroes.

37. For the ephebes, see *Ath. Pol.* 42.2–4.

38. P. Siewert, "The Ephebic Oath in Fifth-Century Athens," argues that ephebic training goes back to the fifth century or earlier. On fifth-century training of youths, see Hornblower, *CT* I.303–4.

39. On this middling group, see Victor Hanson, *The Other Greeks*.

40. It might be argued that Pericles was too young to serve based on the absence of any accounts of his military experience in this war (cf., e.g., Lehmann, *Perikles*, p. 273 n. 1). Yet we know almost nothing of Kimon's exploits in the war (beyond Plut. *Kim.* 5 and *Aristeides* 10, neither of which recounts military matters), and he was certainly old enough to have served. Since we must admit that we cannot answer the question of whether Pericles was old enough to serve in the Persian Wars definitively, we should at least consider the possibility that he might have done so.

41. For the trireme, see J. S. Morrison et al., *The Athenian Trireme*.

42. Hdt. 7. 144; cf. *Ath. Pol.* 22.7.

43. Hdt. 7.141–43.

44. Hdt. 8.61, Thuc. 7.77.

45. Hdt. 8.131.3, 9.114.2, 120.4.

46. Hdt. 9.90–107 (Ionians revolt and join the Greek side: 9.103–4).

242 | Notes to pages 47–52

47. Thuc. 2.13.1.
48. See Hdt. 8.131. D. M. Lewis, *Sparta and Persia*, p. 47, suggests the inherited *xenia*, and notes that it would be "a misunderstanding of the nature of *xenia* to suppose that it connoted necessarily approval of the policies of one's *xenos*, let alone of his state" (citing Xenophon *Hellenika* 4.1.34 to show *xenia*'s irrelevance in times of war). If Xanthippus indeed served as an ambassador to Sparta in 479 (Plut. *Arist.* 10), it is also possible that the *xenia* developed at that time or that the previous relationship encouraged Xanthippus's selection for the embassy.
49. Hdt. 9.114–21, Diod. 11.37.4–5.
50. Hdt. 8.40–41, 53, 9.3–6.
51. Thuc. 1.143.5.
52. On the emergence and development of a "theory of sea-power" in the fifth century, see Raaflaub, "Father of All, Destroyer of All," pp. 315–18.
53. For an excellent modern account of this war, see C. Hignett, *Xerxes' Invasion of Greece*. Useful more recent treatments include J. F. Lazenby, *The Defence of Greece 490–479 B.C.*; P. Green, *The Greco-Persian Wars*; and B. Strauss, *The Battle of Salamis*.
54. ML 27 = Fornara 59, Plut. *Them.* 20.3; cf. Paus. 5.23 (twenty-seven names on the Greek thank-offering at Olympia).
55. Athenian reprisals: Hdt. 8.111–12 (in 480). Spartans: Hdt. 6.72, with Rhodes, *CAH* V².35; cf. Hdt. 9.106.
56. See pp. 61ff.
57. Neither Herodotus's history nor Aeschylus's *Persians* treats the Persians as the kind of two-dimensional villains so often encountered in modern entertainment. Indeed, Herodotus's account earned him the moniker of *philobabaros* ("barbarian lover") from Plutarch (*Mor.* 857a).
58. See pp. 57–58.
59. See pp. 111–23.
60. On the other hand, Kurt Raaflaub suggests to me that Pericles' father Xanthippus, who commanded the Athenian contingent, might have been responsible for Athens' resisting the Spartans' suggestion to move the Ionians across the Aegean to mainland Greece, where they could be more easily protected from Persian aggression (Hdt. 9.106). Such an action could suggest that Xanthippus was positively disposed toward the Ionians. This is certainly possible (if the story is authentic: it reeks of pro-Athenian propaganda stemming from later Athenian imperial relations with Ionia and Spartan-Athenian hostility), but it would not preclude Pericles (or his father) from having developed less than enthusiastic views about the Ionians during the course of the campaign. Leaving them in Asia Minor, after all, may have suited the Ionians' preference but it also did (in fact) expose them to further Persian aggression.
61. The date of Xanthippus's death is unknown, but his absence from any accounts of historical events after the early 470s and the possibility that his son Ariphron (Pericles' brother) was already a candidate for ostracism by the mid-470s (see n. 9) suggests a death early in that decade. Podlecki, *Perikles*, p. 7, puts his death

sometime in the mid-470s. Pericles' *choregia* (in 472: see p. 66) is sometimes held to show that Xanthippus was certainly dead by that year, but this inference is questionable since we do not know that the son of a living father could not perform the service of *choregos* (financial producer).

THREE   EARLY CAREER: THE DOMINANCE OF KIMON (CA. 479–462/1)

1. The Spartans credited Themistocles (along with the Spartan commander) with this victory and rewarded him handsomely: Hdt. 8.124, Plut. *Them.* 17, Diod. 11.27.3.
2. Thuc. 1.94–95, 128.
3. Thuc. 1.128–135.1.
4. Thucydides reports that in 479/8 Themistocles advised the Athenians about rebuilding their city walls, which the Persians had destroyed, and that he devised the stratagem by which this was carried out against Sparta's wishes (Thuc. 1.89–91). This tale contains dubious elements, but it clearly reflects a belief that Themistocles remained influential in the period just after the war ended. For his other activities in the early 470s, see Plut. *Themistocles* 5.4–5, 17 (attends Olympic games and produces a tragedy by Phrynichus in 477/6). F. J. Frost, *Plutarch: Themistocles*, pp. 166–67, suggests that Themistocles was out of office but still touting an anti-Spartan policy in this period.
5. See n. 60.
6. Plut. *Them.* 22. Diodorus implies that Themistocles remained influential for some time after 479 (esp. 11.42–43), but his account has little value in terms of precise chronology. He places Themistocles' downfall in 471 (11.54–55).
7. It is interesting that the prosecutor of Themistocles was an Alkmeonid (Plut. *Them.* 23) and that Kimon prosecuted the man responsible for smuggling Themistocles' family out of Athens (Plut. *Them.* 24), facts that suggest continued cooperation (or at least similar political sympathies) between the Alkmeonid and Kimonid families (and hostility between Themistocles and Kimon: see also Plut. *Them.* 3–5). For Themistocles' relations with other Athenian leaders, see also Diod. 11.42.2–3 (Xanthippus and Aristeides as Themistocles' rivals in the early 470s), with Green, *Diodorus Siculus*, p. 101 n. 167, who believes Themistocles most likely was responsible for Xanthippus's ostracism, and Ed. Meyer, "Kimons Biographie," p. 48 (cf. "Herodots Geschichtswerk," p. 224), arguing that Kimon's marriage to the Alkmeonid Isodike should be placed during the time of this (for him temporary) Alkmeonid/Kimonid alliance (which he believes ended after the fall of Themistocles).
8. Hdt. 8.75, 110.3; Thuc. 1.137.4.
9. On these messages, see Gomme, *HCT* I.440–41; cf. Plut. *Them.* 12, 16, *Arist.* 9.
10. Thuc. 1.135–38, Diod. 11.54–60, Plut. *Them.* 22–31, with many colorful (and often dubious) details.
11. Plut. *Them.* 20 (cf. 5, 9, 24) suggests that Kimon was seen as a natural potential rival of Themistocles, but this may simply be a retrojection based on later events.

244 | Notes to pages 55-56

12. Hdt. 6.132–36, Plut. *Kimon* 4.4; Diod. 10.30–32 contains a very confused fragment about Kimon's early life and family. Diodorus, in fact, does not introduce Kimon as a historical figure until his account of the year 470 (11.60.1), into which year (in typical and perverse fashion) he shoehorns most of Kimon's known activity between ca. 477 and the battle of the Eurymedon, a period of at least a decade. Diodorus's concession (11.59.4) that, in a similar case, he may have spent too long on one subject (in this case praising Themistocles' talents) hardly constitutes a defense of this practice (cf. Green, *Diodorus*, p. 114 n. 203).

13. Plutarch *Kim.* 4 calls the family Kimoneioi and this term has been employed by some (e.g., Bicknell, *Studies*) to designate the descendants of Kimon I (Kimon Koalemos, the later Kimon's grandfather). Bicknell, pp. 86, 92 n. 35, argues that there is no cogent reason to think Stesagoras I (Kimon Koalemos's father) was a Philaid. (For the later stemma, see Figure VI.) See also Sealey, *Essays*, p. 22, who maintains that the Kimonids were not Philaids *per se* but related to them by marriage. For the problematic status of the Philaids as a *genos* (clan), cf. Hdt. 6.35.1, Pherekydes, *FGrHist* 3 F 2, Diog. Laert. 10.1, and Wade-Gery, *Essays*, pp. 164 n. 3. Philaidai was certainly a deme in eastern Attica near Brauron, but the references to a *genos* by that name are very few. Bicknell, *Studies*, p. 88 n. 40, asserts that since Brauron, "in whole or in part, became Philaidai, the family of that name still lived in the district." Lewis, "Cleisthenes and Attica," 26–27, sees the use of the name Philaidai for the deme as a provocative move to annoy the family (whose estates and cult center lay elsewhere). G. Anderson, "Alkmeonid 'Homelands,'" speculates that the Kimonids may have made a home for themselves in eastern Attica during their exile under the tyrants (and that the Alkmeonids did the same in southern Attica), but I believe he misconceives the nature of the (usually close) relationships between the tyrants, Kimonids, and Alkmeonids. The name Philaid is, in any case, convenient and as good as any for referring to the (probably Eupatrid) clan that claimed descent from Ajax's (of Salamis) son Philaeus, whom Herodotus calls the first "Athenian" of the family (Hdt. 6.35.1). Herodotus, we may note, also says that the family ultimately traced its origins from Aegina. For the family's possible deme membership in Lakiadai, see Plut. *Kim.* 4.4, 10.2, Hdt. 6.34–35, with Lewis, "Cleisthenes and Attica," 25–27, and Bicknell, *Studies*, p. 88; but cf. Lavelle, *Fame, Money, and Power*, p. 312 n. 9.

14. For the Peisistratids making certain they had "one of their own" in office, see p. 18 with n. 25.

15. The relevant passages in Hdt. (4.137–42, 6.34–41, 103, 127–36) are discussed by Samons, "Herodotus and the Kimonids." Davies, *APF*, p. 300, believes the Kimonids were at odds with the tyrants in the 540s, and this is accepted by R. Thomas, *Oral Tradition and Written Record*, p. 169 n. 31, who does admit that the family had things to conceal. For a more nuanced (but still basically defensive, Herodotean) view, cf. Stahl, *Aristokraten und Tyrannen*, esp. pp. 111–15; he states: "Principled enmity or alliance between aristocrats and tyrants does not seem to have occurred. The relationship moment-to-moment depended on the circumstances and continuance of the tyrant's power" (p. 115 n. 18; see also pp. 133–36), and this

point may certainly be conceded. Indeed, the interactions between aristocratic families may well have mirrored relations between Greek city-states: both were extremely agonistic (based on competition for predominance). Families could ally and make political war on each other in turn as circumstances and opportunities dictated and no Athenian would have found this surprising. Factions, such as they were, were far more likely to be fluid rather than semipermanent affairs. (On these aspects of the Athenian aristocracy, see Stahl. The study of Roman prosopography has had a clear impact on Greek history in this area, but we must remember that even Roman political alliances were not as fixed as once thought. For the inappropriateness of analogizing archaic Greek aristocratic relations to those of republican Rome, see Stahl, esp. pp. 256–58.) Wade-Gery, *Essays*, pp. 164–65, recognizes that the Alkmeonids and Kimonids made up the ruling coalition with the Peisistratids, but we disagree on much else. In this context, it may be worth noting that although the Peisistratid Hippias is said to have executed many Athenians after his brother's assassination (Thuc. 6.59, *Ath. Pol.* 19.1), no source testifies to his execution of an Alkmeonid, Kimonid, or Keryx/Kalliad, a deed that would surely have been touted by families eager to establish their distance from the tyrants. The fact that none of these families could make such a claim is quite telling and in my opinion testifies to the relatively close connections between these families and the tyrants. Indeed, the Alkmeonids were apparently allowed to go into exile and the other families suffered no retribution whatsoever after the murder of Hipparchus in 514. These facts hardly suggest that these families formed the solid opposition to the tyrants their defenders later claimed.

16. Hdt. 4.97–98, 137–42.
17. Hdt. 4.136–41. In Herodotus's account, the Scythians (whom the Persians had attacked) propose the destruction of the bridge and Miltiades supports them. The other Greek tyrants reject his proposal but decide to break up a small part of the bridge in order to convince the Scythians that they are complying with their wishes.
18. The Kimonids' defense is reflected clearly in the Hdt. passages above (n. 15). A. Fol and N. G. L. Hammond, *CAH* IV².242, recognize the dubious nature of Miltiades' supposed support of the proposal to destroy Darius's bridge and maintain (pp. 234–43) that Darius's invasion was not the disaster Herodotus implies. Beyond the other evidence that suggests the tale of this proposal to destroy the bridge is so much nonsense is the fact that the Persians had a fleet present at the Danube to support the invasion and shuttle troops (Hdt. 4.141): the bridge was therefore merely a convenience rather than absolutely necessary, and its destruction would not have stranded Darius or ensured the Persians' defeat. Any plan to destroy it risked incurring Darius's wrath for little tangible benefit.
19. Hdt. 6.41. We may note as well that Hdt. (6.133) maintains that Miltiades' real motive for the later attack on Paros (in 489) was that a Parian had slandered him to Hydarnes the Persian. This rumor reflects an unflattering strain in the tradition that makes the Kimonids concerned about their standing and reputation with the Persians.
20. Kimon's first generalship was apparently in 478 (Plut. *Kimon* 6), on which basis Ed. Meyer, "Kimons Biographie," p. 42 n. 2, puts his birth ca. 510. Davies, *APF*, p. 302,

also posits a probable birth "in or very close to 510," and see also Blamire, *Kimon*, p. 92. That he was not born much (if at all) before this is suggested by the claim that he was still relatively young at the time of Salamis in 480 (Plut. *Kimon* 5.1–2) and the fact that he is called (by Plutarch) barely more than a boy at the time of his father's trial in 489 (Plut. *Kimon* 4.4); see also *Ath. Pol.* 26.1 (where Kimon is still considered young in 462/1).

21. Kimon's wealth and generosity: Plut. *Kimon* 10, *Ath. Pol.* 27.3–4, with Rhodes, *CAAP*, pp. 338–40.

22. Hdt. 6.136, Plut. *Kimon* 4. Ed. Meyer, "Kimons Biographie," pp. 25–26, believed Kimon would have had little trouble in raising the fifty talents by simply selling off some property.

23. Plut. *Kimon* 4.8. For the possibility that Kimon had no wife before Isodike, see R. Cromey, "The Mysterious Woman of Kleitor." The case against Kimon's first marriage rests on an emendation of the text of Stesimbrotus (which Plutarch consulted) that is (in my opinion) ingenious but uncertain.

24. For my use of the term "Kalliad" to distinguish one branch of the Kerykes, see p. 260 n. 40.

25. Samons, "Democracy, Empire, and the Search for the Athenian Character," p. 156 n. 43, *Empire of the Owl*, pp. 61 n. 155, 203–4, with p. 113 and n. 41.

26. Hdt. 6.136.

27. And the apparent Alkmeonid/Kimonid cooperation against Themistocles: see n. 7.

28. With Kimon's birth date ca. 510 (n. 20) a marriage for him before 489 must be considered very unlikely.

29. It is interesting to note Plutarch's report (*Arist.* 10) that Kimon and Xanthippus served together as ambassadors to Sparta in 479. If true, the report cannot perhaps confirm continued friendship between the families, but it may at least suggest that the two families were not seen as bitter enemies (who would be unlikely to be sent on such a mission together).

30. Hdt. 8.3, Thuc. 1.94, *Ath. Pol.* 23.4.

31. Thuc. 1.94–96; cf. *Ath. Pol.* 23.4–5.

32. Hornblower, *CT* I.143–45 provides bibliography. For the financial aspects, see Samons, *Empire of the Owl*, pp. 84–91.

33. After this victory, the Athenians set up monuments bearing inscriptions that (perhaps somewhat defensively: see p. 230 n. 11) testified to their mastery of "warlike arts": Plut. *Kimon* 7.4–6.

34. Thuc. 1.98, Hdt. 9.105.

35. Some have also argued that Thucydides simply has not told us about other actions that were more in line with the anti-Persian purpose of the organization: Meiggs, *The Athenian Empire*, p. 71. This claim, however, remains unconvincing. Thucydides had little reason to omit any major actions of this type, and there is no evidence that he did so.

36. Hdt. 6.137–40 with Samons, *What's Wrong with Democracy?*, p. 102.

37. Thuc. 1.98.4. The date is uncertain: Hornblower, *CT* I.151–52.

38. Hdt. 5.28–35, 6.96.

39. Azoulay, *Pericles of Athens*, p. 54, strangely does not treat the revolt of Naxos as a "rebellion of any magnitude."

40. Naxos had a considerable fleet according to Herodotus (5.30).

41. Thuc. 1.98–99. For the "imperial moment" at which the Athenians decided to rule rather than merely lead an alliance, see Samons, "Athens – a Democratic Empire," and for the Athenians' earlier "imperial" ambitions see p. 230 n. 7. Although moderns have typically placed the creation of the empire ca. 450 and the alleged peace between Athens and Persia, a treaty that would formally end the need for an alliance against the Persians (see pp. 111ff.), no ancient authority dated the Athenian empire later than the 460s. See Samons, "Athens – a Democratic Empire," p. 17 with n. 19.

42. For the crucial importance of the middling farmer in Greek culture and politics, see Hanson, *The Other Greeks*.

43. Plut. *Kimon* 9–10, 13.

44. Polybius 10.16.2–17.5. Much of the booty seized became public property. Pritchett, *The Greek State at War*, I.85–92, shows that booty tended to become public property after the gods received their portion in the form of a dedication.

45. Plut. *Kimon* 13.7. The agora had apparently been much expanded and adorned with new construction under the Peisistratids, and may also have been used for military training in that period (as it would be later): see Camp, "Before Democracy," pp. 9–11. For the Academy and Kimon's role there, see C. W. Müller, "Kimon und der Akademie-Park," where Müller ingeniously reconstructs a possible dedication by Kimon from *Anthologia Palatina* 6.144 (see also 6.213).

46. Plut. *Kimon* 8.5–7, 13–14, *Thes.* 38.1–4; Pausanias 1.17.2–6, 3.3.7; Parker, *Athenian Religion*, pp. 168–70. For the possible location of the Theseion, see T. Leslie Shear Jr. "*Isonomous t'Athenas epoiesaten*: The Agora and the Democracy," p. 228.

47. Lavelle, *Fame, Money, and Power*, esp. pp. 163–66, notes how early democratic leaders in Athens (like Kimon and Pericles) utilized techniques also employed by the tyrants (such as sponsoring building programs) to gain influence and power in the city. He also notes (p. 165) that the Academy was a district of Athens particularly associated with the Peisistratid Hipparchus. Stahl, *Aristokraten und Tyrannen*, esp. pp. 258–60, emphasizes the continuity between aristocrats and tyrants in terms of gaining and wielding power in archaic Athens.

48. For Kimon's famous generosity, see n. 21.

49. *Ath. Pol.* 23.1–2.

50. Cf. Rhodes, *CAAP*, p. 287, where he writes, "It seems in fact to be the case that in this period the Areopagus was active as a law court and gave verdicts which favored Cimon and his supporters" (referring readers to his own commentary on *Ath. Pol.* 25.3 and 27.1).

51. For the "New Peisistratids," see Plut. *Per.* 16.1.

52. Hdt. 1.61. See p. 35.

53. Plut. *Per.* 7. Lavelle, *Fame, Money, and Power*, pp. 166 with n. 25, 307, considers the possibility that Pericles could actually have been descended from Peisistratus

(through a daughter hypothetically born by his first wife and that daughter's marriage to Hippokrates the Alkmeonid). While this is most unlikely, it surely reflects precisely the kind of speculation in which some fifth-century Athenians indulged (and which perhaps led to stories like Peisistratus's sexual mistreatment of his Alkmeonid wife, a tale designed to make any offspring from that marriage unthinkable).

54. Plut. *Per.* 7.

55. *IG* II² 2318.

56. For Pericles' date of birth, see p. 238 n. 9. The process by which *choregoi* for particular plays were selected at this time is unknown, but Podlecki, *Perikles*, p. 11, reasonably assumes that the *choregos* had some influence over the choice. (For the later period, see n. 62.) Sealey, *Essays*, p. 61, puts Pericles' date of birth as late as 490, based on the fact that he was probably a general at the battle of Tanagra (458/7), thus at least 30, and could still command an expedition in 430 (Thuc. 2.55–56). But in this unlikely case Pericles would have still been a teenager (or younger) when he served as *choregos*.

57. The play does mention the battle of Plataea and gives a certain prominence to the Athenian hoplite action on the island of Psyttaleia.

58. For the relevance of *Persians* to Themistocles, see Podlecki, *Perikles*, pp. 12–14, and Rhodes, *CAAP*, pp. 311–12, where he also notes Aeschylus's association with Kimon's opponents. T. Harrison, *The Emptiness of Asia*, warns against attempting to use this play to divine Aeschylus's political sympathies. Yet the play does not exist in a vacuum, and the evidence taken as a whole clearly points to Aeschylus's support of the "progressive" element in Athenian politics: see pp. 83–84. I admit to having little sympathy for the view that all Athenian tragedies resist political interpretation. Many do, but many others suggest that Athenian playwrights – like great artists of other ages – were able to operate on multiple levels simultaneously. In a society where "religion" and "art" had not been separated in any way from "politics" (all of which are anachronistic divisions reflecting modern, Western notions of a society that is properly divided into particular and separate spheres), it should only surprise us if Athenian tragedies do *not* reflect political issues of the day.

59. Hdt. 7.144 (Themistocles and fleet), Thuc. 1.93 (harbor), Hdt. 8.62 (land of Attica irrelevant). Plut. *Them.* 19 states that Themistocles turned the Athenians back to the sea after the kings of Athens had turned them to the land.

60. Hdt. 8.111–12, Plut. *Them.* 21; for an even earlier attempt at such an act, see Miltiades at Paros in 489 (p. 55).

61. That Pericles' policies reflected Themistoclean ideas: Ed. Meyer, *Forsch.* II.224 (peace with Persia, break with Sparta), Podlecki, *Perikles*, pp. 12–16, 99, 156–57 (use of public money for public purposes, importance of navy/naval superiority, opposition to Sparta as an obstacle to Athens' superiority). On the subject see also Foster, *Thucydides, Pericles, and Periclean Imperialism*, pp. 129–31, and Bloedow, "Implications of a Major Contradiction," pp. 307–8. Podlecki, pp. 15–16, believes Pericles' association with Themistocles demonstrates a break with the Alkmeonid family's anti-Themistoclean policies (see n. 7). Meyer, loc. cit., argues that

Thucydides was the first to see the real significance of Themistocles' career and ideas, but Pericles' career suggests that he (and probably others) had already recognized this. Themistocles' exile and death made praise of him unlikely and the tone of Thucydides' epitaph of the leader (1.138) suggests that he did not expect his opinion to be popular. (It is an interesting question whether Thucydides' digression on Themistocles could have been originally composed before he read Herodotus's history, which presents a sometimes hostile picture of the Athenian but does credit him with considerable intelligence and cunning.)

62. This is denied by Azoulay, *Pericles*, p. 24, largely on the grounds that the *choregoi* (producers) for the plays were appointed by the archons (*Ath. Pol.* 56.3) and thus we have no grounds for believing an Athenian could choose to support a particular play. However, we have no way of determining if the method of appointing *choregoi* in the late fourth century continued earlier practice, and we also know that individuals could in fact volunteer to serve as *choregoi* (see Rhodes, *CAAP*, p. 623).

63. Samons, "Aeschylus, the Alkmeonids, and the Reform of the Areopagos."

64. Davies, *APF*, p. 457, puts the date of birth of Pericles' older son no later than between 460 and 457. Pericles' second wife (or concubine) Aspasia bore him a son who served as a general in 406 BC and thus must have been at least 30.

65. Plut. *Per.* 24 puts the marriage to Hipponikos first; the order has probably been reversed: see Davies, *APF*, pp. 262–63, who puts the second marriage ca. 455 (and believes it produced a daughter later married by Alcibiades), and Fornara/Samons, *Athens from Cleisthenes to Pericles*, p. 162. R. Cromey, "Perikles' Wife: Chronological Calculations," defends Plutarch's order of events.

66. Bicknell, *Studies*, pp. 77–83, speculates that she may have been an Alkmeonid, perhaps the sister of Deinomache (Alcibiades' mother), and Plutarch does imply a relation (*Per.* 24.8). P. Brulé, *Women of Ancient Greece*, pp. 115–16 (*non vidi*), followed by Azoulay, *Pericles*, p. 85, argues that Pericles' first wife was in fact an Alkmeonid named Deinomache and Pericles' first cousin, but this reconstruction posits a relationship so close between Pericles and his first wife's family that it would be very surprising if the tradition omitted her name.

67. Plut. *Per.* 36 with Davies, *APF*, p. 457.

68. Thuc. 1.100.1 provides only the bare facts.

69. Diod. 11.60.3–62; Plut. *Kimon* 12–13.

70. Many scholars hold that the Athenians and their allies meant to form a permanent alliance in 478/7 and that for this reason they sank lumps of iron into the sea (marking the perpetual nature of the agreement: *Ath. Pol.* 23.5): see, e.g., ATL III.326–27. But the permanence envisioned was one of hostility to Persia, not of (say) perpetual tribute payments to Athens after the Persians were defeated, much less of perpetual acquiescence to Athenian acquisition of allied holdings like mines or markets: see Fornara/Samons, *Athens from Cleisthenes to Pericles*, pp. 81–85.

71. Thuc. 1.100–101, Plut. *Kimon* 14.

72. Thuc. 1.100.3. On the date (probably soon after the colony's founding), see Hornblower, *CT* I.155. E. Badian, *From Plataea to Potidaea*, pp. 81–86, argues for a disaster in 453/2 (see n. 77). See also Thuc. 4.102.

73. Thuc. 4.102.3, Diod. 12.32.3, 68.2.
74. Thuc. 1.101. The tale of this (unfulfilled) promise has evoked justifiable skepticism: Athens and Sparta still had good relations in 465, as actual events before and after this (as opposed to reports of secret and unfulfilled promises) show: see Fornara/ Samons, *Athens from Cleisthenes to Pericles*, p. 127 for doubts.
75. Thuc. 1.101.
76. Plut. *Kimon* 14.3–5, *Per.* 10.6.
77. E. Badian, *From Plataea to Potideaea*, p. 85, attempts to use the Athenians' apparent belief that an invasion of Macedon would have been "easy" ca. 463 (Plut. *Kim.* 14.3) to move the Athenian colonists' disaster at Drabeskos (see p. 72) from ca. 465/4 to 453/2. He maintains that no Athenians could have thought operations in Macedon would be "easy" in the immediate aftermath of this disaster. Yet Macedonians and Thracian Edonians (who inflicted the crushing defeat on Athens' colonists) were not the same people, nor were colonists the same as the military assets at Kimon's disposal. Indeed, it is just as likely that the Athenians ca. 463 lusted after influence or control in Macedon *because* of their failure in nearby Thrace. For relations between Athens and Macedon, see the forthcoming work by A. Jarvis, from whose research I have greatly profited.
78. We do not know under what procedure Kimon was tried: Podlecki, *Perikles*, pp. 40–41, believes the case was heard in a regular (jury) court, while others have imagined the *euthyna* (examination at the end of a term of office: see Blamire, *Plutarch: Kimon*, pp. 156–57) or *eisangelia* (impeachment).
79. Plut. *Kimon* 14.5, *Per.* 10.
80. Plut. *Kimon* 4.6–8.
81. One Athenian expressed his views on an *ostrakon* this way: "Kimon son of Miltiades: take Elpinike and go!" See Brenne, "Ostraka and the Process of Ostrakaphoria," p. 14.
82. Plut. *Per.* 5 (from Ion of Chios) and 27; womanizer: Plut. *Per.* 13.
83. Podlecki, *Perikles*, pp. 41–42, believes the story of Pericles' soft prosecution of Kimon may ultimately derive from the anecdote about Elpinike's offer. But the reverse is far more likely: the story about Elpinike was invented to explain Pericles' unusual prosecution. The juicy nature of the Elpinike tale, in turn (and even if invented), then probably became the motive to retain the story of the trial in the tradition. By such means even scurrilous inventions may lead to the retention of factual material in our sources.
84. Plut. *Kimon* 14.5, *Per.* 10.
85. See Fornara/Samons, *Athens from Cleisthenes to Pericles*, pp. 162–63 n. 3, where we do not note the close connection between the Alkmeonid and Kimonid families.
86. Thuc. 6.8 (Nikias chosen against his will).
87. Yet note Plut. *Per.* 10.6 (with Stadter, *Commentary*, p. 127), which maintains Pericles "was chosen" or "put forward" as one of the prosecutors by the people (*hypo tou demou probeblemenos*).
88. The idea of a friendly prosecution is entertained by Bicknell, *Studies*, p. 94 (following an earlier suggestion by R. Sealey).

89. Despite Thucydides' claim that the Spartans had secretly promised to help Thasos (Thuc. 1.101), a story that has the ring of invention (see p. 273 n. 93). The strength of the connection would be demonstrated clearly when the Spartans asked for Athenian aid in 462/1 (see p. 79).

90. Plut. *Kimon* 14.4. Ed. Meyer, "Kimons Biographie," p. 49 n. 1, treats this story as a late invention, disproved by Kimon having named a son Thessalos (indicating a close connection with Thessalians), but see Blamire, *Plutarch: Kimon*, p. 165, who argues that the name may stem from a connection with a particular Thessalian who had become an Athenian citizen.

91. Plut. *Kim.* 16.3.

92. It is possible, though not probable, that Pericles served as a general ca. 463/2. See p. 298 n. 2.

FOUR   THE DEMOCRATIC REVOLUTION (CA. 462/1–444/3)

1. The basic sources are Thuc. 1.102, *Ath. Pol.* 25, Plut. *Per.* 7, 9, *Kimon* 15.2.

2. Rhodes, *CAAP*, pp. 315–19 and *The Athenian Boule*. Raaflaub, in Boedeker and Raaflaub, *Democracy, Empire, and the Arts*, pp. 19–20, id., "Power in the Hands of the People," and "The Thetes and Democracy." J. Ober has argued for a "revolutionary" foundation of democracy in 507: see *The Athenian Revolution*; for a critique of this view, see Samons, "Mass, Elite, and Hoplite-Farmer," and cf. the various views in Raaflaub et al., *Origins of Democracy in Ancient Greece*.

3. Thuc. 1.101–2; cf. Plut. *Kimon* 16–17.

4. Plut. *Kimon* 16.9.

5. As subsequent events show, there were already Athenians by 462/1 who desired that Athens achieve supremacy in Greece, and such a position required a diminished Sparta. Wade-Gery, *Essays*, p. 250 n. 1, notes that the great Wilamowitz believed Pericles himself held this position as early as 462. While there is insufficient evidence to assert this about Pericles personally, events in the 450s (see next chapter) make it certain that a significant number of Athenians already wished to make Athens the first power in Hellas.

6. Plut. *Kimon* 16.10 (from Ion of Chios). Flower, "Panhellenism," pp. 77–84, argues that Kimon was a "panhellenist," who dreamed of a Greek assault on the Persian empire. Such dreams Kimon may have had, but our evidence indicates that any "panhellenism" existed only in the sense that he supported a Greece united against Persia under Spartan and Athenian hegemony. Such a view in no way implied that other Greeks (beyond Sparta) deserved treatment as Athens' equals.

7. Thuc. 1.102.4. For Argos as a de facto "medizing" (supporting the Medes and Persians) state, see Hdt. 8.73.

8. Fornara/Samons, *Athens from Cleisthenes to Pericles*, pp. 127–29, with Rhodes, *CAAP*, p. 311.

9. See Fornara/Samons, *Athens from Cleisthenes to Pericles*, pp. 128–29.

10. It seems unlikely that they intended to take an action that would undermine Kimon, their greatest friend in Athens.

11. *Ath. Pol.* 25.2; cf. Arist. *Pol.* 1274a7, II.12.4.

12. See, e.g., Rhodes, *CAAP*, pp. 314–19.

13. Rhodes, ibid., who provides references to the copious scholarly literature.

14. Popular courts: Arist. *Pol.* 1273b, II.12.2–1274a, II.12.4.

15. Arist. *Pol.* 1294a, IV.9.4–5; 1273b, II.12.2.

16. For the development of the Athenian constitution, see M. Ostwald, *From Popular Sovereignty to the Sovereignty of the Law*, and R. Sealey, *The Athenian Republic*.

17. Raaflaub, *Democracy, Empire, and the Arts*, pp. 19–20 and p. 298 n. 39. This idea also appeared in antiquity: Ps.-Xen. 1.2.

18. *Ath. Pol.* 25.4, Plut. *Per.* 9–10.

19. Plut. *Per.* 10.7.

20. Fornara/Samons, *Athens from Cleisthenes to Pericles*, pp. 27–28, Samons, "Aeschylus, the Alkmeonids, and the Reform of the Areopagos," pp. 225–27; cf. Rhodes, *CAAP*, pp. 311–12. Podlecki, *Perikles*, e.g., pp. 46–54, continues to associate Pericles with the reforms.

21. For earlier treatments of this play's legal/political factors, see Samons, "Aeschylus, the Alkmeonids, and the Reform of the Areopagos."

22. *Eum.* 289–91, 669–73, 754–57.

23. *Eum.* 657ff.

24. Samons, "Aeschylus, the Alkmeonids, and the Reform of the Areopagos," pp. 221–33, where I discuss earlier scholarship.

25. Plut. *Per.* 15 with Thuc. 2.65.8.

26. The comedians made particular sport with the size and shape of Pericles' head, which was said to be "large enough to hold eleven couches" (Plut. *Per.* 3.6). Podlecki, *Perikles*, p. 172, sees the references to Pericles' head as related to the statesman's supposed baldness, but the nature of the jokes make it clear that it was primarily its size and shape that struck some as unusual: see, e.g., Ehrenberg, *The People of Aristophanes*, p. 205.

27. *Gorgias* 515e–519.

28. On Plutarch's treatment of a fundamental change in Pericles (*Per.* 15) – dividing Pericles' career into a demagogic (early) period, in which domestic affairs take center stage, and a statesmanlike (later) period, where foreign policy predominates – see Sicking, "The General Purport of Pericles' Funeral Oration." There is, I believe, something to Sicking's claim that Plutarch drew so little on the Funeral Oration and Pericles' last speech in Thucydides because the content of those speeches could not be reconciled with the image of Pericles he found in Thuc. 2.65 and which he himself hoped to present. This contradiction, as Sicking notes (p. 424), should strengthen our faith in Thucydides as a historian, and it stems, I contend, from the different periods in which Thucydides composed these speeches and his "epitaph" of Pericles (Thuc. 2.65): see pp. 173ff.

29. As, in fact, Plutarch states: *Per.* 7. For Pericles' known military commands, see Appendix 1.

30. *Ath. Pol.* 27.3–4.
31. Samons, *What's Wrong with Democracy?*, esp. pp. 43–45.
32. Hansen, *Athenian Democracy*, pp. 178–203, esp. 182–83, 188–89, and 197–99.
33. Hansen, ibid., and pp. 53, 55 (for citizen numbers).
34. Samons, *Empire of the Owl*, pp. 84–163.
35. *Ath. Pol.* 27.3–4, Plato *Gorg.* 515e2–7, Arist. *Pol.* 1274a8–9, Plut. *Per.* 9.2–3. For the date, see Rhodes, *CAAP*, pp. 338–40 (after 462/1) and Fornara/Samons, *Athens from Cleisthenes to Pericles*, pp. 67–75 (late 450s). It has sometimes been argued that imperial moneys were not used (or not needed) to fund Athens' building program or public payments. Such arguments, however, make little sense in an environment where Athens undertook numerous expensive military, construction, and political projects at the same time. The availability of imperial funds clearly made this nexus of expenditures conceivable and practicable: the issue is not "Could Athens have afforded X without imperial moneys?" but rather "Could and would the Athenians have attempted X, Y, and Z without imperial funds?" See Samons, *Empire of the Owl*, pp. 41–42.
36. Hansen, *Athenian Democracy*, p. 189, estimates 22 to 37 talents per year in the fourth century. By way of comparison, it cost approximately one-half to one talent to pay an Athenian warship's crew of 170 rowers for one month.
37. Samons, *What's Wrong with Democracy?*, esp. pp. 72–99. D. Pritchard, "Costing," emphasizes that although the costs of Athenian festival celebrations (and the Athenian democracy) were high, the Athenians usually spent far more on military expenditures than on domestic programs in any given year. However, this conclusion does not alter the fact that even such smaller domestic expenditures could have a major impact on military policy and effectiveness. It was the expenditure of marginal funds that most affected Athens' foreign policy and military effectiveness, and it is on the margin that public payments potentially impinged on military funding. The important question before the Athenian assembly became not (for example) "Should we spend more on military than on festival/civic matters this year?" (a question Athenians would have easily answered in the affirmative) but rather "Should we spend more on military matters *right now*, or, on *this* particular endeavor (and potentially reduce civic expenditures as a result)?"
38. There is some confusion in our sources between Damon and a certain "Damonides." Podlecki, *Perikles*, pp. 19–20, expresses the orthodox (and reasonable) view that these are in fact variants of the same person. For the view that they are son and father, see Stadter, "Pericles among the Intellectuals," pp. 116–18.
39. Cf. Rhodes, *CAAP*, pp. 38–40. Attempts to date this "event" are unconvincing. The story floats in a vague temporal environment where virtually all things are possible and Kimon, Pericles, and Damon appear more as types than historical personages.
40. Azoulay, *Pericles of Athens*, p. 145, denies that such a proposal to distribute public (vs. private) moneys could form a bond between the proposing politician and the people receiving the money. Surely we may employ modern experience of precisely this relationship and a familiarity with human nature to conclude that Pericles, and

other statesmen who made such proposals, expected and received a reward from the beneficiaries of their proposals in the form of popularity and support.

41. On this aspect of Pericles' personality, see pp. 39, 193 and Plut. *Per.* 7, 16 (Anaxagoras). Contrast Azoulay, *Pericles*, p. 72.

42. For other payments, see Samons, *What's Wrong with Democracy?*, p. 44 with n. 11, and for their effects on Athens' military and foreign policy, pp. 95–99, 143–62. For payments defining democracy, cf. Arist. *Pol.* 1317b, VI.2.6–7.

43. *Ath. Pol.* 26.4.

44. See Hansen, *Athenian Democracy*, pp. 116–20 on metics (legally resident foreigners) in general.

45. J. Blok, "Perikles' Citizenship Law," and Podlecki, *Perikles*, pp. 159–61, provide useful surveys of views on the nature and purpose of the measure. For the law in general, see C. Patterson, *Pericles' Citizenship Law* and "Other Sorts," pp. 168–71. Carter, *The Quiet Athenian*, pp. 47–48, posits that Pericles' measure was aimed at undercutting the type of Athenian aristocrat with "international" connections that tended to favor friendly relations with Sparta and opposed aggressive expansion of the empire. Yet Kimon's career and Athens' actions in the fifth century show that even Athenians who desired close relations with Sparta tended to be active imperialists. Most recently, Blok (op. cit.) has argued that the measure served as an effort at further "democratization" and raising citizens' morale by making poorer Athenians the equals of noble families, who were eligible to hold priesthoods due to their Athenian descent on both the mother's and the father's sides.

46. Fornara/Samons, *Athens from Cleisthenes to Pericles*, pp. 74–75.

47. Thuc. 1.126 (Kylon/Megara); *Ath. Pol.* 17.3–4 (Peisistratus/Argos); Hdt. 6.126–31 (Alkmeonids/Sicyon), 6.39 (Miltiades/Thrace). Themistocles' mother was apparently either Thracian or Carian, and Plutarch suggests that the Athenians saw this connection as a disability for the young Themistocles: *Them.* 1. Since Kimon's father Miltiades had also married a Thracian, it may be that the royal status of the bride in that case somewhat protected Miltiades and his son from the same criticism.

48. The law would, in fact, discourage Athenian settlers in the empire from marrying non-Athenians: Fornara/Samons, *Athens from Cleisthenes to Pericles*, pp. 74–75. For the law's potential relation to Athenians living outside Attica in Athenian cleruchies or colonies, see Carawan, "Pericles the Younger," esp. pp. 390–93.

49. Nonretroactive: see Rhodes, *CAAP*, p. 332, who also notes that by the fourth century the Athenians had a law that actually made marriage with non-Athenian women illegal (as opposed to making the children of such a union noncitizens).

50. But see Susan Lape, *Race and Citizen Identity in Classical Athens*, who argues that from "the mid fifth century onward, citizens [of Athens] increasingly appealed to a language of birth and ancestry to develop narratives about who they were as citizens" (p. ix). For her, "although Athenian racial citizenship does not prefigure modern racisms, it does offer a snapshot of the conditions that can give rise to racial ideologies and racism" (p. x).

51. We may note, for example, that there was apparently no Spartan suitor for the daughter of Cleisthenes of Sicyon (Hdt. 6.127).

52. For other generals ca. 458–439, see Thuc. 1.108, 113, Plut. *Per.* 18.2, Diod. 11.84, 85.1, 12.6.2 (Tolmides), Diod. 11.79.3, 81.4–5, 82.4–5, 83.2–4, 12.1.5 (Myronides), Thuc. 1.117 (Thucydides, Hagnon, Phormion at Samos) with ML 56 (= Fornara 115) with commentary, and Develin, *Athenian Officials*, pp. 74–93. Podlecki, *Perikles*, p. 58, reasonably suggests that Pericles' name may have tended to obscure the successes of generals like Myronides and Tolmides in our tradition. However, Diodorus, who tends to divide his treatment of Athens up into periods of the supposed hegemony of various leaders (Themistocles, then Kimon, then Pericles: see p. 243 n. 12) presents Pericles as a major military figure only after the dominance of Myronides and Tolmides. Indeed, Pericles does not figure prominently as a leader in Diodorus's account until the Samian War of 440–439 (12.27–28).

53. Plut. *Per.* 10, *Kimon* 17–18; for a possible early recall (ca. 452), see Meiggs, *The Athenian Empire*, pp. 111, 422–23.

54. Denied by Azoulay, *Pericles*, p. 144, who calls Kimon's influence at this time "limited." Yet Kimon was able to negotiate a favorable peace treaty for Athens with Sparta and to lead a new campaign against Persian forces in Cyprus.

55. Pericles opposed Tolmides' expedition, which ended in a major disaster at Koroneia: Plut. *Per.* 18.3; cf. id., *Comparison of Pericles and Fabius Maximus* 3.3, Diod. 12.6, and Podlecki, *Perikles*, pp. 60–61. See p. 118.

56. Plut. *Per.* 10.5, with Athenaeus 13.589e and Ed. Meyer, "Kimons Biographie," pp. 34–35.

57. Indeed, Plutarch connects the two events in his account.

58. Plut. *Per.* 11.1, *Ath. Pol.* 28.2. Likewise the precise connection between Thucydides the historian and this family remains uncertain: cf. Markellinos, *Life of Thucydides*, 14–18. For an interesting and influential treatment of the issue, see Wade-Gery, *Essays*, pp. 246–47 (hypothesizing that Thucydides Melesiou married Kimon's sister and was the grandfather of Thucydides the historian) and cf. M. Chambers, "Wilamowitz on Thucydides"; Toepffer, *Attische Genealogie*, pp. 282–86 (Thuc. descended from the daughter of Oloros of Thrace and Miltiades through their daughter and an unknown man [Thuc.'s grandfather]); and Ed. Meyer, "Kimons Biographie," pp. 44–46, who believed the historian's relationship to the family was probably by marriage. Cf. Blamire, *Plutarch: Kimon*, p. 88, and Stadter, *Commentary*, pp. 131–32, for a useful overview of the problem.

59. And perhaps in the courts, if the tale of the court case in the anonymous *Life of Thucydides* (6) actually relates to this Thucydides. Cf. Stadter, *Commentary*, p. 132.

60. Plut. *Per.* 11 (lack of military career and followers in a group in assembly).

61. Samons, *Empire of the Owl*, esp. pp. 107–63.

62. Parthenon: IG I³ 436–51, Plut. *Per.* 13. Azoulay, *Pericles*, pp. 65–66, rightly treats the Parthenon as a symbol of imperialism, but his view that it served as the treasury for the moneys of the Delian League transferred to Athens does not comport with our evidence. For the complicated issue of the money's history in Athens, see Samons, *Empire of the Owl*. Azoulay later (pp. 77–78) seems to endorse the view that the allies willingly participated in Athens' construction on the acropolis, but there is no evidence for this. For the reconstruction on which Azoulay relies, see A.

Giovannini, "Le Parthénon" and "La participation des alliés." For problems with it, see Samons, op. cit., pp. 48–50 with n. 99, 95 nn. 55–56, and 111–12 n. 17.

63. Wycherley, *CAH* V².218. The Hephaisteion was apparently completed some time later: on the building, see Azoulay, *Pericles*, pp. 113–14.

64. Plut. *Per.* 13. For a useful treatment of this structure and its "Periclean" nature, see Azoulay, *Pericles*, pp. 62–65: the building's Persian style "returned the allies to the status of subjects and reminded them that they had, in truth, simply swapped masters" (p. 64).

65. *IG* I³ 435.

66. *IG* I³ 453–60. For the statue, see Lapatin, "Art and Architecture," pp. 135–36 with figure 13.

67. Plut. *Per.* 13 (work at Eleusis). For the work beyond the acropolis and central Athens and the program as a whole, see Wycherley, *CAH* V².211–22.

68. Plut. *Per.* 13, 14 (perhaps to be connected with the work on Athens' water supply: *IG* I³ 49 = Fornara 117: Stadter, *Commentary*, pp. 181–82).

69. W. Burkert, *CAH* V².246, writes that the "programme ... was almost exclusively concerned with public sanctuaries," which is an overstatement, but not a great one. Beyond the new wall to the Peiraeus harbor, Athens dedicated other funds to work on the city's walls, dockyards, water supply, and the like in this period: e.g., *IG* I³.52A = ML 58A = Fornara 119, line 31 (for the date – 433/2 – see Samons, *Empire of the Owl*, pp. 113–38).

70. Plut. *Per.* 12.

71. Some have thought Plutarch's description anachronistic, reflecting the biographer's imperial context and/or relying on an idea of "full employment" where none existed. Stadter, *Commentary*, pp. 153–54, notes that this view is unfounded and Plutarch's account fits the context of fifth-century Athens as well as that of the Roman empire.

72. Plut. *Per.* 11–12, 14.

73. On the debate, see Samons, *Empire of the Owl*, pp. 155–57.

74. Even if it is impossible to reconstruct the source from which Plutarch drew this account, I do not find Stadter's suggestion (*Commentary*, p. 146) that Plutarch essentially created the story himself very likely. This does not seem to reflect Plutarch's method, which relied on the use and interpretation of sources rather than invention.

75. For "glory for all time" (here *doxa aidios*) as an important idea for Pericles, see pp. 100, 170, 177.

76. See n. 68 (with Stadter, cited there) for the possibility that this claim relates to a decree on the Athenian water supply (which mentions Pericles' sons and may have mentioned Pericles).

77. For Nikias, see Plut. *Nikias* and, e.g., Thuc. 3.91.1–3 (expedition against Melos in 426). West, "Pericles' Political Heirs" (I and II), characterizes Nikias as fully "Periclean" in his foreign policy. I would prefer to see him as "Kimonian" (center right rather than center left, to use completely anachronistic language), but the fundamental point is that no one in the mainstream of mid-fifth-century Athenian politics apparently opposed the empire.

78. I should make it clear that I do not mean that we should credit the words reported by Plutarch in his account, only that the report of a debate of this general type and on these issues is credible.

79. Gomme, *HCT* I.137, sees anti-imperialism in Thucydides Melesiou's policy. Carter, *The Quiet Athenian*, pp. 26–51, sees conservative Athenians as increasingly opposed to the empire, and particularly points to Pericles' words in 2.63.2 and 2.64.4 as referring to those who would either give up the empire or resist its acquisition. Nevertheless, I can see no justification for such a view among the supporters of Thucydides beyond a general opposition to Pericles and Periclean policies (so also Stadter, *Commentary*, p. 146). Gomme, indeed, may rightly believe that Pericles expressed the principles of Athenian imperialism more clearly than others, but opposition to the empire *per se* (as opposed to opposition to Pericles or Periclean power) is difficult to identify in mid-fifth-century Athens. It is of course possible that such an anti-imperial view began to develop a following in Pericles' last years, but it left virtually no mark in Athenian politics before the late fifth century (see also Samons, *Empire of the Owl*, p. 188 n. 80). Athenian comedies, as Ehrenberg, *The People of Aristophanes*, pp. 155–56, notes, typically blamed demagogues for profiting personally from the allies' exploitation (rather than condemning the exploitation itself). Ehrenberg, e.g., p. 305, nonetheless confuses a position favoring peace with Sparta (which Aristophanes clearly held) with the opposition to "imperialists." One could oppose war with Sparta (or, rather, *this* war with Sparta) and still fully support the empire.

80. See Samons, *What's Wrong with Democracy?*, pp. 38–39, 143–47. For a rather early expression of the view, see also Ar. *Lys.* 1128ff.

81. Samons, *What's Wrong with Democracy?*, pp. 80–81 with figure 3; *Empire of the Owl*, p. 36; ML 39.

82. Isoc. 8.82 with Samons, *Empire of the Owl*, pp. 197–99.

83. Athenian citizens received other benefits in this period. In 445/4 Psammetichus of Egypt sent a gift of grain to the Athenians that resulted in a review of the citizen roll to determine who could legally share in the distribution of the gift: Philochorus *FGrHist* 328 F 119, Plut. *Per.* 37.4 (the latter connecting the review with Pericles' citizenship law and maintaining that almost 5,000 people improperly listed on the citizen roll were sold into slavery). Gomme, *HCT* I.329, speculates that Psammetichus was perhaps seeking help from Athens against Persia. If so, he is unlikely to have believed that a treaty existed between Athens and Persia.

84. Plut. *Per.* 33, 35, with Frost, "Pericles, Thucydides, Son of Melesias, and Athenian Politics before the War"; for a different view, see Fornara/Samons, *Athens from Cleisthenes to Pericles*, pp. 31–32.

85. One must remember that Athenian "politics" were carried out directly by individual politicians in front of the assembled people (in assembly, council, or courtroom) and not in the way modern parties operate (with platforms, formal organizations, and institutions). The Athenian politician always needed to be able to court the people, whatever his views on particular issues: see K.-J. Hölkeskamp, "Parteiungen und politische Willensbildung," esp. pp. 21–27.

86. Plut. *Per.* 12 (pp. 95–96).
87. Plut. *Per.* 14.3. The date is not quite so certain as is sometimes thought. See Stadter, *Commentary*, pp. 183–84, who notes that Plutarch's evidence "would not exclude a date between 445 and 442" (p. 183). Stadter, pp. 185–86, provides images of *ostraka* bearing Thucydides' or Pericles' name (see also Figure III). These *ostraka* (from unknown years) confirm that Pericles also received votes for ostracism: for images and discussion, see also M. L. Lang, *The Athenian Agora* XXV, nos. 651–52, p. 98, and Tracy, *Pericles*, pp. 35–36.
88. See Samons, *What's Wrong with Democracy?*, esp. chaps. 3, 6.
89. Thuc. 5.26.5. R. S. Stroud, "Thucydides and Corinth," suggests that Thucydides the historian spent considerable time in Corinth.
90. Plut. *Per.* 8.5.
91. For this funeral oration, see pp. 132, 194.
92. Thucydides (2.65) denies that Pericles practiced such demagoguery (at least later in his career), but Plutarch suggests – to my mind convincingly, given the historical record – that the early Pericles employed such methods.

FIVE   A GREEK EMPIRE (CA. 460–445)

1. Thuc. 1.103.4. For Athens' earlier war(s) with Megara, see pp. 12–13. For the First Peloponnesian War in general, see Lewis *CAH* V².111–20.
2. Thuc. 1.103.4.
3. Thuc. 1.105–6.
4. Thuc. 1.104. Athens planted colonies and cleruchies around the Aegean and as far away as the Black Sea in the fifth century, and the Athenians' interests and campaigns in Cyprus and Egypt in the 450s suggest that they saw opportunities for expansion into even such far-flung regions, where (indeed) Greeks had long before already established themselves. It may be, of course, that the Athenians simply believed that a Cyprus or Egypt free of Persian control would make Athenian influence in the Aegean that much more secure.
5. Certainly that number is possible if allied vessels are included in the total. At Hdt. 7.144.1 the Athenians build a fleet of 200 ships (in 483/2). The setting aside of 100 Athenian vessels 431 (Thuc. 2.24.2) probably indicates another 200 were fit for service; 200 ships sent to Egypt in 460 (Thuc. 1.104.2: Athenian and allied vessels) surely imply that at least 100 or more were retained for service in Greece. Diodorus mentions fleets of 200 to 300 vessels in this period (e.g., 11.60.3), but these fleets would often have included allied vessels and Diodorus's value for such details is in any case negligible.
6. Plut. *Per.* 20.3–4; cf. 18, which emphasizes Pericles' caution as a military commander. Podlecki, *Perikles*, p. 64, believes we cannot determine whether Pericles supported or opposed the Egyptian expedition. Bloedow, "The Implications of a Major Contradiction," p. 306, concludes that Pericles supported the effort.

7. For this policy, see pp. 174, 179, 279 n. 41.

8. See Thuc. 1.107–8.

9. It is unclear precisely how Athens exploited this victory and its new control over parts of central Greece. For the possibility that some cities in Boeotia began to make tribute payments, see Hornblower, *CT* I.172.

10. Thuc. 1.108.4 (Aegina) with 105.1, 115.1 (northeast Peloponnese). For the subjection of Aegina, see Meiggs, *Athenian Empire*, p. 98, Hornblower, *CT* I.173. For Aegina's involvement in trade, see Figueira, *Aegina: Society and Politics*, pp. 192–214, 230–86.

11. Meiggs, *Athenian Empire*, p. 98; Plut. *Per.* 8.7, Arist. *Rhet.* 1411a15–16 ("pus in Peiraeus' eye": for this translation and a description of the malady to which it referred, often mistranslated as "eyesore," see Stadter, *Commentary*, p. 108).

12. Hornblower, *CT* I.173.

13. Thuc. 1.111.2. For the date, see Appendix 1, n. 3.

14. See n. 4.

15. Meiggs, *Athenian Empire*, pp. 104–8.

16. E. W. Robinson, "Thucydidean Sieges, Prosopitis, and the Hellenic Disaster in Egypt," p. 150, puts the number of citizen losses at 5,000 to 6,000. Green, *Diodorus*, pp. 242–43, also doubts the loss of the whole Athenian fleet, estimating minimum (Athenian) losses at 8,000 to 9,000 citizens (relying on Holladay, "The Hellenic Disaster in Egypt"). D. Kahn, "Inaros' Rebellion," proposes a new chronology for the Athenian expedition (based on Diodorus and Egyptian evidence) and suggests that Athenian losses were indeed much smaller than Thucydides implies. By his chronology the Athenian relief force was destroyed and the expedition to Egypt ended in 457 BC. I do not find all the evidence he discusses compelling (contemporary indications of who is ruling a disputed territory are not always reliable), but in any case the new chronology would not affect the view of Pericles offered here, although it would cast some doubt on Thucydides' sources of information for mid-fifth-century events.

17. After the Sicilian disaster in 413, the chief proponent of the action (Alcibiades) was already in exile and thus unavailable for blame. The Athenians in the face of that disaster appointed a board of senior statesmen (Probouloi) to advise the state (Thuc. 8.1.3).

18. On the transfer, see Samons, *Empire of the Owl*, pp. 92–104.

19. For Pericles' possible involvement, see Isoc. 8.126, 15.234, Diod. 12.38.2, 54.3, 13.21.3, with Samons, *Empire of the Owl*, p. 101. Green, *Diodorus*, pp. 150–51 n. 302, misreports my views on the amount potentially transferred to Athens and the reasons why 454/3 is a likely – but not certain – date for the transfer. In fact, Green adopts a view in his note similar to my own and on p. 131 n. 240 he accepts, but does not cite, a major conclusion from my research on Athenian finance: namely, that the high-point figure of about 10,000 talents held by Athens (given by Thuc. 2.13.3 and Diod. 12.40.2) contains both moneys transferred from Delos and moneys that already existed in Athens: see Samons, *Empire of the Owl*, pp. 98–102.

20. As it was, the terms of the peace of 451/0 were already quite favorable to Athens: see p. 110.

21. Wade-Gery, *Essays*, p. 248 (an essay originally appearing in the *Journal of Hellenic Studies*, 1932). Compare the views of A. W. Gomme, who, in a candid moment in an early review, expressed the view that "the [Athenian] empire was a fine attempt to solve the Greek political problem": review of H. Willrich, *Perikles* (Göttingen: Vandenhoeck und Ruprecht, 1936), *CR* 50 (1936), p. 192.

22. Some modern scholars continue to reach different conclusions. Compare, for example, R. Balot, "Socratic Courage and Athenian Democracy," who argues that "the Aegean Greeks were unlikely to survive for long as independent states, given the proximity of large expansionist monarchies and aggressive Greek city-states. . . . Seen in this light, the Athenian Empire was better for the other Greeks than all other available alternatives" (p. 53).

23. Thuc. 1.112.1, Theopompus *FGrHist* 115 F88 = Fornara 76, Diod. 11.86.1 (wrong year: 454/3), with Hornblower, *CT* I.168, and Gomme, *HCT* I.325–29, who accepts (wrongly, I believe) Kimon's early recall to Athens ca. 457. Green, *Diodorus*, pp. 165–66 n. 351, speculates about reasons Diodorus could have had for the date he provides, including a possible "*unofficial* truce," supposedly negotiated by Kimon while still ostracized. But given Diodorus's practice elsewhere, a treaty misdated by a few years should hardly surprise us. In this note Green also confuses "public accounting" with the publication of Athenian tribute quota lists. Public accounting and the publication of documents represented separate acts, with the first in no way implying the second: see Samons, *Empire of the Owl*, pp. 312–17.

24. Thuc. 1.112.2–4, Diod. 12.3–4, Plut. *Kimon* 18–19.1.

25. Thuc. 1.112.3.

26. Diod. 12.3–4.

27. Hdt. 7.151. Interestingly, a number of Athenian *ostraka* testify to a (almost certainly different) Kallias's alleged connection with Persia ("Kallias the Mede," etc.): see Brenne, "Ostraka and the Process of Ostrakaphoria," p. 21, and n. 41 below.

28. Isoc. *Paneg.* 4.120.

29. Diod. 12.3–4. Diodorus's account is remarkable in the detail it provides when compared with his skimpy treatment of other major events. He clearly found the treaty intriguing.

30. The sources are conveniently collected and translated at Fornara 95.

31. See, e.g., R. Meiggs, *Athenian Empire*, pp. 152–74.

32. E.g., Meiggs, *Athenian Empire*, p. 152.

33. Samons, "Athens – a Democratic Empire."

34. For the theory that Athens' ended tribute collection for one year as a result of the peace, see p. 116 with n. 52.

35. For my earlier argument in favor of such a treaty, see "Kimon, Kallias, and Peace with Persia." For a good treatment supporting the idea of a formal peace, see Gomme, *HCT* I.331–37. The conventional case is argued by Meiggs, *Athenian Empire*, pp. 129–51, reliant on B. D. Meritt et al., *The Athenian Tribute Lists*, III.275–300, which is still influential for Lewis, *CAH* V².121–27. Azoulay, *Pericles*, e.g., pp. 7, 52, accepts the conventional picture of a peace negotiated ca. 449 but

suggests that it could have been a de facto arrangement. (He strangely places the treaty after a "failure of the Athenian expedition to Egypt" [p. 52] rather than after the victory in Cyprus.) Podlecki, *Perikles*, pp. 66–69, believes in a "tacit agreement" between Athens and Persia rather than a formal treaty, on the possibility of which see also C. Habicht, "Falsche Urkunden," pp. 25–26; A. J. Holladay, "The Détente of Kallias?"; and Knight, *Some Studies*, p. 2. n. 9.

36. *Pace* G. L. Cawkwell, "The Peace between Athens and Persia," p. 116, who calls Herodotus's vague phrase about Kallias "an artful allusion to Athens' trafficking with the Mede." I do find attractive Cawkwell's suggestion (p. 117) that the embassy of Kallias may have been made in conjunction with Athens' new alliance with Argos ca. 462/1; the idea also appears in Fornara/Samons, *Athens from Cleisthenes to Pericles*, p. 175.

37. Badian, *From Plataea to Potidaea*, p. 4, with Fornara/Samons, *Athens from Cleisthenes to Pericles*, p. 175.

38. For Kallias's other acts of diplomacy, see Diod. 12.7 (the Thirty Years Peace of 446/5) and ML 63–64 = Fornara 124–25 (possible involvement with the treaties made with Rhegion and Leontinoi). This may or may not have been the same Kallias: Meritt et al., *ATL* III.277 (yes), ML pp. 173–74 (no). It is possible that the family's status as priests of Eleusis (see p. 113) and perhaps even the clan's name (a *keryx* is a "herald") potentially played some role in their selection for diplomatic missions.

39. Herodotus (7.151) calls Kallias and those sent to Susa with him *aggeloi*, "messengers" or "ambassadors."

40. We do not in fact know how long before the fifth century the Kallias family held this position. For the family's history up to the mid-fifth century, including the relationship with Eleusis, see Davies, *APF*, pp. 254–61; see also Meiggs, *Athenian Empire*, p. 145 with n. 2. The Kallias family may have gained its connection with the larger clan known as the Kerykes only in the seventh century (Davies, *APF*, pp. 254–55, but cf. Toepffer, *Attische Genealogie*, pp. 80–92). I have sometimes called them "Kalliads" to distinguish the family line in which the names Kallias and Hipponikos appeared regularly from the rest of the Kerykes.

41. The family's wealth apparently stemmed at least in part from control of silver mining interests: e.g., Ed. Meyer, "Kimons Biographie," p. 28 (explaining the nickname Lakkoploutos, "pit wealth," that Kallias bore); Bicknell, *Studies*, p. 71 n. 64; and Nepos *Kimon* 1.2–4; cf. Plut. *Arist.* 5. Davies, *APF*, p. 255, apparently accepts the tradition that the family purchased property formerly owned by the Peisistratids (demonstrating their independence), but this story (Hdt. 6.121) likely developed as a defense against the charge that their mining interests had Peisistratid origins (cf. Davies, pp. 260–61, accepting the mines as a source of the wealth of Kallias [II]). Davies himself notes that Kallias (I) was "probably still alive and in Athens in the 520s" and that "we hear nothing of any anti-Peisistratid activity by [his son] Hipponikos," though he resists the natural inference of cooperation between the Kerykes and the tyrants (pp. 255–56; cf. Stahl, *Aristokraten und Tyrannen*, pp. 117–18, who accepts the story that the family opposed the tyrants, while noting that the Herodotean claim of irreconcilable opposition is incredible and that Kallias's

residence in Athens in the 520s may indicate that he had been won over by the Peisistratids). Davies also accepts that Aristeides was related to the family (see Plut. *Arist.* 25.4–8), suggesting that Aristeides' mother was a daughter of Kallias (I). Bicknell, *Studies*, p. 39 (also 62), considers Aristeides an "Alkmeonid fellow-traveller," and Plutarch (*Them.* 2–3, 5; cf. Diod. 11.42.2–3) emphasizes the rivalry between Themistocles and Aristeides (see also p. 242 n. 7) and the latter's support for Miltiades. For the possibility (which I consider slight) of the Alkmeonid family controlling mines in southern Attica, see Camp, "Before Democracy," a fascinating and useful study that nevertheless treats the Alkmeonids and Peisistratids as rivals, rather than as allies, for most of the sixth century. For *ostraka* cast against Kallias Kratiou, who may have served on an embassy to the Persian satrap at Sardis ca. 507, who was probably ostracized in 486/5 (or perhaps received many votes for ostracism in the 470s), who is called "the Mede" on several *ostraka*, and who was either a Keryx/Kalliad or an Alkmeonid, see Bicknell, "Some Pendants," pp. 147–49; Rhodes, *CAAP*, p. 276; and Develin, *Athenian Officials*, p. 53. Develin is hesitant about the embassy ca. 507 (suggested originally by Bicknell: Develin has a typo for the page number of Bicknell's study), but the idea neatly explains both the *ostraka* calling this Kallias "the Mede" and the reason a member of the Kerykes could be chosen for a later embassy to Persia. I therefore believe we should accept that this "Kallias the Mede" was a member of the Kerykes and that he probably served as ambassador to the Persians ca. 507. (It should be noted that Bicknell is inclined to see this Kallias as a member of the Alkmeonid family.)

42. Bicknell, *Studies*, esp. pp. 62, 70–72, notes the close relationship between the families of the Alkmeonids, Kerykes, and Kimonids, claiming (p. 44) that the "Kerykes and Alkmeonids were consistently close." Although I do not share all his conclusions, his work is admirable for its willingness to subject the ancient testimony about these families to a rigorous critique. Likewise, B. M. Lavelle, *Fame, Money, and Power* (e.g., pp. 4, 123), sees the connections and cooperation between the Peisistratid and Philaid/Kimonid families, especially in regard to the latter's control of the Chersonese. Davies, *APF*, p. 305, sees the marriages between these three families in the early fifth century (see p. 58 and Figure VI) as linking "the three most aristocratic families of early fifth-century Athens in an unambiguous way," but does not see that the crucial connections had been forged in the previous century when all three families had cooperated with the Peisistratids. Wade-Gery, *Essays*, p. 164, recognizes that the Alkmeonid and Kimonid families were part of a coalition with the Peisistratids. For a Hipponikos (a name common in the Kallias family) from the time of Solon who is associated with a Kleinias (perhaps from the family of Alcibiades' father of the same name, who himself married an Alkmeonid), see Plut. *Sol.* 15 (cf. *Ath. Pol.* 6) with Ed. Meyer, "Kimons Biographie," p. 30. Davies, *APF*, p. 255, believes this friendship with Solon is likely to be a later invention as the name Hipponikos ("Horse-victor") probably came into the family after the Olympic chariot victories of Kallias (I), the son of Phainippos, in 564 BC.

43. Davies, *APF*, p. 259, accepts a modern hypothesis that Kallias at some point divorced Elpinike (e.g., Ed. Meyer, "Kimons Biographie," pp. 27–28) and that this reflects a political "shift" toward the "Left" (i.e., Pericles). This view of a leftward shift is rightly rejected by Badian, *From Plataea to Potidaea*, p. 192 n. 30; it reflects a misunderstanding of the close relations between these three families in the sixth and fifth centuries.

44. Meiggs, *Athenian Empire*, pp. 124–26, attempts to move Kimon's death back to 451, but this reflects a now discredited hypotheses about events of 450/49 (including supposed financial machinations and the Peace of Kallias).

45. For examples of contradictory views of the (potentially factional) politics here, see Ed. Meyer, "Kimons Biographie," pp. 71–82 (who believes the peace not a success but an admission of failure, because it did not force the Great King to recognize formally the independence of the Greek states: p. 81), Meiggs, *Athenian Empire*, pp. 145–46, and Badian, *From Plataea to Potidaea*, p. 21. My own reconstruction differs from all these.

46. We should recall that Pericles' first wife by this time may already have been married to Kallias's son Hipponikos (p. 68 with n. 65).

47. Even failed negotiations could have resulted in the type of de facto peace that existed in the 440s. Both sides may have come to realize the benefits of standing down. On the other hand, Herodotus's account (7.151) of the Argives' embassy to the Persian Great King and Artaxerxes' answer to them suggests that it was possible to have a relationship of "friendship" with the king without any formal treaty, and this may be precisely what the Argives possessed and the Athenians sought.

48. Plut. *Per.* 17.

49. See Meritt et al., *ATL* III.277–80; cf. Meiggs, *Athenian Empire*, pp. 512–15, 152–53; D. M. Lewis, *CAH* V².125 n. 19; Podlecki, *Perikles*, p. 70; and A. Tronson, "The History and Mythology of 'Pericles' Panhellenic Congress'," for doubts about the Congress Decree. It is defended by Cawkwell, "The Peace between Athens and Persia," pp. 126–29, and Bloedow, "'Olympian' Thoughts," and accepted by Lendon, *Song of Wrath*, pp. 73–74.

50. See especially Meiggs, *Athenian Empire*, pp. 512–15, and n. 49.

51. One account (Diod. 12.3–4) has the Athenians fighting in Phoenicia during this campaign, as they certainly had done at least once before. Meiggs, *Athenian Empire*, pp. 127–28, with ML 33 (= Fornara 78) and commentary.

52. Some scholars believe the Athenians did forgo the collection of tribute for one year around this time. See, e.g., Lewis, *CAH* V².123–25, and ML, pp. 134–35; cf. Meiggs, *Athenian Empire*, p. 154. However, the evidence for this cancellation of tribute and a consequently "missing" tribute quota list is extremely weak. For the probable whereabouts of the "missing list," see Samons, *Empire of the Owl*, p. 80 n. 246 and p. 99 n. 71, where I suggest that the blank portion of the stone on the right lateral face (possibly extending to the missing portion of the top rear of the stone) represents the space left for a (never inscribed) list. This ample space on the right lateral face was clearly left blank intentionally since the lower left lateral face does contain tribute quota lists.

53. Meiggs, *Athenian Empire*, pp. 152–74; Lewis, *CAH* V².121–32.
54. E.g., the decree concerning Erythrai (ML 40 = Fornara 71).
55. For the decree regulating Chalkis, see pp. 119–23.
56. For colonization, see Skyros (Thuc. 1.98.2.). I leave aside the debate over Athenian terminology for different types of settlements and settlers (on which see p. 266 n. 12). There may have been a fairly broad spectrum of types of settlements, but the major (substantive) distinction was whether the particular Athenians who took ownership of property formerly owned by non-Athenians retained their Athenian citizenship (those who are usually called "cleruchs") or became citizens of another (usually new) polis (those we usually call "colonists"). For our purposes this is not a crucial issue, though it undoubtedly affected the territories and poleis in which the Athenians planted settlers.
57. See Meiggs, *Athenian Empire*, pp. 149–51.
58. See p. 129 with n. 14.
59. *Episkopoi*: IG I³ 14 (Erythrai), lines 13–14; Ar. *Birds* 1021–55, with Meiggs, *Athenian Empire*, pp. 585–87; *proxenoi*: IG I³ 19.
60. Plut. *Per.* 12 (pp. 95–96).
61. See, e.g., Polly Low, "Looking for the Language of Athenian Imperialism." Low's argument relies in part on comparing the language in inscriptions with Thucydides' arguably more bald descriptions of Athenian imperialism (which have influenced modern treatments). But the comparison is specious (or, rather, it is relevant only to *us*), since the Athenians' subjects in the fifth century had no Thucydidean language with which to compare Athens' dictates. The pertinent question is whether Athens' allies would have (often) seen the Athenians' actions as violations of their own sovereignty. About this there can be no serious doubt. For the harshness of the Athenian settlement after the Euboean revolt (relevant to Low's treatment of the Chalkis decree), see also Ar. *Clouds* 211–13 with schol. and Plut. *Per.* 7.8.
62. Thuc. 1.113, Xen. *Mem.* 3.5.4.
63. Plato *Alk.* I 112c.
64. Plut. *Per.* 18 and *Comparison of Pericles and Fabius* 3.3 (cf. Diod. 12.6), which emphasize Perikles' *asphaleia* (safety), a quality he arguably demonstrated inconsistently in his career (see pp. 173–74 on Thucydides' view of Pericles' prudence in warfare). Azoulay, *Pericles*, pp. 34–39, mischaracterizes Pericles' policy as avoiding unnecessary wars and then strangely claims that Pericles' "prudent strategy was followed by the Athenians even after the death of its promoter" (p. 39; see also p. 131), an idea that would have surprised the Athenians who occupied Pylos in 425 or invaded Sicily in 415.
65. See also p. 90.
66. Thuc. 1.114, Diod. 13.106.10, Plut. *Per.* 22–23 with Ar. *Clouds* 859.
67. Plut. *Per.* 23.3.
68. ML 52 (Chalkis) = Fornara 103; for Eretria, see the poorly preserved IG I³ 39 = Fornara 102.
69. The *prytaneis* were the presiding subcommittee of the Athenian Council of 500 (for which see Appendix 3).

70. *Euthynai* were audits of officials held at the end of their terms of office. ML, p. 143, however, suggest that the term here is used to refer to "punishments in general" since the Athenians would not wish their oversight to be limited to these audits of magistrates.

71. The *heliaia* was a very large Athenian court, in this case presided over by the Athenian archons known as *thesmothetai*.

72. Trans. Samons, *Athenian Democracy and Imperialism*, pp. 131–34, adapted. Word divisions reflect the lines of the original Greek text. Although H. B. Mattingly has sought to date this decree to the 420s (e.g., *Athenian Empire Restored*, pp. 53–67, 161–63, 374–75, 391–94), the majority of scholars (rightly, I think) place it in the mid-440s, after Euboea's revolt from Athens and subsequent recovery by Pericles (e.g., Rhodes, "After the Three-Bar *Sigma* Controversy," pp. 504–5).

73. ML, p. 141.

74. On the nature of the settlement, cf. Gomme, *HCT* I.342–45; Lewis, *CAH* V².135, calls the document "politely firm," but notices that "the expressions of loyalty required were extreme," and that hostages taken by Athens were not returned. See also Meiggs, *Athenian Empire*, pp. 178–81. Diod. 12.7 refers to the harshness of the settlement after Euboea's revolt.

75. Thuc. 1.75–77.

76. Thuc. 5.89; cf. 1.141.1.

77. Thuc. 5.89.

78. For the so-called Lelantine War between Chalkis and Eretria, see Hdt. 5.99.1, Thuc. 1.15.3, with Hornblower, *CT* I.49.

79. Athens had interests and controlled lands in Euboea from at least ca. 506 BC. See Hdt. 5.77.1–2 with ML 15 = Fornara 42.

80. Phokis, as Gomme, *HCT* I.319 points out, was a traditional friend of Athens (and foe of Sparta, which protected Phokis's rivals in Delphi).

81. See n. 38 and Meiggs, *Athenian Empire*, p. 182.

82. Interpretation of this treaty varies widely. Meiggs, *Athenian Empire*, pp. 181–85, sees the terms as "remarkably favorable to Athens" (p. 182). Podlecki, *Perikles*, p. 76, believes it was most likely touted as a "victory for Athens" and maintains that it provided "de facto recognition that both sides had spheres of influence." Lendon, *Song of Wrath*, p. 79, on the other hand, describes the treaty as "humiliating" in territorial terms, although he notes that some Athenians would admire the fact (in retrospect) that the treaty in some ways recognized Athens as Sparta's equal. Cf. Lewis, *CAH* V².136–37, and Badian, *From Plataea to Potidaea*, pp. 137–45, whose conclusions I do not share.

83. Thuc. 1.140.1 ("no concessions") with 1.127.3.

84. I use the term "faction" merely to represent the (undoubtedly shifting) group of individuals who tended to support Pericles and his policies. Thucydides Melesiou (p. 91) apparently sought to make his own faction tangible in the assembly by having his supporters gather together in a group, but there were no permanent alliances (much less political parties) in fifth-century Athens.

85. If the story that Pericles opposed the operations in central Greece that led to the defeat at Koroneia is true (p. 118), then this could provide another reason he suffered no political fallout from the treaty.
86. Lucan, *Pharsalia* 1.125–26.

SIX PERICLES AND SPARTA: THE OUTBREAK OF THE GREAT WAR
(444/3–431)

1. On Greek settlement in the west (esp. Sicily), see Hornblower, *CT* III.272–8, with bibliography. The term "great Greece" in its Hellenic form may have already been in use by the late fifth century: Hornblower, *CT* I.41.
2. Podlecki, *Perikles*, pp. 91–92, Ostwald, *CAH* V².315–16. Ostwald's speculation that Hippodamus may have been part of a "Periclean brains-trust" (p. 316) exceeds our evidence, though we should probably conclude that Pericles did not disapprove of Hippodamus's selection for the task.
3. Diogenes Laertius 9.50.
4. On Thurii, see esp. Diod. 11.90.3–4, 12.9.1–11.2, 22.1, with Green, *Diodorus* ad locc., esp. pp. 193–94 (notes), Plut. *Mor.* 835c, with other references collected by Hill et al., *Sources for Greek History*, p. 345; Fornara 108; and Lewis, *CAH* V².141–43. For Herodotus at Thurii, see Suda s.v. Herodotus.
5. Despite the absence of good evidence, E. T. Salmon in the *Oxford Classical Dictionary*, 2d ed. (1970), calls Thurii "Pericles' panhellenic foundation." Green, *Diodorus*, p. 192 n. 52, has "no doubt" Pericles "was behind it." On the other hand, Wade-Gery, *Essays*, pp. 256–57, argues that Thucydides Melesiou was responsible for the "panhellenic" aspect of the project. Podlecki, *Perikles*, pp. 81–84, rejects Wade-Gery's arguments and sees the colony as a "Periklean initiative from the beginning" (p. 83). For Podlecki, p. 84, the colony was a "grand enterprise in which Athens took the initiative" rather than a primarily panhellenic affair. For a similar view on the Periclean nature of the foundation, see Ehrenberg, "The Foundation of Thurii." Stadter, *Commentary*, p. 142, cites other scholarship and remains agnostic.
6. Amphipolis: Thuc. 4.102–6, Diod. 12.32.2, schol. Aeschin. 11.31. For Athens' earlier attempt to colonize this region, see p. 72.
7. Athens had established numerous colonies and cleruchies in the Aegean since the 470s. It seems possible that by the mid-440s the city simply did not have the surplus population required to establish a major colony on its own. This could, perhaps, help explain the nature of Thurii and Amphipolis. See also Ehrenberg, "Foundation of Thurii," p. 153, noting Athens' weakness in the years just after 445.
8. Thuc. 6.3.2, Hdt. 7.156–65 (international power in 480).
9. Also like Athens, the Syracusans had established a democratic regime after a period of tyranny. Both states had also exhibited aggressive tendencies under the earlier form of government.

10. Rhegion and Leontinoi: ML 63–64 = Fornara 124–25. Lewis, *CAH* V².143, puts the original alliance with Rhegion near in date to the foundation of Thurii. See also p. 260 n. 38.

11. Plut. *Per.* 20.1–2, with Lewis *CAH* V².145–46. The year may have been 436/5: Develin, *Athenian Officials*, p. 95.

12. Plut. *Per.* 19.1. Dated to the early 440s by Lewis, *CAH* V².127–28, following Meiggs, *Athenian Empire*, pp. 159–61. For other Athenian cleruchies potentially established in the mid-fifth century, see Podlecki, *Perikles*, pp. 62–63, and for Athenian settlements in general in this period (and arguments about what should or should not technically constitute a cleruchy), see Figueira, *Athens and Aigina*, esp. pp. 217–25; cf. Cargill, *Settlements*, pp. xxi–xxiii, 135–38. Azoulay treats cleruchs as "soldier-landlords" (*Pericles*, p. 74) and not "peasants." The institution was probably flexible enough to allow for various arrangements, with Athenians occupying (and working) the lands seized in some cases and simply receiving income from the land in others.

13. Chambers, "Thucydides and Pericles," pp. 83–84, argues that in this period Athens was "using her eastern empire to build empire in the west" (p. 83). Athens had expressed a similarly broad vision in choosing to send a great force to Egypt ca. 460.

14. Samons, *Empire of the Owl*, pp. 195–97. The tribute quota lists for the decade after 440/39 suggest that some states made payments in addition to their assessed tribute.

15. For the techniques of empire, see pp. 117–18 and Samons, "Periclean Imperialism"; cf. Meiggs, *Athenian Empire*, pp. 205–54, and Lewis, *CAH* V².127–46, both relying (however) on some inscriptional evidence that can no longer be dated securely to the mid-fifth century.

16. E.g., Plut. *Per.* 24, 32.1. See Fornara/Samons, *Athens from Cleisthenes to Pericles*, pp. 163–65, and p. 178. Any marriage must have postdated Pericles' citizenship law of 451/0 (since their child Pericles II required a special grant of citizenship) and predated 441/0 (the beginning of the Samian conflict, for which Aspasia was blamed). The evidence taken as a whole, including Aspasia's swift marriage to another political leader after Pericles' death, suggests that Pericles and Aspasia were in fact man and wife. Ed. Meyer, "Kimons Biographie," pp. 55–56, rightly dispenses with the idea that Aspasia was a common prostitute (*porne*) or professional entertainer of men (*hetaira*), ideas that developed from her characterization by Athenian comic poets. He also believes she had real influence on Pericles. For Aspasia in general, see Podlecki, *Perikles*, pp. 109–17, who is basically agnostic on her influence and character.

17. See pp. 143–44.

18. Plut. *Per.* 24, Plato *Menex.*, Athen. 13.589e, with Fornara/Samons, *Athens from Cleisthenes to Pericles*, pp. 164–65. Podlecki, *Perikles*, p. 111, suggests that the lost dialogue *Aspasia* of Antisthenes may have served as a source of such gossip.

19. For the conflict, see Thuc. 1.115–17, Diod. 12.27–28, Plut. *Per.* 24–28. Diodorus and Plutarch claim that the Athenians went to war with Samos after the Samians refused to go to arbitration. On the origins of the quarrel, see Gomme, *HCT* I.349–50, and Meiggs, *Athenian Empire*, p. 428.

20. On Athens' intervention here and its determination to settle everything in Athens' own best interests, see Gomme, *HCT* I.351.

21. Thuc. 1.117.3, ML 55, and Plut. *Per.* 28.

22. See Plut. *Per.* 28.3 (from Duris of Samos). Plutarch himself rejects this story (but see *Per.* 26.4 for an alleged incident of Athenians branding Samian captives on the forehead). Green, *Diodorus*, p. 220 n. 138, accepts this tale, noting that the actual punishment – shackling to posts or boards – is not technically crucifixion. Azoulay, *Pericles*, pp. 56–60, is inclined to accept reports of Pericles' cruelty, even those peddled by a historian of questionable merit such as Duris, despite his own characterization of Pericles as avoiding war wherever possible (p. 284 n. 88) and his criticism of Donald Kagan (on ideological grounds) for (also) portraying Pericles' foreign policy as moderate!

23. Plut. *Per.* 28.6–7.

24. Schol. Ar. *Acharnians* 67 = Fornara 111, with Fornara/Samons, *Athens from Cleisthenes to Pericles*, p. 34. J. Henderson, "Attic Old Comedy," p. 262, writes that "it is plausible to suppose that the intention was to prevent the inflammation of partisan violence, particularly in the presence of foreign allies at the Dionysia," supporting a view propounded by S. Halliwell, "Comic Satire and Freedom of Speech," esp. pp. 57–59, who suggests the Samian War as the precipitating cause. Will, "Perikles," col. 569, attributes the law to Pericles himself, as does Azoulay, *Pericles*, p. 150, but there is no testimony in our sources to this effect. Azoulay goes so far as to argue that comic attacks on Pericles actually affected his public and political life, as he sought to avoid such attacks (p. 151). For this, again, there is no evidence. Given the amount of comic abuse in the record, one must conclude that, if Pericles actually sought to avoid or quash such attacks, he failed miserably. For a translation of contemporary comic attacks on Pericles (with discussion), see Tracy, *Pericles*, pp. 96–108.

25. Fornara/Samons, *Athens from Cleisthenes to Pericles*, pp. 160–61 with schol. Ar. *Peace* 605, Diog. Laert. 2.12, Athenaeus 13.56, 589e = Fornara 116a, b, c.

26. For doubt about the traditions of actual prosecutions and exiles of Periclean associates in this period, see Fornara/Samons, *Athens from Cleisthenes to Pericles*, p. 165 n. 11 (Aspasia); Hornblower, *CT* I.341; Podlecki, *Perikles*, pp. 97–98 (Protagoras), pp. 31–34 (agnostic on date of Anaxagoras's trial, if he was tried), pp. 103–9 (skeptical about Pheidias's trial); and, on the problem as a whole, Stadter, *Commentary*, pp. 284–89, and Gomme, *HCT* II.184–89. Most scholars accept the ostracism of Damon and the exile of Pheidias as historical events (see next note). Diod. 12.39.2 implies that Anaxagoras was charged with impiety (*asebeia*) and Pericles with embezzling sacred funds (*hierosylia*) in the period just before the Peloponnesian War, but skepticism about these details is warranted. For Pericles' relationships with these figures, see chapter 8.

27. See pp. 144–45 with n. 67. Plut. *Per.* 31.5 mistakenly reports that Pheidias died in prison in Athens, but evidence shows that he continued his career as a sculptor at Olympia after his departure from Athens: Stadter, *Commentary*, pp. 285–86. Frost, "Pericles and Dracontides," places Pheidias's downfall and a failed attempt to attack Pericles based on this in the year 438/7.

28. Plut. *Per.* 28.4–7.

29. Some historians have accepted this story and painted Sparta as itching for war with Athens at this time (e.g., Lendon, *Song of Wrath*, pp. 86, 100). But Sparta's actual deeds right up to the moment of (and indeed during) the invasion of Attica in 431 demonstrate clearly that it sought not a *casus belli* but rather an excuse *not* to engage Athens. The Corinthians' later claims rested on something, no doubt, but it hardly can have been more than their agreement with Sparta that the Samians were not worth saving. We may note, in fact, that the Corinthians do not claim (Thuc. 1.40.5) that the Spartans themselves actually favored action to support Samos, as they surely would have done had it been the case. Cf. Hornblower, *CT* I.83–84, with a fanciful discussion of the way this passage "can be adduced as evidence for Spartan aggressiveness towards Athens" (p. 83) and the way Thucydides "reduces or conceals" the significance of certain events.

30. Thuc. 1.116.1–2, where a fleet of fifty Samian warships plus twenty transports engages the Athenians. See Hdt. 6.8.2, for a sixty-ship Samian fleet at Lade in 497.

31. Contrast Hornblower, *CT* I.83, who thinks Athenian-Corinthian relations were good in the period after 446 and before the mid-430s.

32. Thuc. 1.116, Plut. *Per.* 26.2, Diod. 12.27.4.

33. The son of Melesias was probably still ostracized. The historian was perhaps too young, though no evidence assures us of this. See Gomme, *HCT* I.354.

34. Schol. Aristeides 46.136 = Fornara 110, Plut. *Per.* 8.8, with (for the other names) Gomme, *HCT* I.352, 354 and ML 56.

35. On the relationship between election to the generalship and political status or power, cf. Fornara/Samons, *Athens from Cleisthenes to Pericles*, pp. 31–32, where the rivalry between Thucydides Melesiou and Pericles is somewhat understated, as is Pericles' dependence on a military career for his political success.

36. Plut. *Kimon* 8.8–9. Blamire, *Plutarch: Kimon*, p. 124, providing references to other scholarship, discusses the method by which winners at dramatic contests were usually selected (which involved pulling a prescribed number of votes at random out of an urn) and expresses skepticism about Kimon's role in choosing Sophocles as the competition's winner here. If the tale is invented, it nevertheless suggests a belief that Kimon would have favored Sophocles.

37. On Sophocles' views, see pp. 196–97.

38. Podlecki, *Perikles*, esp. pp. 45, 157, admirably notes that Pericles came to realize that Athens would have to "neutralize" the power of the Spartans and the league they led in order to achieve Athenian superiority. For the likelihood that this view had developed already in the 450s, see p. 250 n. 5. Azoulay, *Pericles*, p. 7, strangely characterizes the Peloponnesian League as "designed to counter [Athens'] influence." The league long predated Athens' impingement on the Spartans' sphere of influence and was rather designed to ensure Sparta's predominance in the Peloponnese.

39. On the location and importance of Epidamnus, see Gomme, *HCT* I.158, and Hornblower, *CT* I.68.

40. For these events, see Thuc. 1.24–31, Diod. 12.30–33, and Plut. *Per.* 29.1–3.

41. Thuc. 1.25 with 13.4, dating a conflict between the Corinthians and Corcyreans in the early to mid-seventh century. Hdt. 3.52.3 recounts the subjection of Corcyra by Peisander, tyrant of Corinth, in the late seventh century.
42. Thuc. 1.29–31.
43. Plut. *Per.* 29.1 associates Athens' decision with Pericles, but this is likely to have been an inference.
44. Thuc. 1.32–36.
45. Thuc. 1.37–43.
46. It is unclear whether two actual votes on this issue (on successive days) were taken, although I believe this most likely; cf. Hornblower, *CT* I.86, for another view. In any case, Thucydides' account paints the picture of an uncertain assembly on this question. On the nature of the alliance, see Hornblower, *CT* I.86–87 and de Ste. Croix, *The Origins of the Peloponnesian War*, appendix 13.
47. Thuc. 1.56.
48. Thuc. 1.57.1 notes that Athens' actions against Poteidaia immediately followed the battle of Sybota. The pro-war faction apparently gained strength quite quickly. The speed of this action also casts doubt on the idea of any real Corinthian plot encouraging a revolt in Poteidaia.
49. Thuc. 1.67.2. Hornblower, *CT* I.110, discusses the possible meanings of "autonomy" here. I take it to mean that Athens would not interfere in Aegina's local government.
50. Thuc. 1.67.4, Plut. *Per.* 29–31. The literature on the decree is voluminous and often – in my view – misconceives of the situation and Thucydides' account. See pp. 143ff. and, for an introduction to the problem and some of the literature, see Stadter, *Commentary*, pp. 275–76, and Hornblower, *CT* I.110–12. Lewis, *CAH* V^2.371, suggests that the chronology of the Megarian Decree(s) is impossible to recover from Thucydides' narrative but (rightly) notes that the historian does recognize the popular view that the decree played a major role in the outbreak of the war. Here I tentatively follow Stadter's adaptation of Fornara, "Plutarch and the Megarian Decree," seeing two decrees, one on the motion of Pericles and a second (by Charinos) containing the principal terms of what scholars call the Megarian Decree. One should note, however, that Dover, "Anthemocritus and the Megarians," has argued that Charinos's decree apparently included provisions for regular invasions of the Megarid (suggesting a wartime action), whereas Thucydides' account suggests a decree that was more limited in scope (excluding the Megarians from the Athenian agora and imperial harbors). It remains quite possible that there were more decrees than two (de Ste. Croix, *The Origins of the Peloponnesian*, pp. 246–51, proposes four) and that the Charinos decree was the last in this series of (increasingly broad) measures against Megara.
51. Thuc. 1.68–88, 118–25 (almost a year: 125.1).
52. Thuc. 1.127, 139–40.
53. Thuc. 1.126–27, with p. 36.
54. Thuc. 1.126.1, 127.
55. Thuc. 1.128–135.1, with p. 54.

56. Thuc. 1.126.1–2, 139.
57. Cf. Lendon, *Song of Wrath*, pp. 102–3, who treats the first embassy as an attempt to establish a pretext for war and the later embassies as "a test of Athenian respect for Sparta" (p. 102). The normally sagacious Gomme (*HCT* I.447–52) does not fully comprehend just how much the Spartans actually wanted to avoid this war ("some Spartans": p. 449). On the other hand, even de Ste. Croix, *The Origins of the Peloponnesian War*, pp. 322–23, who sees Sparta as the aggressor in the conflict, admits that some of the embassies just before the war suggest a reluctance to go to war (at least within one faction in Sparta) or a desire to postpone the conflict. Ed. Meyer, "Herodots Geschichtswerk," p. 210, notes that Sparta entered both the first and second Peloponnesian Wars most reluctantly.
58. See Samons, *What's Wrong with Democracy?*, pp. 248–49 n. 31.
59. Pericles had been introduced before: see Thuc. 1.111.2, 127.3; cf. 116. The nature and number of these introductions, especially the repeated material at 127.3 and 139.4, suggest an incomplete revision of this draft of Thucydides' work.
60. Kurt Raaflaub suggests to me that Pericles/Thucydides here perhaps refers rather to an agrarian mind-set shared by the Spartans and other Peloponnesians. This is possible; but the Greek here (*autourgoi*: 1.141.3) refers to individuals who literally work the land themselves and the Spartans did not do this: see Gomme, *HCT* I.455.
61. He will return to this theme in his last speech: Thuc. 2.62, 1–3.
62. "The greatest honors (*megistai timai*) are the result of the greatest dangers" (Thuc. 1.144.3). This is another theme that Pericles will pick up in his other two speeches in Thucydides.
63. For the last, see Kagan, *The Outbreak of the Peloponnesian War*, pp. 328–31, and Sealey, *A History of the Greek City States*, pp. 317–18. Neither, however, believes that the Megarian Decree was the real cause of the war, hidden by Thucydides. For a version of that view, see F. M. Cornford, *Thucydides Mythistoricus*, with the excellent critique of M. Chambers, "Cornford's *Thucydides Mythistoricus*," pp. 61–77, and cf. de Ste. Croix, *Origins of the Peloponnesian War*, esp. pp. 256–59, who argues against the view that the decree was vitally important and of real economic motive or impact, but whose views of the situation ca. 431 and Thucydides' treatment of same I do not share. Lewis, *CAH* V^2.387–88, sees Megara as far more important than Thucydides maintains.
64. Podlecki, *Perikles*, pp. 111–12, believes these lines may be the inspiration for all later accounts connecting Aspasia with the causes of the war.
65. Lines 513–39, trans. J. Henderson.
66. For Pheidias, see pp. 199–201.
67. Podlecki, *Perikles*, pp. 103–4, believes that this passage may form the foundation of all the later stories about Pheidias's troubles in regard to the statue of Athena Parthenos but recognizes that the story must rest on a chronological connection between Pheidias's problems and the outbreak of the Peloponnesian War.
68. Lines 601–18; trans. A. Sommerstein, 1985.
69. De Ste. Croix, *Origins of the Peloponnesian War* (e.g., pp. 2–3), sets out to inveigh against these views of Thucydides and the Megarian Decree. His work, admirable

in its scope and intelligence, nonetheless misreads Thucydides even as it claims to defend his supposed account of the war's causes. Thucydides does not, as de Ste. Croix believes, place "blame" for the war on the Spartans (see later discussion).

70. These passages in Aristophanes (especially the second) apparently encouraged the historian Ephorus to develop a theory of the real cause of the Peloponnesian War that centered on Pericles' need to create a diversion (through war with Sparta) from his personal and political problems, involving charges of financial malfeasance connected with Pheidias. This theory appears in Diodorus 12.38–39, with 12.41.1. Most scholars have rightly rejected the Ephorus/Diodorus hypothesis as dubious (but see Vogt, "The Portrait of Pericles in Thucydides," for the view that Thucydides too much ignored Pericles' personal connections in his account of the war's outbreak). For the likelihood that Pheidias's troubles occurred in the early 430s (rather than just before the war), see pp. 144–45 with n. 67.

71. For an appreciation of Aristophanes' comic genius here, see Gomme, HCT I.449–50.

72. Thus I agree with de Ste. Croix (n. 63) about the minor status of the Megarian Decree (from Athens' point of view), but I disagree on its economic effects, the reasons for the decree's passage, and the Spartans' supposed responsibility for the war. Lewis, CAH V².388, speculates that the decree might have been part of a plan by Pericles to regain control of Megara, and Ehrenberg, The People of Aristophanes, pp. 328–32, treats the decree as an action intended to provoke hostilities with Sparta. Both, I believe, overstate the importance of the decree, but we may accept that Pericles and most Athenians recognized that the measure would be considered a hostile act by an important Spartan ally and that it could serve as a provocation of hostilities. The Athenians' willingness to pass the measure and unwillingness to rescind it make the same statement about Athens' (and Pericles') stance toward Sparta in this period.

73. At 2.13 Thucydides presents the substance of another speech in which Pericles treated the financial situation and some military details.

74. For the possibility of a remark in the Funeral Oration (2.40.2) aimed specifically at the farmers present (and insisting on their political competence), see C. W. Müller, "Perikles über die politische Kompetenz des Attischen Demos."

75. For analysis of this speech, see also Kagan, The Outbreak of the Peloponnesian War, pp. 326–41. I do not agree with Kagan in every detail, but his treatment admirably emphasizes the real strategic and political situation faced (and addressed) by Pericles at this time.

76. Lendon, Song of Wrath, passim, usefully emphasizes the importance of rank or honor (time) in Greek society and, particularly, its role as a cause of wars such as that between Athens and Sparta. (Nevertheless, the passage in Diodorus, 11.65.2–3, on which he places some emphasis, recognizes both the Argives' concern for issues of reputation and their fear of the Mycenaeans' future strength in explaining the conflict between the two states.) Granted that Spartans and Athenians saw the issue of their states' relative rank as extremely important, this fact cannot explain why the two cities went to war in 431 as opposed to (say) 435 or 425. Thucydides clearly

recognized the importance of rank, as Pericles and Archidamus treat the issue in their speeches in the history (as Lendon notes, pp. 120, 169–70). But the historian sought to explain why *this* war occurred at *this* time, and the long-standing wrangling for honor between rival powers (and the Greeks' "ferocious competitiveness": Lendon, pp. 104–5) could not answer those questions in a satisfactory way. Indeed, as a statesman himself, Thucydides sought not to provide the causes of the war in popular terms, but rather to give future leaders a view that peeled back the superficial (but real) layer of continuous competition to reveal a deeper answer that could explain how a particular war occurred at a particular moment in time. The would-be statesman Polybius arguably shared this (political) goal for his history, while academic historians like Livy and Diodorus composed their works to explain history in terms meaningful to the essentially nonpolitical audiences for whom they wrote. Caesar, in a similar way, described his civil war as a struggle over his *dignitas* ("honor": Caesar *BC* 1.7; Cic. *Att.* 7.11.1; Quint. 11.1.80) precisely because he was attempting to win over the views of a popular audience, which would far more readily grasp that issue than the other (no less real) political issues that lay behind his war on his enemies. In emphasizing the ancients' admitted obsession with issues of honor, we need not rob them of their understanding of (and concern about) other issues.

77. See p. 164 on Pericles' claim about "advancing unsupported" against Athens' neighbors.

78. See, e.g., de Ste. Croix, *The Origins of the Peloponnesian War*, pp. 52–58, 60–63; Fornara, *The Nature of History*, pp. 79–81; Fornara/Samons, *Athens from Cleisthenes to Pericles*, pp. 141–43; and Lendon, *Song of Wrath*, pp. 86–90.

79. For discussion of this passage, cf. Hornblower, *CT* I.64–66, and Gomme, *HCT* I.152–54, which is excellent. Trenchant analysis of the complexity of Thucydides' thought here (and its relation to modern "realist" analysis) is provided by A. Eckstein, "Thucydides, the Outbreak of the Peloponnesian War, and the Foundation of International Systems Theory."

80. Lendon, following Kagan (*The Outbreak of the Peloponnesian War*, pp. 345–46), suggests that Athens' power was not in fact growing in the 430s: *Song of Wrath*, pp. 88–89. For the alternative view, see Lewis, *CAH* V^2.145–46, 373, with p. 134. In fact, the issue is not so much Athens' actual power as it is the Spartans' concerns about the Athenians' widening sphere of influence and, especially, their impingement on the Spartans' allies. Thucydides' formulation implies a psychological condition of Spartan concern brought on by Athenian actions and suggests that this Spartan fear of Athens' "growing" power indeed played a major role in bringing about war in 432/1.

81. See Samons, *What's Wrong with Democracy?*, pp. 127–31.

82. Thuc. 1.145.

83. Thuc. 2.12.2.

84. Thuc. 2.13.3–9.

85. Thuc. 2.22.1. Bloedow, "Pericles' Powers," argues that Pericles possessed special powers that allowed him to prevent an assembly, but Thucydides' language here

and elsewhere seems to imply a personal authority based on Pericles' ability to persuade the others holding the power to call or prevent assemblies (including the other generals) rather than a special, legal authority.

86. E.g., Badian, *From Plataea to Potidaea*, pp. 125–69, who sees Thucydides as an apologist for Athens, attempting unfairly to cast blame on Sparta; de Ste. Croix, *The Origins of the Peloponnesian War*, argues that Thucydides' text quite rightly shows that the Spartans were clearly at fault and thus bore the responsibility for the war. In the introduction to his translation of Thucydides' *The Peloponnesian War*, S. Lattimore calls Thucydides' attitude toward the Spartans "critical, perhaps overwhelmingly negative" (p. xiv). I hope it will be obvious that I do not share the view that Thucydides writes as an apologist for Athens and a critic of Sparta. Strasburger, "Thucydides and the Political Self-Portrait of the Athenians," esp. pp. 212–14, argues that Thucydides offers the Spartans as a moderate counterexample to Athenian rashness and imperialism.

87. Badian, *From Plataea to Potidaea*, pp. 234–35, reviews attitudes toward Pericles' responsibility for the Peloponnesian War, noting that the "[i]mperial German tradition tends to take his responsibility for granted and tries to put a favorable interpretation on it" (p. 234).

88. In addition to this spirit of rivalry (see pp. 147–48 for Lendon's emphasis of this issue), there were specifically anti-Spartan feelings in Athens, reflected (for example) in Euripides' *Heraclidae* and *Andromache*, both produced early in the war.

89. See, e.g., de Ste. Croix, *The Origins of the Peloponnesian War*, pp. 64–65; cf. Badian, *From Plataea to Potidaea*, pp. 142–44.

90. Thuc. 1.140.2; cf. 1.78.4, 7.18.2.

91. Hornblower, *CT* I.522 (in another context), notes that Athens may have been somewhat distant from the panhellenic centers at Olympia and Delphi in 431, and certainly Delphi endorsed the Spartans' efforts in the war against Athens (Thuc. 1.118.3). But I do not think it likely in any case that either could have served as an arbitrator here (nor, apparently, did the Athenians, if they knew Delphi and Olympia favored Sparta and their offers of arbitration were sincere).

92. Gomme, *HCT* I.453, notes that the German historian K. Beloch made this point about arbitration, but he dismisses it on the grounds that it was unjustified to refuse arbitration and that such arbitration would not be concerned with the whole empire but only with "Athenian actions in relation to Poteidaia, Megara, and Aegina." That is the whole point, since all these areas concerned Athenian acts: no Spartan actions were under consideration. Lendon, *Song of Wrath*, p. 103, argues that Sparta refused arbitration because the very act would imply an equality of rank with Athens, but surely the terms of the treaty of 451/0 (and even those of the peace of 446/5) had already done that.

93. The tale that Spartans "promised" to help Thasos during their revolt from Athens only to renege on the agreement should be treated as dubious: Fornara/Samons, *Athens from Cleisthenes to Pericles*, p. 127. In any case, the Spartans did not in fact intervene, even diplomatically. See also pp. 249 n. 74, and 250 n. 89.

94. Ed. Meyer, "Herodots Geschichtswerk," p. 210, notes that this idea had an afterlife in Athens and may be seen in such authors as Xenophon and Isocrates. Lendon's ably argued thesis in *Song of Wrath*, that the war of 431 broke out over issues of rank, cannot explain Sparta's acceptance of the Athenians' earlier actions (in the 470s and 460s), which established Athens as (at least) an equal power and (arguably) a superior one by 451/0.

95. Herodotus's account of Miltiades' speech to the Athenian general Callimachus before the battle of Marathon in 490 contains the idea that an Athenian victory over the Persians could not only establish Athens' fame (6.109.1) but also raise Athens to the position of first city of Greece (109.3). Such a claim is unlikely to reflect real Athenian attitudes in 490 but is quite believable for the later fifth century, in which Herodotus worked and gathered information. Perhaps more important, the claim (even if not historical) reflects the Athenians' real knowledge that they were not, in fact, the dominant power in Greece earlier in the fifth century. See also Stahl, *Aristokraten und Tyrannen*, p. 108.

96. For the possibility of another midcentury hoplite battle (at Oinoe), see Hornblower, *CT* I.165, who provides references to the scholarship on this possible, but poorly documented, event. Meiggs, *Athenian Empire*, pp. 95–97, 469–72, treats the battle of Oinoe as a minor engagement, probably in the years 461–454.

97. Thuc. 1.141.6. Note the defensive tone of Pericles' claim (at Thuc. 2.39: see p. 164) that Athens advanced alone ("unsupported," in Crawley's translation) against its enemies and generally won foreign battles, even though the full Athenian force is never assembled (part being required for service in the navy). When, after all, had any Greeks ever faced the *entire* Spartan army? For the importance of fighting alone or as the leader (*hegemon*) of a coalition, see Lendon, *Song of Wrath*, p. 68; although Lendon does not see defensiveness in this speech or this claim, he does admit that the Funeral Oration shows that Athens' confidence in 431 was "fragile" (pp. 133–34).

98. Podlecki, *Perikles*, p. 76, believes the events of 446 inclined Pericles to adopt a policy of "no expansion by land" while maintaining close control over the naval empire. Bloedow, "The Implications of a Major Contradiction," argues that Pericles never recovered from the disaster in Egypt and the failure to acquire and hold a land empire in the 440s.

99. Thuc. 2.13.3–5; cf. 1.140.5.

100. Some scholars (e.g., Lewis *CAH* V².372) have adopted the view that Thucydides believed the war between Athens and Sparta was "inevitable." I find this conclusion unsupportable. Thucydides undoubtedly saw that conflict between Athens and Sparta was always a possibility after the dissolution of their alliance in 462/1, but the historian sought to show why *this war* broke out *when* it did, including documenting the pivotal roles played by Pericles and by the Athenians' ambitions and national character.

SEVEN   PERICLES AND ATHENIAN NATIONALISM: THE CONQUEST OF
HISTORY

1. The Spartan forces' invasion took considerable time, and the Spartan king Archidamus was blamed at home for delaying the actual invasion of Attica with operations on the Attica/Boeotia border: Thuc. 2.13.1, 18–19.1. For the approximate date of the actual invasion of Attica (May), see Thuc. 2.19.1 with Gomme, *HCT* II.70–71.

2. For the Athenians' strong feelings about this action, see Thuc. 2.21 and Plut. *Per.* 33.7–8. For the ignominy and the "moral defeat" it entailed, see Spence, "Perikles and the Defense of Attika," pp. 104–6.

3. For the gravity of this event and its potential importance for the later Athenian psyche, see W. Arrowsmith, "Aristophanes' *Birds*: The Fantasy Politics of Eros," pp. 120–24. Allison, "Pericles' Policy and the Plague," misconceives the move as a regular part of Greek warfare. Rather, the complete abandonment of Attica over an extended period of time reflected Pericles' particular strategy of refusing to meet Sparta in a hoplite battle.

4. Thuc. 2.14.1, 17.

5. Thuc. 2.18–23. For the length of the invasion (between fifteen and forty days), see Hornblower, *CT* 1.278.

6. Cavalry: Thuc. 2.19, 22.2 with Hornblower, *CT* I.276. J. H. Hunter, "Pericles' Cavalry Strategy," treats recent scholarship on Pericles' uses of cavalry here and concludes that the statesman employed a concerted and preconceived strategy; cf. Spence, "Perikles and the Defense of Attika" (the cavalry plan unlikely to have predated the war). In any case, the cavalry could not prevent the Spartan destruction of Athenian lands; it could only limit Spartan activities and harass Peloponnesian forces.

7. Thuc. 2.23, 25–26.

8. Thuc. 2.27. The fact that the Athenians apparently alleged (to themselves and to the Aeginetans) that Aegina had played a pivotal role in bringing about the war with Sparta (see Thuc. 1.67.2) has received too little attention. It seems likely enough that this claim was a pretext for taking long-desired actions against the Athenians' ancient rivals on Aegina, but it tells us something interesting about the Athenians' public claims about the war and their justifications for their actions.

9. Thuc. 2.31–32.

10. For Pericles' strategy (and reservations about it), see Kagan, *The Outbreak of the Peloponnesian War*, pp. 337–42 (with Kagan, "Perikles as General," for a balanced review of his military career), J. Ober, *The Athenian Revolution*, pp. 72–85, with the criticisms of Samons, *What's Wrong with Democracy?*, p. 250 n. 40, de Ste. Croix, *The Origins of the Peloponnesian War*, pp. 208–10, and the review of opinions by Lendon, *Song of Wrath*, pp. 168–69.

11. Thuc. 2.34.8.

12. For the influence of Pericles' speech on Lincoln's Gettysburg address, see G. Wills, *Lincoln at Gettysburg.*
13. Hornblower, *CT* I.294–96, provides an introduction to literature on the speech, but takes no position on many significant issues surrounding the address and its report.
14. An apparent reference to autochthony: see pp. 22–24.
15. It seems likely that Pericles in this passage alludes to Athens' tradition of protecting suppliants (see pp. 25–26). For Pericles and the "unwritten laws," see pp. 196, 212.
16. There has been a trend in recent years to attempt to ameliorate Pericles' stern "advice" to the widows in the audience: see, e.g., L. Hardwick, "Philomel and Pericles," Patterson, "Other Sorts," pp. 171–72, and W. B. Tyrrell and L. J. Bennett, "Pericles' Muting of Women's Voices." Such work has suggested that the most negative interpretations of this passage may be unwarranted and has usefully pointed out the particular circumstances (political and otherwise) within which Pericles addressed these women, but it has not (in my view) shown that the basic attitude expressed here differed from the general Athenian view that respectable women should play a very limited role in public life.
17. Recent scholarship has recognized a nonidealized Pericles in Thucydides; see M. M. Taylor, *Thucydides, Pericles, and the Idea of Athens in the Peloponnesian War,* and E. Foster, *Thucydides, Pericles, and Periclean Imperialism,* who maintains that Thuc. creates the "historical character" Pericles and illustrates the dangers of Pericles' views. Both Taylor and Foster are primarily concerned with "Thucydides' Pericles" (i.e., with Pericles as a character or figure in the work rather than as a historical figure). A similar approach (but producing very different conclusions) is taken by W. Will, *Thukydides und Perikles: Der Historiker und sein Held.* J. Vogt, "The Portrait of Pericles in Thucydides," also sees the statesman as "thoroughly" idealized in the historian's account (p. 224), as (more recently) does Azoulay, *Pericles,* e.g., p. 8. M. Meier, "Probleme der Thukydides-Interpretation," sees Thucydides' treatment of Pericles as developing over time but conflicted or ambiguous from the beginning and sees the praise of Pericles in 2.65 as superficial. The fact that contemporary scholars have held such wildly contrasting views – Thucydides as undercutting Pericles on the one hand or treating him as the "hero" of the work on the other – suggests to me a remarkable achievement in the historian's work: Thucydides' unusually evenhanded approach seemingly provides proponents with opposing views the evidence to make their cases. It also suggests that the historian's views may have changed over time: see at n. 72 below. Podlecki, *Perikles,* p. 208 n. 49, omits discussion of the Funeral Oration as "documentary evidence" because of the uncertainties about responsibility for the views it contains. For other expressions of such doubt, cf. Schubert, *Perikles,* pp. 12–16, and Andrewes, *HCT* V².395–99, and see also Lendon, *Song of Wrath,* pp. 420–25. This approach, in my view, runs the risk of ignoring what may be the most important piece of evidence we possess about Pericles in the strange hope of thereby presenting a more accurate picture of the statesman or of Athenian history.
18. For a somewhat similar view, see P. Hunt, *Slaves, Warfare, and Ideology,* pp. 220–21, who remarks that "the superficial pieties of Pericles' appalling funeral oration purify and sanctify death in war."

19. Bosworth, "The Historical Context of Thucydides' Funeral Oration," and see also Sicking, "The General Purport of Pericles' Funeral Oration," both of whom refer to scholars taking the opposing position. Sicking usefully emphasizes the ways in which Pericles' speech was calculated to meet the needs of a particular politically charged moment. Balot, "Courage in the Democratic Polis," pp. 409–10 n. 12, treats the speech as reflecting Periclean ideas and collects literature on the debate.

20. For potentially Periclean ideas in the speeches, see Appendix 4. For the speeches in Thucydides in general, see pp. 6–7. In an interesting note, M. Haslam, "Pericles Poeta," believes he has identified a piece of verse used by Pericles and quoted by Thucydides. I, however, make no claims for authenticity in these speeches on a verbal level.

21. Sicking, "The General Purport of Pericles' Funeral Oration," p. 414, notes that Pericles himself assumes here something of the role of bard, even referring to his speech as a "hymn" (2.42.2: translated above as "the Athens that *I have celebrated*" [*hymnesa*]). I would emphasize, however, that it is the accomplishments of the Athenians as a whole that will, in Pericles' view, establish Athens' permanent fame.

22. I therefore disagree strongly with Azoulay, *Pericles*, p. 36, who argues that Pericles "turned his back on the heroic ideal, even if it meant paying the ultimate price, in accordance with the ambivalent model set by Achilles." For Achilles, see pp. 43–44. Cf. Mills, *Theseus*, p. 65, for a different comparison of Athens and Achilles: "The Homeric hero defines himself through his services to the community by being both the protector of those less strong and brave than he is, and also the role model for others," drawing on N. Loraux, "Mourir devant Troie" (*non vidi*), pp. 811–13. It is interesting, though I do not believe we can make much of it, that Pericles' advisor Damon is compared in a fragmentary comedy to Cheiron, the centaur that tutored Achilles (Plut. *Per.* 4.4 with Podlecki, *Perikles*, p. 18). F. Cairns, "Cleon and Pericles: A Suggestion," argues that the famous echoes by Cleon of Pericles' last speech in Thucydides are intended to reflect Thersites' echoes of Achilles in Homer (*Iliad* books 1–2), casting Cleon in the role of Thersites and Pericles in that of Achilles. Socrates (in Plato's *Apology* 28b–d) famously compares himself to Achilles, emphasizing the hero's motive of justice: avenging the death of his friend Patroclus even though it will ensure his early death. None of this may indicate anything more than the fact that comparisons with Achilles as the "best of the Achaeans" were commonplace in fifth-century Athens, but they are nonetheless interesting given that Pericles seems to be applying the Achillean ideal to Athens itself.

23. Andrewes, *HCT* V².335 and esp. R. Sealey, *The Athenian Republic*, pp. 101–2, note that Pericles' words about democracy in the speech (2.37.1) reflect (at least) a defensiveness and (at most) a concession about democracy's faults. Cf. Fornara/Samons, *Athens from Cleisthenes to Pericles*, pp. 49–50, and, for recent analysis of the passage in question, R. Winton, "Thucydides 2,37,1," and J. Andrews, "Pericles on the Athenian Constitution."

24. Andrewes, "The Melian Dialogue and Perikles' Last Speech," p. 7 n. 1, may be technically correct that only at Thuc. 2.42.3 does the Funeral Oration comment

directly on the issues of empire, but the speech as a whole clearly strikes a boldly imperialist note.

25. Hornblower, *CT* I.308, speculates that Pericles' actual address may have had a more "elevated and cultural" tone than Thucydides' version. He nevertheless (rightly) notes that Athens' reputation as a cultural leader postdates the context of the Funeral Oration.

26. Thuc. 2.37.2–3, 39.1. Hornblower, *CT* I.301, notes that "there was plenty of suspicion of Alcibiades' habits, [Thuc.] vi.15."

27. The Greek here (2.39.2) emphasizes that the Athenians *themselves* fight such battles (instead of relying on allies as the Spartans do).

28. Hornblower, *CT* I.303–4, notices the odd nature of this chapter but does not comment on the speciousness of the claims.

29. Balot, "Courage in the Democratic Polis," rightly emphasizes that Pericles draws a distinction between the Athenians' ideal of a rational courage based on intelligence and the Spartans' regimented approach. However, I believe he overestimates Pericles' association of this ideal with democracy *per se* (vs. "Athenianness") and underestimates the extent to which Pericles makes a defensive case in the face of Sparta's proven reputation for courage and military success. He does, however, admirably show that Pericles' strategy of avoiding pitched battle opened Athens up to charges of cowardice (pp. 411–12).

30. Hornblower, *CT* I.299, seems to concede that there is a dark side to Pericles' speech.

31. Thuc. 2.47.3–54 (plague narrative). A. J. Woodman, *Rhetoric in Classical Historiography*, pp. 36–40, flirts with the notion that Thucydides invented the plague (or at least its severity) but the latest archaeological evidence has shown that the plague was real and led to mass burials.

32. The actual malady of this plague is perhaps unknowable: see Hornblower, *CT* I.316–17. See recently M. J. Papagrigorakis et al., "DNA Examination," which suggests that typhoid fever may have been the responsible agent, although this finding has been disputed.

33. Plut. *Per.* 36. Plutarch does not in fact say that Paralus died from the plague, but the context suggests this. See also [Plut.] *Cons. Ap.* 118e, Val. Max. 5.10. (ext.) 1, Aelian *VH* 9.6.

34. For Xanthippus's marriage, see pp. 34–36.

35. Thuc. 2.47, 55–57.

36. Plut. *Per.* 33.8: trans. Tracy, *Pericles*, p. 104. On the sexual imagery here, see G. Jones, "Perikles and the Sexual Politics of Hermippos' *Moirai*." The implication of an impotent leader who (as Jones argues from the rest of the fragment) is open to the (sexual) attack of his political enemy Cleon was a conventional attack in Athenian politics and not based on the sexuality of either party. For Pericles' (apparently) strict heterosexuality, see p. 198.

37. Thuc. 2.59.2.

38. Cf. Gomme, *HCT* II.166–67, who notes that Thucydides offers no condemnation of Sparta's refusal here (and who references Aristophanes' condemnation of both sides in *Birds* 211–19).

39. Trans. Crawley. Interestingly, Podlecki, *Perikles*, p. 149, treats this speech as a fairly accurate account of what Pericles must have said in these circumstances, referring to its "unalloyed and even cruel candour" (see also Sicking, "The General Purport of Pericles' Funeral Oration"), where others (Andrewes, "The Melian Dialogue and Perikles' Last Speech") have found this speech (if anything) more incredible than the other two in Thucydides. For an ancient critique of the speech, see Dionysius of Halicarnassus *On Thucydides* 43–47.

40. Pericles again uses imagery implying that any diplomatic concession to Sparta is tantamount to servitude. See also 2.63.1.

41. For excellent analysis of this passage, see Bloedow, "The Implications of a Major Contradiction," who points out that these words illustrate the breadth of Pericles' imperialist policy and ambitions and demonstrate that Athens' imperialist outlook did not alter significantly between Pericles' leadership and that of those who followed him. Nevertheless, there was a real difference in the methods chosen to bring Athenian ambitions to fruition. Pericles had adopted a policy of (in essence) "one war at a time," and his successors abandoned this prudent stance, a change for which Thucydides excoriated them (see pp. 173–74). We may also note that Pericles' reference to the Persian Great King here hardly suggests that a formal peace existed between Athens and Persia.

42. See n. 17 and see also Sicking, "The General Purport of Pericles' Funeral Oration."

43. For Thucydides' bald statement that the moderate oligarchy of 411 was the best regime of his lifetime, see 8.97.2. For somersaults to avoid taking this passage in its natural sense, see Hornblower, *CT* III.1033–36; cf. *CT* I.340, where Hornblower writes that the indications of Thucydides' political views in book VIII of his history are "sometimes difficult." The difficulty evidently stems from the historian's clear preferences for a moderate oligarchic vs. a democratic regime and the discomfort this engenders in many modern scholars (see also n. 62).

44. For a similar view, see Strasburger, "Thucydides and the Political Self-Portrait of the Athenians," p. 215.

45. Gomme, *HCT* II.373. I do not see how a fair reading of book 3, chapters 82–83 (and 84, although it may not be by Thucydides) can support any conclusion other than Gomme's.

46. By "abstract nationalism" I mean in particular that Pericles apparently conceived of the Athenians as a special people with unique qualities and accomplishments that demonstrated that they deserved to rule other Greeks. The Athenians, moreover, inhabited a powerful city that deserved the passionate love of its current citizens and their devotion to the idea of using that power to ensure the city's reputation in history long after it had lost the concrete, material advantages that empire now brought.

47. So also Strasburger, "Thucydides and the Political Self-Portrait of the Athenians." Strasburger, however, believes speeches such as most of those given in Thucydides could never actually have been given in the form presented because of the unabashed imperialism they display (esp. pp. 207–8). I believe Athenian history suggests that Athens' citizens were inured to such ideas and language.

48. This is, in essence, the content of Pericles' first speech in Thucydides.

49. Pericles expressly seeks to encourage the Athenians in the speech summarized beginning at 2.13.3 and in his last speech in Thucydides.

50. E.g., Gomme, *HCT* II.195–96 and *More Essays*, pp. 92–97; H. D. Westlake, "Thuc. 2.65.11," sees an inconsistency between 2.65 and the narrative of books 6 and 7 concerning the role of Alcibiades' recall in the failure at Sicily; cf. Hornblower, *CT* I.342–43. W. E. Thompson, "Thucydides 2.65.11," valiantly attempts to reconcile Thucydides' narrative with his judgment here but does not, in my view, convince.

51. A. H. Rasmussen, "Thucydides on Pericles," p. 40, argues that the verb Thucydides employs here (*perigenesthai*) implies survival rather than victory/superiority, and certainly that is one of its meanings. But the context here – as at 2.65.7 and 1.144.1, both cited by Rasmussen – calls for something more than the notion of mere survival. The emphatic nature of Thucydides' language here and the nature of Pericles' speech at 1.144.1 both suggest that the idea is more than survival: it is a victory (that leads to survival).

52. Gomme, *HCT* II.189, attempts to make sense of this through a contrast with Kimon, but the issue is Pericles' actions (and words) in Thucydides' own history (and not any contrast between the historical Pericles vs. the historical Kimon). That is, how could a Thucydides who wrote "A" about Pericles also write "not A but B"? Thucydides' account of Pericles' actions does not present us with a statesman who made the safety of the city a top priority.

53. This idea, stated explicitly in Pericles' last speech in Thucydides, is implied in the first (1.144: great risks are necessary for honor) and in the second (2.41: perpetual monuments of good and evil left behind by the Athenians).

54. Bloedow, "The Implications of a Major Contradiction," based on analysis of Pericles' last speech (2.62.1–3) when the statesman speaks of the possibility of the Athenians expanding their sea power (where earlier he had encouraged them not to do this), concludes that Thucydides has presented us with "two Pericles, without resolving the contradictions between them" (p. 308). This apparent contradiction stems, I believe, from the differing psychological needs of the Athenian audience (if we assume that Pericles actually said something like this). Bloedow may be right, however, that such a statement about expanding sea power could have influenced Pericles' successors to adopt expansionist strategies and maintain that they were "Periclean." In any case, the apparent contradiction to which I refer here – between Pericles' belligerent policies and Thucydides' claim that he led "moderately" and kept the city "safe" – may be explained in other ways (see later discussion). Rasmussen's attempt ("Thucydides on Pericles," pp. 30–33) to limit the sense of Thucydides' *metrios* (as in "he led *moderately*") here to the idea of a style of action suited to the task at hand is unconvincing.

55. For the unfinished condition of Thucydides work, see below.

56. Once considered the most important issue in Thucydidean studies, the issue of when the historian composed or revised particular portions of his unfinished work has fallen from fashion, especially among Anglophone scholars. Simon Hornblower dismisses the subject in a few pages of the third volume of his commentary, aligning

himself with the current trend treating the text as we have it as a unity and thus brushing aside a wealth of real problems. Contrast the lucid appendices of Gomme's *Historical Commentary on Thucydides*, vol. 5 (1981), written by K. J. Dover and A. Andrewes, who clearly demonstrate inconsistencies in the text as we have it and "strata" of composition. Treating the text as a unity does not make these go away. For recent attempts to address the composition question, see W. Will, *Thukydides und Perikles*, and M. Meier, "Probleme der Thukydides-Interpretation." I do not share many of Will's conclusions, but his work and Meier's are a welcome return to what must remain a fundamental issue for any serious study of Thucydides.

57. See M. Meier, "Probleme der Thukydides-Interpretation," esp. pp. 144–48, for interesting analysis of 2.65. I agree with Meier that Thucydides' presentation of Pericles is not that of an ideal statesman, but I disagree with his view that Thucydides' praise of Pericles in 2.65 is "superficial" and undercut by the fact that it rests on a comparison with the disastrous leaders who followed him. I believe Thucydides in retrospect did (after the war's end: see later discussion) sincerely come to have a higher view of Pericles and Periclean leadership.

58. Thuc. 4.17–21. I thank Kurt Raaflaub for this suggestion. It must be noted, however, that Athens' success at Pylos in 425/4 (when 120 Spartans surrendered and became Athenian captives) and the Spartans' subsequent peace offer arguably stemmed from a violation of Pericles' strategy of nonexpansion during the war.

59. But see p. 133 on the way the Samian War risked potential hostilities with the Peloponnesians and Persians.

60. See also Samons, "Periclean Imperialism."

61. Thuc. 1.138.3 (Themistocles), 2.65 (Pericles), 7.86.5 (Nikias), 8.68.1–2 (Antiphon, anticipating his death). The Spartan general Brasidas (Thuc. 4.81.2, 5.11) presents a potentially related but special case.

62. In this last case we must note that while Thucydides himself praises the moderate oligarchic regime of the 5,000 (8.97.2), his narrative in book 8 taken as a whole suggests that he saw the more narrowly oligarchic regime of the 400 as a net negative for Athens. Andrewes, *HCT* V.171–72, discusses Thucydides' view of Antiphon and the latter's *arete*, reflecting the discomfort many scholars feel with Thucydides' high praise for the oligarch. Hornblower, *CT* III.955, in this context tellingly calls *arete* "one of the hardest words in Th. to translate." But it is hard only if one is predisposed (as many scholars are) to resist the clear implication that Thucydides' political sympathies lay with the moderate oligarchs. Although Thucydides disapproved of the opportunistic oligarchs (as well as the fickle mob), in no way can he be called a supporter of democracy *per se*.

63. Azoulay, *Pericles* (p. 3), argues both that Thucydides envisioned "history solely in relation to the great men who, it was supposed, molded it" and that the historian was "interested in power and its mechanisms more than the individuals themselves" (p. 10). The latter position, in my view, comes closer to the truth, but Thucydides did not neglect the significant role of the individual in determining the directions of events and thus of history.

64. Thuc. 2.63.2.
65. Thuc. 2.64.5.
66. Gomme, *HCT* II.180, maintains that this passage emphasizes "present glory and future fame." He also notes Pericles' "insistence on the glory of Athenian deeds of the last two generations," and notes that some of Pericles' contemporaries shared this view. We must remember that it was only in these generations that Athens had become a first-tier "international" force. For Pericles' emphasis on Athens' inheritance, see R. Balot, "Pericles' Anatomy of Democratic Courage," pp. 513–16.
67. Foster, *Thucydides, Pericles, and Periclean Imperialism*, pp. 217–18, believes this passage "displays both Pericles' talents and his limitations, and prevents easy judgments for or against him. The strategy seems to aim at supporting the maximum complexity over the length of the narrative presentation of the early part of the war" (p. 217). Taylor, *Thucydides*, has a somewhat similar view, maintaining that 2.65 does not offer us "Thucydides' final judgment on either Pericles or the war," and arguing that Thucydides presents contradictory judgments of various issues to force readers to contemplate questions and lead them to their ultimate conclusions. As will be seen, I disagree in that I believe 2.65 does reflect Thucydides' final (expressed) judgment on Pericles, but that does not mean he always held the view there expressed or that he did not allow the context of Pericles' successors to affect his opinion. For an earlier argument that 2.65 should not be seen as a eulogy of Pericles, see Rasmussen, "Thucydides on Pericles."
68. Some historians, on the other hand, do their best to resist the natural implications of Thucydides' words: see, e.g., Hornblower, *CT* III.1033 (Thucydides "has not made it easy for us to pin him down.").
69. For the theory of the defense, see Foster, *Thucydides, Pericles, and Periclean Imperialism*, pp. 1–2, citing a list of scholars with this view, and above all E. Schwartz, *Das Geschichtswerk des Thukydides*; a more subtle — but still in my view incorrect — statement of the defense thesis may be found in J. de Romilly, *Thucydides and Athenian Imperialism*, esp. pp. 153–55, 349–54. For the youthful admirer, see Andrewes, "Thucydides on the Causes of the War" (and, for a similar view, Wade-Gery, *Essays*, p. 260, and Ehrenberg, *Sophocles and Pericles*, p. 4), with the critique of Fornara, "Thucydides' Birth Date," 71–72; cf. J. V. Morrison, *Reading Thucydides*, pp. 195–96, on the possibility that Thucydides in his youth saw "himself as one of Pericles' successors" (as a politician/statesman). For a recent attempt to support Schwartz's thesis, though focusing on the supposed character of the first book of Thucydides as a defense of Athens (as opposed to Pericles himself), see Badian, *From Plataea to Potidaea*, pp. 125–62 (explicitly tying himself to Schwartz at p. 128). Podlecki, *Perikles*, pp. 134–35, rejects Badian's mendacious Thucydides but believes that the historian "has re-cast some of his material *ad maiorem Periclis gloriam*" (p. 135).
70. Cf. de Romilly, op. cit., who believes Thucydides indeed defends Pericles but sees this as a consistent stance taken throughout his treatment of the leader. She identifies passages that are likely early or late but believes that the historian's view of Pericles did not change and that his work "has been fused into a complete

whole" (p. 154). I, on the other hand, would maintain that the *unfinished* nature of Thucydides' work is both apparent and crucially important for evaluating his thought.

71. Gomme, *HCT* II.196 and *More Essays*, pp. 93–97, also posits that (at least portions of) 2.65 were written well after the narrative.

72. A fundamental difference between my understanding of Thucydides and that of many contemporary scholars is that I refuse to force the historian into a perfectly consistent position. The incomplete nature of his work compels us to consider the possibility that Thucydides changed his mind on some subjects and that he never completed the revisions – assuming he wanted to make them – that would have resulted in a thoroughly integrated and uniform presentation. I submit that his presentation of Pericles offers us an excellent example of Thucydides' altered opinion over time. The historian's unfinished text written over a period of many years continues to inspire scholars to take radically opposed views on the question of Thucydides' "admiration" of Pericles (and on other issues).

73. See also n. 22. The Spartan king Archidamus (at Thuc. 2.11.9) also speaks of establishing the Spartans' reputation (implying, but not stating, their future reputation), but is more concerned with not falling short of the standards set by their ancestors (2.11.2).

74. Plut. *Per.* 35.4; see also Diod. 12.45.4 and Gomme, *HCT* II.182–83. Podlecki, *Perikles*, pp. 150–51, speculates that he may have been charged with *klope* (embezzlement), an accusation often employed in political trials. M. H. Hansen, *Eisangelia*, pp. 72–73, believes that Drakontides' decree (which apparently proposed that Pericles be tried on a similar charge involving his management of state funds: see Plut. *Per.* 32.3–4) may belong in this context. But Stadter, *Commentary*, pp. 300–1, following Frost, "Pericles and Dracontides," believes it belongs to another occasion.

75. Thuc. 2.65.3–4. Podlecki, *Perikles*, pp. 150–51, concludes that it is unclear whether Pericles' reelection to office was a special or a regular election.

76. Thuc. 2.65.6, Plut. *Per.* 38.1 with Stadter, *Commentary*, pp. 342–43.

77. This son later became a citizen despite Pericles' own law making the children of non-Athenian mothers ineligible for citizenship. Plutarch's account (*Per.* 37.5) has suggested that the Athenians passed a special law to make this possible for Pericles, but Carawan, "Pericles the Younger," argues that it was a general measure that applied to all who had lost all their legitimate children and wished to adopt the child of a non-Athenian mother in order to carry on the family line.

78. Schol. *Menex.* 235e, Plut. *Per.* 24.6. The sources imply that Lysicles' political success followed (and depended on) this marriage. However, we are surely licensed to conclude that Lysicles was already prominent in 429 and thus able to attract Pericles' widow. For Lysicles' brief post-Periclean career (he died in 428/7), see A. B. West, "Pericles' Political Heirs I," pp. 132–34. West's article (and its continuation, "Pericles' Political Heirs II") is filled with anachronistic terminology (about "parties" and "platforms") but remains useful, demonstrating (among other things) the continued effect of Periclean policies after the statesman's death and showing that

Nikias and other "conservatives" did not constitute an antidemocratic faction supporting peace.

79. Kurt Raaflaub suggests to me that appearances on the comic stage often reflected a political figure's popularity and rarely seem to have done real (political) damage. Aspasia's characterization onstage was of a different type, but it clearly did not harm her enough to prevent a marriage to another politician after Pericles' death.

80. Samons, *Empire of the Owl*, esp. pp. 194, 205.

81. ML 69 (with commentary) = Fornara 136. Some have connected this hike with Cleon, and Hornblower notes (*CT* I.341) that he is the very type of politician compared unfavorably with Pericles in Thuc. 2.65: yet Cleon faced different conditions and "Pericles' financial optimism was misplaced."

82. Samons, *Empire of the Owl*, pp. 205–6.

83. Sicily: Thuc. 3.86, where he notes that the Athenians responded to an appeal based on the Ionian identity of those requesting aid in Sicily (Leontinoi) but in fact wanted to prevent Sicilian grain supplies from reaching the Peloponnese.

84. Thuc. 5.16–25.

85. Thuc. 5.57–74.

86. Melos: Thuc. 5.84–115; Sicily: Thuc. 6.1–26.

87. Plut. *Per.* 38.2. On such amulets, see Stadter, *Commentary*, pp. 343–44. For Pericles' religious views, see pp. 193–95.

88. Azoulay, *Pericles*, e.g., pp. 28, 35–36, somewhat bizarrely portrays Pericles as someone who "refused to engage in warfare unless it was absolutely necessary" (p. 28), but this is to misunderstand both Thucydides and Plutarch. Pericles' policy toward Sparta, for example, very nearly ensured that a war that certainly was not *necessary* would occur. His policy was *to use* warfare whenever necessary in order to achieve his goals for Athens. Our sources do suggest that *within* war, Pericles sometimes pursued a circumspect and perhaps even conservative (by Athenian standards) policy, but that is far different that refusing to engage in anything but "necessary" wars.

89. Stadter, *Commentary*, p. 345.

90. H. N. Couch, "The Last Words of Pericles," p. 499.

91. Cf. Plut. *Per.* 18.1, for Pericles' statement that as far as he was concerned, the Athenians could go on "living forever." His policies certainly did not align easily with such a statement.

92. For a somewhat similar view to that taken here, see Kagan, "Perikles as General," p. 9: "[Perikles'] final words show how deeply he felt the wounds caused by the widespread accusations hurled against him and his stubborn refusal to admit he had been wrong [about the war with Sparta]. He had applied his great intelligence to his city's needs, and reason told him that he was not responsible for the results, which he must have believed to be temporary. . . . Like most generals in history and unlike its few military geniuses, Perikles saw war as essentially a linear phenomenon, subject to reason alone, and understood too little of its other aspects. For that he and his people paid a great price."

93. This tale of Pericles' last words is most likely to have appeared originally in a work hostile to Pericles, as it demonstrates the delusion of a man whose death approaches.

Contrast Azoulay, *Pericles*, p. 121, who maintains that Pericles "displayed an unshakeable lucidity right up to his dying breath."

EIGHT ATHENIAN CULTURE AND THE INTELLECTUAL REVOLUTION: PERICLES AND THE PEOPLE

1. For the importance of non-Athenians in Athens' cultural revolution, see Ostwald, *CAH* V².314–23. For the foreign sophists in particular, see Wallace, "The Sophists in Athens."
2. In this whimsical reconstruction of visitors' reaction to the acropolis, I have omitted mention of the ruins of the "old temple" of Athena Polias, which had been partially destroyed by the Persians. Portions of this temple almost certainly continued to stand as a monument to the barbarians' impiety and Athenian resilience and to be used during later periods (as a treasury, among other things: Samons, *Empire of the Owl*, p. 30, where I should perhaps not have used the term "Peisistratid" to refer to the building). See G. Ferrari, "The Ancient Temple on the Acropolis at Athens."
3. For the low profile of cultural factors in this speech, cf. Hornblower, *CT* I.294–316, esp. p. 308.
4. It is true that the Athenians liked to think of themselves as particularly wise (e.g., Plato *Apol.* 29d), but that is a different matter from admiring intellectual matters *per se*. According to Ehrenberg, *The People of Aristophanes*, pp. 273, 279–80, 291, 295, the populace at large had some acquaintance with, and had been somewhat affected by, the doctrines of the traveling intellectuals known as sophists; but even he recognizes that this knowledge was superficial. Indeed, individual intellectuals beyond Socrates are almost never mentioned in extant Attic comedy, a fact I take to demonstrate how little the common Athenians thought about them and things intellectual in general.
5. Samons, "Democracy, Empire, and the Search for the Athenian Character," and *What's Wrong with Democracy?*, pp. 92–93, 172, 185. Much of what scholars sometimes attribute to interest in "democracy" is rather interest in polis government, which usually depended on votes in citizen assemblies and management by councils and magistrates. For a possible example of democratic/polis-government relevance (from Sophocles' *Ajax*), see p. 197. For the defensiveness in Pericles' description of *demokratia*, see p. 163. Raaflaub, "Contemporary Perceptions of Democracy," pulls together the scattered references and comes to a different conclusion about democracy's profile in Athens, but I would maintain that even when collected in this way the list does not impress.
6. Thuc. 2.38, 40.1.
7. D. Boedeker and K. Raaflaub, *Democracy, Empire, and the Arts*, pp. 8–9. D. Pritchard, "Costing," p. 58, writes that "the clear differential between festival- and military-related spending, the almost constant campaigning of the Athenian

democracy and its general culture of militarism put it beyond doubt that it was not drama or religion but war which was the overriding priority of the Athenian people."

8. Note, for example, that the Athenians' arguments at Thuc. 1.73–77 or 5.85–111 (etc.) are not philosophical expositions but arguments based on experience and a view of human nature that was apparently common. As much as Thucydides' Athenian (and other Greek) speakers use his difficult language and thought, they most often rely on basic, popular notions of expediency and justice to make their points. (But see Appendix 4, where I suggest that some Athenians may in fact have used a type of complex language and thought similar to that found in Thucydides.) That some sophists (e.g., Thrasymachus in Plato *Rep.* I) made similar arguments does not alter the fact that they are not, in fact, newly developed sophistic or intellectual notions. Rather, most of the ideas found in Thucydides' speeches depend ultimately on commonplace notions that went back hundreds of years (see, for example, Hesiod's tale about the hawk and the nightingale and the will of the stronger in *Works and Days* 202ff.). Andrewes, *HCT* V.396, to my mind overemphasizes the philosophical content of most of the speeches (although one must note that he referred only to "some" of the orations as resembling philosophical debates).

9. For issues of advantage and self-preservation and their effects on Athenian citizens, see M. R. Christ, *The Bad Citizen in Classical Athens*, a work to be applauded for its frank look at many of the realities of civic life. Christ, however, in my view often attributes ideals or values that were common to the Greek poleis (and thus to nondemocratic as well as democratic states) to Athens and democracy *per se* (e.g., p. 207). This helps explain why he finds my own praise of Athenian attitudes toward religious, familial, and civic responsibilities "odd," since they come in a book that "rejects the idealization of Athenian democracy" (p. 6 n. 13, referring to Samons, *What's Wrong with Democracy?*, p. 201). The point is that such admirable Athenian attitudes had nothing to do with *demokratia*. They were reflections of *Greek* polis values, and as active in Sparta or Thebes as they were in Athens.

10. Samons, "Democracy, Empire, and the Search for the Athenian Character."

11. I had originally written only "They are like rulers," but a reader for the Press suggested "tyrants," and this characterization comports with Pericles' admission that the Athenians possessed a virtual tyranny over their allies: see Thuc. 2.63.2, with 3.37.2 for Cleon's bald statement of Athens' tyranny.

12. Socrates' father had been a *lithourgos* (stonemason or sculptor): Diog. Laert. 2.18.

13. This fact is frankly admitted by Boedeker and Raaflaub, *Democracy, Empire, and the Arts*, pp. 1–13. For criticism of some of the other contributions to that volume, see Samons, "Democracy, Empire, and the Search for the Athenian Character."

14. See Ehrenberg, *The People of Aristophanes*, and Hanson, *The Other Greeks*.

15. For the trierarchs and trierarchy, see V. Gabrielsen, *Financing the Athenian Fleet*.

16. Nonrowers typically included ten marines (*epibatai*), four archers, and sixteen other *hyperesiai* (officers, assistants): J. S. Morrison et al., *The Athenian Trireme*, pp. 110–15. For debate about whether the marines were usually of the hoplite (roughly middle) class or from the thetic (lower) property class, see Hornblower, *CT* III.815–16.

17. Ehrenberg, *The People of Aristophanes*, pp. 73–94.

18. See Hansen, *The Athenian Democracy*, pp. 246–65, and in general, Rhodes, *The Athenian Boule*. For the basic functions of Athenian government, see Appendix 3.

19. Note Aristophanes *Wasps* 656–60, where the comedy relies in part on the characters' recognition of the profit that empire brings to Athens. For a comic picture of an Athenian farmer in Athens, see Dikaiopolis in Aristophanes' *Acharnians*. On the Attic farmer in general, see Ehrenberg, *The People of Aristophanes*, and for the importance of the independent farmer in Greek history at large, see Victor D. Hanson, *The Other Greeks*.

20. Wealthy Athenians also acquired lands in the empire. Indeed, Athenians' acquisition of non-Athenian land became an infamous feature of the fifth-century Athenian empire, a fact that led to the fourth-century Athenians' need to promise not to acquire such lands when they founded the second Athenian league in 378/7: *IG* II² 43 = Harding 35.

21. The desire to make an intellectual and aesthete out of Pericles goes back to antiquity, as Plutarch's biography shows (see, e.g., *Per.* 4–6). Yet Plutarch still devoted most of his attention to Pericles' military accomplishments. In contrast, modern scholars seem far more interested in Pericles' relationships with intellectuals and artists than in his career as an Athenian general. Stadter, "Pericles among the Intellectuals," presents a refreshingly skeptical account of Pericles' supposed relations with sophists and the intellectual world of Athens, demonstrating that most such tales about the statesman developed in or after the fourth century and rested on precious little evidence (cf. Wallace, in "The Sophists in Athens," pp. 217–18). As Stadter, *Commentary*, p. li, shows, Plutarch makes no real effort to connect Pericles to the literary world, and the influence of intellectuals on him has no reciprocation: "Pericles is not presented as an intellectual, but as a wise ruler."

22. See Hdt. 7.139, which shows a defensive attitude where Athens' credit for the Greek victory in the Persian Wars is concerned. Herodotus states bluntly that his assessment that Athens deserves this credit will not be popular with his readers (7.139.1). This surely reflects Herodotus's knowledge of the anti-Athenian sentiments of his audience. Fornara, *Herodotus*, pp. 37–58, discredits the idea that Herodotus was a bald partisan of Athens or Pericles; for the opposite view, see Ed. Meyer, "Herodots Geschichtswerk," pp. 198–203, 222–25. It may be fair to say that Herodotus was (or his sources were) somewhat predisposed to listen to and report defenses of Athenian actions and calumnies against the Spartans, although this may reflect no more than the likelihood that he had more Athenian than Spartan sources.

23. B. McNellen, "Herodotean Symbolism: Pericles as Lion Cub," and Fornara, *Herodotus*, pp. 51–55.

24. Cf. Fornara/Samons, *Athens from Cleisthenes to Pericles*, p. 35. For Herodotus's religious outlook, see Ed. Meyer, "Herodots Geschichtswerk," esp. pp. 254–56, who argues that Herodotus accepted the existence, activities, and powers of the gods because men experience these things in their lives (see also next note).

25. This theme first appears explicitly in the programmatic speech of Solon to Croesus (Hdt. 1.32; and cf. 1.5.3–4) and reappears thereafter (3.40, 7.10.ε). Ed. Meyer,

"Herodots Geschichtswerk," p. 234, states that Herodotus believed that the reality and power of the gods provided the key for understanding historical events (p. 256), but rejected the attempt (by those like Aeschylus) to justify the gods' actions (pp. 258–59). While the gods at times act based on moral principles, no moral cause is needed: the gods are jealous rather than moral agents. While for Aeschylus, Xerxes presents a monitory example of human pride, for Herodotus the Persian king is primarily a victim of the gods' jealousy of human prosperity (pp. 259–61).

26. Fornara, "Evidence for the Date of Herodotus' Publication." I refer, of course, to the formal publication of the work (consisting primarily of its release for copying), leaving aside the issue of any previous public reading of portions of the work, the evidence for which is (in any case) extremely weak: see W. A. Johnson, "Oral Performance," and J. Kennelly, *Thucydides' Knowledge of Herodotus*. For an opposing view, see R. Thomas, *Herodotus in Context*, pp. 257–69. Despite the lateness of our evidence for public readings, Thomas finds it "impossible to think that Herodotus, of all writers in this period, did not give public lectures or oral performances of some kind" (p. 257).

27. Fornara, *Herodotus*, pp. 54–57, maintains that Herodotus's treatment of the family is objective (p. 56), but I believe Herodotus was inclined to repeat the stories his Alkmeonid (and other aristocratic) informants provided him with perhaps too much credulity or respect. See Samons, "Herodotus and the Kimonids." For the extreme (and, I think, incorrect) position that Herodotus acted as a kind of "house historian" for the Alkmeonids, see Gillis, *Collaboration*, pp. 42, 58. For aristocratic sources for Herodotus's work, see also Ostwald, *CAH* V^2.330–33.

28. At Thuc. 2.64.2 in the context of the plague, Pericles insists that *ta daimonia* ("divine forces") must simply be endured.

29. Ed. Meyer, "Herodots Geschichtswerk," p. 260, notes that Herodotus's stress on the need for moderation rested on a popular view about the jealousy of the gods and the necessary fall of the powerful and emphasizes that both Herodotus and Sophocles suggest that even those who are blameless must endure the actions of the all-powerful gods (pp. 262–64). For Meyer, both demonstrate a "transcendent pragmatism," which recognizes the gods' power and jealousy and is more powerful than any human, intellectual calculation. They are, for Meyer, nearer to epic than to Aeschylus's rationalized morality, which seeks to explain how man's moral failings lead to the gods' (therefore just) reaction. Strasburger, "Thucydides and the Political Self-Portrait of the Athenians," pp. 215–17, finds something like this view of the divine's relationship with man in Thucydides, writing that in the Sicilian disaster we sense "a sort of moral satisfaction at a higher power's settling of accounts" (p. 216) and potentially associating Thucydides' description of the "utter destruction" of the Athenians in Sicily (7.87.6) with a similar phrase (in a context of divine punishment) in Herodotus (2.120.5).

30. Fornara/Samons, *Athens from Cleisthenes to Pericles*, p. 35, with Fornara, *Herodotus*, pp. 51–54.

31. Plato *Apol.* 26d. For Anaxagoras's scientific and philosophical views, see the excellent treatment by Podlecki, *Perikles*, pp. 23–26. The Milesian philosopher

held that all matter consisted of fundamental parts (*spermata*) mixed in various proportions and that *nous* ("intelligence") was "the ultimate creating and controlling principle of the universe" (p. 25).

32. Plut. *Per.* 6. Stadter, "Pericles among the Intellectuals," pp. 120–22, believes that the tradition about Pericles and Anaxagoras as close associates grew out of an ironic account in Plato (*Phaedrus* 269e–70a) describing Pericles adopting Anaxagoras's high-flown style of speech.

33. Plut. *Per.* 16.8–9.

34. Pericles cold and indifferent: Plut. *Per.* 5, 7; open emotion: *Per.* 32.5, 36.7–9.

35. For Pericles' less than sympathetic advice to the fathers and female relatives of the Athenian dead in the Funeral Oration (Thuc. 2.44–45), see Samons, *Cambridge Companion*, pp. 297–98.

36. Plut. *Per.* 32.1–2. On the possible decree against impiety moved by Diopeithes, see Stadter, *Commentary*, pp. 298–300. Plutarch reports that this decree was aimed at Pericles through Anaxagoras, who had unorthodox religious views. This evidence suggests, again, that even Pericles' enemies could not level a charge of impiety directly against him. The most they could say was that he associated with someone who held such views. Azoulay, *Pericles*, pp. 125–26, doubts the authenticity of Diopeithes' decree, but seems to do so largely out of a desire to protect Athens from the charge of becoming a "democracy given to prosecution . . . and bent on punishing the slightest religious deviation" (p. 126). The "slightest" deviation is not at issue: Athenians could clearly bring charges against one another based on religious practice and belief, as the trial of Socrates demonstrates.

37. Ehrenberg, *Sophocles and Pericles*, esp. pp. 46, 92–93, notes the orthodox nature of Pericles' public actions while arguing that "Pericles' mind worked on non-religious lines" (p. 43). In fact, we have little evidence for the latter opinion but ample evidence for the former. Azoulay, *Pericles*, p. 14 (cf. pp. 107–26), believes that Pericles was reproached for "his attitude toward the city gods."

38. Lampon was an important political as well as religious figure, a fact that reminds us that "spheres" (if we may use an anachronistic term that reflects our own biases) of politics and religion were not separate in the ancient Greeks' world. For Lampon, see Thuc. 5.19.2, 24.1, *IG* I³.78, Plut. *Per.* 6, Stadter, *Commentary*, pp. 82–84. Podlecki, *Perikles*, p. 89, accepts F. Jacoby's suggestion that Lampon was Pericles' "'favourite' (i.e., quasi-official) priest." Lampon gave oracles about Thurii: schol. *Clouds* 332, with Diod. 12.10.3–4.

39. Plut. *Per.* 13.13. Even if we doubt the Periclean origin of Plutarch's tale that Athena appeared to the statesman and provided him with the medical treatment necessary to save an injured worker, both the tale itself and sponsorship of the statue make an important point about Pericles' public piety and what could be believed about his religious views.

40. Kagan, *Pericles*, pp. 129, 170–71, 185, in my opinion is somewhat too ready to associate Pericles with "rationalism" and the "secular views of his teachers and friends" (p. 170). The fact that no one accused Pericles himself of heterodox views is surely significant.

41. For an attempt to treat this aspect of Pericles' personal life and its possible political implications, see Azoulay, *Pericles*, pp. 94–106. In my opinion, the evidence is too weak and too heavily reliant on questionable interpretations of comic references to support this analysis.

42. See Plut. *Per.* 4–6, where the biographer describes Anaxagoras's effect on Pericles' bearing and demeanor, before describing his effect on Pericles' outlook (his rejection of superstition). Note, however, that in *Per.* 6, Plutarch provides both the rational (Anaxagoras's) and religious (Lampon's) explanation for an apparent prodigy, ultimately accepting both and implying that Pericles could have done the same. Podlecki, *Perikles*, p. 25–27, posits that Perikles took from Anaxagoras a tendency to look for natural instead of supernatural causes for events. See Plut. *Per.* 35.2 for Pericles calming his helmsman's fears about an eclipse by demonstrating how the sun could be blocked by another object; cf. Thuc. 2.28 (where the eclipse of August 3, 431 BC, is mentioned), Cic. *De Rep.* 1.16.25, Val. Max. 8.11 (ext.) 1, Frontinus *Strat.* 1.12.10, and see below. Podlecki, pp. 28–30, also notes that the notion of Pericles' "high-mindedness" may itself go back to a mocking passage in Plato (*Phaedrus* 269e–270a): "[L]ittle confidence can be put in the anecdotal tradition that connects Perikles and Anaxagoras as far as specific 'doctrines' or, for that matter, a general 'high-mindedness' (which Perikles' enemies were quick to call aloofness) are concerned" (p. 30).

43. See Aristophanes *Knights* 124–44 with MacDowell, *Aristophanes and Athens*, pp. 89–90.

44. Ehrenberg, *Sophocles and Pericles*, p. 46: "Pericles in many ways shared and used popular religion. He was no hypocrite."

45. Plut. *Per.* 8.6. This speech generated another famous quotation, when Pericles said that the loss of the young men was like the "spring being taken out of the year." On this phrase, see Ed. Meyer, *Forsch.* II.221–22.

46. Plut. *Per.* 8.6.

47. *Pace* Wallace, "Plato's Sophists," p. 219.

48. Euripides won his first victory in 441 (*Marm. Par.* 60) but won only four other times during his long career.

49. Sophocles' dominance is demonstrated by the twenty-four victories his tetralogies (four-play groups) won at the City Dionysia and the Lenaia festivals and the fact that his other sets of plays always finished second (of three places) and never third. For the evidence, see W. B. Tyrrell, "Biography," p. 25. Ehrenberg, *The People of Aristophanes*, p. 284: "If Sophokles was the most beloved poet, Euripides was the most admired and the most discussed." The second part of this formulation seems to me open to some disagreement, depending on what one means by "admired" and of what such "discussion" consisted. In *Sophocles and Pericles*, p. 143, Ehrenberg calls Sophocles "the most 'Athenian' of the three great tragedians."

50. B. M. W. Knox, *CAH* V^2.277–78, endorses E. R. Dodds' estimation of Sophocles as "the last great exponent of the archaic world view" (with reference to his views on religious pollution). Ostwald, *CAH* V^2.333–35, notes the similar "tragic view of life"

shared by Herodotus and Sophocles and speculates on possible discussions between the two.

51. For a similar view, see Ehrenberg, *Sophocles and Pericles*, esp. pp. 23–40. However, Ehrenberg argues that Sophocles believed *nomos* was (or should be) an expression of nature (*physis*), which was itself divine. For Sophocles, in Ehrenberg's view, the sophists' distinction between *physis* and *nomos* was false and dangerous. On *physis*, see also T. B. L. Webster, *Introduction to Sophocles*, pp. 46–49, 164: "he believes in *physis* and all that the word implies for an aristocrat."

52. Arist. *Rhet.* 1419a25.

53. Andrewes, *HCT* V².6, says (rightly) that Sophocles and Hagnon (another Proboulos) "were not doctrinaire oligarchs," but it is clear that the Probouloi represented a turn to a more conservative approach to government in Athenian politics and that Sophocles did not oppose this. Ehrenberg, *Sophocles and Pericles*, treats Sophocles as basically apolitical (e.g., p. 140) but argues throughout for the relevance of contemporary experience with Pericles to Sophocles' depictions of Creon and Oedipus.

54. See also Tyrrell, "Biography," p. 25; Webster, *Introduction to Sophocles*, pp. 8–10, 163. Kimon and the other generals famously awarded victory in the dramatic contest of 468 to Sophocles (Plut. *Kimon* 8.8–9 with p. 133).

55. Ehrenberg, *Sophocles and Pericles*: "What [Sophocles] did realize and fear was the danger from within – not so much the imminent menace, but the possible or even necessary results, of a policy relying on the intellectual genius and the overriding power of one man, capable of putting his reasoning intellect over and against the most sacred traditions" (p. 140). Cf. C. Thomas, "Sophocles, Pericles, and Creon." For a different view entirely, see Podlecki, "A Pericles *prosopon* in Attic Tragedy?" esp. pp. 15–22.

56. Thuc. 2.37.3 (unwritten laws). For the importance of (the traditional concept of) shame in Pericles' conception of the Athenian regime, see Balot, "Pericles' Anatomy of Democratic Courage," which, however, in my view overstates the specifically "democratic" nature of Periclean ideas in Thucydides.

57. Gomme, *HCT* II.113, referencing Sophocles *Oed. Rex* 863–70, *Antigone* 450–61. Ehrenberg, *Sophocles and Pericles*, pp. 38–40, also argues that Pericles' unwritten laws are not divine. However, Lysias *Andoc.* 10 mentions Pericles' employment of the phrase "unwritten laws" in a context that suggests their divine origin or (at least) their relevance to the divine (see p. 212). I am inclined to think that Pericles, if he actually used this phrase or something like it, anticipated and intended that his audience would here understand a reference to law that was divine and thus required no codification. For bibliography and discussion, see also Hornblower, *CT* I.302–3.

58. The relevance of this argument to democracy is obvious, but we should note that voting was practiced in all poleis (including Sparta) and not just in democratic city-states.

59. Cf. Ehrenberg, *Sophocles and Pericles*, esp. pp. 178–82. In my opinion, Ehrenberg too quickly dismisses the implied contrast between Ajax and Odysseus (and their

respective worldviews). I will treat the political relevance of this play in another study. Suffice it to say here that the play suggests a potential form of reconciliation between the worlds and outlooks of (essentially) Kimon and Pericles. On this view, cf. March, "Sophocles' Ajax," who dates the play ca. 460 (after Kimon's ostracism) and argues that the play presents "a deliberate rehabilitation of Ajax" (p. 9) and that it presents the hero as a man of "intelligence and action" (p. 18). Kimon's family, it should be remembered, traced their ancestry back to Ajax (p. 55).

60. See, e.g., Fornara/Samons, *Athens from Cleisthenes to Pericles*, p. 2 with n. 4, Foster, *Thucydides, Pericles, and Periclean Imperialism*, p. 133 n. 36.

61. Many scholars date the play to the early to mid-420s: Fornara/Samons, *Athens from Cleisthenes to Pericles*, p. 2 n. 4. Podlecki, *Perikles*, p. 123, rejects the idea that *Oed. Rex* has anything to do with the plague in Athens. Tracy, *Pericles*, pp. 119–27, treats the play as relevant to Pericles and the plague in Athens. He seems to see the implications of the work as positive (overall) for the statesman, although he notes the warnings in the play about overconfidence in man's intelligence.

62. See Ehrenberg, *Sophocles and Pericles*, pp. 51–74 and previous note.

63. See Soph. *Ajax* 130–34, where the "gods love men of steady sense and hate the proud" (trans. J. Moore). S. Esposito, *Odysseus at Troy*, p. 18 n. 53, cautions us against taking these apparent "'words of wisdom' [from Athena] ... as the moral of the whole story." He points out that this is the only place were Sophocles uses the verb *philein* (to love) of the gods. Ehrenberg, *Sophocles and Pericles*, p. 30, notes that Sophocles and Herodotus (3.38) would not have shared the same view on the relativistic nature of law/custom, which, for Sophocles, should stem directly from the divine/natural world.

64. Plut. *Per.* 8.5: "Pericles remarked that a general has to keep his eyes clean, too, and not merely his hands." See also Athen. 13.603e-604f. Interestingly, when asked if he still had relations with women the older Sophocles allegedly responded that he was happy to be past the age when such an insane master could dominate his life: Plato *Rep.* 329b–c.

65. Contrast Kagan, *Pericles*, p. 176, who describes Sophocles' and Pericles' "close and easy friendship;" Wade-Gery, *Essays*, p. 258 n. 1, who sees Sophocles as "one of Pericles' right-hand men;" and Podlecki, *Perikles*, pp. 121–22, who believes the statesman and playwright had a "close personal relationship" and probably an "intellectual and spiritual affinity."

66. Kagan, *Pericles*, p. 176, notes that Pericles seems to have been "strictly heterosexual."

67. So also Stadter, "Pericles among the Intellectuals," pp. 118–19, and Ehrenberg, *Sophocles and Pericles*, p. 140: the two "were on friendly terms, but not friends." (N. O'Sullivan, "Pericles and Protagoras," p. 15, mischaracterizes Ehrenberg's view and the nature of his excellent book.) Ehrenberg also sees Pericles as a somewhat lonely figure, less "human" than Sophocles (pp. 155–57).

68. P. 87.

69. Wallace, "The Sophists in Athens," p. 215.

70. On Damon, see Wallace, "The Sophists in Athens," esp. pp. 215–16, and "Plato's Sophists," pp. 225–27.

71. Wallace, "The Sophists in Athens," pp. 215–16. Stadter, "Pericles among the Intellectuals," pp. 116–18, argues that Damon's influence on Pericles was based largely on his musical interest (and thus probably related to festivals and the construction of the Odeion). For Pericles' relationship with intellectuals in general, see the thorough and justifiably skeptical treatments by Podlecki, *Perikles*, esp. pp. 17–34, and Stadter, "Pericles among the Intellectuals." For Damon's ostracism, see p. 267 n. 26.

72. Plut. *Per.* 13, 31. For those who accept Pheidias's oversight of the program, see Podlecki, *Perikles*, p. 101 with n. 1. Stadter, *Commentary*, pp. 166–67, and "Pericles among the Intellectuals," pp. 119–20, disputes Pheidias's alleged supervisory role and casts doubt on his friendship with Pericles.

73. Plut. *Per.* 31.3.

74. For the vexed question of the date and nature of this accusation, possible trial, and probable expulsion from Athens, cf. Stadter, *Commentary*, pp. 284–93, and Gomme, *HCT* III.186–87.

75. For Pericles' close association with the whole building project, see Plut. *Per.* 12–14. Diod. 12.39.1 calls Pericles *epimeletes* (superintendent, manager) of the Parthenos statue project. Podlecki, *Perikles*, pp. 79, 102, believes Pericles' oversight of the building program as a whole was unofficial. Kagan, *Pericles*, pp. 157–58, and Podlecki, p. 102, assume Pericles served on the board of overseers (*epistatai*) for the Parthenon.

76. For this artwork and the statue of Athena Parthenos within the building, see Lapatin, "Art and Architecture," pp. 135–42 with figs. 13–26.

77. For the potentially discordant note of the Pandora story on the statue's base (beneath Athena's sandals), see Samons, *What's Wrong with Democracy?*, p. 55, and cf. J. J. Pollitt, *Art and Experience*, pp. 98–99.

78. Accepted by Lapatin, "Art and Architecture," pp. 140–41. Pollitt, *Art and Experience*, p. 87, entertains the idea that the frieze casts the Athenians as virtual gods; cf. Kagan, *Pericles*, pp. 165–66. J. B. Connelly, in a series of works culminating in *The Parthenon Enigma*, continues to argue that the frieze represents the mythical king Erechtheus's sacrifice of his daughter in order to save Athens, a view rejected (for example) by E. B. Harrison, "The Web of History." For the possibility that the frieze depicts the Athenian cavalry in its recently expanded (under Pericles) form, see I. Jenkins, "The Parthenon Frieze and Perikles' Cavalry."

79. Lewis, *CAH* V².139. See also Lapatin, "Art and Architecture," p. 142, who notes that the west pediment's depiction of deities vying "for patronage of the city has been cited as evidence of the Athenians' communal self-regard."

80. On Protagoras and Pericles, see Podlecki, *Perikles*, pp. 93–99, and Stadter, "Pericles among the Intellectuals," pp. 112–14.

81. D-K 80 B9, vol. II.268; Plut. *Per.* 36.7–9; and p. 166.

82. Diog. Laert. 9.50 (laws for Thurii); on Thurii, see also pp. 127–28. Stadter, "Pericles among the Intellectuals," p. 112, casts doubt on Protagoras's appointment as lawgiver and the Periclean nature of the project. Protagoras may have visited Athens twice in Pericles' lifetime, ca. 444/3 and 432: Stadter, *Commentary*, pp. 328–29.

83. Plato *Protagoras* 322c–d.

84. Thuc. 2.40.2. For Plato's challenge, see *Apol.* 24c ff. with Samons, *What's Wrong with Democracy?*, pp. 187–98, esp. 194–95.

85. Kagan, *Pericles*, emphasizes the need for any democratic leader who wishes "to be great" (p. 151) to act as a teacher. Although I do not share all the views of his chapter on Pericles as "educator" (pp. 151–71), Kagan's general point is well taken.

86. See, e.g., Pollitt, *Art and Experience*, pp. 94–95 and cf. Podlecki, *Perikles*, pp. 95–96. The saying comes from Protagoras's (lost) work, *On Being*.

87. See also Stadter, "Pericles among the Intellectuals," pp. 114–15, who emphasizes the orthodox piety of Pericles' public career.

88. For the view that Pericles was, in fact, a rationalist, see Podlecki, *Perikles*, p. 30; cf. Kagan, *The Outbreak of the Peloponnesian War*, p. 129, and, for an even more extreme view, Wallace, "Plato's Sophists," p. 219 (probably an atheist).

89. I find it impossible not to speculate that, on this issue, Thucydides' and Pericles' views may well have coincided. In their usual avoidance of treating the divine, the two do seem to share some notion of man's inability to know and/or control this force. Yet neither displays anything like heterodox (much less atheistic) views about the gods.

90. Hornblower, *Thucydides*, pp. 182–84, discusses Thucydides' religious views but one cannot quite divine his conclusions. He seems to treat the historian's views as more or less conventional, yet not strong. He discusses the absence of "divine sanction" for the Athenian empire in Thucydides' account, but the relevance of this idea (to fifth-century Hellenes or for our own evaluation of Thucydides' attitudes) is unclear. For the historian's attitude toward oracles, cf. Hornblower, *CT* I.270 with references there, including N. Marinatos, *Thucydides and Religion*. Gomme, *HCT* II.65–66, rightly notes that Thuc. 2.17.2 does not show that Thucydides did not believe oracles *could* "to some degree, know the future" (p. 66).

91. Cf. L. Kallet, "Thucydides, Apollo, the Plague, and the War," who argues that Thucydides subtly weaves an argument about the divine's role in the Peloponnesian War into his work.

92. See p. 194.

93. See, for example, the Athenians' defense of themselves before the Peloponnesians in Thucydides 1.75–77 for similar views.

94. For the lack of interest in democracy *per se*, see also n. 5.

95. See Plut. *Mor.* 806f, with W. R. Connor, *The New Politicians of Fifth-Century Athens*, pp. 91–98 (on Cleon renouncing his friends) and pp. 119–34 (Pericles as an example for Cleon).

96. Ar. *Knights*, esp. 732.

97. Stadter, *Commentary*, pp. xlii–xliii, observes that Plutarch refutes Plato's negative judgment of Pericles by turning Pericles himself into a Platonist.

98. At Thuc. 2.13.2, Pericles is reported to tell the Athenians that success in war depends on intelligent planning (*gnome*) and surplus wealth (*periousia chrematon*).

99. Thuc. 2.64.5. On the Greek, see Gomme, *HCT* II.180. Hornblower, *CT* I.340, claims that "even here the speaker is granting that 'all this must end' as Macleod

puts it." This is incorrect. Pericles explicitly argues that the *memory* of Athens will survive its loss of empire. Strasburger, "Thucydides and the Political Self-Portrait of the Athenians," suggests that "undying fame" may have been a favorite expression of Pericles, comparing Thuc. 2.64.5 with Plut. *Per.* 12.4 (*doxa aidios*) and noting the similar ideas at 1.144.3 and 2.44.4. The passage in Plutarch is likely to depend on Thucydides, and I would more comfortably conclude that the concept (if not the very words) was employed regularly by Pericles. See Appendix 4.

EPILOGUE: THE PERICLEAN TRADITION

1. Ehrenberg, *The People of Aristophanes*, p. 317: "Pericles had known how to combine martial spirit, intellectual civilization and economic welfare. He found no successor."
2. Samons, *Empire of the Owl*, pp. 212–48.
3. For this aspect of Eupolis's (lost) comedy *Demoi* (demes), see Ehrenberg, *The People of Aristophanes*, pp. 60–61, 109. The other leaders invoked in the passage were probably Solon, Aristeides, Myronides, and perhaps Miltiades.
4. The once fairly common (if not popular) view that stages or strata of composition could be detected in Thucydides' work has been almost completely abandoned in recent years, especially in Anglophone scholarship (see p. 280 n. 56). I do not have the space to defend the view taken here beyond stating that the accounts of 431 to 421 (the so-called Archidamian or Ten Years War) and 415 to 413 (the Sicilian expedition) are, in my opinion, markedly more polished than the section that connects them and the portion that covers the period after 413. Since Thucydides never completed his work, it follows logically that some parts of the text we possess are less finished than others. The popular theory today (as propounded by Simon Hornblower in his *Commentary on Thucydides*, among others) that Thucydides' work was basically written continuously after the war's end (or at least late in the war) fails to explain the condition of the text as we have it. Hornblower rejects the separatist or analytic view of Thucydides, an approach that attempts to identify early or later passages in the text. Somewhat amusingly, however, he actually employs this approach in his analysis of the differing views expressed by A. Andrewes in his commentary on Thucydides. Noting that Andrewes tended to be more circumspect in the body of the commentary than in his appendix on the unfinished nature of Thucydides' work, Hornblower comments, "The appendix in question was undoubtedly written at a later date by many years" (*CT* III.2).
5. For the history of this period, see esp. Xenophon, *Hellenika* books 1–5, and Diod. books 14–16. For a comprehensive modern account, see *CAH* VI.^{2}; for particular periods/issues, see C. D. Hamilton, *Sparta's Bitter Victories*; J. Cargill, *The Second Athenian League*; and J. Buckler, *The Theban Hegemony*.
6. For Agesilaus, see Hamilton, *Agesilaus and the Failure of Spartan Hegemony*, and Cartledge, *Agesilaos and the Crisis of Sparta*; for Epaminondas and Thebes, see V.

D. Hanson, *The Soul of Battle*, which, however, somewhat overstates the "democratic" nature of Epaminondas's achievement.

7. D. M. MacDowell, *The Law in Classical Athens*, p. 43.

8. Plato *Gorgias* 515c–519 (criticism); cf. Isoc. *Antidosis* 234 (with Kagan, *Pericles*, pp. 267–68), for praise based on the very buildings attributed to Pericles.

9. Stadter, *Commentary*, p. lxxxi. For the orators' occasional praise of Pericles, see Lehmann, *Perikles*, pp. 22–24.

10. See esp. Isoc. *Antidosis* 234–35, *On the Chariots* 28.

11. Tracy, *Pericles*, pp. 128–42, 155–56, collects a number of references to the statesman in this period; see also Lysias *Against Eratosthenes* 4, *Against Nichomachus* 28, Xen. *Memorabilia* 2.6.13, *Symposium* 8.39, Lycurgus *Against Demades* fr. 2 (Loeb *Minor Attic Orators* vol. 2).

12. L. Burckhardt, *Bürger und Soldaten*, argues that the ideal of the citizen soldier remained very much alive in the fourth century and that mercenaries supplemented rather than replaced citizen troops. About the ideal I have no doubt that he is correct, but the evidence still shows that mercenaries played a much-increased role in fourth- (vs. fifth-) century Athenian military actions.

13. Samons, *What's Wrong with Democracy?*, pp. 95–99, 143–62. Hansen, *Athenian Democracy*, p. 98, writes that "in the second half of the fourth century many Athenian citizens, on most days of the year, could expect a state payment of one kind or another." For the argument that most public magistracies were paid in the fourth century (a conclusion sometimes denied), see Pritchard, "Public Payment of Magistrates."

14. Pritchard, "Costing Festivals and War."

15. Samons, *What's Wrong with Democracy?*, pp. 143–62. See also Sealey, *Demosthenes*.

16. For the contrary view that "there was nothing fundamentally wrong in the [fourth-century] state of Athens," see P. J. Rhodes, "The Alleged Failure of Athens" (p. 126 for the quotation). I cannot treat Rhodes's interesting paper in detail here, but I do not find at all compelling any analysis that concludes that it was "too late" (p. 123) to oppose Macedon in the late 350s or that Philip was "too clever" (p. 126) for the Athenians. The fourth-century Athenians took decisions that made them and their allies weaker and more vulnerable. We cannot say that they certainly *could* have retained their independence, but we surely can say that they *failed* to do so.

17. For Alcibiades, see recently P. J. Rhodes, *Alcibiades*. Kagan, *Pericles*, pp. 262–63, sees Alcibiades as beginning his career on the model of Pericles (at least in terms of his foreign policy); but he later became a supporter of the very un-Periclean Sicilian expedition.

18. Alcibiades joined Athens' enemies in Sparta and then became an advisor to a Persian satrap before inspiring and then trying to distance himself from an oligarchic revolution in Athens. See Plut. *Alcibiades*, Thuc. books 6–8, and Rhodes, *Alcibiades*.

19. Plutarch relates an interesting anecdote about Pericles attempting to protect Alcibiades' reputation as a youth: Plut. *Alc.* 3. By the time he was a middle-aged

adult, Alcibiades' reputation was beyond repair. Alcibiades' precise relationship to Pericles is problematic: Stadter, *Commentary*, p. 332.

20. Xen. *Memorabilia* 1.2.40–46.
21. See also Diod. 12.38.2–4, where Alcibiades (again portrayed as the cleverer, younger figure), when discussing how Pericles would render his accounts of office, suggests that Pericles should be discovering how *not* to render accounts (instead of how to render them), thus leading Pericles to concoct a plan for a war that would hide his supposed financial malfeasance.
22. For Sophocles on "unwritten laws," see p. 196 above. For Socrates, see (e.g.), Plato *Apol.* 29b.
23. For the striking similarities and differences between Pericles and Socrates, see Samons, *What's Wrong with Democracy?*, pp. 187–202.
24. See Lehmann, *Perikles*, pp. 24–25, who notes that Aristotle's other references to Pericles (beyond those in *The Constitution of Athens*) tend to be respectful.
25. Stadter, *Commentary*, p. lviii.
26. Cicero *De Oratore* 3.34.138.
27. Azoulay, *Pericles*, e.g., pp. 130–31, shows how the negative traditions contained in Plutarch's biography have played a major role in hostile views of Pericles and includes my own work as a prime example of a treatment misled by Plutarch's supposed malevolence: pp. 223–24, with notes.
28. Stadter, *Commentary*, p. xxx, emphasizes Plutarch's attempt to show that Pericles did possess the qualities of self-restraint (*praotes*) and honesty (*dikaiosyne*) against critics who maintained he did not. Plutarch would refer to Pericles frequently as a model of good political behavior in his essay *Advice on Public Life* (Stadter, *Commentary*, pp. xxxlii–xxxliv): Plut. *Mor.* 800c, 802b, 805c, 811e, 812c, 818c.
29. Plut. *Per.* 2; see also 30, and *Comparison of Pericles and Fabius* 1–2, which argues that Fabius's military skill was greater but that Pericles had greater strategic insight. At *Comparison* 3.1, Plutarch criticizes Pericles for his "factious" opposition to good men like Kimon and Thucydides son of Melesias. For the comparison between Pericles and Fabius, see also Lehmann, *Perikles*, pp. 26–27.
30. *Federalist* 6 (Hamilton on Pericles), 10 (Madison on democracies), with Samons, *What's Wrong with Democracy?*, p. 2. Such views paralleled those elsewhere: for the discomfort with Pericles and Periclean Athens in Scotland (and the fascinating story of how the Scots came to begin, but not finish, a monument in Edinburgh imitating the Parthenon), see D. Allan, "The Age of Pericles in the Modern Athens."
31. Azoulay, *Pericles*, pp. 199–202, shows how philhellenism in Germany after ca. 1750 had already led to an improvement in the statesman's reputation in some parts of the continent.
32. For praise of Pericles in the early Germanic scholarly tradition, beginning with E. Curtius's *Griechische Geschichte* (1868), see Lehmann, *Perikles*, p. 254, and Azoulay, *Pericles*, pp. 210–11.
33. For the changing views of Athens and democracy in the nineteenth century, see J. T. Roberts, *Athens on Trial*, pp. 208–55. Azoulay, *Pericles*, pp. 176–226, provides an

extremely useful treatment of changing views of Pericles from the Enlightenment to the present.

34. For the confusion in modern America about "democracy," see Samons, *What's Wrong with Democracy?*

35. Yet even in the democratic twentieth century, views of Pericles have not been universally positive. The Athenian has been more generally admired (especially for his supposed democratic beliefs) in the Anglophone (and particularly American) world. For a treatment of six twentieth-century biographies (five European and one American) of Pericles, see J. A. Dabdab Trabulsi, *Le Présent dans le passé*, a work that emphasizes the influence of the individual authors' historical and political circumstances and perspective on their treatments of Pericles. See also J. P. Sickinger's useful review of the book. For attitudes toward Pericles in German scholarship since the mid-nineteenth century (providing more variety than in the Anglophone tradition), see Lehmann, *Perikles*, pp. 254–56, and Azoulay, *Pericles*, pp. 210–20.

36. Lehmann, *Perikles*, pp. 254–55, points out that some German scholarship of earlier periods praised Pericles for these very traits.

37. Lehmann's biography *Perikles* is notable in that it usefully analyzes (and criticizes) Pericles' foreign policy even as it praises (and perhaps overstates) his contributions to Athenian democratic and cultural advances.

38. Cf. Ed. Meyer, "Herodots Geschichtswerk," pp. 227–28, who maintains that Solon, Cleisthenes, Themistocles, and Pericles all supported policies that led toward democracy not because of theory or ideology but because they believed only that type of government could realize the full power of the city-state.

39. Raaflaub, "Democracy, Power, and Imperialism," admirably traces many advantages that accrued to wealthy and poorer Athenians through Athens' empire. Note especially his argument that the lower classes – especially those rowing Athens' warships – gained political legitimacy and self-confidence through Athens' (largely naval) imperialism: pp. 138–46.

APPENDIX 1   PERICLES' MILITARY CAREER

1 Plut. *Per.* 38.3–4 speaks of Pericles' nine military victories, but we cannot be sure to which campaigns this number refers or what evidence Plutarch (or his source) had for the number. Azoulay's characterization (*Pericles*, p. 34) of Pericles' military "merits" as "less dazzling than those of other *strategoi* who were more familiar with military manoeuvres" does not reflect the evidence we possess.

2 Dated to the late 460s by Badian, *From Plataea to Potidaea*, pp. 13–14 (cf. Samons, "Kimon, Kallias, and Peace with Persia," pp. 137–39), and Blamire, *Plutarch: Kimon*, p. 148, and (hesitantly) to 465/4 by Develin, *Athenian Officials*, p. 71. Others place this event in the context of the Samian War: e.g., Lewis, *Sparta and Persia*, p. 60 n. 68. Plutarch mentions two expeditions in this passage, one by Pericles and one by

Ephialtes, but he does not provide a secure context for them, though of course Ephialtes' must be before his death ca. 461. Podlecki, *Perikles*, pp. 47–48, is rightly dubious about such an early expedition for Pericles, whose career as a general (so far as we are able to judge) began in the 450s.

3 See also Diod. 11.85 with 11.88.1–2, for what appears to be a "doublet," crediting Pericles with this expedition to the Peloponnese in two different years (455 and 453). Develin, *Athenian Officials*, p. 77, accepts only the generalship of 455/4. Green, *Diodorus*, p. 169 n. 362, is inclined to accept both expeditions and, given the differences in Diodorus's accounts of the two incidents, this seems possible. Sufficient doubt remains, however, that I have chosen to list only one command.

4 Diod. 11.88.3 places this event in 453.

5 Diod. 12.7; 12.22.2 describes Pericles commanding a force sent to Euboea the next year (445) to establish a colony of 1,000 Athenians on lands taken from the city of Histiaia.

6 For the uncertainty over these dates, see p. 257 n. 87.

7 Develin, *Athenian Officials*, p. 95, places this expedition in 436/5. See also p. 128 with n. 11.

8 Diod. 12.44.3 puts Pericles' attack on Megara in 430.

9 Diod. 12.45.3 (under the year 430).

APPENDIX 2 PERICLES' LEGISLATION

1. With one exception (the final entry in this list) I have included only references to Pericles actually introducing legislation, excluding examples where he is said to have "persuaded the Athenians" or simply to have taken some action (e.g., Plut. *Per.* 29.1, 34.1–2).

2. Although sources occasionally associate Pericles with these reforms, there is good reason to believe that association was invented or assumed on the basis of Pericles' later prominence and Ephialtes' obscurity: see pp. 82–83 (with further references).

3. Allusions at Plato *Gorgias* 515e, Arist. *Pol.* 1274a8–9, Plut. *Per.* 9.2–3.

4. Ed. Meyer, "Kimons Biographie," p. 58, believes this legislation appeared in a collection of decrees by Krateros, but the measure's authenticity is questionable (pp. 90–91).

5. A weak tradition ascribes the institution of festival payments (*theorika*: providing Athenians with funds to pay for their theater admission) to Pericles, and this has occasionally been accepted by scholars (see, recently, Lehmann, *Perikles*, pp. 106–7 with n. 30). However, I agree with Rhodes (*CAAP*, pp. 514–16) and others that we should expect some contemporary reference to this institution had it existed so early as the mid-fifth century. It certainly existed by the mid-fourth century.

6. For its questionable authenticity, see pp. 115–16.

7. Since the Panathenaia apparently already included musical contests, Podlecki, *Perikles*, pp. 78–80, reasonably suggests that this law may relate to the first contests at the Odeion (probably in 442).

8. It is perhaps unlikely that the refusal (at Pericles' insistence) to hold an assembly after the Spartan army had departed for the invasion of Attica derived from a decree. Thucydides does not mention a vote of the assembly. Podlecki, *Perikles*, p. 146 with n. 43, suggests that during the war Pericles may have had special powers that permitted him to prevent an assembly, as does E. Bloedow, "Pericles' Powers." I consider this possible but unlikely given Thucydides' implication that Pericles' extraordinary powers were largely informal and personal. As Kurt Raaflaub suggests to me, Pericles probably was simply able to convince the Council of 500 not to convene an assembly.

APPENDIX 3   ATHENIAN GOVERNMENT IN THE TIME OF PERICLES

1. Although particularly important in democracies, public speech formed a prominent part of all Greek political life: Samons, "Forms and Forums of Public Speech."

APPENDIX 4   PERICLEAN IDEAS?

1. Athens' regular use for warfare of moneys dedicated to the gods in the Periclean period is confirmed by Athenian inscriptions: see Samons, *Empire of the Owl*.
2. For Thucydides' professed procedure here, see pp. 6–7.

Bibliography

The bibliography on Pericles and mid-fifth-century Athens is huge. I include here only works referred to by short title in the notes and the particular translations of ancient works quoted (sometimes in adapted form) in the text, although I have added a few other works (usually in English) that may be consulted by readers interested in pursuing the questions addressed in this work.

The following standard abbreviations are employed:

AC =	*L'Antiquité classique*
AHB =	*Ancient History Bulletin*
AJA =	*American Journal of Archaeology*
ATL =	B. D. Meritt, H. T. Wade-Gery, and M. F. McGregor. *The Athenian Tribute Lists.* 4 vols. Cambridge, MA: Harvard University Press, and Princeton, NJ: American School of Classical Studies at Athens, 1939–1953.
CA =	*Classical Antiquity*
CAH =	*The Cambridge Ancient History* (various volumes and editions)
CJ =	*Classical Journal*
CP =	*Classical Philology*
CQ =	*Classical Quarterly*
CR =	*Classical Review*
CW =	*Classical World*
Davies, APF =	J. K. Davies. *Athenian Propertied Families, 600–300 B.C.* Oxford: Oxford University Press, 1971.
EMC =	*Échos du monde classique*
FGrHist =	F. Jacoby et al. *Die Fragmente der griechischen Historiker.* Berlin and Leiden: Brill, 1923–.

Fornara =	C. W. Fornara, ed. and trans. *Archaic Times to the End of the Peloponnesian War.* 2d ed. Cambridge: Cambridge University Press, 1983. (References are to item numbers.)
G&R =	*Greece & Rome*
Gomme, *HCT* =	A. W. Gomme, A. Andrewes, and K. J. Dover. *A Historical Commentary on Thucydides.* 5 vols. Oxford: Oxford University Press, 1945–1981.
GRBS =	*Greek, Roman, and Byzantine Studies*
Harding =	P. Harding, ed. and trans. *From the End of the Peloponnesian War to the Battle of Ipsus.* Cambridge: Cambridge University Press, 1985. (References are to item numbers.)
Hornblower, *CT* =	*A Commentary on Thucydides.* 3 vols. Oxford: Oxford University Press, 1991–2008.
HSCP =	*Harvard Studies in Classical Philology*
HZ =	*Historische Zeitschrift*
IG =	*Inscriptiones Graecae*
JHS =	*Journal of Hellenic Studies*
ML =	R. Meiggs and D. Lewis. *A Selection of Greek Historical Inscriptions to the End of the Fifth Century* B.C. Oxford: Oxford University Press, 1969. Rev. ed., 1988.
OAth =	*Opuscula Atheniensia*
PAPhS =	*Proceedings of the American Philosophical Society*
PCPhS =	*Proceedings of the Cambridge Philological Society*
RhM =	*Rheinisches Museum*
Rhodes, *CAAP* =	*A Commentary on the Aristotelian Athenaion Politeia.* Oxford: Oxford University Press, 1981. Rev. ed., 1997.
TAPA =	*Transactions and Proceedings of the American Philological Association*
ZPE =	*Zeitschrift für Papyrologie und Epigraphik*

Adcock, F. E. *Thucydides and His History.* Cambridge: Cambridge University Press, 1963.

Aeschines. *The Speeches of Aeschines.* Translated by Charles Darwin Adams. Loeb Classical Library. Cambridge, MA: Harvard University Press, 1919.

Allan, D. "The Age of Pericles in the Modern Athens: Greek History, Scottish Politics, and the Fading of Enlightenment." *The Historical Journal* 44 (2001): 391–417.

Allison, J. "Pericles' Policy and the Plague." *Historia* 32 (1983): 14–23.

Anderson, G. "Alkmeonid 'Homelands,' Political Exile, and the Unification of Attica." *Historia* 49 (2000): 387–412.

Andreades, A. *A History of Greek Public Finance.* Translated by C. N. Brown. Cambridge, MA: Harvard University Press, 1933.

Andrewes, A. *The Greek Tyrants.* London: Hutchinson, 1956.

"Thucydides on the Causes of the War." *CQ* 9 (1959): 223–39.

"The Melian Dialogue and Perikles' Last Speech." *PCPhS* 186 (1960): 1–10.

"The Opposition to Pericles." *JHS* 98 (1978): 1–8.

"The Growth of the Athenian State." In John Boardman and N. G. L. Hammond, eds., *The Cambridge Ancient History*, 2d ed., vol. 3, pt. 3, pp. 360–91. Cambridge: Cambridge University Press, 1982.

"The Tyranny of Pisistratus." In John Boardman and N. G. L. Hammond, eds., *The Cambridge Ancient History*, 2d ed., vol. 3, pt. 3, pp. 392–416. Cambridge: Cambridge University Press, 1982.

Andrews, J. "Pericles on the Athenian Constitution (Thuc. 2.37)." *AJP* 125 (2004): 539–61.

Aristophanes. *Peace*. Edited and translated by A. Sommerstein. London: Aris & Phillips, 1985.

Aristophanes. Edited and translated by Jeffrey Henderson. 4 vols. Loeb Classical Library. Cambridge, MA: Harvard University Press, 1998–2002.

Aristotle. *The "Art" of Rhetoric*. Translated by John Henry Freese. Loeb Classical Library. Cambridge, MA: Harvard University Press, 1926.

The Nichomachaean Ethics. Translated by H. Rackham. Loeb Classical Library. Cambridge, MA: Harvard University Press, 1934.

The Politics of Aristotle. Edited and translated by Ernest Barker. Reprint. New York: Oxford University Press, 1962.

The Constitution of Athens. In J. M. Moore, ed. and trans., *Aristotle and Xenophon on Democracy and Oligarchy*. Berkeley: University of California Press, 1975.

Arrowsmith, W. "Aristophanes' *Birds*: The Fantasy Politics of Eros." *Arion* n.s. 1.1 (1973): 119–67.

Azoulay, A. *Pericles of Athens*. Translated by J. Lloyd. Princeton, NJ: Princeton University Press, 2014.

Badian, E. *From Plataea to Potidaea: Studies in the History and Historiography of the Pentecontaetia*. Baltimore: Johns Hopkins University Press, 1993.

Balot, R. "Pericles' Anatomy of Democratic Courage." *AJP* 122 (2001): 505–25.

"Courage in the Democratic Polis." *CQ* 54 (2004): 406–23.

"Socratic Courage and Athenian Democracy." *Ancient Philosophy* 28 (2008): 49–69.

Barringer, J., and J. Hurwit, eds. *Periklean Athens and Its Legacy*. Austin: University of Texas Press, 2005.

Bicknell, P. J. *Studies in Greek Politics and Genealogy*. Historia Einzelschriften 19. Wiesbaden: Franz Steiner, 1972.

"Athenian Politics and Genealogy: Some Pendants." *Historia* 23 (1974): 146–63.

Blamire, A. *Plutarch: Life of Kimon*. London: Institute of Classical Studies, 1989.

Bloedow, E. "Pericles' Powers in the Counter-Strategy of 431." *Historia* 36 (1987): 9–27.

"'Olympian' Thoughts: Plutarch on Pericles' Congress Decree." *OAth* 21 (1996): 7–12.

"The Implications of a Major Contradiction in Pericles' Career." *Hermes* 128 (2000): 295–309.

Blok, J. "Perikles' Citizenship Law: A New Perspective." *Historia* 58 (2009): 141–70.

Boardman, John, and N. G. L. Hammond, eds. *The Cambridge Ancient History*, 2d ed., vol. 3, pt. 3. Cambridge: Cambridge University Press, 1982.

Boedeker, D. "Athenian Religion in the Age of Pericles." In L. J. Samons II, ed., *The Cambridge Companion to the Age of Pericles*, pp. 46–49. New York: Cambridge University Press, 2007.

Boedeker, Deborah, and Kurt A. Raaflaub, eds. *Democracy, Empire, and the Arts in Fifth-Century Athens*. Cambridge, MA: Harvard University Press, 1998.

Boersma, J. S. *Athenian Building Policy from 561/0 to 405/4 B.C.* Groningen: Wolters-Noordhoff, 1970.

Bosworth, A. B. "The Historical Context of Thucydides' Funeral Oration." *JHS* 120 (2000): 1–16.

Brenne, S. "Ostraka and the Process of Ostrakaphoria." In W. D. E. Coulson, O. Palagia, T. L. Shear Jr., H. A. Shapiro, and F. J. Frost, eds., *The Archaeology of Athens and Attica under the Democracy*, pp. 13–24. Oxbow Monographs 37. Oxford: Oxford University Press, 1994.

Bruit Zaidman, Louise, and Pauline Schmitt Pantel. *Religion in the Ancient Greek City*. Translated by Paul Cartledge. Cambridge: Cambridge University Press, 1992.

Brulé, P. *Women of Ancient Greece*. Translated by A. Nevill. Edinburgh: Edinburgh University Press, 2003.

Brun, Patrice. *Eisphora–Syntaxis–Stratiotika: Recherches sur les finances militaires d'Athènes au IVe siècle av. J.-C.* Paris: Belles Lettres, 1983.

Buckler, John. *The Theban Hegemony, 371–362 B.C.* Cambridge, MA: Harvard University Press, 1980.

Burckhardt, L. *Bürger und Soldaten: Aspekte der politischen und militärischen Rolle athenischer Bürger im Kriegswesen des 4. Jahrhunderts v. Chr.* Historia Einzelschriften 101. Stuttgart: Franz Steiner, 1996.

Burkert, Walter. *Greek Religion*. Translated by John Raffan. Cambridge, MA: Harvard University Press, 1985.

Cairns, F. "Cleon and Pericles: A Suggestion." *JHS* 102 (1982): 203–4.

Camp, John McK. *The Athenian Agora: Excavations in the Heart of Classical Athens*. London: Thames & Hudson, 1986.

——— "Before Democracy: Alkmaionidai and Peisistratidai." In W. D. E. Coulson, O. Palagia, T. L. Shear Jr., H. A. Shapiro, and F. J. Frost, eds. *The Archaeology of Athens and Attica under the Democracy*, pp. 7–12. Oxbow Monographs 37. Oxford: Oxford University Press, 1994.

Carawan, E. "Pericles the Younger and the Citizenship Law." *CJ* 103 (2008): 383–406.

Cargill, Jack. *The Second Athenian League: Empire or Free Alliance?* Berkeley: University of California Press, 1981.

——— *Athenian Settlements of the Fourth Century B.C.* Leiden: Brill, 1995.

Carter, L. B. *The Quiet Athenian*. Oxford: Oxford University Press, 1986.

Cartledge, Paul. *Agesilaos and the Crisis of Sparta*. Baltimore: Johns Hopkins University Press, 1987.

——— *Sparta and Lakonia: A Regional History, 1300–362 B.C.* 2d ed. London: Routledge, 2002.

Castriota, David. *Myth, Ethos and Actuality: Official Art in Fifth-Century B.C. Athens*. Madison: University of Wisconsin Press, 1992.

Cawkwell, G. L. *Thucydides and the Peloponnesian War*. London: Routledge, 1997.
"The Peace between Athens and Persia." *Phoenix* 51 (1997): 115–30.
Chambers, M. "Thucydides and Pericles." *HSCP* 62 (1957): 79–92.
"Themistocles and the Piraeus." *Studies Presented to Sterling Dow*. GRBS Monographs 10 (1984): 43–50.
"Cornford's *Thucydides Mythistoricus*." In W. M. Calder, ed., *The Cambridge Ritualists Reconsidered: Proceedings of the First Oldfather Conference Held on the Campus of the University of Illinois at Urbana-Champaign, Champaign, April 27–30, 1989*, Illinois Classical Studies, Suppl. 2, 1, pp. 61–77. Atlanta, GA: Scholars Press, 1991.
"Wilamowitz on Thucydides." In W. Calder, et al., eds. *Wilamowitz in Greifswald. Akten der Tagung zum 150. Geburtstag Ulrich von Wilamowitz-Moellendorffs in Greifswald, 19–22. Dezember 1998. Spudasmata* 81, pp. 504–523. Hildesheim: Olms, 2000.
Childs, W. A. P. "The Date of the Old Temple of Athena on the Athenian Acropolis." In W. D. E. Coulson, O. Palagia, T. L. Shear Jr., H. A. Shapiro, and F. J. Frost, eds. *The Archaeology of Athens and Attica under the Democracy*, pp. 1–6. Oxbow Monographs 37. Oxford: Oxford University Press, 1994.
Christ, M. R. *The Bad Citizen in Classical Athens*. Cambridge: Cambridge University Press, 2006.
Clinton, K. "The Eleusinan Mysteries and Panhellenism in Democratic Athens." In W. D. E. Coulson, O. Palagia, T. L. Shear Jr., H. A. Shapiro, and F. J. Frost, eds. *The Archaeology of Athens and Attica under the Democracy*, Oxbow Monographs 37, pp. 161–72. Oxford: Oxford University Press, 1994.
Cohen, E. *The Athenian Nation*. Princeton, NJ: Princeton University Press, 2000.
Connelly, J. B. "Parthenon and *Parthenoi*: A Mythological Interpretation of the Parthenon Frieze," *AJA* 100 (1996): 53–80.
The Parthenon Enigma. New York: Knopf, 2014.
Connor, W. R. *The New Politicians of Fifth–Century Athens*. Princeton, NJ: Princeton University Press, 1971.
Conophagos, C. E. *Le Laurium antique et la technique grecque de la production de l'argent*. Athens: Ekdotike Hellados, 1980.
Cornford, F. M. *Thucydides Mythistoricus*. London: Edward Arnold, 1907.
Couch, H. N. "The Last Words of Pericles." *CJ* 31 (1936): 495–99.
Coulson, W. D. E., O. Palagia, T. L. Shear Jr., H. A. Shapiro, and F. J. Frost, eds. *The Archaeology of Athens and Attica under the Democracy*. Oxbow Monographs 37. Oxford: Oxford University Press, 1994.
Cromey, R. "The Alkmeonidai in Late Tradition." *AC* 47 (1978): 448–57.
"Perikles' Wife: Chronological Calculations." *GRBS* 23 (1982): 203–12.
"The Mysterious Woman of Kleitor: Some Corrections to a Manuscript Once in Plutarch's Possession." *AJP* 112 (1991): 87–101.
Csapo, E., and W. J. Slater. *The Context of Ancient Drama*. Ann Arbor: University of Michigan Press, 1995.

Dabdab Trabulsi, J. A. *Le Présent dans le passé. Autour de quelques Périclès du XXe siècle et de la possibilité d'une vérité en Histoire.* Besançon: Presses Universitaires de Franche-Comté, 2011.

Davies, J. K. *Athenian Propertied Families, 600–300 B.C.* Oxford: Oxford University Press, 1971.

"Corridors, cleruchies, commodities, and coins: the pre-history of the Athenian Empire." In A. Slawisch, ed., *Handels– und Finanzgebaren in der Ägäis im 5. Jh. v. Chr. — Trade and Finance in the 5th c. B.C. Aegean World,* BYZAS 18 (2013): 43–66.

Davis, G. "Mining Money in Late Archaic Athens." *Historia* 63 (2014): 257–77.

Demosthenes. *Demosthenes.* 7 vols. Vol. 1 translated by J. H. Vince; vol. 2 translated by C. A. Vince and J. H. Vince; vol. 3 translated by J. H. Vince; vols. 4–6 translated by A. T. Murray; vol. 7 translated by Norman W. DeWitt and Norman J. DeWitt. Loeb Classical Library. Cambridge, MA: Harvard University Press, 1930–1949.

De Romilly, J. *Thucydides and Athenian Imperialism.* Translated by P. Thody. New York: Barnes and Noble, 1963.

De Ste. Croix, G. E. M. *The Origins of the Peloponnesian War.* London: Duckworth, 1972.

Develin, Robert. *Athenian Officials, 684–321 B.C.* Cambridge: Cambridge University Press, 1989.

Dillon, M. P. J. "Was Kleisthenes or Pleisthenes Archon at Athens in 525 B.C.?" *ZPE* 155 (2006): 91–107.

Dover, K. J. "Anthemocritus and the Megarians." *AJP* 87 (1966): 203–9.

Thucydides. Greece and Rome: New Surveys in the Classics, no. 7. Oxford: Oxford University Press, 1973.

Greek Homosexuality. Cambridge, MA: Harvard University Press, 1978.

Drews, R. *The Coming of the Greeks.* Princeton, NJ: Princeton University Press, 1988.

Eckstein, A. "Thucydides, the Outbreak of the Peloponnesian War, and the Foundation of International Systems Theory." *International History Review* 25 (2003): 757–74.

Mediterranean Anarchy, Interstate War, and the Rise of Rome. Berkeley: University of California Press, 2006.

Ehrenberg, V. "The Foundation of Thurii." *AJP* 69 (1948): 149–70.

The People of Aristophanes. Cambridge, MA: Harvard, 1951.

Sophocles and Pericles. Oxford: Blackwell, 1954.

Esposito, S., ed. *Odysseus at Troy: Sophocles' Ajax and Euripides' Hecuba and Trojan Women.* Newburyport, MA: Focus, 2010.

Euben, J. P., John Wallach, and Josiah Ober, eds. *Athenian Political Thought and the Reconstruction of American Democracy.* Ithaca, NY: Cornell University Press, 1994.

Euripides. *The Suppliant Women.* In D. Grene and R. Lattimore, eds., *The Complete Greek Tragedies,* vol. 3. Chicago: University of Chicago Press, 1992.

Evans, J. A. S. "Herodotus and the Battle of Marathon." *Historia* 42 (1993): 279–307.

Ferrari, G. "The Ancient Temple on the Acropolis at Athens." *AJA* 106 (2002): pp. 11–35.

Figueira, T. J. *Aegina: Society and Politics.* Salem, NH: Ayer, 1981.

"Xanthippos, the Father of Perikles, and the *Prutaneis* of the *Naukraroi*." *Historia* 35 (1986): 257–79.

Athens and Aigina in the Age of Imperial Colonization. Baltimore: Johns Hopkins University Press, 1991.

The Power of Money: Coinage and Politics in the Athenian Empire. Philadelphia: University of Pennsylvania Press, 1998.

Flower, M. "From Simonides to Isocrates: The Fifth-Century Origins of Fourth-Century Panhellenism." *CA* 19 (2000): 65–101.

Fornara, C. W. *The Athenian Board of Generals from 501 to 404*. Historia Einzelschriften 16. Wiesbaden: Franz Steiner, 1971.

Herodotus. An Interpretative Essay. Oxford: Oxford University Press, 1971.

"Evidence for the Date of Herodotus' Publication." *JHS* 91 (1971): 25–34.

"Plutarch and the Megarian Decree." *Yale Classical Studies* 24 (1975): 213–28.

"On the Chronology of the Samian War." *JHS* 99 (1979): 9–17.

Archaic Times to the End of the Peloponnesian War, ed. and trans. Translated Documents of Greece and Rome, 2d ed., vol. 1. Cambridge: Cambridge University Press, 1983.

"Thucydides' Birth Date." In R. M. Rosen and J. Farrell, eds., *Nomodeiktes: Greek Studies in Honor of Martin Ostwald*, pp. 71–80. Ann Arbor: University of Michigan Press, 1993.

Fornara, C. W., and L. J. Samons II. *Athens from Cleisthenes to Pericles*. Berkeley: University of California Press, 1991.

Forrest, W. G. *The Emergence of Greek Democracy, 800–400 B.C.* New York: McGraw-Hill, 1966.

Foster, E. *Thucydides, Pericles, and Periclean Imperialism*. Cambridge: Cambridge University Press, 2010.

Frost, F. J. "Pericles, Thucydides, son of Melesias, and Athenian Politics before the War." *Historia* (1964): 385–99.

Plutarch: Themistocles. A Historical Commentary. Princeton, NJ: Princeton University Press, 1980.

"Pericles and Dracontides." *JHS* 84 (1984): 69–72.

"The Athenian Military before Cleisthenes." *Historia* 33 (1984): 283–94.

Gabrielsen, Vincent. *Financing the Athenian Fleet: Public Taxation and Social Relations*. Baltimore: Johns Hopkins University Press, 1994.

Gagarin, Michael. "The Torture of Slaves in Athenian Law." *CP* 91 (1996): 1–18.

Gillis, D. *Collaboration with the Persians*. Historia Einzelschriften 34. Wiesbaden: Franz Steiner, 1979.

Giovannini, A. "Le Parthénon, le trésor d'Athéna et le tribut des Alliés." *Historia* 39 (1990): 129–48.

"La participation des alliés au financement du Parthénon: *aparchè* ou tribut?" *Historia* 46 (1997): 145–57.

Goldhill, S. *Reading Greek Tragedy*. Cambridge: Cambridge University Press, 1986.

"The Great Dionysia and Civic Ideology." *JHS* 107 (1987): 58–76.

"Civic Ideology and the Problem of Difference: The Politics of Aeschylean Tragedy, Once Again." *JHS* 120 (2000): 34–56.

Gomme, A. W. Review of H. Willrich, *Perikles*. Göttingen: Vandenhoeck und Ruprecht, 1936. *CR* 50 (1936): 191–92.

More Essays in Greek History and Literature. Oxford: Blackwell, 1962.

Gomme, A. W., A. Andrewes, and K. J. Dover. *A Historical Commentary on Thucydides*. 5 vols. Oxford: Oxford University Press, 1945–1981.

Gould, J. "Hiketeia." *JHS* 93 (1973): 74–103.

Green, P. *The Greco-Persian Wars*. Berkeley: University of California Press, 1998.

Diodorus Siculus, Books 11–12.7.1: Greek History, 480–431 B.C. — the Alternate Version. Austin: University of Texas Press, 2006.

Greenwood, E. *Thucydides and the Shaping of History*. London: Duckworth, 2006.

Griffin, J. "The Social Function of Attic Tragedy." *CQ* 48 (1998): 39–61.

Griffith, M. "Public and Private in Early Greek Institutions of Education." In Yun Lee Too, ed., *Education in Greek and Roman Antiquity*, pp. 24–84. Leiden: Brill, 2001.

Grote, George. *A History of Greece*. 12 vols. London: J. Murray, 1846–1856.

Habicht, Christian. "Falsche Urkunden zur Geschichte Athens im Zeitalter der Perserkriege." *Hermes* 89 (1961): 1–35.

Hall, Jonathan M. *Ethnic Identity in Greek Antiquity*. Cambridge: Cambridge University Press, 1997.

Halliwell, S. "Comic Satire and Freedom of Speech in Classical Athens." *JHS* 111 (1991): 48–70.

Hamilton, Charles D. *Sparta's Bitter Victories: Politics and Diplomacy in the Corinthian War*. Ithaca, NY: Cornell University Press, 1979.

Agesilaus and the Failure of Spartan Hegemony. Ithaca, NY: Cornell University Press, 1991.

Hamilton, Charles D., and Peter Krentz, eds. *Polis and Polemos: Essays on Politics, War, and History in Ancient Greece in Honor of Donald Kagan*. Claremont, CA: Regina Books, 1997.

Hammond, N. G. L. "The Expedition of Datis and Artaphernes." In J. Boardman et al., eds., *The Cambridge Ancient History*, 2d ed., vol. 4, pp. 491–517. Cambridge: Cambridge University Press, 1988.

Hammond, N. G. L., and H. H. Scullards, eds. *The Oxford Classical Dictionary*, 2d ed. Oxford: Oxford University Press, 1970.

Hansen, Mogens Herman. *Eisangelia: The Sovereignty of the People's Court in Athens in the Fourth Century B.C. and the Impeachment of Generals and Politicians*. Odense University Classical Studies, vol. 6. Odense, Denmark: Odense University Press, 1975.

The Athenian Assembly in the Age of Demosthenes. Oxford: Blackwell, 1987.

"The Athenian Board of Generals: When Was Tribal Representation Replaced by Election from All Athenians?" In *Studies in Ancient History and Numismatics Presented to Rudi Thomsen*. Århus, Denmark: Århus University Press, 1988.

Was Athens a Democracy? Popular Rule, Liberty and Equality in Ancient and Modern Political Thought. Historisk–filosofiske Meddelelser, 59. Copenhagen: Royal Danish Academy of Sciences and Letters, 1989.

The Athenian Democracy in the Age of Demosthenes. Translated by J. A. Crook. Oxford: Blackwell, 1991.

ed. *The Ancient Greek City–State: Symposium on the Occasion of the 250th Anniversary of the Royal Danish Academy of Sciences and Letters, July 1–4, 1992.* Copenhagen: Royal Danish Academy of Sciences and Letters, 1993.

Hansen, Mogens Herman, and Kurt A. Raaflaub, eds. *Studies in the Ancient Greek Polis.* Historia Einzelschriften 95. Stuttgart: Franz Steiner, 1995.

Hanson, Victor Davis. *Warfare and Agriculture in Classical Greece.* 1st ed., 1983. 2d ed. Berkeley: University of California Press, 1998.

The Other Greeks: The Family Farm and the Agrarian Roots of Western Civilization. New York: Free Press, 1995.

"Hoplites and Democrats: The Changing Ideology of Athenian Infantry." In Josiah Ober and Charles Hedrick eds., *Dēmokratia*, pp. 289–312. Princeton, NJ: Princeton University Press, 1996.

The Soul of Battle: From Ancient Times to the Present Day, How Three Great Liberators Vanquished Tyranny. New York: Free Press, 1999.

Harding, Phillip, ed. and trans. *From the End of the Peloponnesian War to the Battle of Ipsus.* Translated Documents of Greece and Rome, vol. 2. Cambridge: Cambridge University Press, 1985.

Hardwick, L. "Philomel and Pericles: Silence in the Funeral Oration." *G&R* 40 (1993): 147–62.

Harrison, E. B. "The Web of History: A Conservative Reading of the Parthenon Frieze." In J. Neils, ed., *Worshipping Athena*, pp. 198–214. Madison: University of Wisconsin Press, 1996.

Harrison, T. *The Emptiness of Asia: Aeschylus' Persians and the History of the Fifth Century.* London: Duckworth, 2000.

Haslam, M. "Pericles Poeta." *CP* 85 (1990): 33.

Henderson, Jeffrey. "Attic Old Comedy, Frank Speech, and Democracy." In Deborah Boedecker and Kurt A. Raaflaub, eds., *Democracy, Empire, and the Arts in Fifth–Century Athens*, pp. 255–73. Cambridge, MA: Harvard University Press, 1998.

Herodotus. *The Persian Wars.* Translated by G. Rawlinson. New York: McGraw-Hill, 1942.

Hignett, C. *Xerxes' Invasion of Greece.* Oxford: Oxford University Press, 1963.

Hill, G., R. Meiggs, and A. Andrewes, eds. *Sources for Greek History between the Persian and Peloponnesian Wars*, 2d ed. Oxford: Oxford University Press, 1951.

Hodkinson, Stephen. *Property and Wealth in Classical Sparta.* London: Duckworth, 2000.

Hölkeskamp, K.-J. "Parteiungen und politische Willensbildung im demokratischen Athen: Perikles und Thukydides, Sohn des Melesias." *HZ* 267 (1998): 1–27.

Holladay, A. J. "The Détente of Kallias?" *Historia* 35 (1986): 503–7.

"The Hellenic Disaster in Egypt." *JHS* 109 (1989): 176–232.

Homer. *The Iliad*. Translated by R. Lattimore. Chicago: University of Chicago Press, 1951.

Hooker, G. T. W. ed., *Parthenos and Parthenon*, Greece & Rome Supplement to vol. 10. Oxford: Oxford University Press, 1963.

Hornblower, Simon. *Thucydides*. Baltimore: Johns Hopkins University Press, 1987.

A *Commentary on Thucydides*. 3 vols. Oxford: Oxford University Press, 1991–2008.

Hunt, P. *Slaves, Warfare, and Ideology in the Greek Historians*. Cambridge: Cambridge University Press, 1998.

Hunter, J. H. "Pericles' Cavalry Strategy." *Quaderni Urbinati di Cultura Classica* 81 (2005): 101–8.

Hurwit, J. *The Athenian Acropolis*. Cambridge: Cambridge University Press, 1999.

Jenkins, I. "The Parthenon Frieze and Perikles' Cavalry of a Thousand." In J. Barringer and J. Hurwit, eds., *Periklean Athens and its Legacy*, pp. 147–61. Austin: University of Texas Press, 2005.

Johnson, W. A. "Oral Performance and the Composition of Herodotus' *Histories*." *GRBS* 35 (1994): 229–54.

Jones, A. H. M. *Athenian Democracy*. Oxford: Blackwell, 1957.

Jones, G. S. "Perikles and the Sexual Politics of Hermippos' *Moirai*." *CJ* 106 (2011): 273–93.

Jones, J. E. "The Laurion Silver Mines: A Review of Recent Researches and Results." *G&R* 29 (1982): 169–83.

Jones, Nicholas F. *Public Organization in Ancient Greece: A Documentary Study*. Philadelphia: American Philosophical Society, 1987.

The Associations of Classical Athens: The Response to Democracy. Oxford: Oxford University Press, 1999.

Kagan, Donald. *The Outbreak of the Peloponnesian War*. Ithaca, NY: Cornell University Press, 1969.

The Archidamian War. Ithaca, NY: Cornell University Press, 1974.

Pericles of Athens and the Birth of Democracy. New York: Free Press, 1991.

On the Origins of War and the Preservation of Peace. New York: Doubleday, 1995.

"Perikles as General." In J. Barringer and J. Hurwit, eds., *Periklean Athens and its Legacy*, pp. 1–9. Austin: University of Texas Press, 2005.

Kahn, D. "Inaros' Rebellion against Artaxerxes I and the Athenian Disaster in Egypt." *CQ* 58 (2008): 424–40.

Kallet, Lisa. "Did Tribute Fund the Parthenon?" *CA* 20 (1989): 252–66.

Money, Expense, and Naval Power in Thucydides' History 1–5.24. Berkeley: University of California Press, 1993.

"The Origins of the Athenian Economic Arche." *JHS* 133 (2013): 43–60.

"Thucydides, Apollo, the Plague, and the War." *AJP* 134 (2013): 355–82.

Kennelly, J. *Thucydides' Knowledge of Herodotus*. Diss. Brown University, Providence, RI, 1994.

Knight, D. W. *Some Studies in Athenian Politics in the Fifth Century* B.C., Historia Einz. 13. Wiesbaden: Franz Steiner, 1970.

Krentz, Peter. *The Thirty at Athens*. Ithaca, NY: Cornell University Press, 1982.

"The Ostracism of Thoukydides Son of Melesias." *Historia* 33 (1984): 499–504.

Lambert, S. D. *The Phratries of Attica.* Ann Arbor: University of Michigan Press, 1993.

Lang, M. *The Athenian Agora XXV.* Princeton, NJ: Princeton University Press, 1990.

Lapatin, K. "Art and Architecture." In L. J. Samons II, ed., *The Cambridge Companion to the Age of Pericles*, pp. 125–52. New York: Cambridge University Press, 2007.

Lape, S. *Race and Citizen Identity in Classical Athens.* Cambridge: Cambridge University Press, 2010.

Lattimore, S., trans. *Thucydides. The Peloponnesian War.* Indianapolis: Hackett, 1998.

Lavelle, B. M. *Fame, Money, and Power: The Rise of Peisistratos and "Democratic" Tyranny at Athens.* Ann Arbor: University of Michigan Press, 2005.

Lazenby, J. F. *The Spartan Army.* Chicago: Bolchazy–Carducci, 1985.

The Defence of Greece, 490–479 B.C. Warminster, UK: Aris & Phillips, 1993.

Lehmann, G. *Perikles: Staatsmann und Stratege im klassischen Athen.* München: Beck, 2008.

Lendon, J. E. *Song of Wrath.* New York: Basic Books: 2010.

Lewis, D. M. "Cleisthenes and Attica." *Historia* 12 (1963): 22–40.

Sparta and Persia. Leiden: Brill, 1977.

"The Archidamian War." In D. M. Lewis et al., eds., *The Cambridge Ancient History*, 2d ed., vol. 5, pp. 370–432. Cambridge: Cambridge University Press, 1992.

"Megakles and Eretria." *ZPE* 96 (1993): 51–52.

Loraux, Nicole. "Mourir devant Troie, tomber pour Athènes: De la gloire du héros à l'idée de la cité." *Information sur les Sciences Sociales* 17 (1978): 801–17.

The Invention of Athens: The Funeral Oration in the Classical City. Translated by Alan Sheridan. Cambridge, MA: Harvard University Press, 1986.

Born of the Earth: Myth and Politics in Athens. Translated by Selina Stewart. Ithaca, NY: Cornell University Press, 2000.

Low, P. "Looking for the Language of Athenian Imperialism." *JHS* 125 (2005): 93–111.

Lucan. *The Civil War [Pharsalia].* Translated by J. D. Duff. Cambridge, MA: Harvard University Press, 1928.

MacDowell, D. W. *The Law in Classical Athens.* Ithaca, NY: Cornell University Press, 1978.

Aristophanes and Athens. Oxford: Oxford University Press, 1995.

Madison, James, Alexander Hamilton, and John Jay. *The Federalist Papers*, ed. I. Kramnick. New York: Penguin Books, 1987.

March, J. "Sophocles' Ajax: the death and burial of a hero." *BICS* 38 (1991–1993): 1–36.

Marinatos, N. *Thucydides and Religion.* Beiträge zur klassischen Philologie 129. Königstein: Hain, 1981.

Marrou, H. *A History of Education in Antiquity.* Madison: University of Wisconsin Press, 1956.

Mattingly, H. B. *The Athenian Empire Restored.* Ann Arbor: University of Michigan Press, 1996.

McInerney, J. "Pelasgians and Leleges: Using the Past to Understand the Present." In J. Ker and C. Pieper, eds. *Valuing the Past in the Greco-Roman World*, pp. 25–55. Leiden: Brill, 2014.

McNellen, B. "Herodotean Symbolism: Pericles as Lion Cub." *Illinois Classical Studies* 22 (1997): pp. 11–23.

Meier, Chr. *Athens: A Portrait of the City in Its Golden Age.* Translated by R. and R. Kimber. New York: Metropolitan Books, 1998.

Meier, M. "Probleme der Thukydides-Interpretation und das Perikles-Bild des Historikers." *Tyche* 21 (2006): 131–67.

Meiggs, Russell. "The Political Implications of the Parthenon." In G. T. W. Hooker, ed., *Parthenos and Parthenon*, pp. 36–45. Oxford: Oxford University Press, 1963.

"The Dating of Fifth–Century Attic Inscriptions." *JHS* 86 (1966): 86–98.

The Athenian Empire. Oxford: Oxford University Press, 1972.

Meiggs, Russell, and David Lewis. *A Selection of Greek Historical Inscriptions to the End of the Fifth Century* B.C. Rev. ed., Oxford: Oxford University Press, 1988.

Meritt, B. D., and H. T. Wade–Gery. "The Dating of Documents to the Mid-Fifth Century – I." *JHS* 82 (1962): 67–74.

"The Dating of Documents to the Mid-Fifth Century – II." *JHS* 83 (1963): 100–17.

Meyer, Ed. *Forschungen zur alten Geschichte*, vol. 2. Halle: Max Niemeyer, 1899.

"Herodots Geschichtswerk," in *Forschungen*, vol. 2, pp. 196–268.

"Kimons Biographie," in *Forschungen*, vol. 2, pp. 1–87.

Meyer, Elizabeth. "*The Outbreak of the Peloponnesian War* after Twenty-Five Years." In C. D. Hamilton and P. Krentz, eds., *Polis und Polemos*, pp. 23–54. Claremont: Regina, 1997.

Mikalson, J. D. *Athenian Popular Religion.* Chapel Hill: University of North Carolina Press, 1983.

Miller, M. C. *Athens and Persia in the Fifth Century* B.C.: *A Study in Cultural Receptivity.* Cambridge: Cambridge University Press, 1997.

Mills, S. *Theseus, Tragedy, and the Athenian Empire.* Oxford: Oxford University Press, 1997.

Mirhady, D. C. "Torture and Rhetoric in Athens." *JHS* 116 (1996): 119–31.

Mitchell, Lynette G. "A New Look at the Election of Generals in Athens." *Klio* 82 (2000): 344–60.

Montgomery, H. "Silver, Coins and the Wealth of a City State." *OAth* 15 (1984): 123–33.

Moore, J. M., ed. and trans. *Aristotle and Xenophon on Democracy and Oligarchy.* Berkeley: University of California Press, 1975.

Morris, Ian, and Kurt A. Raaflaub, eds. *Democracy 2500? Questions and Challenges.* Archaeological Institute of America Colloquium series. Dubuque, IA: Kendall/Hunt, 1998.

Morrison, J. S., J. F. Coates, and N. B. Rankov. *The Athenian Trireme: The History and Reconstruction of an Ancient Greek Warship.* 2d ed. Cambridge: Cambridge University Press, 2000.

Morrison, J. V. *Reading Thucydides.* Columbus: Ohio State University Press, 2006.

Müller, C. W. "Perikles über die Kompetenz des Attischen Demos (Thuk. 2,40,2)." *RhM* 139 (1996): 1–5.

"Kimon und der Akademie-Park: Zum Epigramm *Anthologia Palatina* 6,144,3 f."
RhM 150 (2007): 225–38.

Mussche, H. F. "Thorikos during the Last Years of the Sixth Century B.C." In W. D. E.
Coulson, O. Palagia, T. L. Shear Jr., H. A. Shapiro, and F. J. Frost, eds., *The
Archaeology of Athens and Attica under the Democracy*, pp. 211–25. Oxbow
Monographs 37. Oxford: Oxford University Press, 1994.

Neils, J., ed. *Worshipping Athena: Panathenaia and Parthenon*. Madison: University of
Wisconsin Press, 1996.

Ober, Josiah. *The Athenian Revolution: Essays on Ancient Greek Democracy and
Political Theory*. Princeton, NJ: Princeton University Press, 1996.

Ostwald, Martin. *Autonomia: Its Genesis and Early History*. Atlanta, GA: Scholars Press,
1982.

———. *From Popular Sovereignty to the Sovereignty of the Law: Law, Society, and Politics in
Fifth–Century Athens*. Berkeley: University of California Press, 1986.

———. "The Reform of the Athenian State by Cleisthenes." In J. Boardman et al., eds., *The
Cambridge Ancient History*, 2d ed., vol. 4, pp. 303–46. Cambridge: Cambridge
University Press, 1988.

O'Sullivan, N. "Pericles and Protagoras." *G&R* 42 (1995): 15–23.

Page, D. L. *Sappho and Alcaeus*. Oxford: Oxford University Press, 1955.

Papagrigorakis, M. J., C. Yapijakis, P. N. Synodinos, and E. Baziotopoulou. "DNA
Examination of Ancient Dental Pulp Incriminates Typhoid Fever as a Probable
Cause of the Plague of Athens." *International Journal of Infectious Diseases* 10 (May
2006): 206–14.

Parker, Robert. *Athenian Religion: A History*. Oxford: Oxford University Press, 1996.

Patterson, Cynthia. *Pericles' Citizenship Law of 451–450 B.C.* Salem, NH: Ayer, 1981.

———. "Other Sorts: Slaves, Foreigners, and Women in Periclean Athens." In L. J. Samons
II, ed., *The Cambridge Companion to the Age of Pericles*, pp. 153–178. New York:
Cambridge University Press, 2007.

Pelling, C. *Literary Texts and the Greek Historian*. London: Routledge, 2000.

———. "Bringing Autochthony Up-to-Date: Herodotus and Thucydides." *CW* 102 (2009):
471–83.

Pickard–Cambridge, Sir Arthur. *Dithyramb, Tragedy, and Comedy*, 2d. ed., rev. T. B. L.
Webster. Oxford: Oxford University Press, 1962.

———. *The Dramatic Festivals of Athens*, 2d ed., rev. John Gould and D. M. Lewis. Oxford:
Oxford University Press, 1988.

Plato. *Apology*. In G. M. A. Grube, trans., *The Trial and Death of Socrates:
Euthyphro, Apology, Crito, Death Scene from Phaedo*, 2d ed. Indianapolis:
Hackett, 1988.

———. *The Laws of Plato*. Translated by Thomas L. Pangle. 1980. Reprint. Chicago:
University of Chicago Press, 1988.

———. *Menexenus*. In S. Collins and D. Stauffer, trans., *Plato's Menexenus and Pericles'
Funeral Oration: Empire and the Ends of Politics*. Newburyport, MA: Focus, 1999.

———. *Phaedrus and Letters VII and VIII*. Translated with an introduction by Walter
Hamilton. London: Penguin Books, 1973.

The Republic. Translated by G. M. A. Grube. Indianapolis: Hackett, 1974.

Plutarch. *The Rise and Fall of Athens. Nine Greek Lives: Theseus, Solon, Themistocles, Aristides, Cimon, Pericles, Nicias, Alcibiades, Lysander.* Translated with an introduction by Ian Scott–Kilvert. London: Penguin Books, 1960.

The Age of Alexander. Nine Greek Lives: Agesilaus, Pelopidas, Dion, Timoleon, Demosthenes, Phocion, Alexander, Demetrius, Pyrrhus. Translated by Ian Scott–Kilvert. Introduction by G. T. Griffith. London: Penguin Books, 1973.

Podlecki, Anthony J. *The Political Background of Aeschylean Tragedy.* Ann Arbor: University of Michigan Press, 1966.

"A Pericles *prosopon* in Attic Tragedy?" *Euphrosyne* 7 (1975/6): 7–27.

Perikles and His Circle. London: Routledge, 1998.

Pollitt, J. J. *Art and Experience in Classical Greece.* Cambridge: Cambridge University Press, 1972.

Pritchard, D. "Costing Festivals and War: Spending Priorities of the Athenian Democracy." *Historia* 61 (2012): 18–65.

"The Public Payment of Magistrates in Fourth-Century Athens." *GRBS* 54 (2014): 1–16.

Pritchett, W. K. *The Greek State at War.* 5 vols. Berkeley: University of California Press, 1971–1990.

Thucydides' Pentekontaetia and Other Essays. Amsterdam: Gieben, 1995.

Pseudo–Xenophon (The "Old Oligarch"). *The Constitution of the Athenians.* In J. M. Moore, ed. and trans., *Aristotle and Xenophon on Democracy and Oligarchy.* Berkeley: University of California Press, 1975.

Raaflaub, Kurt A. "Democracy, Oligarchy and the Concept of the 'Free Citizen' in Late Fifth–Century Athens." *Political Theory* 11 (1983): 517–44.

Die Entdeckung der Freiheit. Vestigia 37. Munich: Beck, 1985.

"Contemporary Perceptions of Democracy in Fifth–Century Athens." *Classica et Mediaevalia* 40 (1989): 33–70.

"Democracy, Power, and Imperialism in Fifth–Century Athens." In J. P. Euben, John Wallach, and Josiah Ober, eds., *Athenian Political Thought and the Reconstruction of American Democracy,* pp. 103–46. Ithaca, NY: Cornell University Press, 1994.

"Equalities and Inequalities in Athenian Democracy." In Josiah Ober and Charles Hedrick, eds., *Dêmokratia,* pp. 139–74. Princeton, NJ: Princeton University Press, 1996.

"Citizens, Soldiers, and the Evolution of the Greek Polis." In Lynette G. Mitchell and P. J. Rhodes, eds., *The Development of the Polis in Archaic Greece,* pp. 49–59. London: Routledge, 1997.

"Power in the Hands of the People: Foundations of Athenian Democracy." In Ian Morris and Kurt A. Raaflaub, eds., *Democracy 2500? Questions and Challenges,* Archaeological Institute of America Colloquium series, pp. 31–66. Dubuque, IA: Kendall/Hunt, 1998.

"The Thetes and Democracy." In Ian Morris and Kurt A. Raaflaub, eds., *Democracy 2500? Questions and Challenges,* Archaeological Institute of America Colloquium series, pp. 87–103. Dubuque, IA: Kendall/Hunt, 1998.

"Father of All, Destroyer of All: War in Late Fifth-Century Athenian Discourse and Ideology." In D. McCann and B. Strauss, eds., *War and Democracy: A Comparative Study of the Korean War and the Peloponnesian War*, pp. 307–56. Armonk, NY: Sharpe, 2001.

"The Alleged Ostracism of Damon." In Geoffrey W. Bakewell and James P. Sikinger, eds., *Gestures: Essays in Ancient History, Literature, and Philosophy Presented to Alan L. Boegehold*, pp. 317–31. Oxford: Oxbow Books, 2003.

The Discovery of Freedom in Ancient Greece. Chicago: University of Chicago Press, 2004.

"War in Athenian Society." In L. J. Samons II, ed., *The Cambridge Companion to the Age of Pericles*, pp. 96–124. New York: Cambridge University Press, 2007.

Raaflaub, K., J. Ober, and R. Wallace. *Origins of Democracy in Ancient Greece*. Berkeley: University of California Press, 2007.

Rahe, Paul A. "The Primacy of Politics in Classical Greece." *American Historical Review* 89 (1984): 265–93.

Republics Ancient and Modern: Classical Republicanism and the American Revolution. Chapel Hill: University of North Carolina Press, 1992.

Rasmussen, A. H. "Thucydides on Pericles: Thuc. 2.65." *CM* 46 (1995): 25–46.

Rhodes, P. J. *The Athenian Boule*. Oxford: Oxford University Press, 1972. Rev. ed., 1984.

A Commentary on the Aristotelian Athenaion Politeia. Oxford: Oxford University Press, 1981. Rev. ed., 1997.

"The Delian League to 449 B.C." In D. M. Lewis et al., eds., *The Cambridge Ancient History*, 2d ed., vol. 5, pp. 34–61. Cambridge: Cambridge University Press, 1992.

"The Athenian Revolution." In D. M. Lewis et al., eds., *The Cambridge Ancient History*, 2d ed., vol. 5, pp. 62–95. Cambridge: Cambridge University Press, 1992.

"Who Ran Democratic Athens?" In Pernille Flensted–Jensen, Thomas Heine Nielsen, and Lene Rubinstein, eds., *Polis and Politics: Studies in Ancient Greek History, Presented to Mogens Herman Hansen on his sixtieth birthday, August 20, 2000*, pp. 465–77. Copenhagen: Museum Tusculanum Press, 2000.

Ancient Democracy and Modern Ideology. London: Duckworth, 2003.

"Nothing to Do with Democracy: Athenian Drama and the *Polis*." *JHS* 123 (2003): 104–19.

"After the Three-bar *Sigma* Controversy: The History of Athenian Imperialism Reassessed." *CQ* 58 (2008): 501–6.

Alcibiades. Barnsley: Pen and Sword, 2011.

"The Alleged Failure of Athens in the Fourth Century." *Electrum* 19 (2012): 111–29.

Rhodes, P. J., with D. M. Lewis. *The Decrees of the Greek States*. Oxford: Oxford University Press, 1997.

Roberts, J. T. *Athens on Trial: The Antidemocratic Tradition in Western Thought*. Princeton, NJ: Princeton University Press, 1994.

Robinson, E. W. *The First Democracies: Early Popular Government outside Athens*, Historia Einzelschriften 107. Stuttgart: Franz Steiner, 1997.

ed. *Ancient Greek Democracy: Readings and Sources*. Oxford: Blackwell, 2004.

"Thucydidean Sieges, Prosopitis, and the Hellenic Disaster in Egypt." *CA* 18 (1999): 132–52.

Rosen, R. M., and J. Farrell, eds. *Nomodeiktes: Greek Studies in Honor of Martin Ostwald*. Ann Arbor: University of Michigan Press, 1993.

Rosivach, V. "Autochthony and the Athenians." *CQ* 37 (1987): 294–305.

Ruschenbusch, E. "Theseus, Drakon, Solon und Kleisthenes im Publizistik und Geschichtsschreibung des 5. und 4 Jahrhunderts v. Chr." *Historia* 7 (1958): 398–424.

Rusten, J., ed. *Oxford Readings in Classical Studies: Thucydides*. Oxford: Oxford University Press, 2009.

Salmon, J. B. *Wealthy Corinth: A History of the City to 338 B.C.* Oxford: Oxford University Press, 1984.

Samons, L. J., II, ed. *Athenian Democracy and Imperialism*. Boston: Houghton Mifflin, 1998.

"Kimon, Kallias, and Peace with Persia." *Historia* 47 (1998): 129–40.

"Mass, Elite, and Hoplite–Farmer in Greek History." *Arion* 5 (1998): 99–123.

"Aeschylus, the Alkmeonids, and the Reform of the Areopagos." *CJ* 94 (1998–99): 221–33.

Empire of the Owl: Athenian Imperial Finance. Historia Einzelschriften 142. Stuttgart: Franz Steiner, 2000.

"Democracy, Empire, and the Search for the Athenian Character." *Arion* 8 (2001): 128–57.

What's Wrong with Democracy? From Athenian Practice to American Worship. Berkeley: University of California Press, 2004.

ed., *The Cambridge Companion to the Age of Pericles*. New York: Cambridge University Press, 2007.

"Athens – a Democratic Empire." In K. Kagan, ed., *The Imperial Moment*, pp. 12–31, 200–8. Cambridge, MA: Harvard University Press, 2010.

"Forms and Forums of Public Speech." In H. Beck, ed., *A Companion to Greek Government*, pp. 267–83. Oxford: Wiley-Blackwell, 2013.

"Periclean Imperialism and Imperial Finance in Context." In S. R. Jensen and T. Figueira, eds., *Athenian Hegemonic Finances*. Swansea: Classical Press of Wales, forthcoming.

"Herodotus and the Kimonids" (forthcoming).

Schubert, Charlotte. *Perikles*. Erträge der Forschung 285. Darmstadt: Wissenschaftliche Buchgesellschaft, 1994.

Schwartz, E. *Das Geschichtswerk des Thykydides*, 3rd ed. Hildesheim: Olms, 1960.

Scully, S. *Homer and the Sacred City*. Ithaca, NY: Cornell University Press, 1990.

Sealey, Raphael. "The Entry of Pericles into History." *Hermes* 84 (1956): 234–47.

Essays in Greek Politics. New York: Manyland, 1966.

A History of the Greek City–States, ca. 700–338 B.C. Berkeley: University of California Press, 1976.

The Athenian Republic: Democracy or the Rule of Law? University Park: Pennsylvania State University Press, 1987.

Demosthenes and His Time: A Study in Defeat. New York: Oxford University Press, 1993.

"Democratic Theory and Practice." In L. J. Samons II, ed., *The Cambridge Companion to the Age of Pericles*, pp. 238–57. New York: Cambridge University Press, 2007.

Shapiro, H. A. "Religion and Politics in Democratic Athens." In W. D. E. Coulson, O. Palagia, T. L. Shear Jr., H. A. Shapiro, and F. J. Frost, eds., *The Archaeology of Athens and Attica under the Democracy*, pp. 123–29. Oxbow Monographs 37. Oxford: Oxford University Press, 1994.

"Autochthony and the Visual Arts in Fifth-Century Athens." In K. Raaflaub and D. Boedeker, eds., *Democracy, Empire, and the Arts*, pp. 127–52. Cambridge, MA: Harvard University Press, 1998.

Shear, T. Leslie, Jr. "*Isonomous t'Athenas epoiesaten*: The Agora and the Democracy." In W. D. E. Coulson, O. Palagia, T. L. Shear Jr., H. A. Shapiro, and F. J. Frost, eds., *The Archaeology of Athens and Attica under the Democracy*, pp. 225–48. Oxbow Monographs 37. Oxford: Oxford University Press, 1994.

Sicking, C. M. J. "The General Purport of Pericles' Funeral Oration and Last Speech." *Hermes* 123 (1995): 404–25.

Sickinger, J. P. *Public Records and Archives in Classical Athens.* Chapel Hill: University of North Carolina Press, 1999.

Review of J. A. Dabdab Trabulsi, *Le Présent dans le passé. Autour de quelques Périclès du XXe siècle et de la possibilité d'une vérité en Histoire.* Besançon: Presses Universitaires de Franche-Comté, 2011. *CR* 63 (2013): 269–71.

"Ostraka from the Athenian Agora," (forthcoming).

Siewert, P. "The Ephebic Oath in Fifth-Century Athens." *JHS* 97 (1977): 102–11.

Sinclair, R. K. *Democracy and Participation in Classical Athens.* Cambridge: Cambridge University Press, 1988.

Spence, I. "Perikles and the Defense of Attika during the Peloponnsian War." *JHS* 110 (1990): 91–109.

Stadter, P. A. *A Commentary on Plutarch's Pericles.* Chapel Hill: University of North Carolina Press, 1989.

"Pericles among the Intellectuals." *Illinois Classical Studies* 16 (1991): 111–24.

Stahl, Michael. *Aristokraten und Tyrannen im archaischen Athen: Untersuchungen zur Überlieferung, zur Sozialstruktur und zur Entstehung des Staates.* Stuttgart: Franz Steiner, 1987.

Stockton, David. "The Peace of Callias." *Historia* 8 (1959): 61–79.

The Classical Athenian Democracy. Oxford: Oxford University Press, 1990.

Strasburger, H. "Thucydides and the Political Self-portrait of the Athenians." In J. Rusten, ed., *Oxford Readings in Classical Studies: Thucydides*, pp. 191–219. Oxford: Oxford University Press, 2009.

Strauss, B. *The Battle of Salamis: The Naval Encounter that Saved Greece.* New York: Simon & Schuster, 2004.

Stroud, R. S. *The Athenian Grain–Tax Law of 374/3 B.C.* Hesperia suppl. 29. Princeton, NJ: American School of Classical Studies at Athens, 1998.

"Thucydides and Corinth." *Chiron* 24 (1994): 267–304.

Taylor, M. M. *Thucydides, Pericles, and the Idea of Athens in the Peloponnesian War.* Cambridge: Cambridge University Press, 2010.

Thomas, C. G. "Sophocles, Pericles, and Creon." *CW* 69 (1975): 120–22.

Thomas, Rosalind. *Oral Tradition and Written Record in Classical Athens.* Cambridge: Cambridge University Press, 1989.

  Herodotus in Context: Ethnography, Science and the Art of Persuasion. Cambridge: Cambridge University Press, 2000.

Thompson, W. E. "Thucydides 2.65.11." *Historia* 20 (1971): 141–51.

Thucydides. *The History of the Peloponnesian War.* Translated by Richard Crawley. London: Longmans, Green, 1876. I have often drawn upon the revisions of T. E. Wick, ed., Thucydides, *The Peloponnesian War.* New York: McGraw-Hill, 1982.

Thür, G. "Reply to D. C. Mirhady, Torture and Rhetoric in Athens." *JHS* 116 (1996): 132–34.

Tod, M. N. *Greek Historical Inscriptions.* 2 vols. in 1. Reprint. Chicago: Ayer, 1985.

Tracy, S. *Pericles: A Sourcebook and Reader.* Berkeley: University of California Press, 2009.

Tronson, A. "The History and Mythology of 'Pericles' Panhellenic Congress' in Plutarch's Life of Pericles 17." *EMC* 19 (2000): 359–93.

Tyrrell, W. B. "Biography." In A. Markantonatos, ed., *Brill's Companion to Sophocles*, pp. 19–38. Leiden: Brill, 2012.

Tyrrell, W. B. and L. J. Bennett. "Pericles' Muting of Women's Voices in Thuc. 2.45.2." *CJ* 95 (1999): 37–51.

Vogt, J. "The Portrait of Pericles in Thucydides." In J. Rusten, ed., *Oxford Readings in Classical Studies: Thucydides*, pp. 220–37. Oxford: Oxford University Press, 2009.

Wade–Gery, H. T. *Essays in Greek History.* Oxford: Blackwell, 1958.

Walker, H. *Theseus and Athens.* New York: Oxford University Press, 1995.

Wallace, R. W. *The Areopagos Council.* Baltimore: Johns Hopkins University Press, 1987.

  "Private Lives and Public Enemies: Freedom of Thought in Classical Athens." In Alan A. Boegehold and Adele C. Scafuro, eds., *Athenian Identity and Civic Ideology*, pp. 127–55. Baltimore: Johns Hopkins University Press, 1994.

  "Law, Freedom, and the Concept of Citizens' Rights in Democratic Athens." In Josiah Ober and Charles Hedrick, eds., *Dēmokratia: A Conversation on Democracies, Ancient and Modern*, pp. 105–19. Princeton, NJ: Princeton University Press, 1996.

  "The Sophists in Athens." In Deborah Boedeker and Kurt A. Raaflaub, eds., *Democracy, Empire, and the Arts in Fifth–Century Athens*, pp. 203–22. Cambridge, MA: Harvard University Press, 1998.

  "Plato's Sophists, Intellectual History after 450, and Sokrates." In L. J. Samons II, ed., *The Cambridge Companion to the Age of Pericles*, pp. 215–37. New York: Cambridge University Press.

Webster, T. B. L. *An Introduction to Sophocles.* Oxford: Oxford University Press, 1936.

West, A. B. "Pericles' Political Heirs I." *CP* 19 (1924): 124–46.

"Pericles Political Heirs II." *CP* 19 (1924): 201–28.

Westlake, H. D. "Thuc. 2.65.11." *CQ* 8 (1958): 102–10.

Will, W. "Perikles." In H. Cancik and H. Schneider, eds., *Der Neue Pauly*, vol. 9, cols. 567–72. Metzler: Stuttgart, 2000.

Thukydides und Perikles. Der Historiker und sein Held. Bonn: Habelt, 2003.

Review of *Lehmann, Perikles: Staatsman und Stratege im klassischen Athen*, H-Soz-u-Kult, H-Net Reviews, May 2008.

Wills, G. *Lincoln at Gettysburg: The Words That Remade America.* New York: Simon & Schuster, 1992.

Winkler, John J., and Froma I. Zeitlin, eds. *Nothing to Do with Dionysos? Athenian Drama in Its Social Context.* Princeton, NJ: Princeton University Press, 1990.

Winton, R. "Thucydides 2,37,1: Pericles on Athenian Democracy." *RhM* 147 (2004): 26–34.

Woodman, A. J. *Rhetoric in Classical Historiography.* London: Routledge, 1988.

Wycherley, R. E. "Rebuilding in Athens and Attica." In D. M. Lewis et al., eds., *The Cambridge Ancient History*, 2d ed., vol. 5, pp. 206–22. Cambridge: Cambridge University Press, 1992.

Xenophon. *A History of My Times [Hellenika].* Edited by George Cawkwell. Translated by Rex Warner. London: Penguin Books, 1979.

Memorabilia and Oeconomicus. Symposium and Apology. Translated by E. C. Marchant and O. J. Todd. Loeb Classical Library. Cambridge, MA: Harvard University Press, 1969.

The Politeia [Constitution] of the Spartans. In J. M. Moore, ed. and trans., *Aristotle and Xenophon on Democracy and Oligarchy.* Berkeley: University of California Press, 1975.

Index